Explaining Illness

Research, Theory, and Strategies

LEA's COMMUNICATION SERIES
Jennings Bryant/Dolf Zillmann, General Editors

Selected titles in Applied Communications (Teresa L. Thompson, Advisory Editor) include:

Beck/Ragan/DuPre • Partnership for Health: Building Relationships Between Women and Health Caregivers

DuPre • Humor and the Healing Arts: A Multimethod Analysis of Humor Use in Health Care

Nussbaum/Coupland • Handbook of Communication and Aging Research

Ray • Communication and Disenfranchisement: Social Health Issues and Implications

Street/Gold/Manning • Health Promotion and Interactive Technology

Williams/Nussbaum • Intergenerational Communication Across the Life Span

For a complete list of other titles in LEA's Communication Series, please contact Lawrence Erlbaum Associates, Publishers

Explaining Illness

Research, Theory, and Strategies

Edited by

Bryan B. Whaley
Department of Communication
University of San Francisco

LEA

LAWRENCE ERLBAUM ASSOCIATES, PUBLISHERS
2000   Mahwah, New Jersey   London

Lawrence Erlbaum Associates, Inc., Publishers
10 Industrial Avenue
Mahwah, NJ 07430

Cover design by Kathryn Houghtaling Lacey

Library of Congress Cataloging-in-Publication Data

p. cm.
Includes bibliographical references and index.
ISBN 0-8058-3111-8 (cloth : alk. Paper) —
ISBN 0-8058-3112-6 (pbk : alk. paper)
1. Physician and patient. 2. Communication in medicine.
3. Interpersonal relations. I. Whaley, Bryan B. II. Series :
Communication textbook series. Applied communication.
[DNLM: 1. Communication. 2. Disease—etiology.
3. Disease—psychology. 4. Physician-Patient Relations.
W 62 E96 1999]
R727.3.E96   1999
610.69'6—dc21
DNLM/DLC
for Library of Congress   99-32748

                                                      CIP

Books published by Lawrence Erlbaum Associates are
printed on acid-free paper, and their bindings are chosen for
strength and durability.

Printed in the United States of America
10   9   8   7   6   5   4   3   2   1

To my daughter,

Reid Cavanaugh Whaley

Contents

COCULTURAL ISSUES AND EXPLAINING ILLNESS

Foreword

The quests to find explanations and meanings are among the defining characteristics of humans. Although they overlap, there are important differences between explanations and meanings. The search for explanations can be a powerful drive for scientific discovery. Indeed, the essence of the scientific method is empirical testing of hypotheses (possible explanations) until one is found that accounts for the observed phenomenon. Better methods of observation and better ways to control or account for confounding factors often lead to increasingly refined and more accurate explanations.

The quest for meaning may include explanation but goes beyond it, often to the realms of philosophy, art, and religion. Explanation involves careful testing of how a phenomenon came to occur at a particular time. With increasing knowledge, the answers usually become increasingly specific, more precise, and more certain. Meaning may include these "how" and "when" questions, but goes on to ask "why." Here, answers may not be certain at all and often involve beliefs that are increasingly broad and difficult to test.

This book is about explaining illness. Much of it concerns the complexities involved in communicating and understanding explanations for illness among different age groups, cultures, and individuals. These are issues of great importance for physicians and other health professionals and also for patients, which includes all of us. This kind of communication is an essential aspect of the patient–physician relationship, which is at the very center of medicine. As a medical editor, I thought it was important to have a forum for scholarly consideration of this relationship and its challenges, so I developed a section of *The Journal of the American Medical Association* (JAMA) to be devoted to it (Glass, 1996). Recognizing, as does this book, the importance of explaining illness to patients in ways that lead to meaningful comprehension and active participation in treatment, JAMA has also established the JAMA Patient Page, as the last editorial page in every issue (Glass, Molter, & Hwang, 1998). The JAMA Patient Page provides reader-friendly information on a topic covered by one or more of the physician-directed articles published in the same issue of JAMA. Physicians are encouraged to copy and save these pages for their patients in order to facilitate and enhance communication about topics that may directly affect their patients or their families or that they hear about through media coverage of medical research.

Communicating understandable and helpful explanations about what is known and not known about an illness is an essential aspect of the patient–physician relationship. This book covers a great deal of information about that communication process and thus offers the potential for physicians and other health professionals to do it better.

But what about those situations that go beyond a need for objective information, as important as that is? What about the powerful, compelling question asked in some way by almost any person facing a severe illness: Why me? Physicians do not like to hear that one, and understandably so. To the extent that it has objective answers, they often involve unhealthy behaviors the patient has engaged in—an issue difficult to discuss without sounding negative or accusatory. To the extent that there are no known objective or scientific answers to the question, it moves from the territory of explanation to that of meaning, as mentioned previously. Should health professionals even be involved in that territory? Or should they just refer patients to a religious counselor when the issue of meaning arises?

Patients committed to a particular faith tradition certainly might benefit from discussion with a religious advisor, and their belief system should be respected as a potential source of strength in coping with illness. But I believe health professionals should be open to hearing this question and helping patients frame it. This framing would usually proceed from an explanation of the biological, psychological, and social realities of the patient's illness in language that is comprehensible to the patient. That includes acknowledging what is uncertain or unknown about those realities. It is often helpful to recognize that the question "why me?" includes the question "what does this mean for me?" where objective explanations and meanings are very closely linked. From that kind of basis, the health professional can facilitate the patient's consideration of the meaning of the illness, with all its subjectivity, irony, and unknowns. This usually involves more listening to, acknowledging, and learning from profound questions than providing direct answers to them. As in other areas of life, the journey can be enlightening if one has a trusted companion and guide, even if the destination is unknown.

The Patient–Physician Covenant states that: "Medicine is, at its center, a moral enterprise grounded in a covenant of trust" (Crawshaw et al., 1995, p. 1553). This moral enterprise surely includes the responsibility to communicate effectively with patients regarding explanations of their illness. I believe it also includes helping patients to struggle with the more difficult question of the meaning of the illness for their life.

—Richard M. Glass, MD
Deputy Editor, Journal of the American Medical Association (JAMA)
Clinical Professor of Psychiatry
University of Chicago

REFERENCES

Crawshaw, R., Rogers, D. E., Pellegrino, E. D., Bulger, R. J., Lundberg, G. D., Bristow, L. R., Cassel, C. K., & Barondess, J. A. (1995). Patient- physician covenant. *Journal of the American Medical Association, 273,* 1553.

Glass, R. M. (1996). The patient–physician relationship: JAMA focuses on the center of medicine. *Journal of the American Medical Association, 275,* 147–148.

Glass, R. M., Molter, J., & Hwang, M Y. (1998). Providing a tool for physicians to educate patients: The JAMA Patient Page. *Journal of the American Medical Association, 279,* 1309.

Preface

The impetus for this book came about from my interest in health-related issues and children, particularly message strategies for explaining illness to this precious and vulnerable population. Concerned with the lack of research conducted, coupled with having no monograph to consult as an updated source of theory and research for this group, I thought it worthy of pursuing such a treatise. Quickly, a broader focus concerning "explaining illness" emerged. The purposes of explaining illness, the methods of explaining illness, and the role illness explanations play in framing and reframing meaning and uncertainty regarding one's health welfare perpetuated my interest in this book. Bound in culture, understanding the nature of illness is foundatonal and an inevitable concern whether it be the inconvenience of a cold or the life-threatening jolt of critical illness.

Primarily, this book is meant to be an initial compilation of the findings regarding explaining illness for researchers to draw on for theorizing and extending research. For students (communication, medical, nursing, public health, and others), the hope is that this text is a source of potential interest and essential information. Serendipitously, when the syringe is empty, health practitioners will find this book useful in serving the populace. For, above all, the research reviewed should ultimately find its way to persons creating the messages to explain illness—those working the health care system. Finally, this work is meant as a foundational source, to be added to periodically as research and theory relegate.

What this book exhibits is the amount of research that has been done in certain areas and, in doing so, the extremely limited amount of work in some domains. The chapters vary in length; some areas of research have garnered far more theoretical and empirical attention than others. For instance, research concerning explaining illness and cocultural groups is long overdue. As encouraging as it is to see efforts progress in this area, much of existing research and treatises are founded on experiential and anecdotal, rather than theoretical grounds. At present, theory-driven systematic investigations have failed to synchronize with interest in this general area. Related concerns hold for explaining illness to children, as well.

All told, this book serves as a corpus from which to examine and evaluate current theory and strategies, and to launch systematic research endeavors. The elegance of this book is the richness depicted by differences between populations and strategies. The intricacies of language, illness, and culture are articulated between the two covers of this text. No matter what the motivation for its examination, may the reader find this book useful.

Be well—however this fits in your system of illness beliefs.

—*B. B. Whaley*
Petaluma, CA

ACKNOWLEDGMENTS

The realization of this book would have well extinguished without contributions from many others. My thanks to Holly Allen—Mayfield Publishing; Pediatric Library of Children's Hospital, Oakland; Sally Higgins—University of San Francisco; Teresa Thompson—University of Dayton; and my daughter's pediatricians—Pitr Conroy, MD and Armando De Pala, Jr., MD.

I am grateful to the contributors of this book for their unwavering commitment to the text from the beginning, their competence, timeliness, and concern for the topic and producing a book of merit. Thank you to: Linda Bathgate—Lawrence Erlbaum—and Austin Babrow—Purdue University—for their trust in my ideas, and John J. Pinelli—University of San Francisco—for funding the essentials needed for this project. Finally, to my partner, Patrica Kathryn Cavanaugh, for her support and trust in me and this book and the daily adjustments made by her to help me see this text to press.

I

FOUNDATIONAL
THEORETICAL ISSUES

The Nature and Language of Illness Explanations

Teresa L. Thompson
Department of Communication
The University of Dayton

An important part of medical interaction includes the provision of explanations from care providers to patients. The central function of all medical systems is to give meaning to illness by naming and defining its cause (Stoeckle & Barsky, 1980). The official medical profession has long advocated full information to patients (Ernstene, 1957; Hayward, 1975), although physicians' behaviors have not always reflected this guideline (Fitts & Ravdin, 1953; Oken, 1961; Rennick, 1960). Lack of explanations from care providers may cause patients to turn instead to "medical hucksters" (Simoni & Ball, 1975). Explanations should focus on describing the medical problem, its etiology, and its effects as well as providing information about procedures, tests, and medications. The goal of this chapter is to illuminate the nature of these explanations and to discuss the language through which they are communicated.

THE NEED

The saliency of explanation in the medical context is made most apparent by an examination of the voluminous amount of research indicating the lack of explanations received by patients and patient dissatisfaction with this (Berkanovic & Marcus, 1976; Cawley, Kistic, & Cappelo, 1990; Fredette, 1990; Gotcher & Edwards, 1990; Korsch, Gozzi, & Francis, 1968; Lazare, Eisenthal, Wasserman, & Harford, 1975; Ley & Spelman, 1967; Northouse & Northouse, 1987; Partridge, 1995; Pendleton, Brouwer, & Jaspars, 1983; Reynolds, 1978; Sheer & Cline, 1995; Ware, Davies-Avery, & Stewart, 1978). Indeed, a request for an explanation of the problem is one of the three most frequent requests made by patients (Stiles, Putnam, Wolf, & James, 1979). One study found that only half of patients studied were able to recall an occasion during their hospitalization when they felt they had received useful health information (Tilley, Gregor, & Thiessen, 1987). The lack of explanations is especially problematic in light of evidence indicating that patients are reluctant to bother care providers with questions (Boreham & Gibson, 1978; Ley, 1988).

Even explanations about such important decisions as a need for dialysis are not provided until right before a decision must be made (Hines, Babrow, Badzek, & Moss, 1997). The same is true of discussions of advanced directives, although patients respond very positively to such communication (Bedell & Delbanco, 1984; Cohen-Mansfield et al., 1991; Ebell, Smith, Seifert, & Polsinelli, 1990; Everhard & Pearlman, 1990; Frankl, Oye, & Bellamy, 1989; Gamble, McDonald, & Lichstein, 1991; Havlir, Brown, & Rousseau, 1989; Lo, McLeod, & Saika, 1986; Schmerling, Bedell, Lilienfeld, & Delbanco, 1988; Schonwetter, Teasdale, Taffet, Robinson, & Luchi, 1991; Schonwetter, Walker, & Robinson, 1995; Smucker, et al., 1993). Receiving more information about a health problem is not associated with increased anxiety, as may be assumed by some care providers (Klafta & Roizen, 1996) but increases the ability to cope (Krantz, 1980; Lazarus & Folkman, 1974; Miller, 1983; Weisman, 1979). More information is not associated with treatment refusal or increased side-effects (Quaid, Faden, Vining, & Freeman, 1990). Physicians communicate their personal views more easily than they do information about treatment options (McCauley, Johnson, & Copley, 1989).

To ascertain whether the positive impact of explanations was caused simply by the act of communicating with patients rather than the content of the explanation, Meyers (1965) compared irrelevant communication, providing explanations, and giving no information. Results indicated that irrelevant information caused tension in the patient and that no information was preferable to irrelevant information. Providing explantions, however, had positive impacts even on very fearful patients.

Typically, doctors underestimate patients' demands for information (Strull, Lo, & Charles, 1984), as do nurses (Tilley, Gregor, & Thiessen, 1987). Physicians also overestimate the quantity, completeness, and effectiveness of the explanations they provide (Waitzkin, 1985). Physicians spend less than 1% of total talking time providing explanations to patients (Wallen, Waitzkin, & Stoeckle, 1979), although pediatricians offer more information when mothers are more interactive (Howell-Koren & Tinsley, 1990) and patients who express more negative affect receive more information (Street, 1992). Family members of patients also report stress from a lack of explanations (Gillis, 1984; Hileman & Lackey, 1990; Hinds, 1985; Houts et al., 1988; Kristanson, 1989; Majerovitz et al., 1997; Wingate & Lackey, 1989; Wright & Dyck, 1984). Cultural differences, however, moderate the desire for explanations (Hepburn & Reed, 1995; Ventres, Nichter, Reed, & Frankel, 1992, 1993).

EFFECTS OF EXPLANATIONS

Explanations are required in the medical context not just because patients want them. Receiving adequate explanations is related to patient compliance with medical regimens (Becker, Drachman, & Kirscht, 1981; Buller & Street, 1991; Clare, 1993; DiMatteo, Reiter, & Gambone, 1994; Francis, Korsch, & Morris, 1969; Gillispie & Ellis, 1993; Kulik & Carlino, 1987; Ley, 1983; Menzies, Rocher, & Vissandjee, 1993; Roter, 1989), fewer malpractice claims (Adamson, Tschann, Gullion, & Oppenberg, 1989; Baird, 1996; Hickson et al., 1994; Hickson, Clayton, Githens, & Sloan, 1992; May & DeMarco, 1986; Vincent, Young, & Phillips, 1994), more rapid recovery (Anderson, 1987; Boore, 1980; Egbert, Battit, Turndorf, & Beecher, 1963; Egbert, Battit, Welch, & Bartlett, 1964; Schmitt & Wooldridge, 1973), less postoperative distress (Anderson, 1987; Padilla et al., 1981), lower blood glucose and more positive attitudes about diabetes (Van Veldhuizen-Scott, Widmer, Stacey, & Popovich, 1995), improved recall (Clare, 1993), less urinary retention (Schmitt & Wooldridge, 1973), reduced postoperative hypertension (Anderson, 1987), decreased chances of infecting others (Ley & Spelman, 1967), less postoperative vomiting (Dumas, Anderson, & Leonard, 1965), less anesthesia (Lemaitre & Finnegan, 1975; Schmitt & Wooldridge, 1973), less reliance on medication (Egbert et al., 1963, 1964; Hayward, 1975; Tarasuk, Rhymes, & Leonard, 1965), improved outcome (Kaplan, Greenfield, & Ware, 1989), fewer clinical visits (Lieberman, 1992), reduced medical costs (Lieberman, 1992), fewer Worker's Compensation claims (Lieberman, 1992), reduced pain (Averill, 1973; Johnson, 1973; King, 1991; McGrath & DeVeber, 1986), earlier discharge (Schmitt & Wooldridge, 1973), reduced anxiety (Miller, Brody, & Summerton, 1988; Partridge, 1989; Raleigh, Lepczyk, & Rowley, 1990; Spencer, 1981; Thompson & Cordle, 1988; Thompson & Meddis, 1990), a more effective working alliance between care providers and patients (Katon & Kleinman, 1980), improved control of asthma (Charlton, Charlon, Broomfield, & Mullee, 1990; Ignacio-Garcia, & Gonzalez-Santso, 1995; Lahdensuo et al.,

1996; Osman, 1996), more success in weight reduction (Himmel, Stolpe, & Kochen, 1994), and reductions in mortality (Lieberman, 1992; Omar & Schiffman, 1995). Patients who do not receive simple etiological explantions of their problem are more likely to seek unorthodox treatments (Cassileth, Lusk, Strouse, & Bodenheimer, 1984). It has also been suggested that patients may sue primarily to receive an explanation of what has gone wrong (Simanowitz, 1985). However, explanations may have less positive outcomes if patients are avoiders, repressors, or especially fearful (Andrew, 1970; Hathaway, 1986; Shipley, Butt, & Horwitz, 1979).

The difficulty of providing adequate explanations is also addressed in the literature. For instance, Hugh-Jones, Tanser, and Whitby (1964) made a special effort to share explanations with patients and to ascertain that the explanations were understood. Nonetheless, 39% of the patients were dissatisfied with the information they were given and 20% reported the wrong diagnosis 4 weeks later. Similar results are reported by Ley and Spelman (1967). The amount of information forgotten rises in direct proportion to the amount of information given (Lichter, 1977) and memory for medical information is particularly low (Ley, 1988). Even written discharge instructions are accurately understood by only 72% of patients (Logan, Schwab, Salomone, & Watson, 1996). Cancer patients indicate hearing almost nothing of what nurses say while chemotherapy is being administered (McCorkle & Ehlke, 1992). The facts—(a) patients have their own theories about illness and interpret new information in light of those theories; (b) patients have many misconceptions about illnesses; and (c) patients' understanding of many illnesses is very low—all make explanation provision even more difficult (Ley, 1988).

THE NATURE OF EXPLANATIONS

Having established the need for explanations in the medical context based on the lack of information received by patients and the positive impacts of explanations, the discussion is now turned to the nature of those explanations. The available research illuminates this discussion in several areas. First, some research identifies the specific information needs of patients to indicate what should be included in explanations. Second, numerous articles by health care providers offer prescriptive suggestions to other care providers about what should be included in explanations and how explanations should be communicated. Third, studies of the effects of different types of explanations are available and are overviewed. Following this, the focus turns on the studies that have been conducted, looking at what is actually said during explanations, including some analyses of care providers who appear to be more effective at offering explanations than is typically the case. Moving to the heart of the chapter, the discussion turns to those studies that have focused on the language or terminology of explanations, including how the language selected by care providers can produce mystification in patients. The chapter concludes with a focus on suggestions for more effective explanation provision, such as frame-switching.

PATIENT INFORMATION NEEDS

One way to determine what should be included in explanations is by an examination of the information needs of patients that typically go unfulfilled. Numerous studies of various health care problems and contexts document these concerns. Consistent themes emerge across these studies. Regardless of medical problem or context, patients indicate that they do not receive explanations about their diagnosis, continuing care, prognosis, and prevention (Hayward, 1975; Sanchez-Menegay & Stalder, 1994). Grounding research in her information-exchange model of physician–patient consultation (Frederiksen, 1993), Frederiksen (1995) reported that patients rated the following explanatory tasks as essential: (a) explaining the cause of the problem, (b) discussing effects of problems with the patient, (c) explaining treatment and how it works, (d) discussing possible side-effects, and (e) informing the patient about what to expect. Her findings indicate that the quality of information is more important than quantity and that an important part of a care-provider's job is to target information toward specific patient needs.

Much research on information needs has focused on cancer patients. These studies lead to the conclusion that cancer patients need more information than they typically receive about the day-to-day routine of the oncology unit (Alexy, 1981–1982). Women who have undergone breast surgery discover a lack of information on the care of the prosthesis and the experiences of other patients (Messerli, Garamendi, & Romano, 1980). Contrary to nurse perceptions of patient information needs, patients themselves emphasize their need to know their diagnosis, plan of care, self-care strategies, and preparation for diagnostic procedures (Lauer, Murphy, & Powers, 1982). Although doctors assume that patients demand more information about treatment, they actually want more explanations of the prognosis (Blinov, Komiakov, & Shipovnikov, 1990; Faden, Becker, Lewis, Freeman, & Faden, 1981; Gilbertson & Wangensteen, 1962; Jonasch, Schwartz, & Buhr, 1989; Kelly & Friesen, 1950; Kindeland & Kent, 1987; McIntosh, 1974; Sell et al., 1993). The desire for information is particularly strong among patients who take a more active role in treatment decision making; these patients report a need for more explanations about diagnosis, treatment alternatives, and treatment procedures (Hack, Degner, & Dyck, 1994). A broad-based Canadian study of cancer patients also documented the need for explanations about treatment and side-effects, practical information about procedures, resources, and daily living issues, and information about emotional issues relating to the impact of cancer on the patients themselves and their family members (Canadian Cancer Society, 1992).

Focusing on the gynecological context, women undergoing surgery for gynecological cancer report a need for explanations about the physical, sexual, and emotional after-effects of their surgery (Corney, Everett, Howells, & Crowther, 1992). Women receiving post-surgical hormone replacement therapy expect their doctors to provide explanations without being asked, but rarely receive them (Lack & Holloway, 1992). These women perceive a particular need for explanations about treatment options and side-effects, and pregnant women need more information about what to expect from prenatal visits, labor, delivery, and about parenting in general. (Omar & Schiffman, 1995). They, too, want to receive this information without having to ask for it. Lack and Holloway's (1992) research indicated that women were sensitive to the nonverbal behaviors of care providers and these behaviors cued them to not take extra time. Thus, they felt reluctant to raise questions.

Pharmacists have recently shown interests in the explanatory needs of patients and have found that most patients do not receive the information they desire about their medications. Although physicians favor disclosing only potential risks with a high probability of occurrence (Christensen-Szalanski, Boyce, Harrell, & Gardener, 1987; Faden et al., 1981), patients prefer detailed and extensive disclosures, particularly regarding risks, and do not want to have to ask for this information (Benson, Gordon, Mitchell & Place, 1977; Joubert & Lasagna, 1975; Keown, Slovic, & Lichtenstein, 1984; Mazis, Morris, & Gordon, 1978). Hesketh, Lindsay, & Harden's (1995) study, which gave patients more extensive explanations about the likely causes of their health problem and how their medication worked, led to positive reactions in patients.

Similar findings are reported in numerous other studies. Following pediatric traumatic brain injury, parents report needs for information about status changes and problem areas as well as comprehensive explanations of the child's physical problem, thinking problems, and medical care (Waaland, Burns, & Cockrell, 1993). Stroke patients find a need for explanations about the problems associated with strokes (McLean, Roper-Hall, Mayer, & Main, 1991), whereas Mauss-Clum and Ryan (1981) and Mathis (1984) indicated needs for explanations that provide realistic expectations for families in which an adult has experienced a traumatic brain injury. Men going through transurethral prostatectomy need explanations about the medical and sexual consequences of surgery, clear instructions about the do's and don'ts during recovery, and information about what is normal and to be expected during the prostatectomy experience (Libman, Creti, & Fichten, 1987). Expectant mothers report high levels of uncertainty regarding what to expect during labor and delivery (Williams & Meredith, 1984). They also need more information about breast feeding but feel that they are given too much information about smoking and drinking and too much written information.

Parents frequently report the need for more adequate explanations regarding their children's health problems. Krauss-Mars & Lachman (1994) found that many parents of disabled children report not being given an explanation of their child's problem, and parents of children with growth problems indicate unrealistic expectations for treatment because of lack of explanations from the doctor (Rotnem, Cohen, Hintz, & Genel, 1979).

HEALTH CARE PROVIDERS' OPINIONS

Based on their knowledge of various health problems as well as years of experience working with patients, numerous health care providers have also offered suggestions about what should be included in explanations. Many emphasize that explanations should begin with an assessment of the patient's understanding of the disease and its treatment (Baker & Feldman, 1993). Among the more general (non-disease-specific) discussions of the issue, Bray (1986) advocated the need to (a) explain procedures; (b) discuss new sensations, postoperative interventions, hospital policy, and the sequence of surgical events; and (c) explain pain reduction adjuncts. In one of the earliest articles on this topic, titled simply "Explanation to the Patient," Aasterud (1963) urged care providers to provide explanations that will help the patient avoid surprises. She noted that patients typically do not need a lot of technical information but that it is helpful for them to have a general summary of what is to be done, the expected action of the patient him- or herself during the procedure, and the approximate length of time involved.

Much of the writing by care providers regarding what should be included in explanations is grounded in Mishel's (1984, 1988) model of uncertainty in illness. Mishel defined *uncertainty* as the inability to determine the meaning of illness-related events and proposed that uncertainty has four forms in the illness experience: (a) ambiguity regarding the state of the illness, (b) complexity of treatment and care, (c) lack of information about the diagnosis and seriousness of the illness, and (d) unpredictability concerning the course of the disease and prognosis. It is argued, then, that explanations should address these four concerns (Bubela et al., 1990; Dodd, 1988; Strull, Lo, & Charles, 1984; Yong-Bronckopp, 1982).

Of particular concern is explanations for patients who have been critically ill and have been in the Intensive Care Unit (ICU). Noting that most intensive care patients have little or no memory of the ICU, Jones and O'Donnell (1994) suggested that their special information need relates to knowledge about the road ahead.

Much other writing about what should be included in explanations is disease-specific. For instance, Abley (1991) encouraged care providers to offer explanations to Parkinson's patients that include discussion of how the disease will affect them, its major symptoms and cause, the drugs used for treatment and how they work, and exercises and tips for daily living. Writing about home apnea monitors for children, Ahmann, Meny, and Fink (1992) documented the need for explanations regarding why the child is on the monitor and how and when to use it. Thyroid cancer patients need explanations about coughing and deep breathing, supporting the neck, side-effects, and airway precautions, as well as signs and symptoms of hypocalcemia (Baker & Feldman, 1993). Patients with diabetes require information about correct medication—insulin administration, side-effects of medication, and the effects of diabetes itself (Draheim, 1995). Women experiencing recurrent pregnancy loss need to have possible causes, aspects of diagnostic testing, and available options explained (Timbers & Feinberg, 1996). And asthma patients need explanations regarding when and how to take medication and competence in the use of an inhaler (Osman, 1996).

A rather unusual point about explanation was made by Evans and Stoller (1993) regarding patients with iatrogenic retroperitoneal stones. They note that a key point of explanation to such patients is the location of the stone so that future misdiagnosis and mismanagement can be avoided.

After finding that patients come to the radiology unit having received inadequate explanations, MacPherson & Gormlie (1995) prepared explanatory materials for these patients. The material included information about the indications for the examinations, required preparation, a description of the exam, the duration of the exam, and required aftercare. Patients responded positively to these explanations. Also focusing on a radiological issue, Stewart (1992) noted that lung cancer patients receiving radiation therapy need to know the rationale, goals, and duration of radiotherapy, not to remove treatment field marks, how to care for the radiated parts, the diagnosis and measures to be taken, likely side-effects and how they should be treated, and required changes in lifestyle.

Solomon and Schwegman-Melton's (1987) outline of what should be included in explanations to patients receiving cardiac catheterization is perhaps the most extensive of those available in the literature. Each of the main issues they identified has several subpoints. The main issues are indications for cardiac catheterization; precathetrization preparation; description of the procedure, equipment, and likely sensations during the procedure; explanation of what the patient will experience after the procedure; risks; and results of medicine versus surgery.

Noting the need for sensitivity to individual differences in patients and the possibility of excessive denial, researchers advocate giving cancer patients more adequate explanations to help reduce pain (Turk & Rennert, 1981; Warner, 1992). They focus on factual information about the challenges that will be faced and decisions that will need to be made as well as realistic information about prognosis.

Another problematic situation is faced by the parents of seriously ill children. Emphasizing that the message may well be distorted by parents. Rae-Grant (1985) suggested that information should not be communicated all at once and should be repeated with opportunities for patient questioning, review, and repetition. Explanations should include the causes, prognosis, and treatment of the problem.

OTHER INFORMATION NEEDS

The studies mentioned earlier documented patient information needs by examining patient or care-provider perceptions on this issue. Other studies have attempted to use empirical description to examine information inadequacies. Observation of physician–patient communication has noted a failure of care providers to give explicit verbal advice about how long or how often to take a prescribed medication (Svarstad, 1976; Wiederholt, Clarridge, & Svarstad, 1992); lack of explanation about the purpose of pulmonary function tests (Khatri, Kaufman, & Baigelman, 1994) or reasons for preoperative fasting (Chapman, 1996); little patient understanding of a chemotherapy drug regimen, side-effects of those drugs, or the purpose and goal of their treatment (Muss et al., 1979); and no discussion of prevention of reinfection in women with sexually transmitted disease (Fleisher, Senie, Minkoff, & Jaccard, 1994). Depending on the STD, from 6.8% to 42.9% of the women studied by Fleisher et al. did not even know the disease for which they were being treated was sexually transmitted. Sixty-seven percent of pediatric respiratory care practitioners do not routinely counsel parents about the negative consequences of second-hand smoke (Wilson & Cohn, 1996), and only one half of referring medical personnel gave a thorough explanation of preparation for and details of barium enema exams (Brown & Silberstein, 1995).

HOW TO COMMUNICATE EXPLANATIONS

Whereas the writing cited previously focused on the content that should be included in explanations, other experts have discussed the manner in which explanations should be communicated. Many recurrent themes emerge across this work. Not surprising, it is suggested that explanations be adapted to the knowledge level and concerns of the individual patient (Righter, 1995; Volker, 1991)—it should be translated to be applicable to the patient's life (Hunt, Jordan, Irwin, & Browner, 1989). Hunt et al. also noted that such an approach will help promote compliance. Tuckett, Boulton, and Olson (1985) ground their recommendation of individual adaptation in the Health Belief Model, which argues that patients must understand the purpose of an action (ameliorative, curative, investigative, or preventive) in order to evaluate it. This notion of individual adaptation is also echoed in Noble's (1991) exhortation to provide explanations at the time the patient is ready to hear them, not at a predetermined point.

Preparatory work is discussed by several authors. Care providers are urged to put the patient at ease (Ley & Spelman, 1967) and to elicit the patient's explanatory model of their illness (Katon & Kleinman, 1981) before offering explanations. Similarly, Webb (1985) suggested first establishing the patient's level of understanding and then providing information that is both brief and directly related to the next important event. Baack's (1993) suggestion of letting the patient set the pace of the conversation is also consistent with the guideline of individual adaptation. Additionally, Baack suggested the use of open-ended questions and reflective statements to encourage verbalization of concerns and clarification of issues.

The need for simplicity of explanations has been oft-repeated (Horder et al., 1972; Jolly, Scott, & Sanford, 1995; Walton et al., 1980). Horder et al. and Walton et al. went so far as to suggest limiting explanations to one or two statements. Fletcher, Fletcher, Thomas, and Hamann (1979) found that simpler explanations were correlated with improved recall and comprehension. Fletcher et al.'s explanations focused on fewer problems and fewer treatments. Similarly, Ley (1987) improved recall by using simpler language, explicit categorization, announcing the categories, repetition, and concrete advice statements. Other examples of simpler, more specific wording were offered by Ley, Bradshaw, Kincey, & Atherton (1976, p. 406). Instead of telling patients to "just take the pills every morning," patients were told to, "take the green ones for 4 days and the red ones for 7 days; wait for 5 days" and "take it when you have your coffee." Ley et al. (1976) also documented improved patient recall. Structured rather than unstructured explanations have been found more effective (Lindeman & Aernam, 1971).

Focusing on patients with low-literacy skills, Mayeaux et al. (1996) provided similar suggestions: simple language, delivering important messages both first and last, repetition, demonstration of procedures or other points, and avoidance of too many directives. They point out that examples should have meaning to the patient and may be communicated most effectively as narratives. They also suggest sitting by the patient and making eye contact (if culturally appropriate) during the conversation. Morton (1996) offered similar guidelines, noting that this can help demystify illness. Morton also suggested a private setting, a gentle manner, and awareness of nonverbals and points out that honesty is essential for morale.

Explanations to reduce anxiety are discussed by several authors. Janis (1983) offered a Stress Inoculation Theory that discusses the need for the communication of realistic information, including details of inherent risks. Patients' feelings of loss of personal control are counteracted by reminding them of their personal resources and abilities to cope and by urging them to develop a personal coping strategy. Janis noted that patients must be allowed to do "the work of worrying," so should be given time to work through their anxiety. These suggestions are also echoed by Teasdale (1993) and Ridgway and Matthews (1982) as they discussed "reframing" techniques. Grew, Stabler, Williams, and Underwood (1983) also discussed reframing, as well as clarifying and redirecting useful techniques to facilitate explanation provision.

Other researchers have suggested that it is not information, per se, that has positive effects for patients but the emotional support that should come with explanations (Dunkel-Schetter, 1984). Roter (1989) argued that the interpreted message from information exchange is one of interest and caring on the part of the doctor. Other research has noted that the main support received from care providers is informational (Yates, 1995). However, Yates reported inadequate support from care providers.

The emotional context of explanations is also discussed by Rusin (1992), who urges care providers to be aware of the affect they communicate and to deal with emotions before content. Other potentially negative aspects of explanations are discussed by Rabinowitz, Beckman, Morse, and Naumburg (1994), who focused on explanations that are controlling. They indicted language that makes a person a possession, such as talking about "my patients." They advocated instead framing the explanation in the patient's context and making the explanation dyadic. This would include incorporating the patient's concerns, fears, and denial; validating feelings; and acknowledging patient control. They noted that sharing expressions of concern and anxiety with the patient may even lead to improved health outcomes. Similarly, Zola (1981) pointed out the need to reassure first so that explanations can then be heard. Patients want information to be provided with a sense of warmth, empathy, and support (DiMatteo, Linn, Chang, & Cope, 1985; Lind, DelVecchio-Good, Seidel, Csordas, & Good, 1989; Martin, 1989). Haas and Puretz (1992) reminded care providers to anticipate questions that patients might be uncomfortable asking, such as those about taboo or embarrassing topics, and initiate such explanations. Finally, the presence of a supportive person at the time of the explanation has also been shown to be helpful (Gerle, Lunden, & Sandblook, 1960; Peteet, Abrams, Ross, & Stearns, 1991; Reid, Bennett-Emslie, Adams, & Kae, 1988).

A PROBLEM

The reader will note that much of the information in the section just completed is in conflict with what has been argued in the previous two sections. Although the research on patient needs indicates a fairly detailed list of the things that patients suggest they need to know and the writing by care providers about what patients should know based on the requirements of various health problems and procedures also leads to a rather lengthy list, the writing about how to communicate explanations argues that doctors should keep those lists rather short. We are told to keep the communication simple—to communicate just a few items to patients. To attempt to address this dilemma, the discussion is turned to the research that has studied the effects of different types of explanations.

EXPERIMENTAL STUDIES OF THE EFFECTS OF EXPLANATIONS

Although the introductory portion of this chapter cited numerous studies indicating the positive effects of increased information to the patient, it would be simplistic to assume that all information has the same impact. Several studies have experimentally manipulated the types of explanations provided.

The majority of these studies have examined the effects of sensory versus procedural information. Results have indicated more positive effects of sensory than procedural information (Hartfield, Cason, & Cason, 1982) but warnings about high pain block the reduction of distress (Leventhal, Brown, Schacham, & Engquist, 1979). Sensory information elicits a cognitive, evaluative response, whereas pain information elicits an affective, emotional response (Leventhal et al., 1979). Other studies have indicated that both sensory and procedural explanations result in less need for medication, but a sensations message also leads to less tension, restlessness, and heart rate acceleration (Johnson, Morrisey, & Leventhal, 1973). Johnson, Kirchhoff, and Endress (1975) found more positive effects of sensory explanations than procedural or no explanations but found that procedural information helped more than no explanation at all. The preferred explanation combines sensory and procedural information, and descriptions of sensations need not be complete to be helpful (Johnson, 1973, 1975; Johnson & Rice, 1974). Such information leads to decreased pain sensation (Ingersoll & Mangus, 1992). Sensory information results in less distress than does typical health education information, especially when the sensory information is coupled with information that helps a patient interpret a potentially threatening event (Fuller, Endress, & Johnson, 1978).

Research has also shown that patients receiving sensory information show greater willingness to repeat the procedure (Padilla et al., 1981). The sensory information described typically includes explanation of such sensations as, in the case of patients undergoing nasogastric intubation, how the passage of the tube will feel; tearing; gagging; discomforts in the nose, throat, or mouth; and feelings of limited mobility (Padilla et al., 1981). Sensory information combined with a description of the procedure and some suggested coping mechanisms, however, decreases discomfort, pain, and anxiety (Padilla et al., 1981).

In cholecystectompy patients, instruction in coping activities, description of sensations, and description of events all dampened negative postoperative moods, especially in fearful patients, but description of typical sensations reduced the length of postoperative hospitalization and time after hospital discharge before patients left their homes. A similar study of herniorrhapy patients, however, found few effects (Johnson, Rice, Fuller, & Endress, 1978).

Characteristics of patients also moderate the impact of explanations. Wilson (1981) reported that sensory information to aggressive patients reduced hospital stay and decreased pain, medication, and epinephrine. Effects were not as strong in nonaggressive patients. Patients using denial were not harmed.

Hjelm-Karlsson (1989) compared a combination of sensory, procedural, and coping explanations to no explanation in patients about to undergo a threatening medical event. Although no differences were reported in physiological reactions, participants receiving the information experienced less pain and discomfort and were calmer, less tense, and more trusting. Other studies have documented positive patient outcomes in reaction to communication about (a) what to expect in the postoperative period, which led to improved pain control, increased mobility, and ability to sleep (Lewin, 1995); (b) explanations about the recommended treatment plan, its rationale, and its link to the patient's complaint (Eisenthal, Koopman, & Lazare, 1983); and (c) increased information about diet, frequency and use of medications, how the medicine is to be used, and potential side-effects (Chwalow et al., 1990). Research by Chwalow and colleagues demonstrated especially strong effects on sicker, less well-educated, poorer patients.

Patient recall has also been enhanced experimentally through providing a tape recording of the interaction with the care provider (North, Cornbleet, Knowles, & Leonard, 1992; Reynolds, Sanson-Fisher, Poole, Harker, & Byrne, 1981; Tattersall, Butow, Griffin, & Dunn, 1994). North et al. (1992) found reduced anxiety in these patients. Tattersall et al. (1994) reported more positive reactions to the tape recording than to a take-home letter.

OBSERVATION OF EXPLANATIONS

Continuing with the theme of observational research of explanation provision are several studies that have looked in depth at such communication. These studies have focused on various contexts. Examining the communication that occurs prior to bone marrow transplantation (BMT), Carney (1987) found that the initial discussion occurs between the doctor and the patient, includes repetition and reinforcement, and is followed up by discussions between nurses and the patient. Although the physicians only provide the patient with the information needed to make a logical decision, such as information on diagnosis and treatment options, nurses provide most of the information about BMT itself, including risks, side-effects, and complications. Nurses emphasize validating the patient's understanding and take an approach that reflects confrontation with quality-of-life issues.

In another cancer-focused study, Dennison (1995) observed the communication that takes place between nurses and patients while chemotherapy is being administered. This study reported that most interactions were initiated by nurses; concentrated on information giving; and included detailed, clear, precise explanations reflecting the highly technical nature of the procedure. Nurses rarely made an attempt to assess patients' understanding of the situation, their preconceptions, or their feelings. This is in contrast, then, to Carney's (1987) findings.

Kalet, Roberts, and Fletcher (1994) were interested in discussions between physicians and patients about risk. They found that risk discussion occurred in only 26% of the cases. Specifically with respect to outcome, however, risk discussions were observed in 48% of the interactions.

Little discussion of risk is also found in communication about medications. Parrott (1994b) studied family practitioners and their patients. Only one half of the doctors named the prescribed medication and only one discussed dosage. There was little mention of possible side-effects and none of possible benefits. The limited discussion of side-effects was typically indirect, characterized by questions about medical history that might lead one to infer potential side-effects. Few physicians discussed cost. No doctor initiated discussion of alternative treatment or drug interactions, repeated information, or provided written instructions. Note that this is in striking contrast to the recommendations available in the literature regarding such communication.

These trends are also reported in Smith, Cunningham, and Hale's (1994) examination of communication between care providers and the ambulatory elderly as it relates to medication. Smith et al. found that physicians provide more explanations about prescription drugs, whereas pharmacists are more active in discussion of over-the-counter medications. This study, too, found that physicians discussed drug interactions and side-effects relatively little.

Overall, however, Smith et al. found a willingness on the part of physicians to provide explanations.

Tannen and Wallat's (1983) study emphasized the different registers or frames pediatricians use when communicating with the child, the family, or medical staff. To the mother, potential risks are downplayed through words such as "only" and "just" as well as conditional phrases that mitigate the seriousness of the information being delivered. By contrast, discussion with medical staff about the same patient includes the terms "sudden death" and "intercranial hemorrhage"—terms that were not included in the physician's communication with the mother. Phrasing to the staff is less conditional, discussing "the possibility" of danger, rather than what danger "would be," as was said to the mother. Tannen and Wallat concluded that physicians may deliberately choose to limit the information patients receive and noted that the physician's choice of wording also limits the mother's understanding of her child's problem.

Beck and Ragan (1995) used a similar microanalytic approach in their study of the provision of patient education to patients. They noted that such interactional resources as repetition, pauses, tag questions, and questions regarding patient understanding prove useful in this process. The discussion returns to their work later in the chapter.

Many of the themes reported are summarized in Sharf's (1990) narrative analysis of physician–patient communication. She concluded that:

> The doctor's story is told in an accounting style that offers medical explanations for selected symptoms (but not for others), reprimands the patient for not having stuck with a diet, and repeatedly warns the patient about further repercussions. It uses medical authority with a paternalistic and overly familiar air; for example, the doctor feels free to address the patient as "chief," but, after a year, knows little about the man's family life. (p. 227)

MEDICAL TERMINOLOGY

Moving beyond a lack of explanation, the most commonly cited problem with the nature of explanations is provider reliance on medical terminology or jargon. As Shuy (1983) argued, jargon is an acceptable and useful tool in the group that knows it. Scott and Weiner (1984) noted that, after having worked hard to acquire a highly specialized vocabulary, care providers are understandably proud of their expertise but frequently lose contact with patients as a result. Jargon is even more problematic because different health care providers may use different terms for the same thing (Gelman, 1980; Swenson, 1984). Use of jargon results in either a lack of comprehension or social one-upmanship (Shuy, 1983). However, use of less jargon increases satisfaction and compliance (Davis, 1971; Korsch et al., 1968). The application of jargon-like labels to patients also colors care providers' perceptions, leading them to perceive only certain characteristics of those patients (Baziak & Dentan, 1960; Gelman, 1980). Ambiguous language is also associated with involuntary noncompliance (Jette, 1982).

Korsch and Negrete (1972) reported that, in more than half of the 800 pediatric visits they studied, physicians used specialized technical terms that were unclear to patients. Terms used included "nares," "peristalsis," and "Coombs titre." Reliance on medical jargon has also been reported in other studies (Boyle, 1970; Ley & Spelman, 1967; McKinlay, 1975; Redlich, 1945; Seligman, McGrath, & Pratt, 1957; Silver, 1979). Misunderstanding of even nontechnical terms such as "arthritis," "diabetes," "stomach ulcer," "asthma," and "chronic bronchitis" has been demonstrated (Ley & Spelman, 1967). Shuy (1976) reported that 38% of patients think that care providers use words that are difficult to understand, and 70% believe that the doctor sometimes withholds information. Shuy's observations of medical interactions concluded that "by far, the largest parts of the medical interviews were conducted in doctor language" (p. 372). Patients tried to adapt their language and speak doctor talk, but doctors did not make it easy for patients.

More recently, Ali and Mahmoud (1993) reported that 22.7% of the patients who are dissatisfied with primary care services in Saudi Arabia feel that way because physicians' explanations are neither clear nor understandable. Orr, Morton, de Leon, and Fals' (1996) study of ethics consultations found that they are helpful because they result in interpretation of jargon, among other things. It is quite a comment on the lack of clarity of explanations that ethics consultations are necessary to improve understanding.

Although the ability of the physician to adapt language to the level of the patient affects patient satisfaction (Comstock, Hooper, & Goodwin, 1982), the implications of jargon use go well beyond this lack of satisfaction. Reliance on technical language leads to lower comprehension and recall (Jackson, 1992). Additionally, Glaser and Strauss' (1965) classic work concluded that use of medical jargon leads to a regressive cycle that can deepen and ultimately lead to a passive patient who feels little control. Because patients are often in trouble or pain when seeing a doctor, they are more willing to be told what to do than would be the case in other contexts; the medical context is "ripe for control" (Shuy, 1983, p. 190). Righter (1995) cited the role of the ostomy nurse in minimizing ambiguity for patients, which may help reverse this cycle.

That patients and doctors use different languages has long been argued (West, 1984). West also noted that physicians do not know what constitutes jargon and that patients do not like jargon. Differences between doctors and patients are especially notable in the area of what is considered common knowledge and in definitions and terms (Blumhagen, 1980; Boyle, 1970; Hadlow & Pitts, 1991; Hawkes, 1974; Pendleton, 1983; Samora, Saunders,

& Larson, 1961; Segal & Roberts, 1980). Physicians are only completely correct in their interpretations of many medical terms 70% of the time, whereas patients are correct a mere 36% of the time (Hadlow & Pitts, 1991). Although it is assumed that patient understanding of medical terminology has improved, Thompson and Pledger (1993) found only slight improvements in word recognition—less than predicted. Almost 30% of patient responses to common medical terms were vague or incorrect, and no word was correctly identified by all participants.

Research is rich with examples of misunderstood terms from medical encounters. Blumhagen discusses the differences between hypertension and "Hyper-Tension," a folk illness that describes a state of being very tense. Silver (1979) noted, "one patient thought that being on a low-salt diet was bad enough. Then, in the hospital, she discovered to her dismay that she was also put on a low-sodium diet" (p. 4). Scott and Weiner (1984) cited a patient who reported no problems with anxiety, when she had been on "nerve pills" for years—she did not understand the term "anxiety." The ambiguity of the word "for" in medical terminology has been noted (Ley, 1988) in that the word has different meanings in "take for pain" or "take for sleeping." In one case "for" means to reduce and in the other to cause. Such ambiguity can prove confusing. Similarly, Reid, Kardash, Robinson, & Scholes (1994) noted that patient literature uses the word "affects" when what is really meant is "hurts." Mayeaux et al.'s (1996) study of patients with low literacy skills found that the phrase "fat in diet" meant anything fattening, including bread, potatoes, and rice to some patients. Other patients did not know what "orally" or "3 times a day" meant. They did not know the difference between a teaspoon and a tablespoon and were not sure if medications for the ear went in the ear or the mouth. Mayeaux et al. noted that 47% of the adult population in the United States has low literacy skills and that low literacy is frequently associated with poor health (see chap. 5, this volume).

Thus, even nonmedical terms can lead to problematic interpretation in the medical context. Zola (1980, pp. 247–248) provided examples of several common problems: (a) "Take this drug four times a day" (must I wake up in the middle of the night to do so?"); (b) "Keep your leg elevated most of the day" (how high? what's "most"? when I sleep?); (c) "Take frequent baths" (what temperature? how long? what's "frequent"?); (d) "Use this pill if you can't stand the pain" (what does "can't stand" mean?); and (e) "Come back if there are any complications" (how bad? must it be unbearable? how do I know if the problem is due to my original concern or to the treatment?).

Shuy's (1976) research notes similar examples: "cardiac arrest" being interpreted as trouble with the police and a patient responding to a question about varicose veins with, "Well, I have veins, but I don't know if they're close or not" (p. 376). Even when not using specialized medical jargon, Shuy indicted physicians for reliance on medical class terminology. He wrote that expressions such as "an infection like pneumonia" or "blood poisoning" are not likely to be understood by all patients because many do not think of pneumonia as an infection and "blood poisoning" is likely to be unclear. "Diabetes" is less likely to be clear to some populations than is the term "sugar" or "sugar diabetes." "Heart trouble" is more understandable to many than "heart disease," especially since "heart trouble" communicates a history of the disease. Some patients use the term "consumption" to refer to a person who drinks him- or herself to death and will talk about "runny bowels" or "running off at the bowels" instead of "diarrhea." Even terms such as "abortion," which, to the doctor, may mean a pregnancy termination that is spontaneous rather than self-induced, will not be interpreted in that way by patients. Shuy concluded by suggesting that "The doctor's over-use of his (sic) technical language tends to estrange him from the patient" (p. 381).

Nonetheless, studies of patient explanations have continued to show reliance on overly complicated terminology, such as "thalassemia trait" (Rowley, Lipkin, & Fisher, 1984). Rowley et al. found that the number of information points in genetic counseling ranged from 25 to 55 but that they could explain all that was necessary with 16. Even under ideal circumstances, the patients they studied could only learn and retain 75% of the information communicated.

Because of concerns about medical terminology, Scott and Weiner (1984) conducted research that led to the development of a "Patientspeak" dictionary. They found that words such as "diastolic," "abnormal," "angina," "bronchus," "chancre," "coitus," "fistula," "hypotension," "mania," "organ," "purulent," and "fracture," although commonly used by care providers, are unclear to patients. Some terms were unclear because of their unique usage in medicine, including "abdomen," "artery," "dizzy," "flex," "full-term," "homosexual," "nausea," "paralysis," "pelvis," "premature," "rotate," "stroke," and "trauma." Regional or ethnic variations in dialect led to different meanings for words such as "boil," "ancestors," "cantaloupe," "compensation," "diaphragm," "dosage," "frankfurter," "spice," and "seasoning." Gender differences were associated with different reactions to "condom," "climax," and "male sex organ" versus "penis." And even nontechnical words such as "alleviate," "apprehensive," "citrus," "deviate," "hereditary," "intermittent," "maladjustment," "nutrition," "radiate," or "ventilate," which were used in explanations provided by physicians, were not always clear to patients.

Other misunderstandings are also evident. Zola (1980) discussed a survey that found that, of a group of patients taking diuretics for fluid retention, over half believed the drugs helped retain fluid and adjusted their use accordingly. This theme is also echoed by anthropologist Lewis (1980), who noted that, even when patients and care providers use the same term correctly, they may give it different significance. Lewis used the example of leprosy and the stigma attached to it by patients. Stoeckle and Barsky (1980) cited similar emotional reactions to such diagnoses as "kidney trouble," in that the patient may have an associated perception of doom.

Related to Scott and Weiner's (1984) categories of types of problematic terms but taking a slightly different perspective, Katon and Kleinman (1980) described five conceptual differences between patients and physicians: (a) using the same term but meaning different things (when a doctor asks about "allergies" to medications, patients sometimes describe side-effects); (b) using the same term but having different etiologic concepts about it (a patient with high blood pressure may attribute it all to stress, whereas the physician includes genetic predispositions and physiologic abnormalities); (c) using the same term but embedding it in different nosologies (the patient may perceive that ulcers lead to cancer); (d) using the same term but having different emotional meanings attached (a diagnosis of "mental illness" is likely to lead to strong patient reactions); and (e) simply not using the same terms. This categorization helps indicate the complexity of the language used in explanations. All of these types of problems are likely to lead to communication difficulties.

I referred earlier to studies of sensory versus procedural information. Building on that line of research, Streator, Ingersoll, and Knight (1995) examined the differential impacts of various types of terms describing sensation. Their study of cold treatments looked at traditional terms (cold, burning, aching, numbness), high-level terms (freezing, crushing, pounding, heavy), moderate-level terms (cold, gnawing, pulsing, aching), or low-level terms (cool, pinching, flickering, dull). They found few differences among the types of terms but concluded that all of those groups reported less pain than did a control group that did not receive sensory information.

A few studies have looked particularly at the euphemisms that are sometimes used by care providers, particularly in discussions of cancer. Some care providers rely on terms such as "tumor," "mass," "malignancy," or "growth" rather than talking about "cancer" (Hardy, Green, Jordan, & Hardy, 1980; Hardy & Hardy, 1979; Oken, 1961). Fisher (1983) cited examples of physicians referring to cancer simply as "it," whereas Mishler (1984) described interactions with cancer patients that never once include the word "cancer" but instead make only vague references to past surgeries. Research indicates that patients prefer messages that do not rely on euphemisms (Woodard & Pamias, 1992). This is especially true of patients who desire a more active role in treatment decisions (Hack, Degner, & Dyck, 1994).

Care providers have been accused of talking at cross-purposes with their patients, evading emotional issues in favor of quasi-scientific explanations that patients do not understand (Raimbault, Cachin, Limal, Eliacheff, & Rappaport, 1975). Raimbault et al. cited numerous examples of patient questions or issues being interrupted and ignored, indicating the doctor's unavailability to the patient. The physician behaviors they cited appear to demonstrate an unwillingness to understand patient concerns. Answers such as, "we are incapable of giving you this information" are offered to patients, although later statements indicate that the physician does indeed have this information. The information he has, however, is not the information that the patient hopes to hear. Other examples provided by Raimbault et al. show the doctor discarding the patient's unscientific reply and imposing a scientific version. "The conversation becomes rather one-sided since the physician acted as if he were teaching about disease to one of his students, giving as much scientific detail as he could" (p. 404). These themes are continued in conversation after conversation with the same patient, as Raimbault et al. demonstrated that the misunderstandings later show up in patients.

Raimbault et al.'s example, "we are incapable of giving you this information," is also an excellent example of nonimmediacy in language use (Wiener & Mehrabian, 1968). Parrott (1994a) applied the concept of nonimmediacy to the physician–patient interaction. She discussed such examples as denotatively nonspecific speech—"Physicians recommend that patients take some time off" rather than the more immediate "I recommend you take some time off"; the first phrasing communicates a message from the body elite of medicine to a patient (a member of a category) rather than a message from a person to a person. She likened spatially and temporally nonimmediate messages to the creation of an "I–It" relationship (Buber, 1958), although she noted that such messages may provide a polite and face-saving way to obtain sensitive and potentially privacy-invasive information. Her empirical results indicate a great deal of nonimmediate speech in medical interaction, that any utterance containing one nonimmediate form is also likely to contain other forms, that gender and experience moderate the likely use of nonimmediate speech, and that nonimmediate speech may also be used to clarify medical information.

The power of nonimmediacy is demonstrated by Fisher's (1983) examples of doctors responses to patients' questions about the need for a suggested hysterectomy. When a physician responds with, "Well, it isn't *absolutely* necessary," the message is communicated that a hysterectomy certainly is preferable. Fisher noted that doctors also use patients' concerns to initiate discussions of morality, which lead to apparent blame for the health problem on the patient.

Echoing a similar theme, Quint (1965) noted physicians phrasing diagnoses generally rather than specifically, which made patient understanding more difficult, or answering questions using "such hedging, evasive, or unintelligibly technical terms" that patients believed their prognosis was more positive than it really was (Davis, 1960, p. 44). Such a discussion leads to the next topic—mystification and control of patients.

MYSTIFICATION AND CONTROL

In response to the question, "Why don't doctors explain a medical problem in simple language that a patient can understand?" noted heart surgeon Michale E. DeBakey once replied, "Most doctors don't want their patients to understand them! They prefer to keep their work a mystery. If patients don't understand what a doctor is talking about, they won't ask him (sic) questions. Then the doctor won't have to be bothered answering them" (Shuy, 1976, p. 369). Implicit in DeBakey's response is the suggestion that care providers deliberately control information. Others have argued a similar point, noting that care providers' use of jargon is intended to mystify the patient, making the provider appear more god-like and in control while actually keeping control over the patient. Fisher (1986) echoed this concern when she wrote that giving the patient more information can serve to change the asymmetry of the relationship, whereas Tate (1983) argued that doctors attempt to maintain power over patients by giving little or cryptic information.

Mystification and other aspects of medical communication can be used to control the patient and health decisions, making the vulnerable even more vulnerable (Gelman, 1980). Todd (1983) provided numerous examples of physicians manipulating the information about treatment benefits and side-effects to lead patients to select the treatment desired by the physician. This may have resulted in unnecessary hysterectomies, in that residents need patients on which to practice such procedures and guide patients accordingly. She noted other instances in which physicians "assumed the role of protector of reproductive function" (p. 178) even when women desired no more children and that the physicians' "power was used in part to reinforce traditional stereotypes of women and their life options" (p. 179). Consistently, "the doctor's reasoning or interpretation took priority over the patient's" (p. 179), and physicians even laughed off patients' concerns. The diminutive "little" is used in many explanations to color patients' perceptions, "I'm just going to do a little exam." Todd concluded, "The doctor ... truncates the patient's social understandings with clinical, technical definitions and with stereotypical social definitions of women's proper roles" (p. 184).

Cicourel (1983) reported physicians recoding the patient's language into fairly abstract categories reflecting explicit medical terminology, interpretations, and factual statements. He noted the same differing linguistic registers to which Tannen and Wallat (1983) referred.

Barnlund (1976) was the first to discuss mystification in the medical context, including an analysis of the role of jargon in mystification and how medical education brings about behavior that is likely to mystify patients. He also noted, however, that mystification may be used "as a constructive

way of protecting the patient from undue anxiety in view of the limited assistance that medicine and surgery can provide" (p. 723). Others agree that
mystification is not always a negative process. Lewis (1980) cited examples of physicians using mystifying jargon explicitly to try to escape from
the unpleasant associations of a term, such as "Hansen's disease" rather
than "leprosy."

EFFECTIVE EXAMPLES

Just as the literature is rich with examples of misunderstood terms from the
provider-patient context, many examples are also found of effective explanation provision. For instance, Cicourel (1983) reported physicians referring to medication by the color of the pill rather than the medical name to
facilitate patient comprehension. Another effective interactional style is
described by Johnson (1993). The nurse practitioner described in this research uses more open-ended questions than do most physicians. She allows for diversion but picks up on teachable moments in which to provide
explanations. Johnson found that this approach helped patients gain a sense
of control over an overwhelming situation.

A nontraditional care provider is also analyzed in Oth's (1994) discussion
of how a Doctor of Chiropracty (D.C.) treats his patients. "Patient satisfaction is enhanced by a practitioner-patient relationship characterized by initial
transmission of large amounts of comprehensible information successively
supplanted by personal affective dialogue" (p. 83). Orth's selection of a D.C.
is especially appropriate because patient dissatisfaction with the communication of traditional care providers leads them to turn to alternatives, especially D.C.s (Howard-Ruben & Miller, 1984). The D.C. explains both his
terminology and the theory underlying his treatment. During the initial
exam, 49% of the dialogue is information exchange. By the time the first spi-
nal manipulation occurs, 34% of the interchange involves the explanation of
information. Even at later reexaminations, 48% of the communication is informational. The content of the information is instrumental and
task-oriented. Woven through the information are such techniques as language consciousness, analogy, negotiation, and repetition of important
points. He details test and x-ray results in ordinary language and actively
demonstrates procedures. He explains etiology by relying on everyday analogies, such as a car. He unpacks and demystifies. Notably, he does not deper-
sonalize by referring to body parts with a definite article ("the neck"), but
uses a possessive pronoun ("your neck"). He uses "we" to indicate mutuality.

In a much more focused context, Chenail et al.'s (1990) analysis of pediatric cardiology referrals contrasted most other physicians with one who
sets up the referral by first underlining the baby's health. He then uses such
phrases as, "send her to the cardiologist here who's going to tell us not to

worry" and "into the no-big-deal category." He ends the interaction by again reassuring the mother. Chenail et al. advocated such an approach because of the highly stressful nature of most such referrals.

Another discussion of effective explanation provision, code-switching, is offered by Mishler (1984). Mishler began with an analysis of the voice of the lifeworld versus the voice of medicine. Noting that "the special asymmetry of the medical interview is that physicians are communicatively competent in both codes" (p. 172), he indicated that most physicians dominate the voice of the lifeworld with the voice of medicine. This has the effect of "absorbing and dissolving the patient's self-understanding of her problems into a system of purposive-rationale action, namely, the framework of technical medicine" (p. 126). He argued that this leads to an objectification of the patient that seriously impairs the potential for human interaction and human medicine. One of the physicians he studied, however, deals in the voice of the lifeworld with his patients. This physician uses patient terms such as "weak spells" and explains why it is important for her to know the names of her medications. He frames problems as concerns on which they should work together, "what I think we should do is" (p. 173). This is in striking contrast to the other physicians studied by Mishler.

Other examples of code-switching—or a lack thereof—have also been noted. Bourhis, Roth, and MacQueen (1989) examined health professionals' and patients' use of medical language (ML) and English language (EL). Although doctors spoke mostly ML and patients mostly EL, patients did not feel that physicians should use EL exclusively. All groups concurred that the use of ML by health professionals leads to communication difficulties, whereas the use of EL rarely does so. In practice, research shows that physicians employ a model of medicine that is somewhere between the textbook biomedical model and folk models (Fitzpatrick, 1984; Gaines, 1979; Helman, 1978; Lock, 1982; Rippere, 1977, 1981).

Beck and Ragan's (1992) discussion of negotiating relational and medical tasks also demonstrates how a nurse practitioner shifts back and forth from medical to interpersonal frames using such devices as verbal hesitations and disfluencies, laughter, transitional words, or references to a physical object. These mark brief asides or temporary shifts from the medical frame and serve to provide identification, transcending differences. These also help save face for the patient and are done without lengthening the exam. Ragan (1990) also demonstrated such verbal play, which enabled the fulfillment of nonmedical and medical goals simultaneously.

Taking a similar perspective, Ragan, Beck, and White (1995) discovered interactions in which explanations that facilitated patient education were interwoven into exams. They concluded that the shifting of frame actually improved the flow of the exam. Humor, empathy and relational asides reduced face threats. Unlike the "morality talk" described earlier by Todd (1983), information in these exams was communicated to broaden the patients' options without chastising or inducing guilt or anxiety. Recommendations are phrased in conversational terms as suggestions that are followed by detailed explanation to provide a rationale. Communication is a dialogue, rather than a monologue. The patients' misunderstanding is not exaggerated.

Similarly, when a physician's verbal responses indicate intent to use the patient's frame of reference, patients are more satisfied (Putnam, Stiles, Jacob, & James, 1985). Although patient satisfaction is related to acknowledgment of patient statements (Mazzuca & Weinberger, 1986), such acknowledgment decreases patient comprehension (Mazzuca & Weinberger, 1986; Mazzuca, Weinberger, Kurpius, Froehle, & Heister, 1983). Comprehension is increased by physician statements demonstrating respect for the patient and by the sharing of current clinical data (Mazzuca et al., 1983).

CONCLUSION

Although some of the information summarized within this chapter has presented contradictory recommendations, enough recognizable patterns emerge across the research to generate some conclusions about the communication of explanations. First, across health problems it appears essential, if possible, to explain to patients the cause of the health problem, as well as its effects and treatment. Explanation should include how the treatment works, possible side-effects, and prognosis. Patients should also be informed about what to expect in terms of procedures and routines they will encounter and lifestyle changes they should make. Additionally, some health problems have special informational needs, as was made clear in the research reviewed earlier. Care providers specializing in any particular health issue should familiarize themselves with the research on information needs relevant to that health concern.

In anticipation of a particular health procedure, explanations should include information about both the procedure itself and, more important, the sensations the patient will experience during the procedure. As much as possible, medical jargon should be avoided or explained and clarified. Care providers should not attempt to communicate too much information at a time and should check for patient understanding of what has been communicated. A tape recording of the explanation may be provided to patients to improve comprehension, understanding, recall, and compliance.

Patients should be encouraged to ask questions, but more is necessary to accomplish this than a perfunctory, "do you have any questions?" at the end of the interaction. A climate of openness during the consultation is required to enable patients to feel comfortable raising issues and expressing a lack of understanding. This can be facilitated by the frame-shifting from the voice of medicine to the voice of the lifeworld described by several of the authors referred to earlier.

Such a climate can also be enhanced by the recognition that all messages, including explanations, have both content and relationship dimensions. The communication of an adequate explanation indicates to patients that the provider cares about whether or not the patient understands the problem, treatment, and related illness domains. This also communicates a relationship of mutuality, an indication that the patient, too, is involved in the health care process.

REFERENCES

Aasterud, M. (1963). Explanation to the patient. *Nursing Forum, 2,* 36–44.

Abley, C. (1991). Learning to live with Parkinson's: A teaching programme to boost patient understanding. *Professional Nurse, 6,* 458–460.

Adamson, T. E., Tschann, J. M., Gullion, D. S., & Oppenberg, A. A. (1989). Physician communication skills and malpractice claims: A complex relationship. *Western Journal of Medicine, 150,* 356–360.

Ahmann, E., Meny, R. G., & Fink, R. J. (1992). Use of home apnea monitors. *Journal of Obstetrics, Gynecology, and Neonatal Nursing, 21,* 394–399.

Alexy, W. D. (1981–1982). Perceptions of ward atmosphere on an oncology unit. *International Journal of Psychiatry in Medicine, 11,* 331–340.

Ali, E. S. M., & Mahmoud, M. E. A. (1993). A study of patient satisfaction with primary care services in Saudi Arabia. *Journal of Community Health, 18,* 49–54.

Anderson, E. A. (1987). Preoperative preparation for cardiac surgery facilitates recovery, reduces psychological distress and reduces the incidence of acute postoperative hypertension. *Journal of Consulting and Clinical Psychology, 55,* 513–520.

Andrew, J. M. (1970). Recovery from surgery, with or without preparatory isntructions, for three coping styles. *Journal of Personality and Social Psychology, 15,* 223–226.

Averill, J. R. (1973). Personal control over aversive stimuli and its relationship to stress. *Psychological Bulletin, 80,* 286–303.

Baack, C. M. M. (1993). Nursing's role in the nutritional care of the terminally ill: Weathering the storm. *The Hospice Journal, 9,* 1–13.

Baird, R. N. (1996). The vascular patient as litigant. *Annuals of the Royal College of Surgeons of England, 78,* 278–282.

Baker, K. H., & Feldman, J. E. (1993). Thyroid cancer: A review. *Oncology Nursing Forum, 20,* 95–104.

Barnlund, D. C. (1976). The mystification of meaning: Doctor-patient encounters. *Journal of Medical Education, 51,* 716–725.

Baziak, A. T., & Dentan, R. K. (1960). The language of the hospital and its effects on the patient. *ETC: A Review of General Semantics, 17,* 261–268.

Beck, C., & Ragan, S. (1992). Negotiating relational and medical talk: Frame shifts in the gynecologic exam. *Journal of Language and Social Psychology, 11,* 47–61.

Beck, C. S., & Ragan, S. L. (1995). The impact of relational activities on the accomplishment of practitioner and patient goals in the gynecologic examination. In G. Kreps & D. O'Hair (Eds.), *Communication and health outcomes* (pp. 73–85). Cresskill, NJ: Hampton Press.

Becker, M. H., Drachman, R. H., & Kirscht, J. P. (1981). A new approach to explaining sick-role behavior in low-income populations. *American Journal of Public Health, 64,* 205–216.

Bedell, S. E., & Delbanco, T. L. (1984). Choices about cardiopulmonary resuscitation in the hospital: When do physicians talk with patients? *New England Journal of Medicine, 256,* 233–237.

Benson, H., Gordon, L., Mitchell, C., & Place, V. (1977). Patient education and intrauterine conception: A study of two package inserts. *American Journal of Public Health, 67,* 446.

Berkanovic, E., & Marcus, A. C. (1976). Satisfaction with health services: Some policy implications. *Medical Care, 14,* 873–879.

Blinov, N. N., Komiakov, I. P., & Shipovnikov, N. B. (1990). The attitude of cancer patients to their own diagnosis. *Vapr Onkol, 36,* 966–969.

Blumhagen, D. (1980). Hyper-tension: A folk illness with a medical name. *Culture, Medicine, and Psychiatry, 4,* 197–227.

Boore, J. (1980). Pre-operative information and post-operative recovery. *NAT News, 17*(1), 16–19,22.

Boreham, P., & Gibson, D. (1978). The informative process in private medical consultations: A preliminary investigation. *Social Science & Medicine, 12,* 408–416.

Bourhis, R. Y., Roth, S., & MacQueen, G. (1989). Communication in the hospital setting: A survey of medical and everyday language use amongst patients, nurses and doctors. *Social Science & Medicine, 28,* 339–346.

Boyle, C. M. (1970). Difference between patients' and doctors' interpretation of some common medical terms. *British Medical Journal, 2,* 286–289.

Bray, C. A. (1986). Postoperative pain: Altering the patient's experience through education. *AORN Journal, 43,* 672–683.

Brown, C., & Silberstein, M. (1995). Patient understanding of the barium enema examination. *Australian Radiology, 39,* 100–101.

Bubela, N., Galloway, S., McCray, E., McKibbon, A., Nagle, L., Pringle D., Ross, E., & Shamian, J. (1990). Factors influencing patients' informational needs at the time of hospital discharge. *Patient Education and Counseling, 16,* 21–28.

Buber, M. (1958). *I and thou.* New York: Scribner's.

Buller, D. B., & Street, R. L. (1991). The role of perceived affect and information in patients' evaluations of health care and compliance decisions. *Southern Communication Journal, 56,* 230–237.

Canadian Cancer Society (1992). *Final report on the needs of people living with cancer across Canada.* Toronto: Canadian Cancer Society.

Carney, B. (1987). Bone marrow transplantation: Nurses and physicians' percepetions of informed consent. *Cancer Nursing, 10,* 252–259.

Cassileth, B. R., Lusk, E. J., Strouse, T. B., & Bodenheimer, B. J. (1984). Contemporary unorthodox treatments in cancer medicine. *Annals of Internal Medicine, 101,* 105–112.

Cawley, M., Kistic, J., & Cappelo, C. (1990). Information and psychological needs of women choosing conservative surgery/primary radiation for early stage breast cancer. *Cancer Nursing: An International Journal for Cancer Care, 13,* 90–94.

Chapman, A. (1996). Current theory and practice: A study of pre-operative fasting. *Nursing Standard, 10*(18), 33–36.

Charlton, I., Charlton, G., Broomfield, J., & Mullee, M. A. (1990). Evaluation of peak flow and symptoms only in self management plans for control of asthma in general practice. *British Medical Journal, 301,* 1355–1359.

Chenail, R. J., Dauthit, P. E., Gale, J. E., Stormberg, J. L, Morris, G. H., Parks, J. M., Sridaromott, S., & Schmer, V. (1990). "It's probably nothing serious, but … ": Parents' interpretations of referral to pediatric cardiologists. *Health Communication, 2,* 165–188.

Christensen-Szalanski, J. J., Boyce, W. T., Harrell, H., & Gardener, M. M. (1987). Circumcision and informed consent: Is more information always better? *Medical Care, 25,* 856–867.

Chwalow, A. J., Mamon, J., Crosby, E., Grieco, A. J., Salkever, D., Fahey, M., & Levine, D. M. (1990). Effectiveness of a hospital-based cooperative care model on patients' functional status and utilization. *Patient Education and Counseling, 15,* 17–28.

Cicourel, A. J. (1983). Hearing is not believing: Language and the structure of belief in medical communication. In S. Fisher & A. D. Todd (Eds.), *Social organization of doctor-patient communication* (pp. 222–239). Washington, DC: Center for Applied Linguistics.

Clare, A. (1993). Communication in medicine. *European Journal of Disorders of Communication, 28,* 1–12.

Cohen-Mansfield, J., Rabinovich, B. A., Lipson, S., Fein, A., Gerber, B., Weisman S., & Pawlson, L. O. (1991). The decision to execute a durable power of attorney for health care and preferences regarding the utilization of life-sustaining treatments in nursing home residents. *Archives of Internal Medicine, 151,* 289–294.

Comstock, L., Hooper, E., & Goodwin, J. (1982). Physician's behaviors that correlate with patient satisfaction. *Journal of Medical Education, 52,* 105–112.

Corney, R., Everett, H., Howells, A., & Crowther, M. (1992). The care of patients undergoing surgery for gynecological cancer: The need for information, emotional support, and counseling. *Journal of Advanced Nursing, 17,* 667–671.

Davis, F. (1960). Uncertainty in medical prognosis: Clinical and functional. *American Journal of Sociology, 66,* 41–47.

Davis, M. S. (1971). Variation in patients' compliance with doctors' orders: Medical practice and doctor-patient interaction. *Psychiatry in Medicine, 2,* 31–54.

Dennison, S. (1995). An exploration of the communication that takes place between nurses and patients whilst cancer chemotherapy is administered. *Journal of Clinical Nursing, 4,* 227–233.

DiMatteo, M. R., Linn, L. S., Chang, B. L., & Cope, D. W. (1985). Affect and neutrality in physician behaviour: A study of patients' values and satisfaction. *Journal of Behavioral Medicine, 8,* 397–409.

DiMatteo, M. R., Reiter, R. C., & Gambone, J. C. (1994). Enhancing medication adherence through communication and informed collaborative choice. *Health Communication 6,* 253–266.

Dodd, M. J. (1988). The efficacy of pro-active information on care in chemotherapy patients. *Patient Education and Counseling, 11,* 215–225.

Draheim, M. A. (1995). Pharmaceutical intervention in diabetes management. *Gastroenterology Nursing, 18,* 190–195.

Dumas, R. G., Anderson, B. J., & Leonard, R. C. (1965). The importance of the expressive function in preoperative preparation. In J. K. Skipper & R. C. Leonard (Eds.), *Social interaction and patient care* (pp. 16–28). Philadelphia: Lippincott.

Dunkel-Schetter, C. (1984). Social support in cancer: Findings based on patient interviews and their implications. *Journal of Social Issues, 40,* 77–98.

Ebell, M. H., Smith, M. A., Seifert, K. G., & Polsinelli, K. (1990). The do-not-resuscitate order: Outpatient experience and decision-making preferences. *Journal of Family Practice, 31,* 630–636.

Egbert, L. D., Battit, G. E., Turndorf, H., & Beecher, H. K. (1963). The value of the preoperative visit by an anesthetist. *Journal of the American Medical Association, 185,* 553–555.

Egbert, L. D., Battit, G. E., Welch, C. E., & Bartlett, M. K. (1964). Reduction of postoperative pain by encouragement and instruction of patients. *New England Journal of Medicine, 270,* 825–827.

Eisenthal, S., Koopman, C., & Lazare, A. (1983). Process analysis of two dimensions of the negotiated approach in relation to satisfaction in the initial interview. *Journal of Nervous and Mental Disease, 171,* 49–54.

Ernstene, A. C. (1957). Explaining to the patient: A therapeutic tool and a professional obligation. *Journal of the American Medical Association, 165,* 1110–1113.

Evans, C. P., & Stoller, M. L. (1993). The fate of the iatrogenic retroperitoneal stone. *Journal of Urology, 150,* 827–829.

Everhard, M. A., & Pearlman, R. A. (1990). Stability of patient preferences regarding life-sustaining treatments. *Chest, 97,* 159–164.

Faden, R. R., Becker, C., Lewis, C., Freeman, J., & Faden, A. L. (1981). Disclosure of information to patients in medical care. *Medical Care, 19,* 718–733.

Fisher, S. (1983). Doctor talk/patient talk: How treatment decisions are negotiated in doctor-patient communication. In S. Fisher & A. D. Todd (Eds.), *Social organization of doctor-patient communication* (pp. 135–157). Washington, DC: Center for Applied Linguistics.

Fisher, S. (1986). *In the patients' best interest: Women and the politics of medical decisions.* New Brunswick, NJ: Rutgers University Press.

Fitts, W. T., & Ravdin, I. S. (1953). What Philadelphia physicians tell patients with cancer. *Journal of the American Medical Association, 153,* 901–904.

Fitzpatrick, R. (1984). Lay concepts of illness. In R. Fitzpatrick, J. Hinton, S. Newman, G. Scrambler, & J. Thompson (Eds.), *The experience of illness* (pp. 11–31). London: Tavistock.

Fleisher, J. M., Senie, R. T., Minkoff, H., & Jaccard, J. (1994). Condom use relative to knowledge of sexually transmitted disease prevention, method of birth control, and past or present infection. *Journal of Community Health, 19,* 395–407.

Fletcher, S. W., Fletcher, R. H., Thomas, D. C., & Hamann, C. (1979). Patients' understanding of prescribed drugs. *Journal of Community Health, 4,* 183–189.

Francis, V., Korsch, B. M., & Morris, M. L. (1969). Gaps in doctor–patient communication: Patients' response to medical advice. *New England Journal of Medicine, 280,* 535–540.

Frankl, D., Oye, R. K., & Bellamy, P. E. (1989). Attitudes of hospitalized patients toward life support: A survey of 200 medical inpatients. *American Journal of Medicine, 86,* 645–648.

Frederiksen, L. G. (1993). Development of an integrative model for medical consultation. *Health Communication, 5,* 225–237.

Frederiksen, L. G. (1995). Exploring information-exchange in consultation: The patients' view of performance and outcomes. *Patient Education and Counseling, 25,* 237–246.

Fredette, S. L. (1990). A model for improving cancer patient education. *Cancer Nursing: An International Journal for Cancer Care, 13,* 207–215.

Fuller, S. S., Endress, M. P., & Johnson, J. E. (1978). The effects of cognitive and behavioral control on coping with an aversive health examination. *Journal of Human Stress, 4,* 18–25.

Gaines, A. D. (1979). Definitions and diagnosis: Cultural implications of psychiatric help seeking and psychiatrists' definitions of the situation in psychiatric emergencies. *Culture, Medicine, & Psychiatry, 3,* 381–418.

Gamble, E. R., McDonald, P. J., & Lichstein, P. R. (1991). Knowledge, attitudes, and behavior of elderly persons regarding living wills. *Archives of Internal Medicine, 151,* 277–280.

Gelman, S. R. (1980). Esoterica: A zero sum game in the helping professions. *Social Casework: The Journal of Contemporary Social Work, 61,* 48–53.

Gerle, B., Lunden, G., & Sandblook, P. (1960). The patient with inoperable cancer from the psychiatric and social standpoints. *Cancer, 13,* 1206–1217.

Gilbertson, V. A., & Wangensteen, O. H. (1962). Should the doctor tell the patient that the disease is cancer? *CA: A Cancer Journal for Clinicians, 12,* 82–86.

Gillis, C. (1984). Reducing family stress during and after coronary artery bypass surgery. *Nursing Clinics of North America, 19,* 103–112.

Gillispie, M. A., & Ellis, I. R. M, (1993). Computer-based education revisited. *Journal of Medical Systems, 17,* 119–125.

Glaser, B., & Strauss, A. (1965). *Awareness of dying.* Chicago: Aldine-Atherton.

Gotcher, J. M., & Edwards, R. (1990). Coping strategies of cancer patients: Actual communication and imagined interactions. *Health Communication, 2,* 255–266.

Grew, R. S., Stabler, B., Williams, R. W., & Underwood, L. E. (1983). Facilitating patient understanding in the treatment of growth delay. *Clinical Pediatrics, 22,* 685–690.

Haas, A., & Puretz, S. L. (1992). Encouraging partnerships between health care providers and women recommended for gynecological surgery. *Health Communication, 4,* 29–38.

Hack, T. F., Degner, L. F., & Dyck, D. G. (1994). Relationships between preferences for decisional control and illness information among women with breast cancer: A quantitative and qualitative analysis. *Social Science and Medicine, 39,* 279–289.

Hadlow, J., & Pitts, M. (1991). The understanding of common health terms by doctors, nurses, and patients. *Social Science and Medicine, 32,* 193–196.

Hardy, R. E., Green, D. R., Jordan, H. W., & Hardy, G. (1980). Communication between cancer patients and physicians. *Southern Medicial Journal, 73,* 755–757.

Hardy, R. E., & Hardy, G. (1979). Patterns of communication to cancer patients: A descriptive analysis. *Journal of the Tennessee Medical Association, 72,* 656.

Hartfield, M. T., Cason, C. L., & Cason, G. J. (1982). Effects of information about a threatening procedure on patients' expectations and emotional distress. *Nursing Research, 31,* 202–206.

Hathaway, D. (1986). Effect of preoperative instruction on postoperative outcomes: A meta-analysis. *Nursing Research, 35,* 269–275.

Havlir, D., Brown, L., & Rousseau, G. K. (1989). Do not resuscitate discussions in a hospital-based home care program. *Journal of the American Geriatric Society, 37,* 52–54.

Hawkes, C. H. (1974). Communicating with the patient—An example drawn from neurology. *British Journal of Medical Education, 8,* 57–63.

Hayward, J. (1975). *Information—A prescription against pain.* London: Whitefriars Press.

Helman, C. G. (1978). "Feed a cold, starve a fever"—Folk models of infection in an English community, and their relation to medical treatment. *Culture, Medicine, & Psychiatry, 2,* 107–137.

Hesketh, A., Lindsay, G., & Harden, R. (1995). Interactive health promotion in the community pharmacy. *Health Education Journal, 54,* 294–303.

Hepburn, K., & Reed, R. (1995). Ethical and clinical issues with Native-American Elders: End-of-life decision making. *Clinics in Geriatric Medicine, 11,* 97–111.

Hickson, G. B., Clayton, E. W., Entman, S. S., Miller, C. S., Githens, P. B., Whetten-Goldstein, K., & Sloan, F. A. (1994). Obstetricians' prior malpractice experience and patients' satisfaction with care. *Journal of the American Medical Association, 272,* 1583–1587.

Hickson, G. B., Clayton, E. W., Githens, P. B., & Sloan, F. A. (1992). Factors that prompted families to file medical malpractice claims following perinatal injuries. *Journal of the American Medical Association, 267,* 1359–1363.

Hileman, J. W., & Lackey, N. R. (1990). Self-identified needs of patients with cancer at home and their home caregivers: A descriptive study. *Oncology Nursing Forum, 17,* 907–913.

Himmel, W., Stolpe, C., & Kochen, M. (1994). Information and communication about overweight in family practice. *Family Practice Research Journal, 14,* 339–351.

Hinds, C. (1985). The needs of families who care for patients with cancer at home: Are we meeting them? *Journal of Advanced Nursing, 10,* 575–581.

Hines, S. C., Babrow, A. S., Badzek, L., & Moss, A. H. (1997). Communication and problematic integration in end-of-life decisions: Dialysis decisions among the elderly. *Health Communication, 9,* 199–218.

Hjelm-Karlsson, K. (1989). Effects of information to patients undergoing intravenous pyelography: An intervention study. *Journal of Advanced Nursing, 14,* 853–862.

Horder, J., Byrne, P., Freeling, P., Harris, C., Irvine, D., & Marinker, M. (1972). *The future general practitioner: Learning and teaching.* London: Royal College of General Practitioners.

Houts, P. S., Yasko, J. M., Harvey, H. A., Kahn, S. B., Hartz, A. J., Hermann, J. F., Schelzel, G. W., & Bartholomew, M. J. (1988). Unmet needs of persons with cancer in Pennsylvania during the period of terminal care. *Cancer, 62,* 627–634.

Howard-Ruben, J., & Miller, N. J. (1984). Unproven methods of cancer management part II: Current trends and implications for patient care. *Oncology Nursing Forum, 11,* 67–73.

Howell-Koren, P. R., & Tinsley, B. J. (1990). The relationships among maternal health locus of control beliefs and expectations, pediatrician–mother communication, and maternal satisfaction with well-infant care. *Health Communication, 2,* 233–253.

Hugh-Jones, P., Tanser, A. R., & Whitby, C. (1964). Patients' view of admission to a London teaching hospital. *British Medical Journal, 2,* 660–664.

Hunt, L. M., Jordan, B., Irwin, S., & Browner, C. H. (1989). Compliance and the patient's perspective: Controlling symptoms in everyday life. *Culture, Medicine, and Psychiatry, 13,* 315–334.

Ignacio-Garcia, J. M., & Gonzalez-Santso, P. (1995). Asthma self-management education program by home monitoring of peak expiratory flow. *American Journal of Respiratory and Critical Care Medicine, 151,* 353–359.

Ingersoll, C. D., & Mangus, B. C. (1992). Habituation to the perception of the qualities of cold-induced pain. *Journal of Athletic Training, 27,* 218–222.

Jackson, L. D. (1992). Information complexity and medical communication: The effects of technical language and amount of information in a medical message. *Health Communication, 4,* 197–210.

Janis, I. L. (1983). Stress inoculation in health care: Theory and research. In D. Meichenbam & M. E. Jeremko (Eds.), *Stress reduction and prevention* (pp. 67–99). New York: Plenum.

Jette, A. M. (1982). Improving patient cooperation with arthritis treatment regimens. *Arthritis and Rheumatism, 25,* 447–453.

Johnson, J. E. (1973). Effects of accurate expectations about sensations on the sensory and distress components of pain. *Journal of Personality and Social Psychology, 27,* 261–275.

Johnson, J. E. (1975). Stress reduction through sensation information. In I. G. Sarason & C. D. Spielberger (Eds.), *Stress and anxiety* (pp. 361–378). Washington, DC: Hemisphere.

Johnson, J. E., Kirchhoff, K. T., & Endress, M. P. (1975). Altering children's distress behavior during orthopedic cast removal. *Nursing Research, 24,* 404–410.

Johnson, J. E., Morrisey, J. F., & Leventhal, H. (1973). Psychological preparation for an endoscopic examination. *Gastrointestinal Endoscopy, 19,* 180–182.

Johnson, J. E., & Rice, V. H. (1974). Sensory and distress components of pain: Implications for the study of clinical pain. *Nursing Research, 23,* 203–209.

Johnson, J. E., Rice, V. H., Fuller, S. S., & Endress, E. P. (1978). Sensory information, instruction in a coping strategy, and recovery from surgery. *Research in Nursing and Health, 1,* 4–17.

Johnson, R. (1993). Nurse practitioner–patient discourse: Uncovering the voice of nursing in primary care practice. *Scholary Inquiry for Nursing Practice, 7,* 143–157.

Jolly, B. T., Scott, J. L., & Sanford, S. M. (1995). Simplification of emergency discharge instructions improves patient comprehension. *Annals of Emergency Medicine, 26,* 443–446.

Jonash, K., Schwartz, R., & Buhr, H. J. (1989). The process of patient education of cancer patients at a surgical clinic. *Chirurg, 60,* 464–469.

Jones, C., & O'Donnell, C. (1994). After intensive care: What then? *Intensive & Critical Care Nursing, 10,* 89–92.

Joubert, P., & Lasagna, L. (1975). Patient package inserts I: Nature, notions and needs. *Clinical Pharmacological Therapy, 18,* 507.

Kalet, R., Roberts, J. C., & Fletcher, R. (1994). How do physicians talk with their patients about risks? *Journal of General Internal Medicine, 9,* 402–404.

Kaplan, S. H., Greenfield, S., & Ware, J. E. (1989). Impact of the doctor–patient relationship on the outcomes of chronic disease. In M. Stewart & D. Roter (Eds.), *Communicating with medical patients* (pp. 228–245). Newbury Park, CA: Sage.

Katon, W., & Kleinman, A. (1980). Doctor–patient negotiation and other social science strategies in patient care. In L. E. Eisenberg & A. Kleinman (Eds.), *The relevance of social science for medicine* (pp. 253–279). Dordrecht, Netherlands: D. Reidel.

Kelly, W. D., & Friesen, S. R. (1950). Do cancer patients want to be told? *Surgery, 27,* 822–826.

Keown, C., Slovic, P., & Lichtenstein, S. (1984). Attitudes of physicians, pharmacists, and laypersons toward seriousness and need for disclosure of prescription drug side effects. *Health Psychology, 3,* 1–10.

Khatri, K., Kaufman, R., & Baigelman, W. (1994). Utilization of pulmonary function tests by primary care internists in a community hospital. *American Journal of Medical Quality, 9,* 49–53.

Kindeland, K., & Kent, G. (1987). Concordance between patients' information preferences and general practitioners' perceptions. *Psychological Health, 1,* 399–409.

King, P. E. (1991). Communication, anxiety, and the management of postoperative pain. *Health Communication, 3,* 127–138.

Klafta, J. M., & Roizen, M. F. (1996). Current understanding of patients' attitudes toward and preparation for anesthesia: A review. *Anesthesia & Analgesia, 83,* 1314–1321.

Korsch, G., Gozzi, E., & Francis, V. (1968). Gaps in doctor–patient communication: I. Doctor-patient interaction and patient satisfaction. *Pediatrics, 42,* 855–871.

Korsch, B. M., & Negrete, V. F. (1972). Doctor–patient communication. *Scientific American, 227*(2), 66–74.

Krantz, D. S. (1980). Cognitive processes and recovery from heart attck: A review and theoretical analysis. *Journal of Human Stress, 6,* 27–38.

Krauss-Mars, A. H., & Lachman, P. (1994). Breaking bad news to parents with disabled children: A cross-cultural study. *Child: Care, Health, & Development, 20,* 101–113.

Kristanson, L. J. (1989). Quality of terminal care: Salient indicators identified by families. *Journal of Palliative Care, 5,* 21–28.

Kulik, J. A., & Carlino, P. (1987). The effect of verbal commitment and treatment choice on medication compliance in a pediatric setting. *Journal of Behavioural Medicine, 10,* 367–376.

Lack, L., & Holloway, I. M. (1992). Post-surgical hormone replacement therapy: Information needs of women. *Journal of Clinical Nursing, 1,* 323–327.

Lahdensuo, A., Haahtela, T., Herrala, J., Fava, T., Kiviranta, K., Kuusisto, P., Pecamaki, E., Poussa, T., Saarelainen, S., & Svaha, T. (1996). Randomized comparison of guided self management and traditional treatment of asthma over one year. *British Medical Journal, 312,* 748–752.

Lauer, P., Murphy, S., & Powers, M. (1982). Learning needs of cancer patients: A comparison of nurse and patient perceptions. *Nursing Research, 31,* 11–16.

Lazare, A., Eisenthal, S., Wasserman, L., & Harford, T. (1975). Patient requests in a walk-in clinic. *Comprehensive Psychiatry, 16,* 467–477.

Lazarus, R., & Folkman, S. (1974). *Stress appraisal and coping.* New York: Springer.

Lemaitre, G., & Finnegan, J. (1975). *The patient in surgery: A guide for nurses* (3rd ed.). New York: Saunders.

Leventhal, H., Brown, D., Schacham, S., & Engquist, G. (1979). Effects of preparatory information about sensations, threat of pain, and attention on cold pressor distress. *Journal of Personality and Social Psychology, 37,* 688–714.

Lewin, J. (1995). Prescribing practice of take-home analgesia for day case surgery. *British Journal of Nursing, 4,* 1047–1051.

Lewis, G. (1980). Cultural influences on illness behavior: A medical anthropological approach. In L. Eisenberg & A. Kleinman (Eds.), *The relevance of social science for medicine* (pp. 151–162). Dordrecht, Amsterdam: D. Reidel.

Ley, P. (1983). Patient's understanding and recall in clinical communication failure. In D. Pendleton & J. Hasler (Eds.), *Doctor-patient communication* (pp. 89–108). London: Academic.

Ley, P. (1987). Memory for medical information. *British Journal of Social and Clinical Psychology, 18,* 245–255.

Ley, P. (1988). *Communicating with patients: Improving communication, satisfaction, and compliance.* London: Croom Helm.

Ley, P., Bradshaw, P. W., Kincey, J. A., & Atherton, S. T. (1976). Increasing patients' satisfaction with communication. *British Journal of Clinical Psychology, 15,* 403–413.

Ley, P., & Spelman, M. (1967). *Communicating with the patient.* London: Staples Press.

Libman, E., Creti, L., & Fichten, C. S. (1987). Determining what patients should know about transurethral prostatectomy. *Patient Education and Counseling, 9,* 145–153.

Lichter, I. (1977). *Communication in cancer care.* Livingstone, Edinburgh, Scotland: Churchill.

Lieberman, D. (1992). The computer's potential role in health education. *Health Communication, 4,* 211–226.

Lind, S. E., DelVecchio-Good, M. D., Seidel, S., Csordas, T., & Good, B. J. (1989). Telling the diagnosis of cancer. *Journal of Clinical Oncology, 7,* 583–589.

Lindeman, C. A., & Aernam, B. V. (1971). Nursing intervention with the presurgical patient—The effects of structured and unstructured preoperative teaching. *Nursing Research, 20,* 319–322.

Lo, B., McLeod, G., & Saika, G. (1986). Patient attitudes to discussing life sustaining treatment. *Archives of Internal Medicine, 146,* 1613–1615.

Lock, M. (1982). Models and practice in medicine: Menopause as syndrome or life transition? *Culture, Medicine, & Psychiatry, 6,* 261–280.

Logan, P. D., Schwab, R. A., Salomone, J. A., & Watson, W. A. (1996). Patient understanding of emergency department discharge instructions. *Southern Medical Journal, 89,* 779–774.

MacPherson, B., & Gormlie, H. (1995). Improving communication in the imaging department. *Nursing Times, 91*(8), 48–49.

Majerovitz, S. D., Greene, M. G., Adelman, R. D., Brody, G. M., Leber, K., & Healy, S. W. (1997). Older patients' understanding of medical information in the emergency department. *Health Communication, 9,* 237–252.

Martin, L. R. (1989). Disclosing a diagnosis of cancer. *Family Practice Research Journal, 11,* 44–58.

Mathis, M. (1984). Personal needs of family members of critically ill patients with and without acute brain injury. *Journal of Neurosurgical Nursing, 16,* 36–44.

Mauss-Clum, N., & Ryan, M. (1981). Brain injury and the family. *Journal of Neurosurgical Nursing, 13,* 165–169.

May, M. L., & DeMarco, L. (1986). *Patients and doctors disputing: Patients' complaints and what they do about them.* (Disputes Processing Research Program, Working Papers Series 7). Madison: University of Wisconsin.

Mayeaux, E. J., Murphy, P. W., Arnold, C., Davis, T. C., Jackson, R. H., & Sentell, T. (1996). Improving patient education for patients with low literacy skills. *American Family Physician, 53,* 205–211.

Mazis, M., Morris, L. A., & Gordon, E. (1978). Patient attitudes about two forms of printed oral contraceptive information. *Medical Care, 16,* 1045–1054.

Mazzuca, S. A., & Weinberger, M. (1986). How clinician communication patterns affect patients' comprehension and satisfaction. *The Diabetes Educator, 12,* 370–373.

Mazzuca, S. A., Weinberger, M., Kurpius, D. J., Froehle, T. C., & Heister, M. (1983). Clinician communication associated with diabetic patients' comprehension of their therapeutic regimen. *Diabetes Care, 6,* 347–350.

McCauley, C. R., Johnson, J. P., & Copley, J. B. (1989). Communication of information about therapeutic alternatives: End-stage renal disease model. *Southern Medical Journal, 82,* 418–422.

McCorkle, R., & Ehlke, G. (1992, August). *Both sides of the fence: A nurse's personal experience with cancer and her rehabilitation needs.* Paper presented at the 7th International Conference on Cancer Nursing, Vienna.

McGrath, P. A., & DeVeber, L. L. (1986). Helping children cope with painful procedures. *American Journal of Nursing, 86,* 1278–1279.

McIntosh, J. (1974). Processes of communication, information seeking and control associated with cancer. *Social Science and Medicine, 8,* 167–187.

McKinlay, J. B. (1975). Who is really ignorant—Physician or patient? *Journal of Health and Social Behavior, 16,* 3–11.

McLean, J., Roper-Hall, A., Mayer, P., & Main, A. (1991). Service needs of stroke survivors and their informal carers: A pilot study. *Journal of Advanced Nursing, 16,* 559–564.

Menzies, R., Rocher, I., & Vissandjee, B. (1993). Factors associated with compliance in treatment of tuberculosis. *Tubercle & Lung Disease, 74,* 32–37.

Messerli, M., Garamendi, C., & Romano, J. (1980). Breast cancer information as a technique of crisis intervention. *American Journal of Orthopsychiatry, 50,* 728–731.

Meyers, M. E. (1965). The effect of types of communication on patients' reactions to stress. In J. K. Skipper & R. C. Leonard (Eds.), *Social interaction and patient care* (pp. 128–140). Philadelphia: Lippincott.

Miller, J. F. (1983). *Coping with chronic illness—Overcoming powerlessness.* Philadelphia: Davis.

Miller, S. M., Brody, D. S., & Summerton, J. (1988). Styles of coping with threat: Implications for health. *Journal of Personality and Social Psychology, 54,* 142–148.

Mishel, M. H. (1984). Perceived uncertainty as a stress in illness. *Research in Nursing and Health, 7,* 163–171.

Mishel, M. H. (1988). Uncertainty in illness. *Image: Journal of Nursing Scholarship, 20,* 225–232.

Mishler, E. G. (1984). *The discourse of medicine: Dialectics of medical interviews.* Norwood, NJ: Ablex.

Morton, R. (1996). Breaking bad news to patients with cancer. *Professional Nurse, 11,* 669–671.

Muss, H. B., White, D. R., Michielutte, R., Richards F., II., Cooper, R., Williams, S., Stuart, J. J., & Spurr, C. L. (1979). Written informed consent in patients with breast cancer. *Cancer, 43,* 1549.

Noble, C. (1991). Are nurses good patient educators? *Journal of Advanced Nursing, 16,* 1165–1189.

North, N., Cornbleet, M. A., Knowles, G., & Leonard, R. C. (1992). Information giving in oncology: A preliminary study of tape-recorder use. *British Journal of Clinical Psychology, 31,* 357.

Northouse, P. G., & Northouse, L. L. (1987). Communication and cancer issues confronting patients, health professionals, and family members. *Journal of Psychosocial Oncology, 5,* 17–46.

Oken, D. (1961). What to tell cancer patients: A study of medical attitudes. *Journal of the American Medical Association, 175,* 1120–1128.

Omar, M. A., & Schiffman, R. F. (1995). Pregnant women's perceptions of prenatal care. *Maternal-Child Nursing Journal, 23,* 132–144.

Orr, R. D., Morton, K. R., de Leon, D. M., & Fals, J. C. (1996). Evaluation of an ethics consultation service: Patient and family perspectives. *American Journal of Medicine, 101,* 135–141.

Osman, L. (1996). Guided self-management and patient education in asthma *British Journal of Nursing, 5,* 785–789.

Oth, K. (1994). Communication in a chiropractice clinic: How a D.C. treats his patients. *Culture, Medicine, & Psychiatry, 18,* 83–113.

Padilla, G. V., Grant, M. M., Rains, B. L., Hansen, B. C., Bergstrom, N., Wong, H. L., Hanson, R., & Kubo, W. (1981). Distress reduction and the effects of preparatory teaching films and patient control. *Research in Nursing and Health, 4,* 375–387.

Parrott, R. (1994b). Exploring family practitioners' and patients' information exchange about prescribed medications: Implications for practitioners' interviewing and patients' understanding. *Health Communication, 6,* 267–280.

Parrott, R. (1994a). Clarifying boundary conditions and extending the motives for nonimmediate language use: A proposed model and test using physicians' role experience and gender. *Discourse Processes, 17,* 353–376.

Partridge, M. R. (1989). Lung cancer and communication. *Respiratory Medicine, 83,* 379–380.

Partridge, M. R. (1995). Asthma: Lessons from patient education. *Patient Education and Counseling 26,* 81–86.

Pendleton, D. (1983). Doctor–patient communication: A review. In D. Pendleton & J. Hasler (Eds.), *Doctor–patient communication* (pp. 5–53). New York: Academic Press.

Pendleton, D., Brouwer, H., & Jaspars, J. (1983). Communication difficulties: The doctor's perspective. *Journal of Language and Social Psychology, 2,* 17–36.

Peteet, J. R., Abrams, H. E., Ross, D. M., & Stearns, N. M. (1991). Presenting a diagnosis of cancer: Patients' views. *Journal of Family Practice, 32,* 577–581.

Putnam, S. M., Stiles, W. B., Jacob, M. C., & James, S. A. (1985). Patient exposition and physician explanation in initial medical interviews and outcomes of clinic visits. *Medical Care, 23,* 74–83.

Quaid, K. A., Faden, R. R., Vining, E. D., & Freeman, J. M. (1990). Informed consent for a prescription drug: Impact of disclosed information on patient understanding and medical outcomes. *Patient Education and Counseling, 15,* 249–259.

Quint, J. C. (1965). Institutionalized practices of information control. *Psychiatry, 28,* 119–132.

Rabinowitz, B., Beckman, H. B., Morse, D., & Naumburg, E. H. (1994). Discussing preventive services with patients: Can we make a difference? *Health Values, 18*(4), 20–26.

Rae-Grant, Q. (1985). Psychological problems in the medically ill child. *Psychiatric Clinics of North America, 8,* 653–663.

Ragan, S. L. (1990). Verbal play and multiple goals in the gynecologic exam interaction. *Journal of Language and Social Psychology, 9,* 67–84.

Ragan, S. L., Beck, C. S., & White, M. D. (1995). Educating the patient: Interactive learning in an OB-GYN context. In G. H. Morris & R. J. Chenail (Eds.), *The talk of the clinic: Explorations in the analysis of medical and therapeutic discourse* (pp. 185–207). Mahwah, NJ: Lawrence Erlbaum Associates.

Raimbault, G., Cachin, O., Limal, J. M., Eliacheff, C., & Rappaport, R. (1975). Aspects of communication between patients and doctors: An analysis of the discourse in medical interviews. *Pediatrics, 55,* 401–405.

Raleigh, E. H., Lepczyk, M., & Rowley, C. (1990). Significant others benefit from preoperative information. *Journal of Advanced Nursing, 15,* 941–945.

Redlich, F. C. (1945). The patient's language: An investigation into the use of medical terms. *Yale Journal of Biology and Medicine, 17,* 427–453.

Reid, A., Bennett-Emslie, G., Adams, L., & Kae, S. B. (1988). What should we tell patients with cancer? *Scottish Medical Journal, 33,* 260.

Reid, J. C., Kardash, C. M., Robinson, R. D., & Scholes, R. (1994). Comprehension in patient literature: The importance of text and reader characteristics. *Health Communication, 6,* 327–325.

Rennick, D. (1960). What should physicians tell cancer patients? *New Medical Material, 2,* 51–53.

Reynolds, M. (1978). No news is bad news: Patients' views about communication in hospitals. *British Medical Journal, 1,* 1673–1676.

Reynolds, P. M., Sanson-Fisher, R. W., Poole, A. D., Harker, J., & Byrne, M. J. (1981). Cancer and communication: Information-giving in an oncology clinic. *British Medical Journal, 282,* 1449–1451.

Ridgway, V., & Matthews, A. (1982). Psychological preparation for surgery: A comparison of methods. *British Journal of Clinical Psychology, 21,* 271–280.

Righter, B. M. (1995). Uncertainty and the role of the credible authority during an ostomy experience. *Journal of Wound, Ostomy, and Continence Nursing, 22,* 100–104.

Rippere, V. (1977). Commonsense beliefs about depression and antidepressive behaviour: A study of social consensus. *Behavioral Research Therapy, 15,* 465–473.

Rippere, V. (1981). Depression, commonsense and psychosocial evolution. *British Journal of Medicine Psychology, 54,* 379–387.

Roter, D. (1989). Which facets of communication have strong effects on outcome—A meta-analysis. In M. Stewart & D. Roter (Eds.), *Communicating with medical patients* (pp. 183–196). Beverly Hills, CA: Sage.

Rotnem, D., Cohen, D. J., Hintz, R. L., Genel, M. (1979). Psychological sequelae of relative "treatment failure" for children receiving human growth hormone replacement. *Journal of the American Academy of Child Psychiatry, 18,* 505–520.

Rowley, P. T., Lipkin, M., & Fisher, L. (1984). Screening and genetic counseling for beta-thalassemia trait in a population unselected for interest: Comparison of three counseling methods. *American Journal of Human Genetics, 36,* 677–689.

Rusin, M. J., (1992). Communicating with families of rehabilitation patients about "Do Not Resuscitate" decisions. *Archives of Physical Medicine and Rehabilitation, 73,* 922–925.

Samora, J., Saunders, L., & Larson, M. (1961). Medical vocabulary knowledge among hospital patients. *Journal of Health and Human Behavior, 2,* 83–89.

Sanchez-Menegay, C., & Stalder, H. (1994). Do physicians take into account patients' expectations? *Journal of General Internal Medicine, 9,* 404–406.

Schmerling, R. H., Bedell, S. E., Lilienfeld, A., & Delbanco, T. L. (1988). Discussing cardiopulmonary resuscitation: A study of elderly outpatients. *Journal of General Internal Medicine, 3,* 317–321.

Schmitt, F. E., & Wooldridge, P. J. (1973). Psychological preparation of surgical patients. *Nursing Research, 22,* 108–116.

Schonwetter, R. S., Teasdale, T. A., Taffet, G., Robinson, B. E., & Luchi, R. J. (1991). Educating the elderly: Cardiopulmonary resuscitation decisions before and after intervention. *Journal of the American Geriatric Society, 39,* 372–377.

Schonwetter, R. S., Walker, R. M., & Robinson, B. E. (1995). The lack of advance directives among hospice patients. *The Hospice Journal, 10*(3), 1–11.

Scott, N., & Weiner, M. F. (1984). "Patientspeak": An exercise in communication. *Journal of Medical Education, 59,* 890–893.

Segal, A., & Roberts, L. W. (1980). A comparative analysis of physician estimates and levels of medical knowledge about patients. *Sociological Health Illness, 2,* 317–333.

Seligman, A. W., McGrath, N. E., & Pratt, L. (1957). Level of medical information among clinic patients. *Journal of Chronic Diseases, 6,* 497–509.

Sell, L., Devlin, B., Bourke, S. J., Munro, N. C., Corris, P. A., & Gibson, G. J. (1993). Communicating the diagnosis of lung cancer. *Respiratory Medicine, 87,* 379–380.

Sharf, B. F. (1990). Physician–patient communication as interpersonal rhetoric: A narrative approach. *Health Communication, 2,* 217–236.

Sheer, V. C., & Cline, R. J. (1995). Testing a model of perceived information adequacy and uncertainty reduction in physician–patient interactions. *Journal of Applied Communication Research, 23,* 44–59.

Shipley, R. H., Butt, J. H., & Horwitz, E. A. (1979). Preparation to reexperience a stressful medical examination: Effect of repetitious videotape exposure and coping style. *Journal of Consulting and Clinical Psychology, 47,* 485–492.

Shuy, R. (1976). The medical interview: Problems in communication. *Primary Care, 3,* 365–386.

Shuy, R. (1983). Three types of interference to an effective exchange of information in the medical interview. In S. Fisher and A. D. Todd (Eds.), *The social organization of doctor–patient communication* (pp. 190–202). Washington, DC: Center for Applied Linguistics.

Silver, J. M. (1979, November). Medical terms: A two way block? *Colloquy: The Journal of Physician–Patient Communications, 4*–10.

Simanowitz, A. (1985). Standards, attitudes, and accountability in the medical profession. *Lancet, 334,* 546.

Simonil, J. J., & Ball, R. A. (1975). Can we learn from medical hucksters? *Journal of Communication, 25,* 174–181.

Smith, D. H., Cunningham, K. G., & Hale, W. E. (1994). Communication about medicines: Perceptions of the ambulatory elderly. *Health Communication, 6,* 281–295.

Smucker, W. D., Ditto, P. H., Moore, K. A., Druley, J. A., Danks, J. H., & Townsend, A. (1993). Elderly outpatients respond favorably to a physician-initiated advance directive discussion. *Journal of the American Board of Family Practice, 6,* 473–482.

Solomon, J., & Schwegman-Melton, K. (1987). Structured teaching and patient understanding of informed consent. *Critical Care Nurse, 7,* 74–79.

Spencer, J. J. (1981). Telling the right patient. *British Medical Journal, 283,* 291–292.

Stewart, G. S. (1992). Trends in radiation therapy for the treatment of lung cancer. *Nursing Clinics of North America, 27,* 643–651.

Stiles, W. P., Putnam, S. M., Wolf, M. H., & James, S. A. (1979). Interaction exchange structure and patients' satisfaction with medical interviews. *Medical Care, 17,* 667–681.

Stoeckle, J. D., & Barsky, A. J. (1980). Attributions: Uses of social science knowledge in the doctoring of primary care. In L. Eisenberg & A. Kleinman (Eds.), *The relevance of social science for medicine* (pp. 223–240). Dordrecht, Netherlands: D. Reidel.

Streator, S., Ingersoll, C. D., & Knight, K. L. (1995). Sensory information can decrease cold-induced pain perception. *Journal of Athletic Training, 30,* 293–295.

Street, R. L. (1992). Communicative styles and adaptations in physician–patient consultations. *Social Science and Medicine, 34,* 1155–1163.

Strull, W. M., Lo, B., & Charles, G. (1984). Do patients want to participate in medical decision making? *Journal of the American Medical Association, 252,* 2990–2994.

Svarstad, B. L. (1976). Physician–patient communication and patient conformity with medical advice. In D. Mechanic (Ed.), *Growth of bureaucratic medicine: An inquiry into the dynamics of patient behavior and the organization of medical care* (pp. 220–235). New York: Wiley.

Swenson, P. (1984). Communicating with surgeons. *American Organization of Registered Nurses Journal, 40,* 784–785.

Tannen, D., & Wallat, C. (1983). Doctor/mother/child communication: Linguistic analysis of a pediatric interaction. In S. Fisher and A. D. Todd (Eds.), *The social organization of doctor–patient communication* (pp. 203–219). Washington, DC: Center for Applied Linguistics.

Tarasuk, M. B., Rhymes, J. P., & Leonard, R. C. (1965). An experimental test of the importance of communication skills for effective nursing. In J. K. Skipper & R. C. Leonard (Eds.), *Social interaction and patient care* (pp. 110–120). Philadelphia: Lippincott.

Tate, P. (1983). Doctor's style. In D. Pendleton & J. Hasler (Eds.), *Doctor–patient communication* (pp. 74–85). New York: Academic Press.

Tattersall, M. H. N., Butow, P. N., Griffin, A., & Dunn, S. M. (1994). The take-home message: Patients prefer consultation audiotapes to summary letters. *Journal of Clinical Oncology, 12,* 1305–1311.

Teasdale, K. (1993). Information and anxiety: A critical reappraisal. *Journal of Advanced Nursing, 18,* 1125–1132.

Thompson, C. L., & Pledger, L. M. (1993). Doctor–patient communication: Is patient knowledge of medical terminology improving? *Health Communication, 5,* 89–98.

Thompson, D. R., & Cordle, C. J. (1988). Support of wives of myocardial infarction patients. *Journal of Advanced Nursing, 13,* 223–228.

Thompson, D. R., & Meddis, R. (1990). A prospective evaluation of in-hospital counseling for first-time myocardial infarction men. *Journal of Psychosomatic Research, 34,* 237–248.

Tilley, J. D., Gregor, F. M., & Thiessen, V. (1987). The nurse's role in patient education: Incongruent perceptions among nurses and patients. *Journal of Advanced Nursing, 12,* 291–301.

Timbers, K. A., & Feinberg, R. F. (1996). Recurrent pregnancy loss: A review. *Nurse Practitioner Forum, 7,* 64–75.

Todd, A. D. (1983). A diagnosis of doctor–patient discourse in the prescription of contraception. In S. Fisher & A. D. Todd (Eds.), *Social organization of doctor–patient communication* (pp. 159–187). Washington, DC: Center for Applied Linguistics.

Tuckett, D. A., Boulton, M., & Olson, C. (1985). A new approach to the measurement of patients' understanding of what they are told in medical consultations. *Journal of Health and Social Behavior, 26,* 27–38.

Turk, D. C., & Rennert, K. S. (1981). Pain and the terminally ill cancer patient: A cognitive–social learning perspective. In H. Sobel (Ed.), *Behavior therapy in terminal care: A humanistic approach* (pp. 95–123). Cambridge, MA: Ballinger.

Van Veldhuizen-Scott, M. K., Widmer, L. B., Stacey, S. A., & Popovich, N. G. (1995). Developing and implementing a pharmaceutical care model in an ambulatory care setting for patients with diabetes. *Diabetes Educator, 21,* 117–123.

Ventres, W., Nichter, M., Reed, R., & Frankel, R. (1992). Do-not-resuscitate discussions: A qualitative analysis. *Family Practice Research Journal, 12,* 157–169.

Ventres, W., Nichter, M., Reed, R., & Frankel, R. (1993). Limitation of medical care: An ethnographic analysis. *Journal of Clinical Ethics, 4,* 134–145.

Vincent, C., Young, M., & Phillips, A. (1994). Why do people sue doctors? A study of patients and families taking legal action. *Lancet, 343,* 1609–1613.

Volker, D. L. (1991). Needs assessment and resource identification. *Oncology Nursing Forum, 18,* 119–123.

Waaland, P. K., Burns, C., & Cockrell, J. (1993). Evaluation of needs of high- and low-income families following paediatric traumatic brain injury. *Brain Injury, 7,* 135–146.

Waitzkin, H. (1985). Information giving in medical care. *Journal of Health and Social Behavior, 26,* 81–101.

Wallen, J., Waitzkin, H., & Stoeckle, J. D. (1979). Physician stereotypes about female health and illness. *Women & Health, 4,* 371–388.

Walton, J., Duncan, A. S., Fletcher, C., Freeling, P., Hawkins, C., Kessel, N., & McCall, I. (1980). *Talking with patients.* London: Nuffield Provincial Hospitals Trust.

Ware, J. E., Davies-Avery, A., & Stewart, A. L. (1978). The measurement and meaning of patient satisfaction. *Health and Medical Care Services Review, 1,* 1–15.

Warner, J. E. (1992). Involvement of families in pain control of terminally ill patients. *The Hospice Journal, 8,* 155–170.

Webb, P. (1985). Getting it right: Patient teaching. *Nursing, 2,* 1125–1127.

Weisman, A. (1979). *Coping with cancer.* New York: McGraw-Hill.

West, C. (1984). *Routine complications.* Bloomington: Indiana University Press.

Wiederholt, J. B., Clarridge, B. R., & Svarstad, B. L. (1992). Verbal consultation regarding prescription drugs: Findings from a statewide study. *Medical Care, 30,* 159–173.

Wiener, M., & Mehrabian, A. (1968). *Language within language: Immediacy, a channel in verbal communication.* New York: Appleton- Century-Crofts.

Williams, M. L., & Meredith, V. (1984). Physician–expectant mother communication: An analysis of information uncertainty. *Communication Research Reports, 1,* 110–116.

Wilson, J. F. (1981). Behavioral preparation for surgery: Benefit or harm? *Journal of Behavioral Medicine, 4,* 79–102.

Wilson, T. N., & Cohn, R. C. (1996). A national survey on the prevalence of cigarette smoking in pediatric respiratory care departments and its effect on smoking cessation efforts. *Respiratory Care, 41,* 202–205.

Wingate, A. L., & Lackey, N. R. (1989). A description of the needs of noninstitutionalized cancer patients and their primary caregivers. *Cancer Nursing, 12,* 216–225.

Woodard, L. J., & Pamias, R. J. (1992). The disclosure of the diagnosis of cancer. *Primary Care, 19,* 657–663.

Wright, K., & Dyck, S. (1984). Expressed concerns of adult cancer patients' family members. *Cancer Nursing, 6,* 371–374.

Yates, B. C. (1995). The relationship among social-support and short- and long-term recovery outcomes in men with coronary heart disease. *Research in Nursing and Health, 18,* 193–203.

Yong-Bronckopp, D. (1982). Cancer patients' perception of five psychosocial needs. *Oncology Nursing Forum, 9*(4), 31–35.

Zola, I. K. (1980). Structural constraints in the doctor-patient relationship: The case of non-compliance. In L. Eisenberg & A. Kleinman (Eds.), *The relevance of social science for medicine* (pp. 241–252). Dordrecht, Netherlands: D. Reidel.

2

Managing Uncertainty in Illness Explanation: An Application of Problematic Integration Theory

Austin S. Babrow
Department of Communication
Purdue University

Stephen C. Hines
Department of Communication Studies
West Virginia University

Chris R. Kasch
Department of Communication
Bradley University

Case One. The parents of a newborn observe that their daughter's pupils are different sizes. A pediatric opthamologist diagnoses her condition as Horner's syndrome. Although the syndrome has no effects of its own, it may be symptomatic of a brain stem tumor, lung cancer, or a traumatic head injury. The physician recommends a CAT scan to explore these possibilities. The parents carefully investigate the desirability of this test. In the process, they learn that they must withhold food from their child for 9 hours and take a small risk that complications from anesthetizing her will result in death. They also learn that there is little chance that the problems a CAT scan might reveal will be treatable. Ultimately, they decide to refuse the test and the opportunity to fully understand the cause of their child's condition.

Case Two. After 2 years in remission following treatment for breast cancer, Marie learns from her doctor that cancer has reappeared in another part of her body. Although survival is possible, Marie correctly recognizes that the cancer will probably be fatal. Her best friend attempts to encourage Marie by increasing her uncertainty about whether she will survive.

Case Three. Jason's kidneys failed at age 21. Rather than accepting a family member's offer to donate a kidney, he chose the rigors of dialysis for 6 years. When prompted by doctors to consider a transplant, he indicates that he wants to defer the transplant in the hope that advances in posttransplant immunosuppressant therapy will decrease his complications and the possibility that his body will reject the kidney.

THE SIGNIFICANCE OF UNCERTAINTY IN ILLNESS AND ILLNESS EXPLANATION

Although the three cases that open this chapter illustrate differing health problems, they are united by the theme of uncertainty. Indeed, uncertainty is widely believed to be a central feature of illness experiences (see Atkinson, 1984, 1995; Babrow, Kasch, & Ford, 1998; Fox, 1957; Katz, 1984). An individual's need to believe that the world is predictable and that what has been true will continue to be true (Schutz, 1970) is challenged by illness. Illness raises questions about how the body will feel and perform; about how relationships with others will change; and, most generally, about who we are in the world, what we are doing, and where our life is going. In all these ways, illness creates uncertainty and leads to a search for new ways of understanding our new, sick selves (Cohen, 1993).

Although illness creates uncertainty, the uncertainty it creates, in turn, exacerbates both stress and threats to health. A wide range of research, from that on the attitudinal effects of mere exposure (Bornstein, 1989; Zajonc, 1968) to tests of uncertainty in interpersonal communication (Berger & Gudykunst, 1991), tells us that encounters with novel, ambiguous, or unknown stimuli are unsettling. The reason for this appears to be simple; we are discomfited by not knowing how to react to such stimuli. This discomfort adds directly to the stress associated with illness.

Uncertainty about how to respond to a stressor is not only unpleasant and directly stress-enhancing, it is also indirectly stressful. An enduring sense of uncertainty can threaten one's general sense of coherence, the belief that the world is understandable, manageable, and meaningful (see Antonovsky,

1990). It also threatens our sense of control or efficacy (see Abramson, Garber, & Seligman, 1980; Abramson, Seligman, & Teasdale, 1978). Both the general sense of coherence and sense of control are thought to be prerequisites of psychological and physical well-being (Brenders, 1987; Friedman, 1993).

Finally, a considerable body of research indicates that stress has significant negative effects on health through its direct impact on the sympathetic–adrenal–medullary and the pituitary–adrenocortical systems (Stroebe & Stroebe, 1995). Stress also threatens health indirectly by causing maladaptive behaviors such as substance abuse (again, see Stroebe & Stroebe, 1995). In all of these ways, uncertainties such as those illustrated at the beginning of the chapter exacerbate illness experiences.

Although the chapter's initial cases illustrate the critical role of uncertainty in illness, they also challenge the assumption that reducing uncertainty is always the most appropriate means of dealing with it. The parents in the first scenario chose to accept one set of uncertainties in order to avoid other consequences they viewed as even more undesirable. In the second scenario, Marie's friend attempted to increase uncertainty about her chances of survival rather than assuring Marie that she would die or fostering an overly optimistic belief that she is sure to live. Recent research studying social support among women with breast cancer confirms the appropriateness of this choice in the context of dealing with initial reactions to a cancer recurrence (Ford, Babrow, & Stohl, 1996). Jason's decision in the third scenario to postpone a kidney transplant suggests that uncertain but potential advances in medical therapy provided him with a source of hope that enabled him to tolerate years of painful dialysis treatments.

Together, these three cases suggest that efforts to come to terms with illness must be attuned to the uncertainty that permeates illness experiences. The cases also suggest that uncertainty must be *managed*—at times reduced, at other times maintained, and at still other times increased (see Brashers & Babrow, 1996; Ford et al., 1996). Much remains to be learned about how illness-related uncertainty may be most effectively managed, but one thing is clear: To be effective, illness explanations must be designed to manage uncertainty.

In this chapter, we discuss three questions that must be addressed by those attempting to manage illness-related uncertainty. First, we must ask, "What type(s) of illness-related uncertainty is the person experiencing?" Much prior research has defined uncertainty loosely or in conflicting ways (see Atkinson, 1995; Babrow, Kasch, & Ford, 1998) and, clearly, people use the term "uncertainty" with a wide variety of meanings in mind. Health communicators must be able to determine the form of uncertainty a person is experiencing if they are to formulate effective messages and interaction strategies. The second question we must ask is, "How do illness-related uncertainties create difficulties for the sick person?" Not all instances of uncertainty are equally troubling. Understanding how uncertainties are problematic and when they are more and less troublesome is essential to formulating sensible illness explanations and related messages. Third, we must ask, "What obstacles must be anticipated by those attempting to communicate about illness-based uncertainties?" In many cases, no means of managing uncertainty will be fully satisfying or indefinitely sustainable. Thus, competent uncertainty management, and therefore skillful illness explanation, require the ability to anticipate challenges and adapt as changes occur in the source and nature of the uncertainty. These three questions are answered in turn by each of the following sections of the chapter.

TYPES OF UNCERTAINTY IN ILLNESS

Because of the pervasiveness of uncertainty in illness experiences, scholars have sometimes failed to make important distinctions between differing types of uncertainty. This imprecision led Atkinson (1995) to characterize the term as a "linguistic wastebasket" into which writers place a wide variety of problems. Moreover, Babrow, Kasch, and Ford (1998) noted that scholars have approached the topic of uncertainty in illness from many perspectives, ranging from individual–psychological to interactional and discourse analytic and to broad historical and sociocultural frames. Although much of value can be learned from each of these viewpoints, the failure to consider ways in which each of these perspectives is connected to the others confounds our understanding of uncertainty.

Babrow, Kasch, and Ford (1998) synthesized numerous analyses and, in so doing, identified five distinct senses of the term "uncertainty" in the scholarly literature on illness experiences (see Table 2.1). These various meanings characterize not only the research literature but also major variations in the actual experience of uncertainty in illness. First, complexities inherent in the illness itself are often the source of uncertainty. A second set of uncertainties relates to the sufficiency, reliability, and validity of information about the illness. For instance, patients often struggle to decide whether their doctor really knows what is wrong with them and is fully disclosing what they know. A third form of uncertainty relates to the nature of one's judgment about the likelihood of particular outcomes. Those affected by illness may come to believe in a specific probability of some event (e.g., a positive test result), or they may have only a general sense of the chances of the event. A fourth set of uncertainties relates to how to integrate new pieces of information with existing beliefs, attitudes, and values; intentions and plans; and ongoing behavior. For example, people must integrate information that a loved one is dying with very strongly held negative attitudes toward this loss. It is at times unclear whether it would be more appropriate to deny the impending death or to accept it as a blessing. Such integrations entail considerable uncertainty. Finally, uncertainty has different meanings depending on one's basic understanding of what can be known. Some people believe that nothing can be known with absolute certainty; others find great comfort in things that they view as absolutely certain. For some, certainties provide a framework to make sense of things that are less certain. For others, absolute truths are obstacles to knowledge.

Understanding these different meanings or types of uncertainty is essential to scholarly work. This understanding is also necessary for the practical matters of managing uncertainty and formulating effective illness explanations. To support this claim, we detail the nature and implications of two of the five dimensions summarized in Table 2.1.

TABLE 2.1
Types of Uncertainty in Illness
(adapted from Babrow, Kasch, & Ford, 1998)

1. Complexity
   a. Multicausality
   b. Contingency
   c. Reciprocity
2. Qualities of information
   a. Sufficiency of information
      i. Clarity
      ii. Completeness
      iii. Volume
   b. Reliability and validity
      i. Accuracy
      ii. Confidence in the source (ethos)
      iii. Ambiguity
      iv. Applicability
      v. Consistency
3. Probability
   a. Belief in a specific probability
   b. Belief in a range of probabilities
   c. Belief that eve is unpredictable
4. Structure of information
   a. Order
   b. Integration
5. Lay epistemology

Complexity

Uncertainty can be understood to reflect the very nature of an illness and, in particular, its complexity (see Bursztajn, Feinbloom, Hamm, & Brodsky, 1990; Fox, 1980; Jones, 1982; Nuland, 1993). Although some diseases are characterized by a relatively simple pathology with a single, clearly identifiable cause and a straightforward treatment mechanism (e.g., common bacterial infections treatable by an antibiotic), other diseases are far more complex (e.g., HIV; see Nuland, 1993). As simple, curable diseases are controlled and life is extended, increasingly complex diseases are becoming more common. This trend has led a number of scholars to note that the very nature of illness is becoming more complex (e.g., Bursztajn et al., 1990; Callahan, 1993; Fox, 1980; Jones, 1982; Nuland, 1993). It is also clear that there are several distinct sources of complexity in illness processes. As a result, several different meanings are possible when one says that she or he is uncertain about some aspect of an illness.

Types of Complexity

One complexity in illness processes is multicausality. For example, diminished cognitive capacity may result from Alzheimer's disease, a stroke, uremia, depression, or a combination of these and many other factors. Whereas some factors might be sufficient to produce a symptom independently, other diseases stem from an extensive number of contributory factors (e.g., cardiovascular disease). As a result, understanding what caused a disease or what disease is suggested by an observable symptom can be quite complex.

A second complexity relates to the contingent nature of many symptoms and illnesses. Consider the following examples. Doctors prescribing medications may not be aware of other medications the patient is taking that place the patient at elevated risk. The effects of many drug combinations on patient health have never been studied clinically. Patients taking multiple medications frequently do not understand that specific medications should not be taken at the same time or their effects will be nullified. Convincing dieters to avoid faddish and sometimes dangerous approaches to weight loss may be difficult because dieters must be made to understand the complex relations among caloric intake, exercise, metabolic rate, and other factors. These and other medical contingencies are another form of complexity that patients and health care providers must confront.

A third form of complexity stems from the presence of reciprocal causal processes such as those constituting mind–body relationships (see Borysenko, 1987; Brown, 1998). For example, the belief that one is ill might lead to depression, risk taking, or the cessation of exercise, all of which might exacerbate the illness. When serious illnesses are treated aggressively (e.g., chemotherapy, bone marrow transplantation, brain surgery), patients can suffer both from the initial illness and from the treatments they receive. Frequently, even the doctors cannot be sure whether side effects have resulted from the illness or how it is being treated.

Implications

Distinguishing among types of complexity-based uncertainty is important to the formulation of adequate and effective messages. As teachers of empirical research methods, we know from experience the difficulty people have in understanding complex causal processes, including the tendency to confuse the types described here. If classroom learning about complex causal processes is difficult, the emotion and diminished cognitive capacity that often accompany illness must necessarily increase the challenge of understanding a complex disease etiology and its treatment. Hence, the first step in formulating an appropriate message to someone confronted with the uncertainty of a complex illness is for the communicator to understand the form of complexity that characterizes the malady. This understanding, combined with assessments of the message receiver's cognitive capacity and current (mis)understanding of the illness, become the building blocks of effective explanatory messages (also see chap. 3, this volume).

Quality of Information

A second dimension in the meaning of uncertainty in the experience of illness has to do with the quality of available information. Uncertainties about the quality of information can be classified into one of two general subtypes: qualities related to the sufficiency of information and qualities related to its reliability and validity.

Sufficiency of Information

Clarity. Simple lack of clarity can produce uncertainty (Sheer & Cline, 1995). Patient understandings are often challenged by a garbled message, imprecise wording, unfamiliar technical jargon, and emotional interference in message processing (see chap. 1, this volume). For example, Kimball (1971) wrote:

> The physician speaks a strange and often unintelligible dialect. He (sic) calls everyday common objects by absurd and antiquated terms. He speaks of mitral feedback ... (and a) world peopled with cirrhotics, greensticks, and

hebephrenics. The professional dialect creates a communication gap between physicians and patients that is generally acknowledged by neither. (p. 137)

Completeness. Incomplete information is another source of uncertainty reflecting the quality of available information (Babrow, 1992; Folkman, Schaefer, & Lazarus, 1979; Mishel, 1988; Sheer & Cline, 1995). Several further distinctions are relevant here. Fox's (1957) classic study of the socialization of medical students identifies some of these variations in meanings of uncertainty: (a) students must face the limits of medical knowledge, (b) they must face the limits of their own knowledge, and (c) they must learn to distinguish "between personal ignorance or ineptitude and the limitations of present medical knowledge" (Fox, 1957, p. 214). This analysis can be further refined. Notably, concerns about a lack of information take on different meanings depending on whether one believes that the desired information is unknown but conceivably knowable in some time frame, unknown but conceivably knowable at some unspecified time in the future, or fundamentally unknowable (e.g., questions of faith). For example, the prospective kidney transplant recipient in the third case at the start of this chapter was gambling that a substantial advance in therapeutic knowledge would occur before he became substantially sicker. So, in a variety of senses, we may experience uncertainty because our information is incomplete.

Volume. Although the previous argument suggests that uncertainty may at times be reduced by information seeking, it is less common but equally important to realize that too much information can confuse and overwhelm us. As the volume of available information grows, it is increasingly difficult to understand the relevance and importance of particular pieces of information. So, for example, "although doctors were once taught to believe that more information is better ('marshalling all the facts'), there are limits to the amount of data anyone can handle" (Schwartz & Griffin, 1986, p. 39). Information can accumulate to the point that it causes uncertainty, overload, "operational failure" (e.g., missing important diagnostic steps, losing or failing to act on data), and decreased diagnostic accuracy (Schwartz & Griffin, 1986). As Simon (1978) argued, "we cannot afford to attend to information simply because it is there" (p. 13); we have to be willing and able to attend only to the most relevant information. For this reason, advances in medical knowledge and diagnostic technology have created a practical paradox for practitioners. As the amount of available information increases, the need to screen individual pieces for their relevance increases, but the ability to screen decreases. Hence, superabundant information may create uncertainty for health care providers, patients, and their families.

Reliability and Validity of Information

Accuracy. Aside from the sufficiency of information, concerns about its reliability and validity also give rise to uncertainty. Perhaps the most basic of these is concern about the accuracy of available information. All manner of errors can enter into data gathered from patient histories, physical examinations, and laboratory tests. "Errors may be due to inaccurate recordings by the observer, faulty observation, or misrepresentation of the data by an instrument or by the patient" (Weinstein & Fineberg, 1980, p. 2). Moreover, errors made during observation of symptoms contribute to misdiagnoses, which in turn create errors in statistics on the prevalence of diseases (see Edwards, 1972). Such errors produce uncertainty about the accuracy of every piece of available data.

Source Ethos. An issue that is closely related to the accuracy of information is our attitude toward its source, or source ethos. Although there has been considerable debate over the content of ethos (see Cronkhite & Liska, 1976), two characteristics of sources appear to be especially relevant to receivers: perceived expertise and trustworthiness (see Stiff, 1994). For example, a patient might question her physician's competence on numerous grounds (e.g., intelligence, training, clinical skill). An important example in contemporary medicine can be found in a paradoxical consequence of the explosive advances in medical knowledge and technology. Given the enormous volume and pace of medical discovery and invention, patients have reason to suspect the competence of all but the most renowned specialist in a given area. This suspicion may be reinforced by the common practice of referring patients to specialists. Such referrals carry with them the seeds of uncertainty about physician competence; the referring physician is less expert than the doctor to whom the patient is referred. Hence, patients are primed to wonder about the referring doctor's competence to refer (Chenail et al., 1990).

Even if a doctor's competence is not questioned, issues of trustworthiness may create uncertainty. In recent years, increasing numbers of patients have questioned whether information from doctors is skewed by medical paternalism or personal avarice. In the environment of managed care, patients have questioned whether doctors have chosen to forgo referrals or to conceal treatment options because of their contracts with health care organizations. Moreover, just as patients may question the competence and trustworthiness of their doctors, research also indicates that care providers also experience considerable uncertainty related to patients' competence and trustworthiness (see Atkinson, 1995).

Ethos is a function not only of inferences about the speaker's competence and character but also of markers of the source's attitude toward her or his own messages. In other words, hearers (or readers) judge ethos in part by listening for markers of the speakers' own view of the credibility of what they say. Studies of discourse reveal abundant evidence that talk is permeated with such markers. Consider, for example, Prince, Frader, and Bosk's (1982) study of linguistic hedges in the discourse on a pediatric ward. The researchers identified hedges used both to ambiguate the fit between observations and analytic categories (approximators) and to soften or qualify the speaker's commitment to information (shields). Prince et al. counted an average of one such hedge every 15 seconds in their study of 12 hours of tapes made on morning rounds. More generally, doctors (and other sources) signal attitudes toward their information by adopting various voices, ranging from authoritatively certain declaration to educated, although qualified, testimony to skeptical recapitulation of others' (e.g., patients') reports (see Atkinson, 1995). In the face of doubts about source ethos, a person can be said to be uncertain about the meaning or significance of the information offered by the source.

Ambiguity.   Yet another subdimension of uncertainty rooted in reliability and validity of information is the idea that the information might be more or less ambiguous or open to varied meanings (Folkman et al., 1979; Lazarus & Folkman, 1984; Mishel, 1988; Norton, 1975; Sheer & Cline, 1995). Consider, for example, the meaning of symptoms or signs and, in particular, their relation to disease processes. Weinstein and Fineberg (1980) noted that:

> The relations among clinical signs, symptoms, and disease are not the same in every patient. Even if one could accurately and unambiguously determine the patient's clinical signs and symptoms, uncertainty would often remain about the presence or absence of disease. Pathognomonic signs, that is, signs whose presence indicates that a particular condition is undoubtedly present, have been recognized for only a few diseases. Even then, these signs are not typically manifest in very many cases of those diseases and are, therefore, rarely helpful. In a typical situation a symptom or sign often occurs in the presence of the disease in question but may be absent, and that same sign is sometimes present even in the absence of the disease. (p. 2)

Indeed, particular symptoms or signs are typically indicative of several different diseases.

The meaning of physical symptoms depends on a number of contexts. Any one symptom takes on a different meaning depending on other available information about current physical functioning, the pathology of the disease, and the patient's personal and medical history. Meanings are further ambiguated by changes in medical science that destabilize and transform the meaning of symptoms, diseases, and diagnostic labels. Edwards (1972) suggested that "the usefulness of disease categories is so much a function of available treatments that these categories themselves change as treatments change" (p. 140; also see Kramer, 1993).

In short, uncertainty may be rooted in the ambiguity of available information. Efforts to interpret and make sense of this information reveal the inherent ambiguity of health, illness, and health care experiences (see Mishler, 1984, 1986; Mokros, 1993). Metaphorical understandings of illness illustrate, in a general way, the variety of ways in which individuals attempt to cope with this ambiguity. Whereas some people view illness as a challenge, others see it as an invasion by hostile forces, as a punishment, as a weakness or sign of failing, or as an irreparable loss (Lipowski, 1970; Sontag, 1978, 1989). Still others see illness as a liberating experience, allowing them to escape from the world for a while. For others, it is a challenging occupation (Herzlich & Graham, 1973). Similarly, we see ambiguity in evolving metaphorical understandings of specific diseases such as tuberculosis, cancer, and AIDS (see Martin, 1994; Sontag, 1978, 1989). Hence, the signs we interpret and the words we use to inform ourselves about our condition are inherently ambiguous, and this ambiguity is a major form of uncertainty in the experience of illness.

Applicability. Yet another subdimension of uncertainty related to information quality arises when one is unsure of the applicability of information to a given circumstance (Mishel, 1988). For example, Folkman et al. (1979) pointed out that uncertainty about the likelihood of an event (e.g., that a diagnostic test will confirm the presence of a disease; that one will survive a particular illness) may entail concern about the applicability of available relative frequency data. In a short personal essay about his battle with cancer, Gould (1985) used uncertainty about data suggesting he would live about 8 months to help him cope with his disease. Because he was young, otherwise healthy, receiving experimental treatments, and optimistic about his survival, Gould reasoned that this data was not relevant to his situation. Thus, uncertainty about the applicability of information may be a source of stress or a means of coping with illness.

Consistency. Uncertainty is experienced to the extent that information is internally or externally contradictory (see Norton, 1975). One type of contradiction stems from symptoms that do not agree (e.g., all the tests are negative but the patient is very tired and dizzy). Contradictions also may be embedded within messages, particularly when providers need to deliver threatening or bad news (Maynard, 1991, see also chap. 4, this volume). For example, Chenail et al. (1990) observed physician referrals such as the following that put families into a double bind: "The heart murmur was (sic) not serious, but your child should be sent to a heart specialist in order to be really sure" (p. 174). Finally, contradictions may occur when the physician's message is inconsistent with a patient's experiences. This, too, was powerfully illustrated in Chenail et al.'s study of physician referrals. Their work revealed that families are often "faced with a situation in which they must reconcile two seemingly contradictory positions: the doctor's diagnosis of a referable heart murmur and the family's observations of what they believed was a healthy child" (p. 174). Similarly, Kreps and Thornton (1992) noted various common "double" or contradictory messages occurring in practitioner–patient interactions (e.g., "This [shot] won't hurt"). Finally, Cassell (1985) pointed out that past experience, personal contacts in- and outside of professional health care settings, and information from the mass media provide abundant and often inconsistent information.

Implications

Distinguishing among types of uncertainty rooted in qualities of the available information is vital to the formulation of adequate and effective explanatory messages. For instance, the remedy for information overload is diametrically opposed to the strategy for dealing with incomplete information. As another example, determining whether a person seeks information that is not yet known or information that is fundamentally unknowable is important in order to know who the person should be talking with and how this conversation should be focused. Other responses are appropriate when uncertainty is rooted in doubts about the source of information. Under these circumstances, efforts by the suspect source to provide more information may be of little benefit. Moreover, efforts by the suspect source to prevent information overload by providing less information may raise further doubts about her or his credibility. Instead, information that enhances source ethos or corroborating information from other sources may be the most appropriate response.

More generally, Babrow, Kasch, and Ford's (1998) analysis of types of uncertainty reveals numerous distinctions that have not been recognized clearly in past writing on the topic. Scholars' tendency to obscure these distinctions with general references to the term "uncertainty" reflects what is probably a common tendency among the ill and those with whom they interact. Hence, when patients use the term "uncertain" and its synonyms (e.g., unsure, doubt, ignorance, risky, insecure, chancy, unstable, puzzled, hazy, vague, confused), providers must respond by probing for a clearer understanding of what the person means. Only after the patient's uncertainty is clarified can the care provider formulate sensible interactional goals, strategies, and explanatory messages.

UNDERSTANDING THE TROUBLE
WITH UNCERTAINTY IN ILLNESS

Determining the type of uncertainty a person is experiencing is clearly necessary. However, this step is not sufficient for effective communication with her or him. One must also understand the importance of uncertainty to the person. Although some instances of uncertainty are very troubling, others may be only mildly disturbing. In still other cases, uncertainty provides a resource for coping with an illness. Hence, understanding how uncertainties are problematic and when they are more and less troublesome is essential to formulating sensible illness explanations and related messages. Problematic integration (PI) theory provides a useful framework to answer the second question about uncertainty that we posed at the start of this chapter. Specifically, the theory explains how and when illness-related uncertainties create difficulties for patients and those with whom they interact.

The theory of problematic integration is a general perspective on uncertainty and communication. It is based on two widely held ideas (Babrow, 1992, 1995; see Table 2.2). One common idea is that people need probabilistic orientations to their world. Probabilistic orientations may take the form of conscious beliefs or expectations or of tacit and unconscious assumptions about the nature and structure of the world.[1] For example, a young adult who has discovered a hard lump on one of his testicles is likely to wonder, "Do I have cancer?" Moreover, he may wonder "What are the chances that I will have to have the testicle removed? Was this caused by sexual activity?" Answers to questions such as these would constitute probabilistic orientations. Moreover, as these examples illustrate, such orientations may be contemporaneous with experience, prospective, or retrospective (respectively). Further, probabilistic orientations may take the form of certainty, and thus they may be routinized, automatic, and relatively mindless (see Langer, 1989). In other words, they may be held as tacit or unconscious assumptions about the nature of the world (e.g., I will be able to get out of bed, feed myself, and watch today's sunset). The term *probabilistic orientation* is used as an overarching label, including relatively mindful and mindless orientations, to acknowledge that all answers to questions such as those sketched previously are subject to revision and doubt. In other words, even though we may be cer-

---

[1]These include beliefs about the nature of the physical world as well as beliefs about abstractions (e.g., freedom, eternity; see Babrow, 1995).

[2]Using somewhat different terms, Lazarus (1991) offered the following clarification of the distinction between probabilistic orientations (what he called "knowledge") and evaluative orientations ("appraisals" in his terms): People are continually seeking knowledge (i.e., beliefs about how things work in general and in the specific adaptational encounter) and appraisals of the significance of the person–environment relationship for personal well-being, whether about a specific encounter or life as a whole (p. 127).

TABLE 2.2
Main Propositions of Problematic Integration Theory

1. People need probabilistic orientations to their world.

2. People need evaluative orientations to their world.

3. Probabilistic and evaluative orientations are integrated in experience.

4. Integration is at times problematic.

5. Illness is essentially the ongoing experience of interwoven problematic integrations.

6. The experience of integrative dilemmas entails processes in which given forms of PI are transformed in a variety of ways.

7. Communication is integral to the ways that PI is formed and transformed.

tain of—and therefore take for granted—most of our understandings of the world, even the most basic articles of faith can be challenged and made uncertain by experiences such as illness.

PI theory is founded on a second widely accepted idea; that is, people need evaluative orientations to their world. In other words, however some perceived aspect of the world is identified and understood, it must be appraised in terms of its implications for a person's well-being.[2] Continuing the previous example, the young man must answer questions such as the following: "How bad is testicular cancer? How bad would it be to lose a testicle? How bad would it be to have brought on the cancer by my own behavior?" Answers to questions such as these would constitute evaluative orientations. And, like probabilistic orientations, some evaluations are relatively simple, routine, or automatic. However, even well-established, routine judgments may be revised by a serious illness. Thus, a painful and rapidly progressing disease may prompt the person to rethink their evaluation of whether it is bad to die. Revising evaluations of stressful events is central to efforts to successfully cope with the stressors (see Babrow, 1992; Lazarus & Folkman, 1984).

PI theory builds on the preceding ideas in several distinctive ways. It recognizes that probabilistic and evaluative orientations are not merely separate, cooccurring phenomena. A central claim in PI theory is that probabilistic and evaluative orientations are integrated in experience (Babrow, 1992, 1995). Integration occurs in three distinct but interrelated ways. One way that integration occurs is in the reciprocal influences of these two orientations. Continuing the previous example, a person's assessment of the likelihood that his testicular cancer will be fatal can influence his evaluation of this outcome. Indeed, it is often said that life is valued most when it is in jeopardy. In addition, the person's evaluation of dying may influence his judgment of the likelihood of dying (see Babrow, 1991, 1992). Probabilistic and evaluative orientations are also integrated when they are connected with the probabilities and evaluations of other things. A belief in a loving, all-powerful god might affect estimates of the likelihood that the cancer will be fatal or evaluations of how bad it would be to die. But the belief that one is dying may also result in changes in these religious beliefs and values (see Hines, Babrow, Badzek, & Moss, 1997). Finally, probabilistic and evaluative orientations must be integrated with ongoing intentions, plans, and actions (see Eagly & Chaiken, 1993). In summary, probabilities and values are not isolated from one another or from such orientations to other aspects of experience. Rather, they are integrated with one another and with broader complexes of knowledge, feelings, and behavioral intentions (Ajzen & Fishbein, 1980; Babrow, 1992, 1995; Fishbein & Ajzen, 1975).

Another basic claim in PI theory is that integration is, at times, problematic. For example, persons confronting medical problems face various forms of integrative dilemmas, including diverging expectations and desires (e.g., the high probability of particular side-effects of chemotherapy), impossible wishes (e.g., that death can be postponed indefinitely), ambivalence (e.g., prolonging a painful life), and one or more of the types of uncertainty and ambiguity discussed previously. Most important, PI theory suggests that illness is essentially the ongoing experience of interwoven problematic integrations (e.g., symptoms, diagnosis, prognosis, treatment, remission, recurrence; see Babrow, 1995; Brashers & Babrow, 1996)

PI theory develops the preceding notion in two additional, closely related claims. One is that the experience of integrative dilemmas entails processes in which given forms of PI are transformed in a variety of ways. The other is that communication is integral to the ways that PI is formed and transformed (see Babrow, 1995). One of the ways that PI is altered is by transformation in its basic form (see Babrow, 1992). For example, what is at first perceived as an impossibility (or certainty) is often transformed by information that creates uncertainty. For instance, a couple who believes that it is impossible for them to conceive a child may obtain new information that leads them to believe that conception may be difficult but that it is not impossible. Second, because probabilistic and evaluative orientations to a given object must be integrated with such orientations to other objects of thought, the problematic integration arising from a particular focal issue can be expected to give rise to various related concerns. For example, a person diagnosed with a fertility problem might, in turn, experience doubts about her or his sexuality, attractiveness, and general health. Third, although PI is an individual psychological experience, it is also often linked with interpersonal and broader social dynamics. In other words, PI is frequently experienced as an interactional dilemma and a manifestation of topics of broad social concern. For example, a person who must reconcile the information that she is dying with her terror of death probably receives this information from a doctor who views himself as a healer who must admit he cannot heal her. This conversation may take place in a hospital that is poorly prepared to care for dying patients within a culture actively debating how to improve care for the dying (see Babrow, 1995; Callahan, 1993; Maynard, 1991).

In summary, PI theory provides a general perspective on health communication. It suggests that illness is essentially the ongoing experience of problematic integrations of a person's expectations or beliefs with their values or desires. More specifically, the theory proposes that health-related probability judgments must be seen as distinguishable but not independent from evaluative judgments. From this, it follows that probabilistic judgments about consequences of an illness will both affect and be affected by evaluations of the desirability or undesirability of these consequences. Because these integrations of probability and evaluation are unlikely to remain satisfying (e.g., denial of illness is unlikely to continue indefinitely), PI theory suggests that particular forms of problematic integration will often be replaced by other forms. Moreover, particular dilemmas produced by illness are likely to create additional dilemmas. Uncertainty about whether a breast must be removed to prevent the spread of breast cancer may easily raise other troubling questions about how this event will affect self-image or relations with others. As a result, uncertainty and the stress associated with it are likely to spread as the illness continues. Finally, when the uncertainty resulting from an illness involves important consequences and persists for an extended period, it will be influenced by persons who interact with the patient as well as the broader culture in which these conversations take place. In other words, problematic integrations are formed, sustained, and transformed by communication. The practical implications of these ideas for illness explanations are discussed in the following section.

PRACTICAL IMPLICATIONS FOR EXPLAINING ILLNESS

Explaining illness is always an important task and patients are always entitled to complete explanations of their condition (Beauchamp & Childress, 1994; President's Commission, 1982). However, illness explanations become the most important under the same conditions that they become the most difficult. Specifically, explanations of illness may be most important when the illness has serious long-term consequences that cannot be prevented easily or, in some cases, at all. Explanations of these illnesses are also substantially more challenging. Treatment options are more difficult to explain. Because the physical, psychological, and relational consequences of the illness are more threatening and uncertain (Gotcher, 1995; Hines, Babrow, et al., 1997; Spiegel, 1992), communication is often reduced. Emotional and physical stress make the reception of explanatory messages by patients and family members more difficult and the formulation of these messages more challenging (Buckman, 1992; Strauss, Sharp, Lorch, & Kachalia, 1995). Moreover, because persons experiencing serious long-term illness are typically treated by a medical team consisting of multiple specialists, explanatory messages can easily contain incomplete or conflicting information (Clark, 1995; SUPPORT, 1995). Finally, because such illnesses frequently require patients to be actively involved in their own treatments over an extended period of time, explanations must be more detailed and must be restated to compensate for memory distortion or loss (Badzek, Hines, & Moss, 1998; Ramsdell & Annis, 1996; Wilson, 1995).

Basic Sources of Missed Understanding in Illness Explanation

We previously argued that these kinds of illnesses are instances of problematic integration for patients, their families, and health care providers. This section uses the preceding analysis to identify challenges and practical guidelines for illness explanation. It begins with a discussion of basic sources of missed understanding in illness explanation. Next, the section identifies circumstances in which explanation of illness is most likely to be difficult, including major conversational dilemmas that must be overcome for explanations of illness to meet the needs of patients and their families.

PI theory and the analysis of variations in the meaning of uncertainty make it clear that there are broad opportunities for patients and practitioners to talk past one another. One major source of this missed communication is when a patient's focal concern is not clear to the practitioner (see Babrow, Kasch, & Ford, 1998; Mishel, 1988). For instance, a patient who says that she is "uncertain about an upcoming medical procedure" may be taken to mean that she is (a) not sure what to expect in the process of the procedure itself, (b) worried about immediate and longer term outcomes, (c) doubtful about her physical and–or emotional readiness for the procedure, (d) concerned about her family's supportiveness, (e) undecided about the advisability of the procedure, and–or a host of other potentially relevant issues. Unless the ambiguity is resolved, the practitioner is likely to offer an irrelevant explanation. Therefore, a most basic practical implication of the current analysis is that the hearer must clearly understand the focal point of the speaker's uncertainty.

A second basic source of missed communication is the possibility of a hearer misunderstanding the form of uncertainty expressed by the speaker. The preceding analysis reveals that the term "uncertainty" and its variants can refer to a wide variety of substantively different issues (Table 2.1). For example, assume that the practitioner in the earlier illustration learns that the patient is concerned specifically about outcomes of the impending medical procedure; the care provider still may not know what the patient means by her uncertainty. Does she want more information, or is she unsure due to information overload? Does she want to know more, or is she ambivalent about learning more? Does she wish that medical science had more information to offer, or does she think that the practitioner is holding something back? If her uncertainty is rooted in personal ignorance, the practitioner might help her best by providing and explaining new information (Sheer & Cline, 1995). By contrast, uncertainty rooted in ambivalence might require attention to the patient's motives for avoiding illness explanations (see later this chapter). And, when uncertainty is rooted in doubts about others as sources of information, patients and health care providers must find ways to reestablish trust. Hence, the hearer must clarify and adapt illness explanations (or other relevant responses) to the form of uncertainty underlying a speaker's expression of doubt.

A third basic source of missed communication is the complex dynamic process at the heart of problematic integration; both the focus and form of uncertainty are likely to shift repeatedly over the course of an interaction. In other words, any one integrative dilemma can be expected to provoke a cascading sequence of troubles. This is because of the very nature of integration. Recall that integration entails not only the synthesis of probabilistic and evaluative orientations to a given issue (e.g., what is the likelihood that my kidneys will fail, and how bad is kidney failure?); it also entails synthesis of these orientations with probability and value judgments about related issues (e.g., related to dialysis, organ transplantation, mortality, marital relations, financial considerations). This means that, over the course of conversation about some particular uncertainty, there are likely to be numerous shifts in the focus of concern. Moreover, the form of uncertainty is likely to change over time (e.g., uncertainty rooted in ignorance may change to doubts about informational accuracy, doubts about source ethos, and so on). Hence, communicators must be sensitive to shifts in focal issues and forms of uncertainty lest they miss the point of one another's cares. Although sensitivity to these basic sources of misunderstanding increases the chance for effective communication, it is also important to recognize circumstances where illness explanations are especially problematic.

Circumstances in Which Explaining Illness is Especially Problematic

When Certainty About the Illness is Highly Desirable But Impossible

Aside from the basic challenges reviewed previously, PI theory and the analysis of types of uncertainty suggest several specific conditions in which the explanation of illness will be especially troublesome. The first of these conditions reflects diverging expectations and desires in orientations to uncertainty itself. In other words, (un)certainty is neither inherently good nor bad; its value must be appraised. Moreover, people also form probabilistic judgments about (un)certainty. They may assess the possibility of achieving certainty. Alternatively, people may judge the likelihood of being or remaining uncertain. In illness, for example, people frequently experience diverging expectations and desires in relation to uncertainty itself. Hence, one situation where illness explanation is especially challenging is when certainty is highly desirable but highly unlikely or impossible.

When certainty is most desired but impossible, explanation of illness becomes quite challenging. On the one hand, this situation evokes substantial emotion, unsettles thought processes, and raises the stakes in the patient–care provider interaction. On the other hand, the situation places great demands on intellectual capacities and interactional skills. When complexity, such as multiple contingencies, is the cause of uncertainty, direct attempts to explain the illness will be extremely difficult. For instance, a person diagnosed with a brain tumor cannot know whether the tumor is malignant. Surgery to remove the tumor may or may not produce particular side-effects, which, in turn, may or may not be easily remedied. The tumor may or may not recur, depending in part on the type of follow-up treatments that are selected. Because each of these uncertainties requires the discussion of additional contingencies, the explanatory task cannot be clearly defined. Moreover, any such discussion will be well supplied with emotion. Also, the same explanation that overwhelms one person might be painfully incomplete for another. Doctors faced with this dilemma often respond by acting as if these uncertainties do not exist (Katz, 1984), giving patients the illusion of certainty and control.

We believe that there are three essential practical implications of the foregoing, one attitudinal and the other two behavioral. First, care providers must understand and accept that the practice of medicine is a form of principled gambling rather than either art or science (Bursztajn et al., 1990). Bursztajn et al. argued that, at base, this requires that care providers acknowledge a degree of uncertainty in the world, a fact that doctors have been loath to admit (Katz, 1984). In addition, they argued that principled, skilled gambling also clearly requires estimates of not only probabilities but also values and emotions. Moreover, the principled gambler consciously attempts to identify and understand the effects of various typically unconscious decision heuristics, such as the gambler's ("If I am losing, perhaps now I'll win") and postmortem fallacies ("If I am losing, I must be doing something wrong"; Bursztajn et al., 1990, p. 189). The principled gambler also tries to understand the effects of social context on gambling decisions. In short, the principled gambler attempts to consciously manage uncertainty, continually honing this skill rather than hiding from it as either an artist guided by inarticulate intuition or a scientist clinging to the belief in a mechanistically determined world.

Aside from the foregoing attitudinal implication of our analysis, there are two practical behavioral implications. One is that care providers must teach their patients to understand that medicine is principled gambling. Patients are undoubtedly threatened by losing faith in medical certainty, but the threat may be substantially reduced by helping them to understand that medical uncertainties can be managed in highly informed, reasoned, and skillful ways. Moreover, care providers must be willing to assure patients that, although they confront medical uncertainties, they can be confident in the constant, caring service of the health care team. In other words, the uncertainty of a biological outcome can be managed more confidently by assurance of social–structural support.

When Certainty About the Illness is Possible But Highly Undesirable

A related situation in which the explanation of illness is especially troublesome is when certainty about the illness is possible but highly undesirable. PI theory asserts that one circumstance that makes communication difficult is the need to confront a highly undesirable outcome that also is highly probable (also see Maynard, 1991). Although conversations about illnesses that are easily managed or cured enable participants to pursue multiple conversational goals with little difficulty, incurable illness is more difficult to address. For example, a doctor explaining strep throat to a concerned parent can readily blend a discussion of the effects of antibiotics on the illness with reassurance that the child will soon be well. But when the illness entails predictable outcomes such as death or a debilitating condition that is highly undesirable, explanation is often viewed as counterproductive (Ford et al., 1996; Gotcher, 1995; Jones, 1979; Lazarus, 1983).

For centuries, doctors have advised each other to provide patients with hope, even if concealing or lying about undesirable outcomes was needed. Hippocrates advised doctors to "Give necessary orders with cheerfulness and serenity, turning his (sic) attention away from what is being done to him; sometimes reprove sharply and emphatically, and sometimes comfort with solicitude and attention, revealing nothing of the patient's future or present condition" (in Katz, 1984, p. 4). The first code of ethics developed by the American Medical Association cautioned doctors that:

> the life of a sick person can be shortened not only by the acts, but also by the words or the manner of a physician. It is, therefore, a sacred duty to guard himself carefully in this respect, and to avoid all things which have a tendency to discourage the patient and to depress his spirits. (in Katz, 1984, p. 20)

Although legal changes have altered standards for disclosure in the United States (Kodish & Post, 1995), efforts to discuss highly undesirable consequences of illness continue to be problematic.

For doctors, such discussions require an admission that their efforts to preserve health have been unsuccessful (Buckman, 1992; Katz, 1984). For patients and their families, these explanations require an acknowledgment that serious impairment or death is in their future. Depending on the patient's culture, these conversations may violate norms that proscribe the discussion of bad news (Blackhall, Murphy, Frank, Michel, & Azen, 1995; Carrese & Rhodes, 1995; Gostin, 1995; Jecker, Carrese, & Pearlman, 1995). Hence, when an explanation of illness requires the discussion of outcomes that are both certain and highly undesirable, all of the participants may be inclined to collaborate to avoid a thorough and impartial discussion of prognosis (Hines, Badzek, & Moss, 1997). More generally, the effectiveness of illness explanation will depend directly on interactants' ability to manage the dialectical tension between the pain of clarity and the hope preserved by uncertainty.

When Reducing Uncertainty About the Illness is Irrelevant

Efforts to explain illness are problematic when patients and–or members of their families do not want to maintain control over their illness through reducing uncertainty about it. Although PI theory suggests that experiencing an event that is both quite probable and very undesirable is troublesome, it also asserts that a range of communicative responses may be used to manage this condition. Attempting to maintain control is one potential response. However, individuals from different cultures may employ a variety of responses (see the chapters on cultural issues in explaining illness, this volume). Field and Cassel (1997) noted that Western bioethics has defined the ideal patient as one who clearly understands his or her condition, prognosis, and treatment options, wants to maintain individual control over future treatment, and does not believe that the condition will be affected by miracles or divine intervention (p. 370). Field and Cassell argued convincingly that this ideal patient is relatively uncommon, particularly among the growing numbers of patients (and care providers) from non-Western cultures (also see Blackhall et al., 1995; Carrese & Rhodes, 1995; Gostin, 1995; Jecker et al., 1995). Thus, the assumption that patients want autonomous control is questionable for many persons confronting illness.

Even when control is a personal goal, persons will not necessarily want clear and unambiguous information. A variety of forms of secondary control entail conscious choices to adapt to negative events rather than attempting to avoid, change, or control them (Fiske & Taylor, 1991; Rothbaum, Weisz, & Snyder, 1982). From this perspective, a person may maintain secondary control by deciding to place others such as medical personnel or family members in charge of responding to a major illness. Our research has shown this tendency may be relatively common, particularly among older individuals (Hines, Moss, & Badzek, 1997a). When persons do not want individual control or use a form of secondary rather than primary control, explanations of illness may be unsatisfying for both themselves and their health care providers. Providers may find it unsettling to perform medical procedures on patients who do not understand or want to understand them. And efforts to meet the standards needed for informed consent may be distressing for patients who would prefer not to know about their condition (Hines, Badzek, & Moss, 1997). Hence, care providers must attempt to understand and adapt to patients' level of desire to maintain control over their treatment (see Babrow, Hines, et al., 1998).

Mutual Avoidance of Illness Explanation

Many discussions of why illness explanations are unsatisfactory have attempted to place the blame on a particular party. Thus, some have suggested that patients or their families avoid talking about medical problems with serious consequences because they are afraid to do so (Buckman, 1992). Others have argued that doctors are responsible, perhaps because they are unconcerned that patients be fully informed or because they cannot admit to a patient that they are incapable of effecting a cure (Addington & Wegescheide-Harris, 1995; Buckman, 1992). We have argued that this avoidance is a collaborative accomplishment in which families, patients, and health care providers all willingly participate (Hines, Babrow et al., 1997; Hines, Moss, & Badzek, 1997b). For example, our research has shown that doctors had frequently concealed the need for dialysis from older patients for months after that diagnosis could have been made; nonetheless, patients reported little distress with this delay even when they ultimately had no time to plan for this eventuality. Although denial may violate norms regarding full disclosure of a patient's condition, patients, families, and health care providers may collectively choose to reduce stress by avoiding conversation about a severe illness or approaching death. Although mutual avoidance may accomplish this goal for a period, research suggests that this strategy may ultimately produce greater stress (Fiske & Taylor, 1991; Thompson, 1981). Such a result is fully consistent with the assertion of PI theory that efforts to manage instances of PI, such as serious illness or impending death, are inherently unstable.

In summary, particular strategies may be temporarily acceptable. The wise practitioner will anticipate, prepare the patient for, and together manage change. In other words, care providers must enact new communication strategies before those such as mutual avoidance become ineffective. This means only in part that care providers must closely track a patient's condition and anticipate changes for the worse; in addition, it means that members of the health care team must look for opportunities and methods for shifting from avoidance to consideration of unpleasant potentialities. Moreover, to manage this shift effectively, it must begin well before a patient's health takes a serious downturn because it would then be either difficult or impossible to collaborate effectively. A promising approach for this sort of managed shift in strategies for coping with problematic integration is to begin the process of replacing mutual avoidance with collaborative health care planning on a day when the patient is doing well.[3] In other words, when the doctor can say with assurance that all is well, she or he should go on to note that this may not always be the case and that it is wise to plan for the possibility of a turn for the worse. At this point, the patient can be drawn in to the process of advance care planning (see Doukas & Reichel, 1993; Singer, Robertson, & Roy, 1996).

CONCLUSION

It is clear that the experience of illness is permeated with uncertainty. Uncertainty is, in its most general sense, the justification and motivation for explanatory health communication. However, there are many significant variations in the nature of illness-related uncertainty. This variance requires sensitive probing of the nature of uncertainty in a given situation and adaptation of illness-explanatory strategies. Moreover, the need to integrate beliefs with desires further challenges health communication. For instance, straightforward explanations are at times threatening or damaging to both patients and care providers, and at other times they can be irrelevant. Health communication strategies, whether or not they ultimately entail explanatory messages, must be adapted to the dynamics of our need to integrate beliefs and expectations with values, desires, and hopes.

REFERENCES

Abramson, L. Y., Garber, J., & Seligman, M. E. P. (1980). Learned helplessness in humans: An attributional analysis. In J. Garber & M. E. P. Seligman (Eds.), *Human helplessness: Theory and applications* (pp. 3–57). New York: Academic Press.

Abramson, L. Y., Seligman, M. E. P., & Teasdale, J. D. (1978). Learned helplessness in humans: A critique and reformulation. *Journal of Abnormal Psychology, 87,* 49–74.

Addington, T., & Wegescheide-Harris, J. (1995). Ethics and communication with the terminally ill. *Health Communication, 7,* 267–281.

---

[3]Our recommendation here is patterned after the approach of Alvin Moss, M.D., a nephrologist and Director of the Center for Health Ethics and Law, Robert C. Byrd Health Sciences Center, West Virginia University.

Ajzen, I., & Fishbein, M. (1980). *Understanding attitudes and predicting social behavior.* Englewood Cliffs, NJ: Prentice-Hall.

Antonovsky, A. (1990). Personality and health: Testing the sense of coherence model. In H. S. Friedman (Ed.), *Personality and disease* (pp. 155–177). New York: Wiley.

Atkinson, P. (1984). Training for certainty. *Social Science and Medicine, 19,* 949–956.

Atkinson, P. (1995). *Medical talk and medical work.* London: Sage.

Babrow, A. S. (1991). Tensions between health beliefs and desires: Implications for a health communication campaign to promote a smoking cessation program. *Health Communication, 3,* 93–112.

Babrow, A. S. (1992). Communication and problematic integration: Understanding diverging probability and value, ambiguity, ambivalence, and impossibility. *Communication Theory, 2,* 95–130.

Babrow, A. S. (1995). Communication and problematic integration: Milan Kundera's "Lost Letters" in The Book of Laughter and Forgetting. *Communication Monographs, 62,* 283–300.

Babrow, A. S., Hines, S. C., Glover, J. J., Badzek, L. A., Holley, J. L., & Moss, A. H. (1998, April). *Do dialysis patients want autonomy in advance medical care planning? An examination of patient views about communication and decision making.* Paper presented at the Kentucky Conference on Health Communication, Lexington, KY.

Babrow, A. S., Kasch, C. R., & Ford, L. A. (1998). The many meanings of "uncertainty" in illness: Toward a systematic accounting. *Health Communication, 10,* 1–24.

Badzek, L., Hines, S. C., & Moss, A. H. (1998). Inadequate self-care knowledge among elderly hemodialysis patients: Assessing its prevalence and potential causes. *ANNA Journal, 25,* 293–300.

Beauchamp, T. L., & Childress, J. F. (1994). *Principles of biomedical ethics* (4th ed.). New York: Oxford University Press.

Berger, C. R., & Gudykunst, W. B. (1991). Uncertainty and communication. In B. Dervin (Ed.), *Progress in communication science* (Vol. X, pp. 21–66). Norwood, NJ: Ablex.

Blackhall, L. J., Murphy, S. T., Frank, G., Michel, V., & Azen, S. (1995). Ethnicity and attitudes toward patient autonomy. *Journal of the American Medical Association, 274,* 820–825.

Bornstein, R. F. (1989). Exposure and affect: Overview and meta-analysis of research, 1968–1987. *Psychological Bulletin, 106,* 265–289.

Borysenko, J. (1987). *Minding the body, mending the mind.* Reading, MA: Addison-Wesley.

Brashers, D. E., & Babrow, A. S. (1996). Theorizing health communication. *Communication Studies, 47,* 243–251.

Brenders, D. A. (1987). Perceived control: Foundations and directions for communication research. In M. McLaughlin (Ed.), *Communication yearbook 10* (pp. 86–116). Beverly Hills, CA: Sage.

Brown, W. A. (1998). The placebo effect. *Scientific American, 278,* 90–95.

Buckman, R. B. (1992). *How to break bad news.* Baltimore, MD: John Hopkins University Press.

Bursztajn, H. J., Feinbloom, R. I., Hamm, R. M., & Brodsky, A. (1990). *Medical choices, medical chances: How patients, families, and physicians can cope with uncertainty.* New York: Routledge.

Callahan, D. (1993). *The troubled dream of life: In search of a peaceful death.* New York: Simon & Schuster.

Carrese, J. A., & Rhodes, L. A. (1995). Western bioethics on the Navajo reservation. *Journal of the American Medical Association, 274,* 826–829.

Cassell, E. J. (1985). *Talking with patients: Volume 2: Clinical technique.* Cambridge, MA: MIT Press.

Chenail, R. J., Douthit, P. E., Gale, J. E., Stormberg, J. L., Morris, G. H., Park, J. M., Sridaromont, S., & Schmer, V. (1990). "It's probably nothing serious, but … ": Parents' interpretation of referral to pediatric cardiologists. *Health Communication, 2,* 165–188.

Clark, P. G. (1995). Quality of life, values, and teamwork in geriatric care: Do we communicate what we mean? *Gerontologist, 35,* 402–411.

Cohen, M. H. (1993). The unknown and the unknowable—Managing sustained uncertainty. *Western Journal of Nursing Research, 15,* 77–96.

Cronkhite, G., & Liska, J. R. (1976). A critique of factor analytic approaches to the study of credibility. *Communication Monographs, 43,* 91–107.

Doukas, D. J., & Reichel, W. (1993). *Planning for uncertainty: A guide to living wills and other advance directives for health care.* Baltimore, MD: Johns Hopkins University Press.

Eagly, A. H., & Chaiken, S. (1993). *The psychology of attitudes.* New York: Harcourt Brace Jovanovich.

Edwards, W. (1972). N = 1: Diagnosis in unique cases. In J. A. Jacquez (Ed.), *Computer diagnosis and diagnostic methods* (pp. 139–151). Springfield, IL: Thomas.

Field, M. J., & Cassel, C. K. (Eds.). (1997). *Approaching death: Improving care at the end of life.* Washington, D.C.: National Academy Press.

Fishbein, M., & Ajzen, I. (1975). *Belief, attitude, intention, and behavior.* Reading, MA: Addison-Wesley.

Fiske, S. T., & Taylor, S. E. (1991). *Social cognition* (2nd ed.). New York: McGraw Hill.

Folkman, S., Schaefer, C., Lazarus, R. S. (1979). Cognitive processes as mediators of stress and coping. In V. Hamilton & D. M. Warburton (Eds.), *Human stress and cognition: An information processing approach* (pp. 265–298). New York: Wiley.

Ford, L. A., Babrow, A. S., & Stohl, C. (1996). Social support messages and the management of uncertainty in the experience of breast cancer: An application of problematic integration theory. *Communication Monographs, 63,* 189–207.

Fox, R. (1957). Training for uncertainty. In R. K. Merton, G. G. Reader, & P. L Kendall (Eds.), *The student–physician* (pp. 207–241). Cambridge, MA: Harvard University Press.

Fox, R. (1980). The evolution of medical uncertainty. *Milbank Memorial Fund Quarterly/Health and Society, 58,* 1–49.

Friedman, H. S. (1993). Interpersonal expectations and the maintenance of health. In D. Blank (Ed.), *Interpersonal expectations: Theory, research, and applications* (pp. 179–193). Cambridge, England: Cambridge University Press.

Gostin, L. O. (1995). Informed consent, cultural sensitivity, and respect for persons. *Journal of the American Medical Association, 274,* 844–845.

Gotcher, J. M. (1995). Well-adjusted and maladjusted cancer patients: An examination of communication variables. *Health Communication, 7,* 21–34.

Gould, S. J. (1985). The median isn't the message. *Discover, 6,* 40–42.

Herzlich, C. & Graham, D. (1973). *Health and illness: A social psychological analysis.* London: Academic Press.

Hines, S. C., Babrow, A. S., Badzek, L., & Moss, A. H. (1997). Communication and problematic integration in end of life decisions: Dialysis decisions and the elderly. *Health Communication, 9,* 199–218.

Hines, S. C., Badzek, L., & Moss, A. H. (1997). Informed consent among chronically ill elderly: Assessing its (in)adequacy and predictors. *Journal of Applied Communication Research, 25,* 151–169.

Hines, S. C., Moss, A. H., & Badzek, L. (1997b, November). *Making medical choices when all of the options are bad: Problematic integration for the seriously ill.* Paper presented at the Annual Meeting of the National Communication Association, Chicago.

Hines, S. C., Moss, A. H., & Badzek, L. (1997a). Being involved or just being informed: Communication preferences of seriously ill, older adults. *Communication Quarterly, 45,* 268–281.

Jecker, N. S., Carrese, J. A., Pearlman, R. A. (1995). Caring for patients in cross cultural settings. *Hastings Center Report, 25,* 6–14.

Jones, R. A. (1982). Expectations and illness. In M. S. Friedman & M. R. DiMatteo (Eds.), *Interpersonal issues in health care* (pp. 145–167). New York: Academic Press.

Jones, R. B. (1979). Life-threatening illness in families. In C. A. Garfield (Ed.), *Stress and survival: The emotional realities of life-threatening illness* (pp. 353–362). St. Louis, MO: Mosby.

Katz, J. (1984). *The silent world of doctor and patient.* New York: The Free Press.

Kimball, C. P. (1971). Medicine and dialects. *Annals of Internal Medicine, 74,* 137–139.

Kodish, E., & Post, S. G. (1995). Oncology and hope. *Journal of Clinical Oncology, 13,* 1817–1822.

Kramer, P. D. (1993). *Listening to Prozac.* New York: Viking.

Kreps, G. L., & Thornton, B. C. (1992). *Health communication theory and practice* (2nd ed.). Prospect Heights, IL: Waveland Press.

Langer, E. J. (1989). *Mindfulness.* Reading, MA: Addison-Wesley.

Lazarus, R. S. (1983). The costs and benefits of denial. In S. Breznitz (Ed.), *The denial of stress* (pp. 1–30). New York: International Universities Press.

Lazarus, R. S. (1991). *Emotion and adaptation.* New York: Oxford University Press.

Lazarus, R. S., & Folkman, S. (1984). *Stress, appraisal, and coping.* New York: Springer.

Lipowski, Z. J. (1970). Physical illness, the individual, and the coping process. *Psychiatry in Medicine, 1,* 91–102.

Martin, E. (1994). *Flexible bodies: Tracking immunity in American culture from the days of po-lio to the age of AIDS.* Boston: Beacon Press.

Maynard, D. W. (1991). Bearing bad news in clinical settings. In B. Dervin (Ed.), *Progress in communication science* (Vol. X, pp. 143–172). Norwood, NJ: Ablex.

Mishel, M. H. (1988). Uncertainty in illness. *Image: Journal of Nursing Research, 20,* 225–232.

Mishler, E. G. (1984). *The discourse of medicine: Dialectics of medical interviews.* Norwood, NJ: Ablex.

Mishler, E. G. (1986). *Research interviewing: Context and narrative.* Cambridge, MA: Harvard University Press.

Mokros, H. B. (1993). Communication and psychiatric diagnosis: Tales of depressive moods from two contexts. *Health Communication, 5,* 113–128.

Norton, R. W. (1975). Measurement of ambiguity tolerance. *Journal of Personality Assessment, 39,* 607–619.

Nuland, S. B. (1993). *How we die: Reflections on life's final chapter.* New York: Knopf.

President's Commission for the Study of Ethical Problems in Medicine and Biomedical and Behavioral Research. (1982). *Making health care decisions.* Washington, DC: U.S. Government Printing Office.

Prince, E. F., Frader, J., & Bosk, C. (1982). On hedging in physician–physician discourse. In R. J. DiPietro (Ed.), *Linguistics and the professions* (pp. 83–97). Norwood, NJ: Ablex.

Ramsdell, R., & Annis, C. (1996). Patient education: A continuing repetitive process. *ANNA Journal, 23,* 217–221.

Rothbaum, F., Weisz, J. R., & Snyder, S. S. (1982). Changing the world and changing the self: A two-process model of perceived control. *Journal of Personality and Social Psychology, 42,* 5–37.

Schutz, A. (1970). *On phenomenology and social relations: Selected writings.* In H. Wagner (Ed.), Chicago: University of Chicago Press.

Schwartz, S., & Griffin, T. (1986). *Medical thinking: The psychology of medical judgment and decision making.* New York: Springer-Verlag.

Sheer, V. C., & Cline, R. J. (1995). Testing a model of perceived information adequacy and uncertainty reduction in physician–patient interactions. *Journal of Applied Communication Research, 23,* 44–59.

Simon, H. (1978). Rationality as a process and product of thought. *American Economic Review, 68,* 1–16.

Singer, P. A., Robertson, G., & Roy, D. J. (1996). Bioethics for clinicians: 6. Advance care planning. *Canadian Medical Association Journal, 155,* 1689–1692.

Sontag, S. (1978). *Illness as metaphor.* New York: Farrar, Strauss, & Giroux.

Sontag, S. (1989). *AIDS and its metaphors.* New York: Anchor.

Spiegel, D. (1992). Effects of psychosocial support on patients with metastatic breast cancer. *Journal of Psychosocial Oncology, 10,* 113–121.

Stiff, J. B. (1994). *Persuasive communication.* New York: Guilford.

Strauss, R. P., Sharp, M. C., Lorch, S. C., & Kachalia, B. (1995). Physicians and the communication of "bad news": Parent experiences of being informed of their child's cleft lip and/or palate. *Pediatrics, 96,* 82–89.

Stroebe, W., & Stroebe, M. S. (1995). *Social psychology and health.* Buckingham, England: Open University Press.

SUPPORT (1995). A controlled trial to improve care for seriously ill hospitalized patients. *Journal of the American Medical Association, 274,* 1591–1598.

Thompson, S. C. (1981). Will it hurt less if I control it? A complex answer to a simple question. *Psychological Bulletin, 90,* 89–101.

Weinstein, M. C., & Fineberg, H. V. (1980). *Clinical decision analysis.* Philadelphia: Saunders.

Wilson, B. (1995). Promoting compliance: The patient–provider partnership. *Advances in Renal Replacement Therapy, 2,* 199–206.

Zajonc, R. B. (1968). Attitudinal effects of mere exposure. *Journal of Personality and Social Psychology, 9,*(2), 1–27.

3

Explaining Illness Through the Mass Media: The Problem-Solving Perspective

Katherine E. Rowan
Department of Communication
Purdue University

In 1998, the *New England Journal of Medicine* published a study saying that the number of false positives, or false alarms, resulting from mammogram screening was unacceptably high (Elmore et al., 1998). Shortly after the national media covered this news, a Midwest radiologist attended a neighborhood party. He spent the evening responding to questions generated by an Associated Press story (Haney, 1998), which had been on the front page of the local paper. Some party guests interpreted the news to mean that mammography was unreliable and that obtaining mammograms was pointless. Others interpreted the news cynically. Mammograms are money-making ventures for hospitals, they reasoned. It is not surprising that these tests are given repeatedly, perhaps far more often than necessary.

The radiologist was upset by this turn of events. In his view, undue publicity for the *New England Journal of Medicine* study misled and confused the public. Elmore et al. (1998) may have exaggerated the false positive rate[1], but the news story gave no indication that this could be the case. The people the doctor talked with at the party seemed more misled than aided by their exposure to this news. Many did not know what false positives were and did not think about the fact that false positives are preferable to false negatives when dealing with a life-threatening disease.

In contrast, journalists looking at the same news coverage assessed it differently. Several said the news was informative and important. The fact that people were talking about the study with a radiologist was an indication that the media had done their job in getting the word out. Further, if a prestigious medical journal says the rate of false positives in mammograms is unacceptably high, the public has a right to know.

This chapter argues that the radiologist's, journalists', and citizens' reactions to this story reflect intuitive beliefs about the ideal ways in which mass media should share health and illness information. When these beliefs are unexamined, they undermine physicians' and journalists' capacities to work with one another. Consequently, the first half of this chapter identifies two common beliefs about the reasons for inadequacies in mass media coverage of health and illness. It then analyzes these beliefs and describes ways in which they fuel physicians', journalists', and the public's doubts about and distrust of one another. Because learning is hampered by distrust, this section offers research-supported advice for earning trust from the public and fellow professionals.

The chapter's second half focuses on steps for explaining complex medical subject matter. Research shows that some intuitive assumptions held by expert explainers are useful; others are not. The chapter critiques the less useful assumptions. It then offers a diagnostic framework for anticipating likely sources of confusion for lay audiences and research-informed steps for addressing and overcoming these difficulties.

EDUCATION VERSUS EMPOWERMENT: WHICH ROLE SHOULD MASS MEDIA PLAY?

Physicians, journalists, and the public often have differing views of how the mass media should communicate medical information. One perspective says that the mass media should educate the public. Typically, physicians

---

[1]One criticism of Elmore et al. (1998) is that the study exaggerated the number of false positives women received. Another is that news reports did not include some important information needed to contextualize its findings. As Feig (1998), a radiologist and chair of the American College of Radiology Committee on Screening Mammography Guidelines, wrote: Most news reports did not mention that in this study the false positive rate was only 6.5% for a single mammographic examination and 3.7 for a single clinical breast examination. More important, the cumulative 49% false positive rate was an extrapolated value because women had a median of only four mammograms during the 10-year period. The author failed to realize that such extrapolation will overestimate recall rates (p. 8).

adopt this view. The other view says that the public is sufficiently expert and what it needs from mass media is greater empowerment; that is, greater accountability from health professionals. Frequently, journalists and members of the public are sympathetic to the empowerment notion. Although proponents of these views typically see them as being in opposition to one another, I find that each has strengths and weaknesses. By recognizing these conflicting orientations, physicians, journalists, and citizens can understand and ease some of the tensions affecting them when they attempt to explain health and illness through the mass media.[2]

Education

According to the education view, news coverage, public service announcements, and mass media public health campaigns do the greatest public good when they educate the public about health and illness. That is, they are effective when they convey accurate information from authoritative medical experts to wide audiences. These outlets do the greatest harm when they convey inaccurate or misleading information, which leads the public to behave in ways that harm health. According to this view, the role of the media is to serve as a conduit through which clear and accurate information flows from medical experts to the targeted public.

Some evidence supports the education view. News coverage, health campaigns with mass media components, and even single public service announcements or television programs can promote public health. Research shows that certain effects are achieved more easily than others. Generally, increases in awareness of medical information are more easily achieved through mass-mediated messages than are changes in understanding of health and illness information, attitude change, or behavioral compliance (Freimuth & Taylor, 1994; McGuire, 1984; Rogers & Storey, 1987). Nevertheless, research shows that even the most difficult changes to achieve have occurred as a result of mass media messages. One study found that exposure to television and radio public service announcements significantly predicted knowledge of measles vaccination among Philippine mothers (McDivitt, Zimicki, & Hornik, 1997). Further, knowledge of the reasons for vaccinating children against measles and the steps to acquiring vaccinations accounted

---

[2]In this chapter, the terms mass media, illness, and explanation are intended in specific ways. *Mass media* refers to contexts where shared meaning is created through an intermediary vehicle for large numbers of people. The definition includes news stories, news features, explanatory graphics, advertisements, press releases, web sites, magazines, brochures, books, and other similar materials. Following Kaplan (1997), *illness* is distinguished from disease. Kaplan wrote that illness is the broader term. *Disease* refers to biological processes. Illness refers to "the impact of the disease as well as social, psychological, and environmental factors on patient outcome" (p. 76). *Explaining* refers to efforts to deepen understanding of complex subject matter. It does not refer to discourse designed to prove claims to fellow experts (Martin, 1970; Rowan, 1988, 1995a).

for three fifths of increased compliance in getting children vaccinated (McDivitt et al., 1997). Other studies show connections between exposure to media messages and awareness of health news. For example, Johnson, Meischke, Grau, and Johnson (1992) found that 82% of randomly sampled U.S. women over 40 said they had received cancer-related information from the media. More dramatic evidence of the educational role that media messages can play is found in contexts where beloved public figures fall ill. According to Freimuth and Taylor (1994), "in the first 60 days following Earvin 'Magic' Johnson's announcement of his HIV-seropositive status, the Centers for Disease Control AIDs Hotline received more than 1.7 million attempted calls" (p. 8). Daily calls in the 2 months following news coverage of the announcement were four times greater than the daily average call rate in the prior 3 months (also see Brown & Basil, 1995).

Unfortunately, there is ample evidence that mass media frequently convey inaccurate or misleading health information that can harm public health. For example, Freimuth, Greenberg, DeWitt, and Romano (1984) reported that "instead of offering information on … prevention, risks, detection, and treatment of cancer, newspapers provide material that leads the public to believe that 'everything causes cancer" (p. 70). Bazell (1990) said that since the mid-1980s, the mass media have been suggesting that a cure for AIDs was just around the corner but that expectations created by this message of hope were repeatedly dashed. Signorelli and Staples (1997) found that children who watched large amounts of television were more apt to believe that sugary breakfast foods were healthful than did their counterparts who watched less television.

Another criticism leveled at mass media coverage of medicine and science from the education perspective is that whereas individual news stories may contain accurate information, mass media presentations frequently fail to provide audiences with sufficient context and explanation. For instance, Dunwoody (1982) reviewed studies assessing the accuracy of science news stories. She found that in most cases, when scientists said a science story was inaccurate, they meant that the story failed to include some important information. Long (1995) found that there was surprisingly little explanatory content in newspaper science stories. Typically, less than 10% of the text in a story was classifiable as an effort to deepen understanding of complex information. Pellechia (1997) noted that science news stories in major newspapers did not differ appreciably in terms of methodological information they included between 1960 and 1990 despite the fact that reporters are urged frequently to report a study's methods in addition to its conclusions.

In the education view, then, the mass media can and should play the role of accurate and thorough information conveyer. Improvements in mass media communication of health and illness information must chiefly come by having professional communicators strive harder for accuracy and clarity because omissions and mistakes in health communication can cause injury, illness, or death.

Empowerment

The second view of mass media's role regarding public health says that the education view is flawed in several ways. First, it has the wrong goals—those of making mass media reflect perfectly what medical experts say and of achieving passive acceptance of medical advice by lay audiences. Second, its understanding of relationships among messages, media, and behavior is naive.

Proponents of the empowerment view maintain that the education view, although well intentioned, is paternalistic and dysfunctional. A compliant, passive public, critics say, is ultimately a public whose health is more at risk than a public confident in its health knowledge and decision-making abilities. For example, Kerr, Cunningham-Burley, and Amos (1998) argued that:

> Critiques of public understanding of science are traditionally based on a "deficit model" wherein professionals bemoan the public's ignorance of, and lack of interest in, science. However, a strong critique of this position is emerging from the sociology of science literature, in which it is argued that many different groups make up the public—and that their knowledge is not simply a matter of technical detail, but involves a broader understanding of scientific practice and institutions. (p. 41)

These authors went on to argue that the public is expert in a number of areas, including its own experiences with medical professionals. Constant focus on people's lack of medical knowledge may reduce public confidence and physicians' appreciation of the public's common sense. Further, medical decision making that proceeds without input from affected people can be poor.

The empowerment view looks for ways mass media can increase physicians' appreciation of the public's knowledge and ability to make wise decisions about health and illness. Kaplan (1997) argued that doing so is a necessity in the late 20th century because the nature of medicine has changed. Early 20th-century medicine worked on an acute-care model. In it, physician–patient communication was not especially important: Physicians found the source of illness in brief, initial encounters with patients, provided remedies, and patients went on about their business. In the latter part of the century, chronic illnesses such as cancer and heart disease were the main killers. As Kaplan (1997) wrote, "The chronic care model requires long-term interactions between providers and patients. Self-management is the key feature" (pp. 75–76). Others have made similar arguments, saying that improving patients' abilities to manage their own health care should be the principal role of health communication (e.g., Lambert et al., 1997; Rimal, Ratzan, Arnston, & Freimuth, 1997). Additionally, empowerment advocates want to enhance the decision-making capacities of communities as well as individuals. Empowerment can come from having communities play key roles in health-care policy development (e.g., Butterfoss et al., 1998; Lugo, 1996). Scholars making these arguments say that health-care policy is substantially harmed when affected citizens are not included in such decision making. For instance, Kerr et al. (1998) described the disappointment felt by disabled people who see policy about pregnancy termination for certain disabilities made without input from those who live with these conditions.

A second plank of the empowerment view is its alternative perspective on how mass communication works. Empowerment advocates criticize the education view for unreflectively assuming that communication about health and illness can effectively occur in a one-way flow of expert advice to uninformed public. Additional inadequacies come from its failure to appreciate the conditions in which people encounter mediated health messages. On a daily basis, such messages are generated by numerous groups, all vying to guide people through thickets of confusing health decisions (e.g., Clarke, 1986; Durant, Evans, & Thomas, 1992). A grocery store checkout line suggests some of the many business, religious, and governmental groups spewing claims about their cures for impotence, allergies, memory loss, obesity, and other common maladies. Popular magazines with titles such as *Healthy Living, Men's Health,* and *Prevention* flourish. Even if some of this information is accurate and thorough, empowerment advocates say, a free-market economy ensures that there will always be misleading health information in the mass media. Consequently, the public must be empowered to sort through it all.

Further, empowerment advocates argue, even when medical information is clear, the range of effects it can have varies from random attention to understanding to analysis, acceptance, or rejection. As Freimuth and Taylor (1994), Rogers and Storey (1987), Witte (1992, 1997), and many others have shown, mass-mediated messages are good at raising public awareness, somewhat good at increasing understanding, and occasionally effective at changing attitudes and motivating healthful behavior. Consequently, assuming, as the education view does, that accurate media messages will improve health is naive. Even when media messages are accurate, thorough, and uncontroversial, the extent to which they result in behavioral change is affected by many conditions, chiefly wealth and education. Studies frequently show that wealth and education affect the likelihood that such messages are understood, believed, and effective in motivating behavioral change (e.g., Marshall, Smith, & McKeon, 1995; O'Keefe, Boyd, & Brown, 1998).

In sum, the empowerment view of media's role in enhancing public health holds that medical experts' reasons for wanting their advice followed should be suspect and that it is the public who must decide how medical decisions are made. Consequently, from this perspective, the most important steps one can take to improve mass media health messages involve increasing the medical professionals' accountability to the public and enhancing citizens' decision-making powers. In the empowerment view, mass media can improve public health by functioning as watchdogs of the medical community, alerting the public to contexts where their views are ignored or where their power should be bolstered.

Not surprisingly, there are critiques of the empowerment view. For example, numerous studies suggest the empowerment view is unduly generous in its assessment of public understanding of health, medicine, and scientific research (Durant et al., 1992; Ley, 1983; Majerovitz et al., 1997; Missed Messages, 1998; Thompson & Pledger, 1993). The strengths of this view, however, come from its identification of conditions under which people attend to and benefit from mass media presentations of scientific information. The empowerment view reminds medical and communication scholars that science "is relevant when they think that it directly affects them and when they feel they have the opportunity to influence the way in which it affects their lives" (Kerr et al., 1998, pp. 43–44).

Limitations of Both Perspectives

Viewing the mass media solely as an educational tool or solely as a tool for creating social accountability are appealing but limited notions. These views of mass media inadequacies limit communicators' abilities to analyze their specific difficulties when they are personally faced with talking to a reporter, reflecting on how best to explain a complex medical phenomenon on television in 30 seconds, or reacting to a medical news story at a neighborhood party. Instead, physicians and journalists need a diagnostic framework that assists them in thinking about the distinctive ways mass communication about illness is apt to be hampered by predictable tensions or confusions, along with research-informed ways to overcome these problems.

THE PROBLEM-SOLVING APPROACH
TO RISK COMMUNICATION

Drawing from past work, I offer a problem-solving framework (Rowan, 1991, 1994b, 1995b) for anticipating difficulties likely to occur when communicating about physical risks. This approach assumes that communicating about a physical risk such as an illness is similar to any communication situation except in one important respect: Discussing physical risk creates a distinctive cluster of five difficulties. First, because the risk of illness threatens some of life's most precious commodities (e.g., life itself, feelings of well-being, freedom, attractiveness, responsibility to others), communicating about it is inherently upsetting, uncomfortable, and sometimes very frightening. Therefore, risk communicators explaining mild or severe illnesses need strategies for empathizing, overcoming suspicion, and earning trust. Second, because risk communication situations are often characterized by a lack of awareness (e.g., about new drugs, new dietary guidelines, or new technologies), risk communicators require skills for enhancing awareness. Third, because illnesses, their prevention, and treatment are complex topics, communication about these topics will be hindered by absences of understanding (e.g., about what anemia is; how human hearing works, or why women can inherit a gene for breast cancer from their fathers). So, those who communicate about illness need strategies for explaining complex subjects. Fourth, because risk communication situations involve frequent disagreements among the well-informed (e.g., about whether the dietary guidelines for salt intake should be changed or whether men in their 80s should undergo prostrate surgery), there is a need for strategies designed to gain agreement. Fifth, because risk communicators must sometimes motivate people to move from agreement to action (e.g., to move from promising to exercise regularly to doing so; or from merely purchasing hypertension medications to taking them), there is a need for communication strategies designed to motivate action.

The problem-solving framework's identification of five common tensions likely to beset explaining illness transcends and integrates the education and empowerment perspectives. Thinking about this cluster of likely difficulties and the communication goals they suggest may assist professionals whose first reaction to a difficult communication encounter involving the mass media and a medical topic is that the sole problem is ignorance or the sole problem is the inordinate power of health professionals. This framework does not offer magic words. Instead, it suggests ways of analyzing challenging communication situations and locating research on the best ways to address these difficulties.

To keep this set of common tensions and goals in risk communication situations in mind, the mnemonic CAUSE can be used. That is, risk communication involves earning trust or establishing Credibility; creating Awareness; deepening Understanding of complex material; gaining agreement on Solutions to problems, and moving from agreement on solutions to Enactment.

Earn trust	Credibility
Create awareness	Awareness
Deepen Understanding	Understanding
Gain agreement on solutions	Solutions
Motivate action	Enactment

Communication theorists have maintained for centuries that these goals are generally best pursued in this order (e.g., Campbell, 1776/1988). That is, usually people are uninterested in understanding a subject more deeply if they do not trust those individuals wishing to explain it or do not believe that these individuals have their best interests at heart. Similarly, it makes little sense to urge action if there is not, first, agreement on the nature of a situation and the desirability of a given action. Individuals need to determine first if communication in a given situation has faltered principally because of suspicion, lack of awareness, and so forth. Instead of assuming communication has faltered because of ignorance or a lack of justice, the problem-solving model of risk communication encourages individuals to think about the particular difficulty most likely to be hindering shared meaning creation in a given case and to analyze and address that difficulty.

Once a communicator has determined that, for example, lack of trust is the principal obstacle and trust building or credibility management must be pursued, the problem-solving framework provides sets of heuristics for determining how that goal might be best achieved. These analyses of the principal obstacles to enhancing credibility, awareness, understanding, agreement, and action are developed by reviewing research in fields such as communication, rhetoric, social psychology, instructional design, educational psychology, science education, counseling, negotiation, marketing, and disaster response (Rowan, 1991, 1994a, 1994b, 1995b; also see Lambert et al., 1997). Knowing about frequent obstacles encountered in achieving these goals assists communicators in anticipating the challenges they are apt to face.

The problem-solving framework can be illustrated and applied to mass media communication of illness information by focusing on two particularly important goals: earning trust and explaining complex material. This chapter describes ways medical and communication professionals can analyze difficult communication situations and generate careful messages in mass media contexts. It does not describe the coaching one might seek to gain personal feedback on one's choice of messages or delivery skills during an on-camera interview. There are other resources for professionals who wish this kind of feedback (e.g., Wright, 1997).

USING THE PROBLEM-SOLVING FRAMEWORK TO EARN TRUST

Earning Audience Trust

Because illness is frightening and frequently distasteful, people have trouble paying attention to information about it. Audiences may be somewhat better able to attend to explanations of illness if they know the explainer cares about them. As an office desk sign puts it, "I don't care how much you know until I know how much you care." In mass media contexts, there are likely to be audience members who are suspicious of the orthodox medical community or frightened of the topic discussed (e.g., cancer, AIDS, Alzheimer's, arthritis, mental illnesses). To communicate in fear- or suspicion-filled contexts, physicians and health communicators need to think about how first to earn an audience's trust. According to research, a number of steps may help.

Acknowledge the Public's Concerns and the Existence of Problems Before Attempting to Educate. Research suggests that people are better able to listen to others when their concerns are initially acknowledged (e.g., Sypher, Bostrom, & Seibert, 1989; chap. 1, this volume). In mass media contexts, physicians may be tempted to begin their remarks by noting that a problem that people view as serious is actually not. That approach may work when an individual has earned trust. For example, the *New York Time's* Jane Brody can report a story headlined, "Health Scares That Weren't So Scary" (Brody, 1998) and have people pay attention to it. The same message from a highly credentialed but not well-known physician could engender suspicion.

Endorse Fundamental Values Before Attempting to Explain. Physicians may want to educate, but beginning one's remarks by doing so can make them seem unconcerned about audience values. Research by Petty and Cacioppo (1986) suggests that people reason differently depending on whether they have high or low involvement in an issue. That is, if people are very knowledgeable about a topic, they have high involvement. In this context, they are likely to think about the merit of the arguments presented. In contrast, when a topic is unfamiliar, Petty and Cacioppo would view them as low-involvement audiences. In such contexts, people use peripheral cues when deciding whether they agree or disagree with a message. *Peripheral cues* include matters such as whether the speaker seems likeable and whether the speaker seems to care about the audience's concerns.

Physicians' and scientists' intuitive orientations toward explaining complex medical information may cause them to seem less likeable to low-involvement audiences. If physicians determine that a mass media context is likely to be hampered by suspicion of their motives, they may want to re-earn audience trust by prefacing explanations with an endorsement of a value held by the audience. No words by themselves earn an individual trust, but some words can be less effective than others in establishing credibility. In this era, people are well aware that some recommendations could be tinged by profit motives. Asked about the risk of getting AIDS in a dental office, a dentist being interviewed on television could respond:

In terms of your safety, consider these statistics. Your chances of dying from general anesthesia are 1 in 10,000. ... Your chances of contracting AIDS from an HIV-infected dentist are 1 in 250 million. So, you see, your chance of contracting AIDS in the dental office is minimal. (Wright, 1997, p. 70, citing Siew, Chang, Gruninger, Verrusio, & Neidle, 1992)

This answer is one that a dentist's colleagues (a high-involvement audience) might appreciate. Audiences with low topic involvement—that is, audiences who are unfamiliar with infection control procedures—are not likely to find this answer reassuring. In fact, they may be unduly skeptical because they suspect a profit motive or a lack of respect for their concerns may be coloring the dentist's reply.

Wright (1997) suggested that dentists respond to patients' concerns about safety not by belittling the concern but rather by focusing on patients' values and ways in which patients can control their health care. For example: "Your safety in the dentist office or any other medical office is very important. We think we should always protect patients from infection. Ask your dentist to describe his or her infection control procedures in the office. Good dental offices will be proud to do so." Although one may not want to pursue like ability for its own sake, it may be effective to endorse audience values before beginning an explanation or questioning a set of questionable facts.

Cast a Positive Identity. Physicians asked about a medical topic can use such opportunities to bolster people's sense of their ability to learn. Research suggests that the public finds medical news more interesting than many other topics, but they do not feel especially well-schooled in science (e.g., Burgoon, Burgoon, & Wilkinson, 1983; Durant et al., 1992). To encourage people's confidence in their ability to learn, a physician may want to begin an explanation by noting that a certain topic fascinated him or her, too, and that there is information about it on several authoritative web sites and medical encyclopedias. Presenting a short, effective explanation after such prefatory remarks may allow a health care provider to earn trust, establish likeability, and educate. A licensed nutritionist in Maryland talks with young women about the popular magazines they read. In the course of conversation, she supports her patients' interest in nutrition and mentions magazines she finds reliable. This approach of legitimating people's interest in learning is likely to be more effective than that of an oncologist who told the wife of a cancer patient to stop consulting web sites for cancer information. He gave this advice because he believed the wife could not understand the material she read. When motivated to learn complex material, people sometimes surprise themselves and others.

Increasingly, reputable medical information is available through the Internet. For example, the U.S. Department of Health and Human Services promotes reputable health information web sites and databases through

Healthfinder (www.healthfinder.org). Additionally, professional medical literature is available free on Medline, which contains abstracts from over 4,000 peer-reviewed journals (www.ncbi.nlm.hih.gov/PubMed/).

Earning Trust in Physician–Journalist Encounters

When journalists contact physicians for interviews, the communication efforts of both parties may be hindered by suspicion of one another's motives and competence. Physicians, who intuitively expect the mass media to educate the public, are suspicious that journalists merely want to sell newspapers and television air time. Journalists may be skeptical of physicians who contact them. Certainly some medical professionals seek the public limelight principally as a way of making money. Journalists may also feel intimidated by medical subject matter, and physicians may be cowed by the prospect of on-camera communication.

To work through these suspicions and fears, there are a number of steps physicians and journalists can take. First, physicians and journalists may find it useful to expect that each will orient toward the point of a medical news story using either the education or the empowerment perspective. That is, journalists should expect that physicians may want to educate the public, and physicians may expect that journalists will resist this stance and want instead to focus on accountability issues such as inadequacies in medical care. Recognizing these tendencies makes it easier to manage them. Public relations officers for medical organizations or universities can help both groups cope with these differences by creating contexts where professionals can meet one another and discuss their concerns.

A second step in managing suspicions is to seek out professionals each party admires. The National Association of Science Writers can help physicians and public relations professionals locate good science writers in their geographic areas (www.nasw.org). Professional medical associations such as the American Medical Association or the American Dental Association can assist reporters in locating physicians who are skilled communicators. Each group can watch and read the work of top medical and science reporters. Many respect the reporting of Jane Brody with the *New York Times,* Robert Bazell with NBC-TV, Boyce Rensberger of the *Washington Post* (now at Massachusetts Institute of Technology), and David Shaw of the *Los Angeles Times.* Deborah Blum and Mary Knudson (1997), two accomplished science journalists, showcase outstanding science and medical writers in their field guide to science writing. Gastel (1983) is a physician and professor who studies health communication. Dr. Zorba Paster's "On Your Health" is a respected program on Public Radio International.

A third step that physicians and journalists can take to navigate through mutual suspicions is to talk about their differing professional norms. One context where differences are likely concerns checking back. *Checking back* refers to the practice of having a news source read or listen to a portion of a story before the story's publication or airing. From reporters' perspective, no news source has the right to shape their reporting. This perspective developed in the context of political reporting, where a high premium is placed on ensuring that politicians do not control news coverage. However, as a documentary by King (1991) shows, such views are alarming to medical professionals who view resistance to checking back as flagrant disregard for accuracy. In general, however, reporters who cover medical and science news routinely know that the check back norms for science and medical reporting differ from those of political reporting. Seasoned medical reporters are likely to welcome efforts to ensure accuracy. Checking back to determine accuracy makes sense to journalists. Checking back to censure or withhold information does not.

Using the Problem-Solving Framework to Explain Complex Subject Matter

Once fear has subsided and concerns about a communicator's motives or competence are not at issue, audiences can focus on the substance of an expert's remarks. Just as there are strategic challenges associated with earning trust, there are also strategic challenges associated with explaining complex information. The first such question concerns anticipating or diagnosing the principal source of likely confusion.

Intuitively, many assume that explaining complex material is principally a matter of using simple, familiar words and short sentences. Research supports this view to some extent (e.g., Broberg, 1973; chap. 5, this volume; Jackson, 1992; Klare, 1963; Missed messages, 1998). There is no question that frequent use of unfamiliar terms harms the understandability of an explanation. In one memorable study (Hayes, 1992), a researcher analyzed mothers' talks with their children and farmers' conversations with cows. Not surprisingly, these discourse forms were found "less lexically taxing" than those in scientific journals. Lexically taxing texts contained a high percentage of unfamiliar words. However, there are problems with assuming that explaining complex medical matters is solely a matter of using simple words (e.g., Duffy, 1985; Kantor, Anderson, & Armbruster, 1983; Reid, Kardash, Robinson, & Scholes, 1994; Shuy & Larkin, 1978). Consider the statements, "Women can inherit a tendency toward breast cancer from their fathers," or "the weather has no effect on arthritis." The difficulty of these ideas results not from word or sentence length but from their inconsistency with strongly held lay theories about genetics and illness. Clearly, there are multiple sources of difficulty in understanding medical news.

In a series of publications, I have offered a way of diagnosing common sources of confusion and selecting research-supported steps for overcoming these anticipated difficulties (Rowan, 1988, 1991, 1999; also see Reid et al., 1994). In brief, this framework says that there are three principal obstacles to understanding difficult ideas. These are difficulties in (a) distinguishing essential from associated meanings of terms (e.g., the difference between nervousness and hypertension or the meaning of "false positive"); (b) difficulties in visualizing complex, unseen, or unfamiliar phenomena (e.g., the body's multiple defenses against cancer or why infants are more susceptible to inner-ear infections than older children); and (c) obstacles in understanding ideas that seem counterintuitive to lay audiences, such as the fact that one may be ill without feeling bad or that a tendency toward a female disease may be inherited by a woman from her father (Richards, 1996). Although there is no substitute for directly testing audiences' understanding of and interest in the subject one is writing about, research has identified ways of formally identifying aspects of a topic that are likely to be confusing to many people. This section of the chapter summarizes this work and analyzes illness accounts in the mass media.

Methods of Addressing the Three Key Sources of Confusion

Scholars in several fields have studied text features that are effective at overcoming each of the three main obstacles to understanding complex ideas (e.g., Anderson & Smith, 1984; diSessa, 1982; Gentner, 1988; Hewson & Hewson, 1983; Mayer, 1983; Mayer & Anderson, 1992; Mayer, Bove, Bryman, Mars, & Tapangco, 1996; Merrill & Tennyson, 1977; Rowan, 1988, 1995b; Rukavina & Daneman, 1996). I refer to people's efforts to overcome each of these difficulties as a certain type of explanation. So, there are *elucidating explanations,* which establish the meaning and use of terms; *quasi-scientific explanations,* which help audiences envision complex structures and processes; and *transformative explanations,* which help people understand counterintuitive or implausible ideas. Research has identified text and graphic features that make each type of explanation most effective.

Elucidating Explanations.   Elucidating explanations are designed to help people understand the meaning and use of a term. The name "elucidating" is used because this sort of discourse clarifies meanings. When people struggle to understand the meaning of a term, they are, in fact, struggling to distinguish a concept's essential meaning from its associated meaning. Good elucidating explanations focus attention on this distinction. Specifically, good elucidating explanations contain (a) a typical instance of the concept, (b) a definition that lists each of the concept's essential features,

(c) an array of varied examples and nonexamples (nonexamples are instances likely to be mistaken for examples), and (d) opportunities to practice distinguishing examples from nonexamples (Merrill & Tennyson, 1977; Tennyson & Cocchiarella, 1986).

Because medicine is replete with unfamiliar terms, physicians and medical writers often substitute a more familiar term rather than using a technical term and explaining it. Sometimes this approach makes sense, especially when there is no time or space to explain an unfamiliar word to a mass audience. The phrase "osteoporatic bone" may be more precise than "brittle bone," but in a brief radio news story, mass audiences may decipher the phrase "brittle bones" more easily. However, research suggests that it is not the use of a single technical term that makes messages difficult to comprehend. Instead, it is the density or frequency of unfamiliar terms that creates confusion (Halliday & Martin, 1993). Communicators may want to think about keeping their message simple but using one precise term and explaining it carefully.

Typically, when precise terms are used, good explainers know that audiences are uncertain about a word's medical meaning, so they address this confusion immediately. Writing for *Parade* magazine, Dr. Isadore Rosenfeld (1998) highlighted the distinction between essential and associated meanings for the term, hypertension. He wrote, "It's called 'hypertension,' but it has nothing to do with being tense. Calm people have it, you can 'feel good' and still have it—and, untreated, it can be deadly" (p. 4). Confusion arises about hypertension for a number of reasons, but one source is the similarity of the illness' name with the common notion, tension. A second is the fact that experiencing stress or tension can exacerbate the condition. Rosenfeld's immediate focus on this common confusion was probably informative to many.

Second, in addition to noting a term's unessential meanings, good elucidating explanations define concepts by their essential meanings. This point may seem obvious, but it is a step frequently not taken. Because mass media explanations need a wide readership, concepts are sometimes defined by associated meanings and never redefined more carefully. Unfortunately, in the article just cited, Rosenfeld defined diuretics by their common name, "water pills" (p. 5) but did not characterize their essential meaning. One study showed less than half of 224 adults aged 18 to 83 years could adequately define this term; some people called it a "diet pill, a laxative, or a blood thinning agent" (Thompson & Pledger, 1993, p. 92). A better definition of diuretics was presented in a *John Hopkins Medical Letter* (A basic guide, 1992). It said diuretics "cause kidneys to eliminate sodium and water, thus reducing overall fluid volume—including blood volume—in the body, and lowering blood pressure" (p. 3). This latter definition focuses on the term's precise meaning and describes the reason for taking a diuretic if one is hypertensive, rather than offering a vaguer sense of its connection with water.

A third feature of a good, elucidating explanation is an array of varied examples. Intuition tells writers to give an example of a confusing concept, but research suggests that the best elucidating explanations offer several examples that instantiate the concept's essential meaning in differing ways (Merrill & Tennyson, 1977). This effort to illustrate a concept's essential features in multiple guises minimizes the likelihood that a random feature of some single example will be interpreted as essential. A *Reader's Digest* article on the benefits of dietary fiber contained an effective elucidating explanation of what counts as fiber:

> The term "dietary fiber" refers to the parts of plants that pass through the human stomach and small intestine undigested—ranging from the brittle husks of whole wheat to the stringy pods of green beans to the gummy flesh of barley grains ...
> Fiber gives digesting food a soft and bulky consistency, helping it move at a steady pace—neither too fast nor too slow—through the digestive tract. For centuries doctors have prescribed dietary fiber for patients suffering from both constipation and diarrhea. (Murray, 1990, p. 76)

This passage is a good elucidating explanation because it defines fiber by its essential meaning and then offers several varied examples (from "the brittle husks of whole wheat to the stringy pods of green beans to the gummy flesh of barley grains"). Had the writer discussed only grain products, audiences might have wrongly inferred that those materials have dietary fiber and other plant foods like green beans do not. Differing examples help readers understand the array of fiber sources.

A final important step in elucidating explanation is discussion of nonexamples. Research shows that considering ways in which an apparent example does not have this status helps audiences see important distinctions (Merrill & Tennyson, 1977; Tennyson, Woolley, & Merrill, 1972). Clayman (1989) discussed a nonexample of depression in *The American Medical Association Encyclopedia of Medicine* entry on this illness. The entry says depression involves:

> feelings of sadness, hopelessness, pessimism, and a general loss of interest in life, combined with a sense of reduced emotional well-being. Most people experience these feelings occasionally, often as a normal response to a particular event. For example, it is natural to feel sad when a close relative dies. However, if the depression occurs without any apparent cause, deepens, and persists, it may be a symptom of a wide range of psychiatric illnesses. (p. 344)

This explanation helps audiences focus on the nature of depressive illness by distinguishing it from a nonexample, that being shorter-term feelings of sadness over tragic events.

Effective Quasi-scientific Explanations. The second difficulty in comprehending illness has little to do with words and their associations. Instead, this difficulty concerns picturing the complex. For instance, genetic mutation, the anatomical reasons for frequent ear infections in the very young, or typologies used to classify illnesses are each phenomena that are difficult to understand chiefly because they are complicated or infrequently seen and therefore hard to envision. The term "quasi-scientific explanation" is used for explanations designed to address this source of difficulty. The goal of these accounts is similar to that of science. Science attempts to represent aspects of reality; quasi-scientific explanations make these representations clear to nonscientists.

Research has identified the functions and features of effective quasi-scientific explanations. Functionally, quasi-scientific discourse assists audiences by first giving them a simplified image of something intricate. Text features that convey these simplified images include model-suggesting headlines; ("New View Sees Breast Cancer as 3 Diseases," Kolata, 1997); organizing analogies ("Scientists starve cancer tumors," Neergaard, 1997); headings, captions, and topic sentences, and signaling phrases ("The key point is"). Research has shown that, in general, messages enhanced by these text features are more likely to be understood than are passages without them (e.g., Mayer, 1983; Mayer et al., 1996; McDaniel & Donnelly, 1996; cf. Whaley, 1994). Interestingly, researchers also have shown that omitting transitional phrases to adhere rigidly to readability formulas, which mandate short sentences, may harm the understandability of a quasi-scientific explanation (Duffy, 1985; Loman & Mayer, 1983). Transitions and longer sentences sometimes depict links within a process or structure. Audiences may need this information to construct clear mental models of difficult-to-visualize phenomena.

Graphics are another set of tools for helping audiences picture the complex. Studies have explored graphic aids such as diagrams, cartoons, and animation (e.g., Mayer et al., 1996; McDaniel & Donnelly, 1996). In general, graphics that assist audiences in scaffolding simple mental models of complicated structures or processes are associated with greater understanding of these phenomena.

Interestingly, exposure to text and graphic aids that present a simple model of the complex not only improves comprehension, it also improves knowledge use (Harp & Mayer, 1997; Mayer, 1983; Mayer et al., 1996). For example, in one study, Loman and Mayer (1983) gave randomly selected groups of high school students the same account of why red tides form in the ocean. (*Red tides* occur when microscopic organisms called dinoflagellates proliferate. Warm, calm water encourages population explosions of these organisms, which secrete a poison that kills fish). In this study, the control and treatment group received the same text passage accounting for red tides. The treatment passage differed only in that its causal structure was more overt. This was accomplished by inserting headings that highlighted key phases in the organisms' life cycle ("Dinoflagellates Bloom; Dinoflagellates Secrete Poison; Dinoflagellates Die") and signaling phrases emphasizing connections between events (e.g., "the result is" or "because of this"). Students who received the enhanced text were not only better able to explain dinoflagellate population changes, they were also better able to apply their knowledge to solve newly encountered problems. For example, they were more likely to have viable ideas for reducing the likelihood of a red tide (e.g., make the water rough) than were their counterparts.

This type of finding has been replicated in dozens of studies over the last two decades. That is, text and graphics that help audiences see how to-be-learned information should be structured enhance both understanding and application of scientific information (Mayer, 1983, 1989; Mayer et al., 1996). The implications of this finding are important for medical writers. They suggest that under certain conditions, effective text and graphic features may be associated with greater patient understanding and possibly with enhanced compliance in treatment regimens. Not surprising, some award-winning medical writing uses text and graphic features in ways research has found effective. For example, the Consumer Health Information Corporation (CHIC) has won awards for its work explaining complex illnesses and their treatments through brochures and ads (D. L. Smith, CHIC President, personal communication, Oct. 21, 1998). One pamphlet developed by CHIC explained obsessive-compulsive disorder to patients. Text and a figure help readers visualize the ways inadequate "free" serotonin may be associated with OCD. The text reads:

What Causes OCD?

Although the exact cause of Obsessive Compulsive Disorder (OCD) is unknown, the condition seems to be linked to low levels of a substance in the brain. The substance is serotonin.

Serotonin is one of many natural chemicals stored in the nerves. Brain nerve cells need serotonin to send messages [electrical impulses] to each other so that you can walk, eat, and live.

Serotonin is stored inside nerve cells. When a nerve cell starts to send a message, it releases this "stored" serotonin into the space the message must cross to get to the next nerve cell. Once the serotonin is outside the nerve cell, it is "free" to work. Because it helps carry the message from one nerve cell to another, serotonin is also called a neurotransmitter.

Once the message has crossed successfully to the next nerve, the serotonin goes back into the nerve cell where it is stored until needed again. (Consumer Health Information Corporation, 1994, p.2)

This text is followed by a simple, captioned graphic (see Fig. 3.1). The text and graphic have the features of effective quasi-scientific explanations. For instance, the first paragraph of the text passage presents a very simple causal account of OCD: "the condition seems to be linked to low levels of a substance in the brain" (p. 2). The graphic re-enforces this simple account of OCD by representing a normal amount of serotonin as six small dots and an abnormal amount as two serotonin dots. Patients reading this pamphlet may have a better understanding of why a serotonin re-uptake inhibitor,

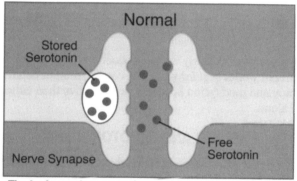

The body needs a normal amount of serotonin that is "free" between the nerve cells.

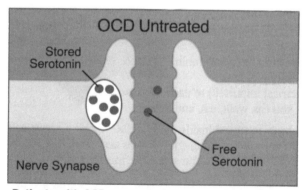

Patients with OCD appear to have a lower than normal level of "free" serotonin between the nerve cells.

FIG. 3.1. This illustration shows that clinical depression is associated with low levels of "free" serotonin. Research suggests that seeing both captions and visuals may help lay audiences both understand this disease and use their knowledge in problem-solving tasks. Graphic from Solvay Pharmaceuticals. Reprinted with permission.

drugs like Prozac or Luvox, may have been prescribed for them than they would without the pamphlet. They may also be more motivated to continue their medication than they would without an understanding of the medication's function. The effectiveness of this specific text and graphic would have to be tested to reach this conclusion definitively, but this approach to explaining complex information seems consistent with research-supported recommendations.

Not all visuals help audiences picture the complex. In two related studies, Harp and Mayer (1997) and Mayer et al. (1996), found that dramatic photograghs did *not* make a passage explaining lightning more understandable. Photographs may have had an attention-getting effect, but they did not improve college students' abilities to use their new-found knowledge. In contrast, students who read the same passage accompanied by captioned cartoons depicting conditions necessary for lightning were more able to explain how to avoid lightning than were their counterparts. Mayer et al. (1996) explained this result by saying that carefully constructed annotated illustrations focus attention on key components in complex processes. Additionally, the annotations and accompanying graphics assist people in making links between visual and verbal information.

With advances in computerized layout and design, the features of effective quasi-scientific explanations are increasingly evident in popular media. For instance, a story about cancer research used a set of annotated illustrations that probably assisted readers in understanding a new development in cancer research (Neergaard, 1997). The story, "Scientists starve cancer tumors," was published with a set of set of diagrams. As Fig. 3.2 shows, three illustrations depict a tumor being fed by blood vessels, a clotting agent with a special homing device being injected into the tumor, and a cancer cell's blood supply being cut off by the clotting agent. Concise labels are presented below each illustration. They read: "Cancer tumor grows; antibody with homing device [is injected intravenously]; blood clot forms; tumor starves" (p. A5). These illustrations, along with brief explanatory text, are precisely the sort of discourse that Mayer and his associates found most effective in helping students to both understand and use scientific explanations of complex processes. Additionally, the news story wrapped around this graphic does an effective job of helping readers understand challenges associated with this research, such as the task of getting the blood-clotting protein to affect only the cancerous tumor's blood supply rather than that of any noncancerous regions.

A special envisionment problem is created when there is no expert consensus on a complex medical topic that of integrating conflicting information. For example, experts looking at many of the same data may disagree about whether to change guidelines for dietary salt intake (e.g., Alderman, & Kotchen, 1998; Neufeldt, 1997). In an effort to provide balanced cover-

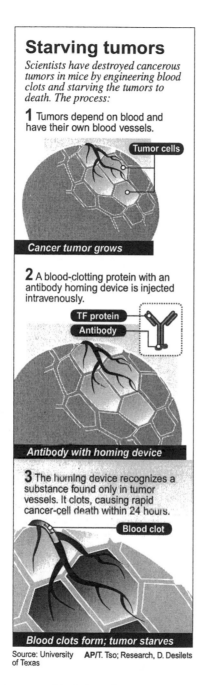

Starving tumors

Scientists have destroyed cancerous tumors in mice by engineering blood clots and starving the tumors to death. The process:

1 Tumors depend on blood and have their own blood vessels.

Tumor cells

Cancer tumor grows

2 A blood-clotting protein with an antibody homing device is injected intravenously.

TF protein
Antibody

Antibody with homing device

3 The homing device recognizes a substance found only in tumor vessels. It clots, causing rapid cancer-cell death within 24 hours.

Blood clot

Blood clots form; tumor starves

Source: University of Texas   AP/T. Tso; Research, D. Desilets

FIG. 3.2. Research says graphics help audiences envision complex phenomena more than text-only explanations, particularly when a graphic uses headings, captions, and simple visuals as this one does. Source: Associated Press. Reprinted with permission.

89

age, reporters typically present at least two sides to any news event. They carry this practice to reporting on medicine. From a journalist's perspective, this approach is balanced, careful, and fair.

Unfortunately, research suggests that, rather than helping audiences cope with complex issues, news articles that present conflicting medical information sometimes breed confusion or cynicism (Qian & Alvermann, 1995; Rukavina & Daneman, 1996; Schommer, 1990).

There are some research-supported steps that physicians and medical reporters can take to help audiences interpret conflicting medical information. For example, a step as simple as labeling such situations as puzzles may help. A recent line of work suggests that the ways writers frame or package science news may assist audiences in interpreting conflicting findings (e.g., Qian & Alvermann, 1995; Rukavina & Daneman, 1996). In brief, this research shows that when writers cast information as a puzzle or a dilemma where there is no single answer, some individuals are better able to comprehend it. Specifically, Rukavina and Daneman (1996) found that labeling conflicting accounts as an unsolved puzzle with two possible answers and then discussing the strengths and weaknesses of each answer significantly improved comprehension of these ideas among many high school and college students. In contrast, students who received the same information in texts that presented the two theories successively were less likely to understand the theories or even note that they conflicted.

A second step is to present an analysis of each side's strengths and weaknesses. This is not always possible, but, when it is, it allows audiences to puzzle through the problem along with researchers. A story on breast cancer research does an effective job of alerting lay readers to a puzzle in research on breast cancer and of showing them current best guesses about its solution:

> For years, cancer specialists repeated their hypothesis as if it were a mantra: virtually all breast cancer has spread by the time it is detected. But now, seemingly overnight, that prevailing view of breast cancer has changed.
>
> At a recent meeting at the National Institutes of Health, speaker after speaker said, as though it was indisputable, that breast cancer was really three separate diseases whose boundaries were indistinct. ...
>
> Dr. John Wasson of Dartmouth College ... explained the cancer types this way: "There is the mean type that spreads so quickly that current technology can't de-tect it or treat it. ... The second type is one that is growing at a rate where it will cause trouble and begin to spread within 5 to 10 years. Then there is a third type that may take even longer to spread, if it spreads at all. ..."
>
> One implication of the new view of cancer, Dr. Jay Harris said, is that better and better mammograms cannot magically turn the breast cancer statistics around. ... Many [researchers] ... are now studying molecular markers, like aberrant can-

cer genes, that might indicate a tumor's potential to be lethal. (Kolata, 1997, reprinted in Hart & Chappell, 1997, pp. 84–86)

Kolata's (1997) story offered a simple model of very complicated information (i.e., think of breast cancer as several diseases); it also seems to frame a frustrating situation (that of mammograms not being as effective as hoped in detecting cancer) into a puzzle that audiences can mull over along with medical researchers.

Transformative Explanations. The third type of explanation, transformative explanations, helps audiences understand ideas that are difficult to comprehend because they are counterintuitive. That is, some scientific notions can be expressed with simple words and can easily be envisioned, but they are still profoundly difficult to understand. For instance, people struggle to understand why they should take a medication if they do not feel ill, why frozen meat should not thaw on counter tops, or why going outdoors without a jacket is not the cause of colds. In these cases, powerful lay theories are the principal source of confusion. Research in science education shows that to help audiences recognize, test, and overcome lay theories, one must use a form of text I call transformative explanation. Transformative explanations are so-named because they assist audiences in recognizing implicit lay theories, understanding their strengths and limitations, and understanding the reasons for scientists' endorsements of other accounts.

Scholars have explored lay theorizing in detail, for it particularly blocks mastery of Newtonian principles and scientific accounts of familiar phenomena such as weight, light, or disease (e.g., Alvermann, Smith & Readance, 1985; Anderson & Smith, 1984; diSessa, 1982; Guzzetti, Snyder, Glass, & Gamas, 1993; Hewson & Hewson, 1983; Hewson & Hewson, 1984; Richards, 1996). Fortunately, it is possible to predict the contexts in which lay theories are most likely to develop. People develop lay theories about very familiar aspects of life that have great import. Lay theories develop to explain weather, accidents, gender relations, nutrition, and so forth. For example, powerful lay theories once said that "bad air" was the cause of a "mal–aria," an implicit theory still suggested in the disease's name. Contemporary lay notions erroneously assure people that everything natural is good, that expensive cuts of meat do not house harmful pathogens, or that infants riding in cars are just as safe in a parent's arms as they are in a car seat. Unfortunately, because lay theories guide people's actions, they endanger health and safety.

Lay theories are difficult to overcome for several reasons. First, they are often tacit or unspoken, although they still guide thought and action (e.g., Rowan, 1991). People who memorized "force equals mass times acceleration" may be surprised when they learn a train traveling "only" 10 miles an hour can cause a horrific accident. Their unspoken lay theory says that impact or force is a function of speed. Second, lay theories often exist side-by-side with their more orthodox scientific counterparts (e.g., Anderson & Smith, 1984). As in the train example, everyday experiences may seem to support the lay notion that slowness equals lightness. To reconsider a lay notion, people must sometimes be surprised into awareness of the discrepancy between a lay theory and its more accepted scientific counterpart. Media coverage of an accident caused by a slow train may be the impetus creating this surprise. News reporters can take advantage of such opportunities and help people rethink the connections among mass, acceleration, and force.

Researchers have identified message features that help audiences recognize and reflect on lay theories. In general, good transformative explanations treat audiences like scientists: Scientists do not give up their theories until they receive compelling reasons to do so. Similarly, people do not give up lay notions simply because someone says they are wrong. Specifically, good transformative explanations help audiences overcome lay theories when they (a) state the lay theory, (b) acknowledge its apparent merit, (c) create dissatisfaction with it, and (d) show how a more orthodox notion better explains the phenomenon in question (Alvermann et al., 1985; Anderson & Smith, 1984; Guzzetti et al., 1993; Hewson & Hewson, 1983; Hewson & Hewson, 1984; Kuhn, D., 1989; Schommer, 1990; Shymansky & Kyle, 1988).

News coverage of food safety is one arena where counterintuitive recommendations (transformative explanations) are frequent. For example, the U.S. Food Safety and Inspection Service (USDA, 1997, 1998) said it is impossible to tell whether a hamburger is safe to eat without taking its temperature. This view is a radical departure from the everyday notion that if a hamburger patty turns pinkish or brownish when cooked, it is safe to eat. A story in the *Washington Post* covered a campaign designed to alert the public to the need to use a thermometer when cooking hamburger (Sugarman, 1999). In the story, the writer does a good job of getting the surprising news in the lead. She also addressed the most likely lay theory critiqued in this story, that being that "browness equals doneness in hamburger cooking." However, given the many everyday views that this news contradicts, the story should probably have more text devoted to discussing lay notions this advice calls into question, acknowledging their apparent merit, and then presenting the experts' reasons for saying these notions are inadequate. The story follows, with points noted where it does or does not include the four steps in effective transformative explanation:

Giant Introduces a New Way to Take a Burger's Temperature

[Step 4: *State the scientifically endorsed view*]: The only way to make sure a burger is safe to eat is to take its temperature, says Giant Food. So last week, all packages of ground beef sold at its supermarkets started carrying bright yellow labels that say "Use a Thermometer" and "Cook to 160 degrees F." And in every Giant meat department, disposable thermometers (and regular reusable ones) popped up for sale.

"Many people are concerned about the safety of ground beef since the discovery of E. coli 0157:H7 bacteria that can cause serious or fatal illness," said Odonna Mathews, Giant's vice president of consumer affairs, in announcing the information campaign. "The good news is that cooking ground beef to an internal temperature of 160 degrees kills any harmful bacteria."

[Step 2: *Acknowledge the plausibility of the lay view*]: But why not just cook it until it's no longer pink inside—as some experts have recommended?

[Step 3: *Create dissatisfaction with the lay view*]: It's not that simple, as it turns out. U.S. Department of Agriculture researchers recently found that more than a quarter of the fresh ground beef patties and as many as two-thirds of the previously frozen burgers they cooked prematurely brown before reaching 160 degrees.

Conversely, nearly half of all burgers retained some pink when cooked to the safe temperature. Aside from whether the ground beef was fresh or frozen, the color variations were a result of how the meat was thawed, whether seasonings were added and the age of the animal the patties came from. ...

Still, many home cooks don't feel comfortable using a meat thermometer; about half of all Americans own one, but only 3 percent use it regularly when cooking ground beef, according to the USDA.

The disposable thermometers being sold at Giant, called T-Sticks, may help. ... "Based on my experience, once you get used to using a thermometer, it's easy," said Giant's Mathews. Another benefit, she said, is that you're less likely to overcook your burgers—and "end up with hockey pucks." (Sugarman, 1999, p. E2)

This expert-endorsed recommendation is asking for change in centuries-old practices for cooking meats. The obdurateness of habit, as well as tacit and explicit lay beliefs, may make it extremely difficult for people to accept this message. Research on lay theories suggests that further discussion of likely objections or questions could help. For example, news coverage could address the question of whether this advice is simply another instance of extreme caution on the part of large companies to protect themselves from lawsuits. Everyday experiences, such as the fact that people know they are not using thermometers when cooking hamburger, and they do not see themselves becoming ill as a result, are likely to legitimate these objections and call the advice in question.

One individual who deals routinely with lay theories about food safety is Bessie Jones Berry of the USDA's Meat and Poultry Hotline. In an interview, she described her responses to questions from inexperienced cooks

(B. J. Berry, personal communication, Nov. 4, 1998). Note in this summarized account of Ms. Berry's comments that there is considerable attention to stating common lay notions and providing multiple reasons to be dissatisfied with them:

> "I grew up with my mother cooking the turkey overnight at low temperatures and no one got sick. So why can't I do that now?"—question asked by callers to USDA's Meat and Poultry Hotline
>
> Answer:
>
> *[Steps 1 and 2: State the lay view and acknowledge its apparent plausibility]*: You may be right that no one got sick. People adjust to levels of pathogens over time, so if the cook in the family followed the same practices repeatedly but family members were the only ones eating the meals, it may be that people adjusted to certain food pathogens over time.
>
> *[Step 3: Create dissatisfaction with the lay view]*. On the other hand, as adults, our memories of the past are not always complete. There was a lot of infant mortality in the past. If your family had guests for dinner, those people may have gotten ill but did not attribute their illness to food poisoning or did not feel it was polite to report their illness to their hosts.
>
> In the distant past, people did not have access to refrigeration as we do. Because they did not, they cooked and cooked and cooked their food. They kept it HOT on the stove all day. People cooked enough food for the day and kept it hot all day until it was gone.
>
> People frequently get sick around the holidays. They may attribute their illness to the flu, rather than to food poisoning. Because we have become used to refrigeration, we may be more casual about leaving food out without it being hot than people were years ago. Food left out without refrigeration for long periods of time produces a hazard.
>
> *[Step 4: State scientifically supported views, noting their relevance to the lay theory]*. Bacteria may be introduced into food during the preparation process in many ways. There are bacteria in nasal passages and eye sockets that may be transmitted to food during its preparation. If you are cooking, you should not be touching your face and hair, but if you watch people on televised cooking shows, they touch their faces and hair repeatedly. Today, television chefs may be someone's model for cooking guidance, rather than a home economics teacher, for example, who might have been more likely to alert a future cook to improper food preparation practices.

Berry's reply suggests a variety of ways in which people could become ill from improperly handled meat. She may have created dissatisfaction with the lay view that "the old way of cooking was a good way" by describing a variety of plausible ways in which harmful bacteria could develop in a poultry dish. Her explanatory expertise develops because she and her colleagues at the USDA Meat and Poultry Hotline handle numerous questions about food safety, particularly around the holidays. Researchers interested in effective explaining may want to study the explanatory efforts of those who respond to the public's questions and inquiries frequently. These individuals' explanations may, because of constant challenge, practice, and refinement, be especially effective.

Given the tacitness and obdurateness of lay theories, addressing these notions and overcoming them is not easy. A further complication is that people may have lay theories that contradict long-established domains of science (e.g., Newton's Laws) as well as emerging science (e.g., genetics). Explainers need to know how to help people become dissatisfied with lay perspectives but also to appreciate that today's orthodox science may have the status of lay theory in decades to come. This perspective on learning is enjoyable when one is simply trying to understand. Unfortunately, when the topic being explained is illness, it is hard for listeners to distance themselves from frightening personal consequences and focus on intriguing intellectual puzzles. One advantage to mass media messages is that they can be turned off or tuned out when emotional or physical factors are not conducive to learning.

CONCLUSION

The New England Journal of Medicine's false alarms story was lauded by journalists because it seemed to empower the public and lamented by physicians because it seemed to mislead more than educate them. This chapter argues that these reactions to such news coverage are predictable outcomes of strongly held intuitive notions, perhaps lay theories, about how the mass media should explain illness information to the public. Undue adherence to these views may limit health communicators' abilities to think carefully about why people might find some medical information upsetting or confusing in a specific context.

As an alternative to these intuitive orientations, this chapter offers a problem-solving approach, or diagnostic framework, for explaining illness through the mass media. This approach maintains that effective explanation depends not on constant efforts to replace jargon with familiar words or on any single explanatory procedure but rather on carefully diagnosing, or identifying, principal obstacles thwarting communication about illness and research-tested steps to overcome these tensions. The tensions arise from the subject matter—illness—and its consequences for the audience. Because illness is inherently frightening and upsetting as well as confusing, those communicating about it should expect that suspicion and fear are likely obstacles to comprehension. Prior to offering explanations, communicators may first need to consider how best to earn an audience's trust. Research suggests that beginning one's remarks by criticizing people's ideas can create needless suspicion.

If trust has been earned but a subject is difficult to understand, the problem-solving approach says that communicators need to identify the principal source of confusion. Drawing from research, this chapter identifies three common difficulties. These involve (a) distinguishing intended from associated meanings of medical terms, (b) picturing the complex, and (c) overcoming misunderstandings that arise because of powerful but tacit lay theories. Frequently, good medical writers anticipate these confusion sources and address them. By viewing their work through the lens of research on effective explanation, this chapter suggests some reasons why their efforts may be effective and some ways in which their work may be even more so.

Physicians often succeed in their professions because of their diagnostic prowess. It may be that the most effective physician–explainers and medical writers are so because of their intuitive skill in anticipating likely confusions, their interest in respectfully addressing these difficulties, and the welcoming manner in which they encourage medical inquiry.

ACKNOWLEDGMENTS

I would like to thank individuals who helped me think about this chapter and locate media examples for it. They include: Julie Catherine Klish, Purdue Dean's Scholar; Christopher Dowden, Purdue graduate student; Professor Bryan Whaley, University of San Francisco; Len Carey, U. S. Department of Agriculture; Professor Brant Burleson, Purdue; Michael Rowan of WEAR-TV, Pensacola, FL; and Mrs. Ellen and Dr. Chad Phelps, Lafayette, IN. I thank George Mason University for providing me an office during a sabbatical when this chapter was written.

REFERENCES

A basic guide to hypertension medications. (1992, June). Health after 50. *The Johns Hopkins Medical Letter, 4*, 3.

Alderman, M. H., & Kotchen, T. A. (1998, September 29). Time to change guidelines for dietary sodium? *Washington Post Health*, p. 19.

Alvermann, D. E., Smith, L. C., & Readance, J. E. (1985). Prior knowledge activation and the comprehension of compatible and incompatible text. *Reading Research Quarterly, 20*, 420–436.

Anderson, C. W., & Smith, E. L. (1984). Children's preconceptions and content-area textbooks. In G. Duffy, L. Roehler, & J. Mason (Eds.), *Comprehension instruction* (pp. 187–201). New York: Longman.

Bazell, R. (1990). Medicine show. *The New Republic, 202*, 16–19.

Blum, D., & Knudson, M. (1997). *A field guide for science writers: The official guide of the National Association of Science Writers.* New York: Oxford University Press.

Broberg, K. (1973). Scientists' stopping behavior as indicator of writer's skill. *Journalism Quarterly, 50,* 763–767.

Brody, J. E. (1998, August 19). Health scares that weren't so scary. *The New York Times on the Web.*

Brown, W. J., & Basil, M. D. (1995). Media celebrities and public health: Responses to "Magic" Johnson's HIV disclosure and its impact on AIDS risk and high-risk behaviors. *Health Communication, 7,* 345–370.

Burgoon, J. K., Burgoon, M., & Wilkinson, M. (1983). Dimensions of content readership in 10 newspaper markets. *Journalism Quarterly, 60,* 74–80.

Butterfoss, F. D., Morrow, A. L., Rosenthal, J. R., Dini, E., Crews, R. C., Webster, J. D., & Louis, P. (1998). CINCH: An urban coalition for empowerment and action. *Health Education & Behavior, 25,* 212–225.

Campbell, G. (1776/1988). *The philosophy of rhetoric.* (L. F. Bitzer, Ed.). Carbondale: Southern Illinois University Press.

Clarke, J. N. (1986). Cancer meanings in the media: Implications for clinicians. In T. McCormack (Ed.), *Studies in Communications* (Vol. 3, pp. 175–215). Greenwich, CT: JAI.

Clayman, C. B. (Ed.). (1989). Depression. *The American Medical Association Encyclopedia of Medicine.* New York: Random House.

Consumer Health Information Corporation (1994). *I'm tired of doing these things over and over again.* Marietta, GA: Solvay Pharmaceuticals.

diSessa, A. A. (1982). Unlearning Aristotelian physics: A study of knowledge based learning. *Cognitive Science, 6,* 37–75.

Duffy, T. M. (1985). Readability formulas: What's the use? In T. M. Duffy & R. Waller (Eds.), *Designing usable texts* (pp. 113–143). New York: Academic Press.

Durant, J., Evans, G., & Thomas, G. (1992). Public understanding of science in Britain: The role of medicine in the popular representation of science. *Public Understanding of Science, 1,* 161–182.

Dunwoody, S. (1982). A question of accuracy. *Institute of Electrical and Electronics Engineers Transactions on Professional Communication, PC25,* 196–199.

Elmore, J. G., Barton, M. B., Moceri, V. M., Polk, S., Arena, P. J., & Fletcher, S. W. (1998). Ten-year risk of false positive screening mammograms and clinical breast examinations. *New England Journal of Medicine, 338,* 1089–1096.

Feig, S. A. (1998, June). A perspective on false positive screening mammograms. *The American College of Radiology, 54,* 8, 13.

Freimuth, V. S., & Taylor, M. K. (1994, November). *Are mass media health campaigns effective? A review of the empirical evidence.* Paper presented at the annual meeting of the National Communication Association, New Orleans, LA.

Freimuth, V. S., Greenberg, R. H., DeWitt, J., & Romano, R. M. (1984). Covering cancer: Newspapers and the public interest. *Journal of Communication, 34,* 62–73.

Gastel, B. (1983). *Presenting science to the public.* Philadelphia: Institute for Scientific Information.

Gentner, D. (1988). Are scientific analogies metaphors? In D.S. Miall (Ed.), *Metaphor: Problems and perspectives* (pp. 106–132). Atlantic Highlands, NJ: Humanities Press.

Guzzetti, B. J., Snyder, T. E., Glass, G. V., & Gamas, W. S. (1993). Promoting conceptual change in science: A comparative meta-analysis of instructional interventions from reading education and science education. *Reading Research Quarterly, 28,* 117–155.

Halliday, M. A. K., & Martin, J. R. (1993). *Writing science: Literacy and discursive power.* Pittsburgh, PA: University of Pittsburgh Press.

Haney, D. Q. (1998, April 6). Study finds mammograms often give false alarms. Lafayette [Ind.] *Journal and Courier,* p. A1.

Harp, S. F., & Mayer, R. E. (1997). The role of interest in learning from scientific text and illustrations: On the distinction between emotional interest and cognitive interest. *Journal of Educational Psychology, 89,* 92–102.

Hart, J., & Chappell, R. (1997). *Worlds apart: How the distance between science and journalism threatens America's future.* Nashville, TN: First Amendment Center.

Hayes, D. P. (1992, April 30). The growing inaccessibility of science. *Nature, 356,* 739–740.

Hewson, M. G., & Hewson, P. W. (1983). Effect of instruction using students' prior knowledge and conceptual change strategies on science learning. *Journal of Research in Science Teaching, 20,* 731–743.

Hewson, P. W., & Hewson, M. G. (1984). The role of conceptual conflict in conceptual change and the design of science instruction. *Instructional Science, 13,* 1–13.

Jackson, L. D. (1992). Information complexity and medical communication: The effects of technical language and amount of information in a medical message. *Health Communication, 4,* 197–210.

Johnson, J. D., Meischke, H., Grau, J., & Johnson, S. (1992). Cancer-related channel selection. *Health Communication, 4,* 183–196.

Kantor, R. N., Anderson, T. H., & Armbruster, B. B. (1983). How inconsiderate are children's textbooks? *Journal of Curriculum Studies, 15,* 61–72.

Kaplan, R. M. (1997). Health outcomes and communication research. *Health Communication, 9,* 75–82.

Kerr, A., Cunningham-Burley, S., & Amos, A. (1998). The new genetics and health: Mobilizing lay expertise. *Public Understanding of Science, 7,* 41–60.

King, D. (1991). *Whatever happened to Mr. Wizard, or how do we really find out about science.* Video available from Oregon State University Agricultural Experiment Station, Corvallis, OR.

Klare, G. R. (1963). *The meaning of readability.* Ames, IA: Iowa State University.

Kolata, G. (1997, April 1). New view sees breast cancer as 3 diseases. *The New York Times,* p. C1.

Kuhn, D. (1989). Children and adults as intuitive scientists. *Psychological Review, 96,* 674–689.

Lambert, B. L., Street, R. L., Cegala, D. J., Smith, D. H., Kurtz, S., & Schofield, T. (1997). Provider-patient communication, patient-centered care, and the mangle of practice. *Health Communication, 9,* 27–43.

Ley, P. (1983). Patients' understanding and recall in clinical communication failure. In D. Pendleton & J. Hasler (Eds.), *Doctor–patient communication* (pp. 89–108). London: Academic Press.

Loman, N. L., & Mayer, R. E. (1983). Signaling techniques that increase the understandability of expository prose. *Journal of Educational Psychology, 75,* 402–412.

Lugo, N. R. (1996). Empowerment education: A case study of the resources sisters/companeras program. *Health Education Quarterly, 23,* 281–289.

Long, M. (1995). Scientific explanation in U. S. newspaper science stories. *Public Understanding of Science, 4,* 119–130.

Majerovitz, S. D., Greene, M. G., Adelman, R. D., Brody, G. M., Leber, K., & Healy, S. W. (1997). Older patients' understanding of medical information in the emergency department. *Health Communication, 9,* 237–251.

Marshall, A. W., Smith, S. W., & McKeon, J. K. (1995). Persuading low-income women to engage in mammography screening: Source, message, and channel preferences. *Health Communication, 7,* 283–299.

Martin, J. R. (1970). *Explaining, understanding, and teaching.* New York: McGraw-Hill.

Mayer, R. E. (1983). What have we learned about increasing the meaningfulness of science prose? *Science Education, 67,* 223–237.

Mayer, R. E. (1989). Systematic thinking fostered by illustrations in scientific text. *Journal of Educational Psychology, 81,* 240–246.

Mayer, R. E., & Anderson, R. B. (1992). The instructive animation: Helping students build connections between words and pictures in multimedia learning. *Journal of Educational Psychology, 84*, 444–452.

Mayer, R. E., Bove, W., Bryman, A., Mars, R., & Tapangco, L. (1996). When less is more: Meaningful learning from visual and verbal summaries of science textbook lessons. *Journal of Educational Psychology, 88*, 64–73.

McDaniel, M. A., & Donnelly, C. M. (1996). Learning with analogy and elaborative interrogation. *Journal of Educational Psychology, 88*, 508–519.

McDivitt, J. A., Zimicki, S., & Hornik, R. C. (1997). Explaining the impact of a communication campaign to change vaccination knowledge and coverage in the Philippines. *Health Communication, 9*, 95–118.

McGuire, W. J. (1984). Public communication as a strategy for inducing health-promoting behavioral change. *Preventive Medicine, 13*, 299–319.

Merrill, M. D., & Tennyson, R. D. (1977). *Teaching concepts: An instructional design guide.* Englewood Cliffs, NJ: Educational Technology Publication.

Missed messages. (1998, July 20). *American Medical News, 14*, 17.

Murray, M. (1990, July). Confused about fiber? *Reader's Digest, 137*, 75–78.

Neergaard, L. (1997, January 24). Scientists starve cancer tumors. *The (Santa Rosa, CA) Press Democrat*, p. A5.

Neufeldt, V. (1997, January 9). (Executive Producer). *Junk science.* (ABC News Special). New York: American Broadcasting Corporation.

O'Keefe, G. J., Boyd, H. H., & Brown, M. R. (1998). Who learns preventative health care information from where: Cross-channel and repertoire comparisons. *Health Communication, 10*, 25–36.

Pellechia, M. G. (1997). Trends in science coverage: A content analysis of three U. S. newspapers. *Public Understanding of Science, 6*, 49–68.

Petty, R. E., & Cacioppo, J. T. (1986). *Communication and persuasion: Central and peripheral routes to attitude change.* New York: Springer-Verlag.

Qian, G., & Alvermann, D. (1995). Role of epistemological beliefs and learned helplessness in secondary school students' learning science concepts from text. *Journal of Educational Psychology, 87*, 282–292.

Reid, J. C., Kardash, C. M., Robinson, R. D., & Scholes, R. (1994). Comprehension in patient literature: The importance of text and reader characteristics. *Health Communication, 6*, 327–335.

Richards, M. (1996). Lay and professional knowledge of genetics and inheritance. *Public Understanding of Science, 5*, 217–230.

Rimal, R. N., Ratzan, S. C., Arnston, P., & Freimuth, V. S. (1997). Reconceptualizing the "Patient": Health care promotion as increasing citizens' decision-making competencies. *Health Communication, 9*, 61–74.

Rogers, E. M., & Storey, J. D. (1987). Communication campaigns. In C. Berger & S. Chaffee (Eds.), *Handbook of communication science* (pp. 817–846). Thousand Oaks, CA: Sage.

Rosenfeld, I. (1998, Sept. 13). Don't be blasé about your blood pressure. *Parade Magazine*, pp. 4–5.

Rowan, K. E. (1988). A contemporary theory of explanatory writing. *Written Communication, 5*, 23–56.

Rowan, K. E. (1991). When simple language fails: Presenting difficult science to the public. *Journal of Technical Writing and Communication, 21*, 369–382.

Rowan, K. E. (1994a). The technical and democratic approaches to risk situations: Their appeal, limitations, and rhetorical alternative. *Argumentation, 8*, 391–409.

Rowan, K. E. (1994b). Why rules for risk communication are not enough: A problem-solving approach to risk communication. *Risk Analysis, 14*, 365–374.

Rowan, K. E. (1995a). A new pedagogy for explanatory public speaking: Why arrangement should not substitute for invention. *Communication Education, 44*, 236–250.

Rowan, K. E. (1995b). What risk communicators need to know: An agenda for research. In B. R. Burleson (Ed), *Communication yearbook, 18,* (pp. 300–319). Thousand Oaks, CA: Sage.

Rowan, K. E. (1999). Effective explanation of uncertain and complex science. In S. Friedman, S. Dunwoody, & C. L. Rogers (Eds.), *Communicating new and uncertain science* (pp. 201–223). Mahwah, NJ: Lawrence Erlbaum Associates.

Rukavina, I., & Daneman, M. (1996). Integration and its effect on acquiring knowledge about competing scientific theories from text. *Journal of Educational Psychology, 88,* 272–287.

Schommer, M. (1990). Effects of beliefs about the nature of knowledge on comprehension. *Journal of Educational Psychology, 82,* 498–504.

Shuy, R. W., & Larkin, D. L. (1978). Linguistic considerations in the simplification/clarification of insurance policy language. *Discourse Processes, 1,* 305–321.

Shymansky, J. A., & Kyle, W. C. (1988). A summary of research in science education–1986 [Special issue]. *Science Education, 72,* (3).

Siew, C., Chang, S. B., Gruninger, S. E., Verrusio, A. C., Neidle, E. A. (1992). Self-reported percutaneous injuries in dentists: Implications for HBV, HIV transmission risk. *Journal of the American Dental Association, 123,* 37–44.

Signorelli, N., & Staples, J. (1997). Television and children's conceptions of nutrition. *Health Communication, 9,* 298–301.

Sugarman, C. (1999, Jan. 13). Giant introduces new way to take a burger's temperature. *The Washington Post,* p. E2.

Sypher, B. D., Bostrom, R. N., & Seibert, J. H. (1989). Listening, communication abilities, and success at work. *Journal of Business Communication, 26,* 293–303.

Tennyson, R. D., & Cocchiarella, M. J. (1986). An empirically based instructional design theory for teaching concepts. *Review of Educational Psychology, 56,* 40–71.

Tennyson, R. D., Woolley, F. R., & Merrill, M. D. (1972). Exemplar and nonexemplar variables which produce correct concept classification of behavior and specified classification errors. *Journal of Educational Psychology, 63,* 144–152.

U.S. Department of Agriculture (1997, October). *Kitchen thermometers.* Washington, DC: Author.

U.S. Department of Agriculture (1998, August). *Thermometer use for cooking ground beef patties.* Washington, DC: Author.

Thompson, C. L., & Pledger, L. M. (1993). Doctor-patient communication: Is patient knowledge of medical terminology improving? *Health Communication, 5,* 89–97.

Whaley, B. B. (1994). "Food is to me as gas is to cars??": Using figurative language to explain illness to children. *Health Communication, 6,* 193–204.

Witte, K. (1992). The role of threat and efficacy in AIDs prevention. *International Quarterly of Community Health Education, 12,* 225–249.

Witte, K. (1997). Preventing teen pregnancy through persuasive communications: Realities, myths, and the hard-fact truths. *Journal of Community Health, 22,* 137–154.

Wright, R. (1997). *Tough questions, great answers: Responding to patient concerns about today's dentistry.* Carol Stream, IL: Quintessence.

4

Explaining Illness as Bad News: Individual Differences in Explaining Illness-Related Information

Catherine M. Gillotti
Department of Communication
Purdue University Calumet

James L. Applegate
Department of Communication
University of Kentucky

Recent changes in the medical industry in the United States have influenced the approach of practitioner and medical educators to the clinical, daily operations of practicing medicine. These alterations have produced, among other things, a growing concern for the importance of communication and training in the health care context. For instance, communication is being recognized by medical educators as an important component of the medical students' social and clinical training (Novack, Volk, Drossman, & Lipkin, 1993).

Health communication researchers have repeatedly investigated communication as an important component in the health care interaction (Thompson, 1994). Factors such as patient satisfaction, patient cooperation, and recovery all point to important outcomes for the patient's well-being. The study of communication in this context is particularly salient for physicians and other care providers given the responsibility attached to information giving and information gathering in life-and-death situations. For instance, health care providers are faced with challenges of gaining patients' and family members' understanding of complex procedures under extreme anxiety, performing difficult clinical procedures while trying to comfort patients and explaining the complexities of illness and courses of treatment.

Often, communication concerns explaining illness as bad news. This practice is of particular importance because bad news delivery, although routine in some respects, can also be one of the most challenging communicative events faced by care providers (Maynard, 1991). Although the impact of news on patients is unique to their experience and influenced by the communication ability of both the health professional and the patient, two factors confound carrying out this responsibility. First, there is a lack of theoretical and systematic research concerning the best ways to explain illness as bad news. Second, several authors suggest that little is known about how health professionals are trained for explaining illness (Sharp, Strauss, & Lorch, 1992). What is understood, however, suggests health care providers are inadequately trained during their formal medical education for the challenge of bad news delivery (Davis, 1991; Fallowfield, 1993; McLauchlan, 1990; Miranda & Brody, 1992; Quill & Townsend, 1991; Speck, 1991). For instance, Miranda and Brody (1992) stressed that although medical schools are attempting to incorporate bad-news delivery in the curricula, not enough is done to facilitate the education of clinicians: "Despite the importance of this function, which falls to almost all clinicians, no clear research is available to guide this process, and little has been written to help practitioners deliver bad news in the most constructive manner possible" (p. 83).

What has been overlooked in medical education is that not only do care providers treat, diagnose, and educate their patients, they also potentially shatter these same patients' lives when relaying information on serious illnesses (Speck, 1991). Additionally, there are ethical factors to be considered in explaining illness. Some authors directly involved in the health care delivery system have discussed the implications of the patient's wishes to know the extent of the news and severity of the prognosis (Beyene, 1992; Charlton, 1992; Waitzkin, 1985). These issues have direct relevance to the content and context of explaining illness. Hence, it is important to understand how physicians explain illness to patients and their families as well as the subsequent evaluations of those explanations.

This chapter contains a representative literature review on medical disclosure, factors concerning bad news delivery, and communication issues related to medical education and provides a constructivist communication theoretical framework as a foundation for the study of explaining illness as bad news and the development of communication education programs for care providers.

MEDICAL DISCLOSURE

Early notions concerning medical disclosure are founded on the ideas of Hippocrates. He argued that it was physicians' responsibility to determine how much information patients should receive concerning their condition (Maynard, 1991; Waitzkin, 1985). Patients usually want as much information as possible, which can cause a conflict if the physician embraces Hippocrates' view of disclosure (Maynard, 1991; Waitzkin, 1985).

However, Charlton (1992) addressed the concern about medical disclosure by tracing the change in patient attitudes over the past decades, specifically in the United States. Since the 1950s, both patients and physicians have lobbied for more information to be given to the patient by the physician. Charlton stated that, in the past, the delivery of bad news to the patient was believed to lower patients' morale; thus, full disclosure meant running the risk of affecting the health of the patient. However, Sell, Devlin, and Bourke (1993) found that 46 out of 50 patients diagnosed with lung cancer wanted to know the truth about their diagnosis and felt the physician had done the right thing by telling them. Whatever the physician's view of disclosure, patients are demanding more information, making the ability to explain illness effectively all the more urgent.

There are, of course, extreme cases where the disclosure of the diagnosis and prognosis might endanger the patient or others; cases that may force the physician to consider withholding information. However, some contend that humans are more resilient than typically thought; individuals deserve to know the truth about their health status if they want it and providers should err on the side of disclosure (Davis, 1991; Morton, 1996). As Cousins (1976) wrote about his own fight against an incurable disease, "I have learned never to underestimate the capacity of the human mind and body to regenerate—even when the prospects seem most wretched" (p. 1463).

Legal issues have intervened to change care providers' and patients' views of explanations of illness, as well. Charlton (1992) suggested "The principle of informed consent requires respect for individuals and their autonomy, and so their right to be informed, and discourages a paternalistic attitude which deems the deceit may be beneficial for the patient's welfare" (p. 617).

Disclosure issues tied to explanation of illness are complicated and require consideration of what is wanted by the patient, what the physician feels is the appropriate amount and kind of information to be given, and what binds both parties in the law (Charlton, 1992). Although the ethics debate over issues about medical disclosure continues, the delivery of medical information, in particular bad news, is a more frequent demand of the communication skills of health providers than ever before. The following section reviews current thinking about bad news delivery by medical professionals.

BAD NEWS DELIVERY

As paramount as the communicative task of explaining illness as bad news, there are surprisingly few treatises concerning strategies and messages to accomplish this goal. However, a review of the current medical literature on explaining bad news to patients and their families reflects what has been offered.

Strategies for Explaining Illness as Bad News

A perusal of the literature suggests numerous common strategies for delivering bad news, which emphasize using sound interpersonal communication skills: (a) breaking the bad news to the patient or family members in a quiet place where interruptions will not intrude on news delivery; (b) spending adequate time with the patient after the news is delivered; (c) being empathetic, sincere, compassionate, and sympathetic; (d) touching the patient; (e) answering any questions the patient or families might have; (f) assessing the emotional stability of the patient following the delivery of the news; (g) avoiding information overload; (h) scheduling a follow-up consultation within a few days of the initial delivery of the news in order to give more details about the prognosis; (i) using simple language that the patient and family members will understand; (j) providing any written materials that would be helpful to the patient; and (k) ensuring there is someone present to support the patient after the news is delivered (Brewin, 1991; Charlton, 1992; Davis, 1991; Fallowfield, 1993, Graham, 1991; McLauchlan, 1990; Miranda & Brody, 1992; Ptacek & Eberhardt, 1996; Quill & Townsend, 1991; Speck, 1991; Statham & Dimavicius, 1992).

The most comprehensive experiential advice offered is a six-step protocol by Buckman (1992). He suggested that, "Our own experiences in practice—in medical oncology and in family medicine—have stimulated us to draw up guidelines that are, above all, practical" (pp. 4–5). Reflecting many of the strategy suggestions offered by others, Buckman made the following recommendations for explaining bad news: (a) get started by setting the appropriate context; (b) find out how much the patient knows; (c) find out how much the patient wants to know; (d) share the information; (e) respond to the patient's feelings; and (f) plan and follow through. He specifically recognized that responding to the patient's feelings is the most important aspect of delivering bad news and further advocated being adaptable in the interaction. Buckman provided a seemingly sound set of examples and suggestions for explaining illness from the clinician's perspective and discussed many of the same challenges faced by care providers and patients in this situation (to be outlined in upcoming sections). Importantly, however, he recognized that these recommendations are only one approach to explaining illness.

Brewin (1991) offered a descriptive analysis of three ways to deliver bad news, which he referred to as (a) the unfeeling way, (b) the kind and sad way, and (c) the understanding way. For example, the "unfeeling" way might be characterized by the physician standing at the foot of the bed when delivering the news. The "kind and sad" way is characterized by excessive sympathy and compassion that leads to decreased patient morale and may be interpreted as paternalistic. Finally, the "understanding" way focuses on subtlety and sensitivity. For example, the physician might say, "I'm afraid the tests show ... but I'm glad to say that the position is at least more hopeful than some cases we see ... " (p. 1208). Brewin advocated the understanding and positive way because it is characterized by flexibility, feedback, and reassurance. The method of achieving this feeling of positiveness, according to Brewin, is to convey genuine sincerity and avoid any kind of formula deliveries of the news. This is an essential point because it emphasizes adaptability in challenging communicative situations. Specifically, it calls for the care provider to be person-centered in the delivery of bad news and adaptive to the perspective of the patient as person.

Learning as much about patients and their coping styles as possible has been suggested as part of the advanced preparation for the delivery of bad news (Brewin, 1991; Platt & Keller, 1994; Quill & Townsend, 1991). In other words, this advice concerns reducing the relational uncertainty and creating common ground. In general practice situations, such as those referred to by Quill and Townsend (1991) and Brewin (1991), the relationship between physician and patient can transcend a purely professional level and reach an interpersonal one. This development better enables the care provider and patient to anticipate the other's reactions while using adaptive communication skills.

All of this advice appears consistent, sensible, and could be defined by many as practicing good communication skills. However, these recommendations have originated without independent analysis or scientific scrutiny. As Ptacek and Eberhardt (1996) noted, many of the authors of the bad news articles based their recommendations on their work experience, which has merit; however, only systematic observations grounded in a coherent theoretical perspective allows for supported generalizations. Thompson (1994) suggested that the lack of empirical rigor is a recurring criticism of the studies conducted on communication by health professionals and that the impact of the process should be pursued empirically.

Moreover, although the advice contained in this literature seems intuitively sound and the call for individual adaptation appropriate, two concerns surface. First, what is often viewed as common sense is frequently incorrect. For instance, some literature on expressed emotion in the health care context suggests that the emotion expressed by health care providers in interaction is beneficial and wanted by patients and or family members (Krahn, Hallum, & Kime, 1993; Maynard, 1989; Sharp, Strauss, & Lorch, 1992; Wesley, 1996). Interestingly, Wesley (1996) found that patients generally preferred high levels of affect from the physician but no affect was preferred over a low affective expression. The relationship between expressed emotion and patient satisfaction may be curvilinear. This contradiction points to a need for more empirical research and obscures what course of action health care providers should take in a bad news situation. Second, it is unclear what constitutes the nature of many suggestions for explaining illness as bad news (e.g., "the understanding way"). The conflicting demands and difficult nature of bad news situations make implementation of abstract recommendations all the more difficult.

Difficulties In Explaining Illness As Bad News

Several factors have been identified that help to account for the difficulty in explaining illness when the news will be perceived as bad. These factors include the lack of certainty in predicting the exact course of a disease, the potential feelings of failure experienced by the care providers, the inevitable emotion to be expressed in the provider–patient interactions, and the lack of training provided to health professionals in handling this kind of communicative challenge.

Uncertainty. All interactions contain some degree of uncertainty. Interactants are searching to reduce the uncertainty about themselves and each other (Berger & Bradac, 1982). This assumption applies to both health care providers and patients in the delivery of medical information. The bad news context, in particular, presents a high degree of uncertainty where expectations for certainty are high. Often, physicians and other health professionals are unable to predict the future of the patient's health status once a diagnosis has been made. This uncertainty may cause the care provider and patient some psychological discomfort. Miranda and Brody (1992) stated that health care providers must learn to be comfortable with uncertainty while conveying hope to the patient (see chap. 2, this volume). Additionally, many care providers must treat patients who they have just met (e.g., emergency and trauma units), which increases the uncertainty present in the interaction (McLauchlan, 1990).

Feelings of failure. Another reason for the difficulty in explaining illness as bad news is the feeling of failure that some health care providers experience. For instance, Miranda and Brody (1992) suggested, "The physician may have feelings of impotence, or even guilt or failure: 'If only I'd done that mammogram/stool guaiac/Pap smear/got him to stop smoking'" (p. 85). Health care providers simultaneously strive to treat patients while maintaining their public identity as a healer (i.e., face, Goffman, 1959). Losing patients or not being able to fully restore a patient's health contradicts the provider's identity or image of a competent healer.

Expressed emotion. A third difficulty of delivering bad news centers around the emotional expression of both providers and patients (Maynard, 1991; Ptacek & Eberhardt, 1996). Fallowfield (1993) agreed that the delivery of bad news places stress on the care provider as well as the patient. As such, care providers must learn to express and cope with their feelings of the situation as well as the patient's. Often, health care providers fail to spend enough time dealing with their emotional responses to patients and their condition. In some specific areas of health care, formal programs have been instituted to encourage care providers to explore their emotional reactions to their work through formal debriefing sessions (Swanson, 1993).

DiMatteo (1979) suggested that the relationship between the physician and patient is an emotionally charged one because of the accessibility to the patient's body as well as the dependency that usually develops between the patient and the physician. He advised that the physician's role be seen as an interdependent interplay of technical expertise and affect because, historically, physicians have relied on their ability to express emotion and to support the emotions of the patients in their efforts to heal.

In response to this stress, Ptacek and Eberhardt (1996) offered a model of stress and coping to understand bad news delivery and to frame future studies. The stress and coping model operates through consideration of two cognitive factors: primary and secondary appraisals. The primary appraisal is an assessment of what is initially at stake, whereas the secondary appraisal considers the amount of resources needed to cope with the situation. Ptacek and Eberhardt further stated that once an individual has completed a cognitive appraisal of the situation, efforts are made to resolve the issue through the elimination of external stress and through the reduction of negative feelings regarding the situation. What this model offers is a transactional approach to the interaction with recognition of the stress and emotion involved for both care providers and patients. However, the authors noted that even when physicians acknowledge the patient's perspective, they still tend to discount it.

Similarly, other research has indicated that the show of emotion by physicians and other care providers appears to be beneficial for the patient and family members receiving the news and for the care providers themselves; thus, scholars encourage health professionals to express emotion when explaining illness (Kaiser, 1993; Krahn, Hallum, & Kime, 1993; Maynard, 1989; Sharp, Strauss, & Lorch, 1992). However, this is sometimes challenging for physicians because of patient expectations regarding the physician's role and demeanor. That is, "Physicians are intimately familiar with the natural history of disease and can discuss serious illness with stoic objectivity and precision, but they view illness from an emotional distance that their patients do not—a separation that should be recognized" (Kaiser, 1993, p. 13).

Recognizing the necessary emotional distance required by the care providers does not negate patients' need to express emotion. In a retrospective study of communication preferences of parents of children with developmental disabilities, Sharp et al. (1992) found that the parents indicated they appreciated emotional displays by the physician and the opportunity to show feelings themselves. Simultaneously, the researchers discovered that when delivering bad news to the parents, the physician maintained control of the interaction, limiting opportunities to comfort and display emotion. The authors suggested that, "The physician was often perceived as in control, confident, and able to allow the parents to talk, although less likely to allow the parents to show feelings" (p. 121).

Although work demonstrates the positive effects of care provider emotional displays (Krahn et al., 1993; Maynard, 1989; Sharp et al., 1992), health care personnel, especially physicians, tend to distance themselves emotionally from their patients. Additionally, Wesley (1996) demonstrated that even though patients tend to prefer high levels of emotional expression, they also would prefer no expression as opposed to low levels of expression. This body of literature contains contradictory premises concerning the value of emotional expression from the care provider and may lead the reader to contemplate the causes for the lack of expressed emotion on the part of care providers, in particular physicians, when explaining illness.

Historically, physicians have been encouraged to stay detached in order to objectively diagnose the patient (Flynn & Hekelman, 1993; Hafferty, 1991; McWhinney, 1989; Mizrahi, 1991). The primary factor contributing to this detachment is the socialization process of medical students and residents. Researchers believe this socialization process leads physicians to be distant and to dehumanize their patients (Flynn & Hekelman, 1993;

Hafferty, 1991; Mizrahi, 1991). For instance, Hafferty (1991) contended that as a result of the medical students' training, there is ambiguity in role expectations imposed by patients in life-and-death situations because of the demand for duplicity. This means that patients expect their care providers to think and feel differently about disease, disability, and death, but at the same time share the same perspective of these as we do. Hafferty offered support for his claims by exploring the reactions of medical students to anatomy lab. He poignantly demonstrated that a physician's first patient is a cadaver. In order to cope with mutilating and quartering a human body while being accepted by their peers, many medical students have to learn to numb their emotions. Emotional displays were met with severe criticism from peers, who suggested that maybe those students who showed emotion were not destined to be physicians.

Confounding the situation further, research suggests the continuation of physicians' emotional detachment through various residency programs (Flynn & Hekelman, 1993; Mizrahi, 1991). In order to cope and survive their residency programs, residents are forced to accept a powerful value system that often contradicts the values these same individuals brought to medical school with them. Moreover, other care providers also are enculturated with similar values within the health care context (Jensen, 1993).

Lack of Training. Finally, explaining bad news is difficult due to a lack of training of health professionals during medical school. Fallowfield (1993) contended that even though more communication skills training is occurring in medical schools, there is still a disparity in relationship to the amount of clinical skills. Additionally, Krahn et al. (1993) stated that medical training has emphasized information gathering instead of information giving and counseling once news is delivered.

Novack et al. (1993) conducted a survey of 130 programs in the 126 medical schools across the United States in an effort to assess the quantity and quality of interpersonal skills training in medical schools. The results indicated that although there has been an increase in the number of medical interviewing and interpersonal skills training courses offered in the curricula, these offerings vary in terms of quality and intensity. However, some efforts are being made during the clinical years to train health care providers. Graham (1991) advocated the teaching of communication skills, in particular the explanation of bad news, by allowing his residents to attend the sessions with him when the news is delivered to the patient in order to allow his students first hand observation. However, Graham did not describe how he typically approaches the delivery of bad news.

Some institutions utilize tutorial programs to educate medical students on the delivery of bad news (Pearse & Cooper, 1993); however, these types of tutorial programs are not the norm. Rappaport and Witzke (1993) conducted a study on the education of third-year medical students during their internal medicine–surgical rotations on issues of death and dying. The researchers found that 41% of their respondents had never been present when a staff physician spoke to a dying patient. Thirty-five percent stated that they had never spoken to an attending physician about how to handle patients with terminal diseases (Rappaport & Witzke, 1993). More vivid were the results from the students on the surgical rotation. Seventy-three percent indicated that they had never been present when a surgeon delivered bad news to a patient's family members and 85 percent had never been present when a surgeon told family members of the death of the patient. Rappaport and Witzke (1993) concluded that this training is essential for physicians to learn compassion—"If we are to turn out both competent and compassionate physicians, education in this area must be stressed during the clinical years by house staff and attending physicians" (p. 165).

Clearly there is need for systematic, integrated education programs based on theory-driven research with strong validity claims that allow for the development of basic communication-relevant abilities (e.g., perspective taking, autonomy-granting strategies, and listener adaptive lines of action in the health care context). Suggestions for the need for perspective-taking, a transactional perspective, and the importance of communication effectiveness are well intentioned (Maynard, 1991). However, this advice lacks a theoretical grounding from which to foster this research. A theory that provides an integrative approach and addresses all of these important issues is constructivism.

CONSTRUCTIVISM AS A FRAMEWORK
FOR EXPLAINING ILLNESS AS BAD NEWS

The aforementioned discussion has revealed that the literature concerning explaining illness as bad news, as a critical communicative skill, contains a plethora of anecdotal suggestions and lacks systematic empirical efforts to ascertain the credence of strategies (Ptacek & Eberhardt, 1996). What is needed to resolve these concerns, is constructivism, which provides a sound theoretical framework from which to examine the essential facets of explaining illness as bad news and provides a basis for comprehensive training in delivering bad news.

The following sections provide an overview of the theory of constructivism and explain the relationship between key forms of social cognitive and communicative development as these relate to effective communication between health provider and client as outlined in the theory. Specifically, the relationship between interpersonal cognitive complexity and the development of person–patient-centered verbal and nonverbal communication ability is explored, as these affect important outcomes in the explanation of illness. Finally, research using constructivist theory to investigate communication in the health care context is reviewed.

Constructivism

The core of constructivism concerns individual differences in persons' social cognitive abilities that underlie communication adaptation and effectiveness: dimensions of a more global construct of communication competence (Delia, O'Keefe, & O'Keefe, 1982). Specifically, constructivists argue that the more developed and differentiated persons' interpersonal constructs, the greater their ability to take the perspective of others while meeting the instrumental and interpersonal goals of that interaction.

Constructivist researchers in communication have examined the relationship between individual differences in social cognitive development and communication behavior for 20 years. Over the last decade, the focus of investigations has been on the person-centered quality of communication (see reviews in Applegate 1990; Burleson, 1989). *Person-centeredness* is a global characteristic of communication, tapping a variety of ways in which people demonstrate the ability to recognize and strategically adapt to the autonomy and individuality of fellow interactants while accommodating the constraints imposed by the communicative situation (e.g., conflicting goals, norms of appropriateness).

Personal Constructs. Centrally, constructivist study of social perception processes underlying person-centered communication is grounded in an integration of Kelly's (1955) theory of personal constructs (Kelly, 1955) with a Wernerian conception of development (Werner, 1957; Werner & Kaplan, 1963). Specifically, constructs are the bipolar dimensions that people utilize in their perceptual processes to make sense of the social world (e.g., hot–cold, friendly–unfriendly, smart–dumb). Differences in the quality of persons' social cognitive schemes (i.e., constructs) used in communication are indexed hierarchically to reflect such increases in the complexity and organization of individual social perception. Although recognizing the multiple forms that social schemes may take (e.g., causal, temporal), constructivist research has focused on Kelly's (1955) theory of systems of interpersonal constructs used to understand people and social contexts.

Orthogenetic Principle. As a developmental theory, constructivism casts both social cognitive and communication development in terms of Werner's (1957) orthogenetic principle that defines all development in terms of increasing differentiation, articulation, and hierarchic integration of forms of thought and behavior. Specifically, the complexity (i.e., number of constructs), abstractness (i.e., psychological versus physical focus), and integration (i.e., organization) of interpersonal constructs have been studied in relation to construction of more sophisticated impressions of others and more adaptive, person-centered communication messages. In more than 100 studies, constructivist research has consistently demonstrated significant relationships between these forms of social-cognitive and communicative development.

Constructs and Listener Adaptation.   Early research cast individual communication differences tied to construct development in terms of the "listener-adaptation" of communication strategies (especially persuasive strategies). The explanation for the relationship seemed straightforward—more constructs produced more attributions about others' needs, wants, desires, and concerns that were incorporated into strategies (i.e., incorporating counterarguments for perceived persuadee objections to a persuasive argument). Increased perspectivism was the key to the construct–communication relationship.

However, as research showed relationships between construct development and an increasingly broad array of communicative behaviors (e.g., sensitivity to norms for face support, higher levels of persuasive reasoning generally), the simple "perspectivism" account proved inadequate. This led O'Keefe and Delia (1982) to offer an influential alternative account of how constructs related to more sophisticated communication behavior. That account informs our present effort in the following way. Measures show that a more complex, psychologically focused, organized interpersonal construct system taps a generally more person-centered orientation to communicative contexts. Person-centered communication embraces a variety of separable aspects including the extent to which the communicator: (a) is responsive to the changing aims and utterances of the interactional partner; (b) adapts messages to the specific characteristics and needs of a particular listener; (c) integrates concerns for positive relational and identity goals within the instrumental goal context, producing a generally more complex set of goal structures; and (d) acknowledges the autonomy of the listener and encourages reflection and reasoning by another about his or her circumstance (Applegate et al., 1985).

The use of this orientation in specific conversations allows the individual to generate a more complex set of beliefs for defining the situation and the embedded instrumental, relational, and identity goals. These situated beliefs about contexts and persons are taken to be the most direct guides for communicative behavior by constructivist researchers. The more complex understanding of the means, ends, and obstacles to goal attainment (with special attention to the characteristics of other persons' perspectives in defining these factors) are, we believe, best thought of as generated and organized, not in the abstract, but within more complex and sophisticated plans of action.

Constructivist theory would predict that in defining the desired goals, means, and obstacles of a context in which illness is to be explained, the more sophisticated provider evidences a more interpersonally complex set of constructs for viewing social contexts generally. These, then, would facilitate his or her ability to: (a) define a more complex set of goals addressing both the informational and affective issues present, (b) infer more potential means or plans for achieving those goals, and (c) select strategies that anticipate potential obstacles to achieving goals while adapting to the unique perspective of an autonomous, reasoning patient.

Person-Centered Versus Position-Centered Communication

Level of interpersonal cognitive complexity has been associated with greater sophistication in various areas of social behavior (Applegate, Kline, & Delia, 1991; Burleson, 1984; Burleson & Waltman, 1988). As noted, constructivist research on communication ability has focused on the development of person-centered communication skills (Applegate & Delia, 1980).

Person-Centered Communication. Person-centered communication in comforting, social influence, information transmission, or face maintenance strategic performances reflects an ability to adapt effectively to another's individual perspective and grant autonomy to the other in the course of a reasoning process that focuses communication on a proactive effort to accomplish goals. Specifically, high levels of interpersonal cognitive complexity have been positively associated with the production of a greater number of proactive plans for dealing with problematic communicative situations (Waldron & Applegate, 1994), more comforting strategies designed to provide social support (Burleson, 1984), greater proficiency in completing tasks requiring only verbal communication (Hale, 1982), more effective and listener-adaptive influence and conflict resolution strategies (Applegate & Woods, 1991; Burleson, Delia, & Applegate, 1992; Clark & Delia, 1979), the utilization of face-saving strategies in face-threatening contexts (Applegate & Woods, 1991), and the ability to produce supportive messages in a nursing context (Willihnganz, 1987).

Position-Centered Communication. Person-centered communication contrasts with less sophisticated approaches to the accomplishment of communication goals, often characterized as more position centered. Position-centered communication grounds interaction in ascribed role-based characteristics of participants (e.g., physician to patient) and typically assumes a shared definition of those positional roles as defining communication. For example, a physician who maintains a position-centered approach to explaining an HIV-positive result to a patient would produce communication limited to an ascribed conception of the role relationship that exists between the expert and the patient. The physician might say something like, "We have your test results back. They are positive. Do you have any medical questions for me?" This might be followed with a clinical explanation of the difference between being HIV positive and having full-blown AIDS. Conversely, a person-centered approach in the same situation would embody a more complex focus on the informational and affective needs of the patient. Provider communication could exhibit informational strategies that more explicitly acknowledge limited processing capacity due to the shock of the news: "I know this news must hit you hard. Let me just try to cover the most important things for you to remember from today's visit." We would expect to see more in the way of explicit responses to assuage patient responses reflecting fear: "We're not going to leave you. You're not alone. There is more that is being developed, so there are things to hope for." Although the content of the delivery of the diagnosis in these examples might be the same, the second example focuses not only on adapting information dissemination itself but also on the social support and comfort implicitly called for in this type of interaction.

Person-Centered Behavior and Nonverbal Immediacy.   Recent studies have broadened constructivism analyses of person-centered communication behavior to include nonverbal behavior. Nonverbal researchers generally have given special attention to the role of nonverbal behavior in the communication of immediacy and altercentrism (Burgoon, 1985; Coker & Burgoon, 1987; Manusov, 1991), two concepts that Woods (1993) argued are conceptually parallel to the verbal dimension of person-centered communication. Immediacy is defined by approach, arousal, and warmth and closeness. As Woods (1993) stated, "Approach and arousal are basic elements that project acknowledgment of the conversational partner in person-centered communication, while warmth and closeness certainly overlap the relational facet of person-centered communication" (p. 40). Altercentrism is defined by attending to the other interactant and being empathetic (Spitzberg & Hecht, 1984).

   In an effort to integrate verbal and nonverbal contributors of communication competence framed in a constructivist approach, Woods (1993) studied 109 participants in a video taped, persuasive interaction in which dyads were paired for disagreement on an assigned issue. After the interaction, participants completed an evaluation of the other's communication competence, social attractiveness, and persuasiveness.

Woods (1993) based his nonverbal measures on Coker and Burgoon's (1987) research. His results indicated that immediacy and altercentric nonverbal behaviors (eye contact, in particular) were related to person-centered measures of verbal interaction. Additionally, head nodding and verbal interaction scores were predictors of third-party evaluations of the communication competence of participants. Woods' (1993) results argue for the inclusion of person-centered measures of nonverbal communication (i.e., of immediacy and altercentrism) in constructivist analyses of communication development and its impact on important outcome variables. Of course, the physician–patient relationship also is typically developed in face-to-face interactions, with both physician and patient utilizing nonverbal cues in their interpretations of the interaction. For these reasons, it is important to incorporate nonverbal measures in analyses of interactions in which illness is explained.

Person-Centered Communication in the Health Context

A limited number of studies have directly applied constructivist analyses of social cognitive and communicative ability to the health care context. For instance, Kasch and Dine (1988) called for person-centered communication to operate as a theoretical underpinning to effective nursing action. The authors conducted a literature review of relevant person-centered communication research and urged future researchers to account for perspective taking because they believed that nurses are likely to show great variation in perspective-taking ability. Further, they suggested that perspective taking can be used as a resource in accomplishing nursing goals (Kasch & Dine, 1998).

Willihnganz (1987) directly examined social cognitive ability and more sophisticated communication in a nursing context with a sample of 88 nurses. She investigated the relationship between social cognitive complexity and communicative performance in a context requiring social support. The results indicated that nurses with higher construct-differentiation scores viewed more of their peers as supportive than those with lower differentiation scores. Further, Willihnganz contended that more differentiated individuals help "create" more support from the individuals with whom they interact: "One might actually receive more support because one can more effectively negotiate it" (p. 23). The results also indicated that those individuals who attended to positive face wants in the interaction were perceived as supportive. This finding further supports research on cognitive complexity and face preservation (Applegate & Woods, 1991).

Kline and Ceropski (1984) studied the person-centered communication skills of 46 medical students in interviews with newly admitted patients. Participants completed measures of interpersonal cognitive complexity and scored each participant on measures of differentiation and abstraction.

Students were asked to respond to two hypothetical patient scenarios. In the first situation, the medical student was to instruct a patient on diet options to lower cholesterol levels. The second scenario involved advising a relative of an alcoholic patient. Students also completed a mailed questionnaire asking them to outline their goals of a medical interview along with a description of their role as physician in the interview. Finally, each student was videotaped while interviewing a newly admitted patient.

The results indicated that construct abstractness and empathy served as predictors to person-centered regulative communication strategies. Construct abstractness and role differentiation served as significant predictors of person-centered regulative communication strategies in the second scenario. Kline and Ceropski concluded that although many of the students demonstrated person-centered communication skills in their videotaped interactions, whether they employed them in the interaction depended on how the student evaluated the patient's motivational characteristics and how the student viewed the medical encounter, which is central to highly cognitive complex persons.

Gillotti (1996) examined the ways in which 54 third-year medical students at a large Southern university delivered bad news. Using the general constructivist framework outlined previously, Gillotti measured the interpersonal complexity of the students as well as the complexity of 527 third-party evaluators. The students then engaged in videotaped interactions with a standardized patient in which the student had 11 minutes to tell the patient she was HIV positive.

These videotaped interactions were evaluated for evidence of patient-centered verbal communication strategies utilized by the medical students in their attempts to comfort the patient and for nonverbal immediacy and altercentricism. Coders used a modified version of Burleson's (1984) comforting scale for assessment of patient-centered communication. The interviews were analyzed first for the number of attempts to comfort the patient that were displayed by the medical student. The patient-centered quality of the comforting attempts was then coded. Each was given a numerical rating from 1 to 9, with 9 being the most sophisticated, patient-centered form of comforting. The scale divides interactions into three major levels with three levels embedded within each major level. The major levels are divided as follows: (a) denial of the patient's perspective, (b) implicit recognition of patient's feelings–perspective, and (c) explicit recognition of patient's feelings–perspective (Burleson, 1984).

Detailed data analyses from this study point to the promise of extending a communication theory like constructivism to study bad news delivery in health contexts. The study captured clear individual differences in the person-centered communication abilities of students. As predicted, medical students with high-cognitive complexity scores were evaluated as more person- centered in the interaction by expert and lay evaluators. Overall, the average comforting strategy utilized by the medical students was a 6, which indicates an implicit attempt to comfort the patient. However, the most frequently used strategy was a 7, indicating explicit attempts to comfort the patient. Perhaps most interesting, evaluations of the medical students' communication by 527 third-party evaluators who viewed the videotapes suggested that those medical students exhibiting more person-centered verbal comforting strategies and more immediate nonverbal behaviors were rated higher in communication competence.

FUTURE DIRECTIONS

On first examination, the explanation of illness may appear to be a minor, communicative task to be accomplished in the health care setting. However, this chapter has revealed that the explanation of illness should be considered and executed as carefully as any clinical procedure. The outcome of delivering health care information, especially bad news, has serious implications for the physician–patient interaction and, like all communication in this context, is directly related to important outcome variables such as patient satisfaction and compliance (Thompson, 1994).

This chapter has noted that much of the work done in explaining illness as bad news is anecdotal in nature. Although it may prove to be sound advice, it fails to grant researchers the luxury to make theoretical and empirical generalizations about this important communicative responsibility. We believe that to take a step closer to certainty in explaining illness as bad news requires using constructivism as the theoretical perspective.

As the previous literature demonstrates, the higher a person's construct differentiation and abstraction scores, generally the more person-centered they are in the interaction. For this reason, constructivism serves as an important theoretical underpinning to the study of the individual differences in the person-centered communication skills of health professionals because it examines the communicative ability, skills development, and overall communicative competence of individuals. The utilization of constructivism to study and to train health care providers will emphasize developing the individual holistically as a competent communicator, who will then be able to negotiate varying communication challenges, including comforting patients while explaining their diagnosis and prognosis. Recent studies utilizing constructivism as the theoretical underpinning have extended the theory by examining nonverbal behaviors as well as verbal in defining competent communication.

These results—and those in the admittedly limited number of studies that have applied constructivism analyses of person-centered communication in health contexts—provide evidence for the continued application of constructivism to explaining illness as bad news and provider–patient communication. This theoretical framework will not only allow us to capture the nature of the differences in communication ability that exist among health care providers but also to understand why those differences exist and how to develop educational practices that enhance person-centered communication as an effective and adaptive communication response in health settings.

Scholars conducting research about health and communication are committed to contributing to the quality of communication training for health professionals. Communication research offers the theoretical basis that identifies the essential skills needed for the medical education curricula of the 21st century. Adopting a person-centered approach to communication—or, in this case, a patient-centered approach—has begun the transformation of the medical culture called for by Stewart et al. (1995). There is struggle in all change, but responding to the call and the needs of the changing health care system will lead to a more complete educational experience for health care providers and, more important, to competent communication in the health-care context.

REFERENCES

Applegate, J. L. (1990). Constructs and communication: A pragmatic integration. In G. Neimeyer & R. Neimeyer (Eds.), *Advances in personal construct psychology* (Vol. 1, pp. 203–230). Greenwich, CT: JAI.

Applegate, J. L., & Delia, J. G. (1980). Person-centered speech, psychological development, and the contexts of language usage. In R. St. Clair & H. Giles (Eds.), *The social and psychological contexts of language.* (pp. 245–282). Hillsdale, NJ: Lawrence Erlbaum Associates.

Applegate, J. L., Kline, S. L., & Delia, J. G. (1991). Alternative measures of cognitive complexity as predictors of communicative performance. *International Journal of Personal Construct Psychology, 4,* 193–213.

Applegate, J. L., & Woods, E. (1991). Construct system development and attention to face wants in persuasive situations. *The Southern Communication Journal, 56,* 24–31.

Berger, C. R., & Bradac, J. J. (1982). *Language and social knowledge: Uncertainty in interpersonal relations.* London: Edward Arnold Ltd.

Beyene, Y. (1992). Medical disclosure and refugee: Telling bad news to Ethiopian patients. *Western Journal of Medicine, 157,* 328–332.

Brewin, T. B. (1991). Three ways of giving bad news. *The Lancet, 337,* 1207–1210.

Buckman, R. (1992). *How to break bad news, A guide for health care professionals.* Baltimore, MD: The Johns Hopkins University Press.

Burgoon, J. K. (1985). Nonverbal signals. In M. L. Knapp & G. R. Miller (Eds.), *Handbook of interpersonal communication* (pp. 344–390). Newbury Park, CA: Sage.

Burleson, B. R. (1984). Age, social-cognitive development and the use of comforting strategies. *Communication Monographs, 51,* 140–153.

Burleson, B. R. (1989). The constructivist approach to person-centered communication: Analysis of a research exemplar. In B. A. Dervin, L. Grossberg, B. J. O'Keefe, & E. Wartella (Eds.) *Rethinking communication, Vol. 2: Paradigm exemplars* (pp. 29–46). Newbury Park, CA: Sage.

Burleson, B. R., Delia, J. G., & Applegate, J. L. (1992). Effects of maternal communication and children's social-cognitive and communication skills on children's acceptance by the peer group. *Family Relations, 41,* 264–272.

Burleson, B. R., & Waltman, M. S. (1988). Cognitive complexity: Using the role category questionnaire. In C. H. Tardy (Ed.), *A handbook for the study of communication* (pp. 1–36). Norwood, NJ: Ablex.

Charlton, R. C. (1992). Breaking bad news. *The Medical Journal of Australia, 157,* 615–621.

Clark, R. A., & Delia, J. G. (1979). Topoi and rhetorical competence. *The Quarterly Journal of Speech, 65,* 187–206.

Coker, D. A., & Burgoon, J. K. (1987). The nature of conversational involvement and nonverbal encoding patterns. *Human Communication Research, 14,* 167–202.

Cousins, N. (1976). Anatomy of an illness (as perceived by the patient). *The New England Journal of Medicine, 295,* 1458–1463.

Davis, H. (1991). Breaking bad news. *The Practitioner, 235,* 522–526.

Delia, J. G., O'Keefe, B. J., & O'Keefe, D. J. (1982). The constructivist approach to communication. In F. E. Dance (Ed.), *Human communication theory.* 147–190. New York: Harper & Row.

DiMatteo, M. R. (1979). A social-psychological analysis of physician–patient rapport: Toward a science of the art of medicine. *Journal of Social Issues, 35,* 12–33.

Fallowfield, L. (1993). Giving sad and bad news. *The Lancet, 341,* 476–478.

Flynn, S. P., & Hekelman, F. P. (1993). Reality shock: A case study in the socialization of new residents. *Family Medicine, 25,* 633–636.

Gillotti, C. M. (1996). *Individual differences in the delivery of bad news among third year medical students to patients.* Unpublished doctoral dissertation, University of Kentucky, Lexington.

Goffman, E. (1959). *The presentation of self in everyday life.* Garden City, NY: Doubleday.

Graham, J. R. (1991). Touching and imparting of bad news. *The Lancet, 337,* 1608–1609.

Hafferty, F. W. (1991). *Into the valley: Death and the socialization of medical students.* New Haven, CT: Yale University Press.

Hale, C. L. (1982). An investigation of the relationship between cognitive complexity and listener-adapted communication. *Central States Speech Journal, 33,* 339–344.

Jensen, K. (1993). Care-beyond virtue and command. *Health Care for Women International, 14,* 345–354.

Kaiser, R. M. (1993). The challenge of breaking bad news. *Hospital Practice, 28*(10A) 8–14.

Kasch, C. R., & Dine, J. (1988). Person-centered communication and social perspective taking. *Western Journal of Nursing Research, 10,* 317–326.

Kelly, G. A. (1955). *The psychology of personal constructs* (2 vols). New York: W. W. Norton.

Kline, S. L., & Ceropski, J. M. (1984). Person-centered communication in medical practice. In G. M. Phillips & J. T. Wood (Eds.), *Emergent issues in human decision-making* (pp. 120–141). Carbondale: Southern Illinois University Press.

Krahn, G. L., Hallum, A., & Kime, C. (1993). Are there good ways to give 'bad news'? *Pediatrics, 91,* 578–582.

Manusov, V. (1991). Perceiving nonverbal messages: Effects of immediacy and encoded intent on receiver judgments. *Western Journal of Speech Communication, 55,* 235–253.

Maynard, D. W. (1989). Notes on the delivery and reception of diagnostic news regarding mental disabilities. In D. T. Helm, W. T. Anders, A. J. Meehan, & A. W. Rawls (Eds.), *The interactional order: New directions in the study of social order* (pp. 54–67). New York: Irvington.

Maynard, D. W. (1991). Bearing bad news in clinical settings. In B. Dervin & M. J. Voigt (Eds.), *Progress in communication sciences,* (Vol. 10, pp. 143–172). Norwood, NJ: Ablex.

McLauchlan, C. A. J. (1990). Handling distressed relatives and breaking bad news. *British Medical Journal, 301,* 1145–1149.

McWhinney, I. (1989). The need for a transformed clinical method. In M. Stewart & D. Roter (Eds.), *Communicating with medical patients* (pp. 25–40). Beverly Hills, CA: Sage.

Miranda, J., & Brody, R. V. (1992). Communicating bad news. *Western Journal of Medicine, 156,* 83–85.

Mizrahi (1991). *Getting rid of patients.* Brunswick, NJ: Rutgers University Press.

Morton, R. (1996). Breaking bad news to patients with cancer. *Professional Nurse, 11,* 669–671.

Novack, D. H., Volk, G., Drossman, D. A., & Lipkin, M. (1993). Medical interviewing and interpersonal skills teaching in US medical schools: Progress, problems, and promise. *Journal of the American Medical Association, 269,* 2101–2105.

O'Keefe, B. J., & Delia, J. G. (1982). Impression formation and message production. In M. E. Roloff & C. R. Berger (Eds.), *Social cognition and communication.* Beverly Hills, CA: Sage Publications.

Platt, F. W., & Keller, V. F. (1994). Empathic communication: A teachable and learnable skill. *Journal of General Internal Medicine, 9,* 222–225.

Ptacek, J. T., & Eberhardt, T. L. (1996). Breaking bad news: A review of the literature. *Journal of American Medical Association, 276,* 496–502.

Quill, T. E., & Townsend, P. (1991). Bad news: Delivery, dialogue, and dilemmas. *Archives of Internal Medicine, 151,* 463–468.

Rappaport, W., & Witzke, D. (1993). Education about death and dying during the clinical years of medical school. *Surgery, 113,* 163–165.

Sell, L., Devlin, B., & Bourke, S. (1993). Communicating the diagnosis of lung cancer. *Respiratory Medicine, 87,* 61–63.

Sharp, M. C., Strauss, R. P., & Lorch, S. C. (1992). Communicating medical bad news: Parents' experiences and preferences. *Journal of Pediatrics, 121,* 539–546.

Speck, P. (1991). Breaking bad news. *Nursing Times, 87,* 25–26.

Spitzberg, B. H., & Hecht, M. L. (1984). Component model of relational competence. *Human Communication Research, 10,* 575–599.

Statham, H., & Dimavicius, J. (1992). How do you give the bad news to parents? *Birth, 19,* 103–104.

Stewart, M., Brown, J. B., Weston, W. W., McWhinney, I. R., McWilliam, C. L., & Freeman, T. R. (1995). *Patient-centered medicine: Transforming the clinical method.* Thousand Oaks, CA: Sage.

Swanson, R. W. (1993). Psychological issues in CPR. *Annuals of emergency medicine, 22*(2), 350.

Thompson, T. L. (1994). Interpersonal communication and health care. In M. L. Knapp & G. R. Miller (Eds.), *Handbook of interpersonal communication* (pp. 696–725). Newbury Park, CA: Sage.

Waitzkin, H. (1985). Information giving in medical care. *Journal of Health and Social Behavior, 26,* 81–101.

Waldron, V., & Applegate, J. L. (1994). Cognitive complexity and conversational planning as antecedents to person-centered conflict communication. *Human Communication Research, 21,* 3–35.

Willihnganz, S. C. (1987, November). *Impact of individual differences in social cognition and message strategy use on perceptions of social support in nurses.* Paper presented at the annual meeting of the Speech Communication Association, Boston.

Werner, H. (1957). The concept of development from a comparative and organismic point of view. In D. B. Harris (Ed.), *The concept of development.* Minneapolis, MN: University of Minnesota.

Werner, H., & Kaplan, B. (1963). *Symbolic formation.* New York: John Wiley & Sons.

Wesley, G. (1996). *Affective orientation: Its role in compliance- gaining in physician-patient and nurse-patient interactions.* Unpublished doctoral dissertation, University of Kentucky, Lexington.

Woods, E. (1993). *An integration of the assessment of verbal and nonverbal components of interpersonal communication competence from a constructivist perspective.* Unpublished doctoral dissertation, University of Kentucky, Lexington.

POPULATIONS
AND NEW SOURCES
OF EXPLANATION

5

Explaining Illness to Patients with Limited Literacy

Terry C. Davis
Departments of Medicine and Pediatrics
Louisiana State University Medical Center, Shreveport

Mark V. Williams
Division of General Medicine
Emory University School of Medicine

William T. Branch, Jr.
Division of General Medicine
Emory University School of Medicine

Kristen W. Green
Department of Medicine
Louisiana State University Medical Center, Shreveport

Physicians' core clinical skill is communication; however, many patients have difficulty understanding their doctors' instructions (Cohen-Cole, 1991; Mayeaux et al., 1996). Even immediately after leaving their physicians' offices, patients are able to correctly identify only about 50% of the critical information just given to them (Cohen-Cole, 1991; Kitagawa &

123

Hauser, 1973; Stamler, Hardy, & Payne, 1987). Patients with poor literacy skills probably account for a substantial portion of these patients, and they certainly have a poorer understanding of common medical terms (Gibbs, Gibbs, & Henrich, 1987; Mayeaux et al., 1996) and written health materials than literate patients (Davis, Bocchini et al., 1996; Davis, Fredrickson et al., 1998; Davis, Holcombe, Berkel, Pramanik, & Divers, 1998; Williams et al., 1995).

Health care providers implicitly assume patients comprehend their written and oral explanations of illness. However, more than 40 million U.S. citizens with limited literacy are unable to process adequately and use the health information they receive. Another 50 million with marginal literacy skills struggle with health messages (Kirsch, Jungeblut, Jenkins, & Kolstad, 1993).

These individuals are at a disadvantage in navigating the health care system (Baker, Parker, Williams, Pitkin et al., 1996; Weiss & Coyne, 1997; Weiss, Coynes, & Michielutte, 1998). The ramifications of this deficit are missed doctors' appointments, pills taken at incorrect times or inappropriate dosages, and consent not informed because patients cannot adequately understand the written or oral health communication that is taken for granted by health care providers (Doak, Doak, Friedell, & Meade, 1998; Mayeaux et al., 1996; Miles & Davis, 1995; Weiss, Hart, & Pust, 1991; Williams et al., 1995). Simplifying written materials, relying solely on oral explanation, or both cannot be assumed to be adequate substitutes (Davis, Fredrickson et al., 1998; Davis, Holcombe et al., 1998).

Understanding the factors that contribute to (mis)understanding illness explanations by persons with limited literacy is paramount to solving the problem. This chapter discusses the high prevalence of inadequate literacy in the United States and the impact of patients' literacy skills on health communication. After a review of current research examining the issue, we provide recommendations to optimize explaining illness to patients with limited literacy.

INADEQUATE LITERACY IN AMERICA

According to the National Adult Literacy Survey (NALS; Kirsch et al., 1993), considered to be the most accurate portrait of literacy in our society, almost half (48%) of U.S. adults lack the necessary skills to function adequately in our society. These 90 million citizens lack the ability to "read, write, and speak in English, and compute and solve problems at levels of proficiency necessary to function on the job and in society, to achieve one's goals, and develop one's knowledge and potential" (Kirsch et al., 1993, p.3).

The NALS assessed practical, everyday reading and math skills needed to function in the United States in the 1990s. This household survey of over

26,000 adults required participants to respond to a series of diverse literacy tasks that were scored on five levels (Table 5.1). NALS found 40 to 44 million Americans, or 21 to 24%, scored in the lowest level and another 50 million or 27% in Level 2. Thirty one percent scored in Level 3 and could be considered to have marginal literacy skills. The 15% in Level 4 and 3% in Level 5 are considered to have adequate literacy skills to face the 21st century (Kirsch et al., 1993). These statistics are important for health providers because they show that only about 18% of adults, those in Levels 4 and 5 (Table 5.1), can adequately handle most explanations of illness, oral and written health instructions, and patient education.

There is no direct conversion between functional literacy as measured by the NALS and reading grade level as measured by standardized reading tests. However, Doak, Doak, and Root (1996) estimated that people who score on NALS Level 1 are reading below a fifth-grade level. This means about 1 in 5 Americans reads below a fifth-grade level. Rates double for Americans over 65 and inner-city minorities, the primary users of Medicare and Medicaid. Yet, Americans are reportedly more educated now than at any previous time in our history, with the average educational attainment of adults being above the 12th-grade level (Kirsch et al., 1993; Stedman & Kaestle, 1991). However, education level does not necessarily translate into a corresponding level of reading. Despite increasing educa-

TABLE 5.1

Example of Functional Literacy Tasks by Level in the National Adult Literacy Survey

Level	Task
Level 1	Total an entry on a deposit slip.
	From a form, locate the time or place of a meeting.
Level 2	Determine the difference in price of two items.
	Locate an intersection on a street map.
Level 3	Write a brief letter explaining an error on a bill.
	Use a bus schedule.
Level 4	Determine correct change using a menu.
	Explain the difference in two types of employee benefits.
Level 5	Interpret a lengthy newspaper article.
	Use a calculator to determine the cost of carpet to cover a room.

Note. Adapted from Kirsch et al. (1993).

tion, average reading skills of U.S. adults are between the 8th and 9th grade level (Stedman & Kaestle, 1991).

People with inadequate literacy skills come from a variety of backgrounds; they are native-born and immigrant, come from all races and classes, and have no visible signs of disability. However, functionally illiterate adults are more likely to have more health problems, to live in poverty, to have fewer years of education, and to be older. These are many of the people cared for in our public hospitals. Among adults who reported having health problems in NALS, 45% were in Level 1 and 30% were in Level 2. Thus, 75% were in the lower literacy range and only 1% of adults reporting health problems scored in Level 5 (Kirsch et al., 1993).

INADEQUATE LITERACY IN HEALTH CARE SETTINGS

The findings in NALS have been corroborated in the health care setting. People who score in Levels 1 and 2 on the NALS survey also probably lack the basic reading and numerical tasks required to function in the health care environment. Williams et al. (1995) were the first to quantify health literacy. *Functional health literacy* is defined as the ability to perform health-related tasks requiring reading and computational skills (Parker, Baker, Williams, & Nurss, 1995). An evaluation of more than 2,500 patients at two public hospitals, using their native language (English or Spanish), revealed that 42% could not understand directions for taking medication on a empty stomach, 26% could not understand an appointment slip, and 60% could not understand a standard informed consent document. In all, 35% of the English-speaking patients and 62% of the Spanish-speaking patients had inadequate or marginal functional health literacy. The prevalence of inadequate or marginal functional health literacy was more pronounced among the elderly (those over age 60). More than 80% of English-speaking patients over the age of 60 at the public hospital in Atlanta had inadequate health literacy (Williams et al., 1995).

Impact of Literacy on Patient–Provider Communication

Limited health knowledge, inability to understand basic health vocabulary, and impaired ability to assimilate new information and concepts play varying roles in low-literate patients' ability to communicate with health care providers and care for themselves (Doak, Doak, & Root, 1996; Gibbs et al., 1987; Mayeaux et al., 1996; Miles & Davis, 1995; Samora, Saunders, & Larson, 1961; Seligman, McGrath, & Pratt, 1957; Weiss et al., 1991; Williams et al., 1995). Simple instructions such as take medicine orally, on an empty stomach, or three times a day are daunting to many low-literate patients. They commonly do not understand the context, detail, or significance of their diagnoses (Jolly, Scott, & Sanford, 1995; Logan, Schwab, Salomone, & Watson, 1996; Spandorfer, Karras, Hughes, & Caputo, 1995), and discharge instructions are too complex for them (Jolly, Scott, Feied, & Sanford, 1993; Williams, Counselman, & Caggiano, 1996). A study in senior citizens' public-assistance housing complexes found that participants with the poorest literacy skills reported greater difficulty understanding information given to them by health care providers (Weiss, Reed, & Klingman, 1995). Patients with poor literacy who suffer from a chronic disease such as diabetes or asthma are also less likely to understand their disease and treatment (Williams, Baker, Honig, Lee, & Nowlan, 1998; Williams, Baker, Parker, & Nurss, 1998).

Differences in the Communication Process.   An unidentified problem in provider–patient communication is that individuals with low literacy skills deal with communication differently than those with higher skills (Doak et al., 1998). This often results in a mismatch between the provider's communication process of explaining illness or giving medical advice and the patient's ability to understand and remember the information. For example, patients with low literacy may take instructions literally, miss the context, and not make inferences from factual data (Doak, Doak, & Root, 1996).

Doak et al. (1998) believed that there needs to be a reasonable overlap in the language and logic of health information that providers give and the patient's language, logic, and experience. Patients need advice that they understand and makes sense to them; they need information that, from their perspective, is logical, achievable, and worthwhile.

Patients with low literacy may not get a relevant explanation of illness because physicians' explanations are based on their perspective and conceptualization of illness, not the patients'. There is often an unrecognized contrast between physicians' and patients' health education and health logic (Doak et al., 1998). Physicians' health logic is based on a medical model. For example, physicians' thinking about risks and benefits of cancer screening is based on scientific studies and statistics. On the other hand, low-literate patients' education and thinking about the risks and benefits of cancer screening may be based on stories from family and friends or those seen on television programs like *20/20*. These messages may be perceived as more relevant and motivational than statistics. If patients with low literacy are given only factual information, they are not likely to be able to infer needed behavioral direction. In fact, for these patients, the factual information may obscure behavioral information that focuses on patient action and motivation (Doak et al., 1998).

Vocabulary and Medical Terms.   Patients' limited health vocabulary, compounded by physicians' overuse of medical terms, is perhaps the major source of inadequate communication between patients and their health care providers. The types of words providers use can be very difficult for patients. For example, concept words ("normal range"), category words ("ACE inhibitors"), and value judgment words ("excessive bleeding") are often misunderstood (Doak et al., 1998). Not surprising, patients commonly complain that physicians do not explain their illness or treatment options to them in terms they can understand (Mayeaux et al., 1996; Samora et al., 1961). Samora et al. (1961) assessed 125 hospitalized patients' comprehension of 50 of the most common health words found in transcripts of physician–patient interviews. To facilitate comprehension, each word was placed in a simple sentence and read to the patient. For example, patients were asked what "pulse" meant when used in "let me feel your pulse." There was a high variation in patient comprehension of commonly used terms, ranging from 13% of patients having an adequate understanding of "terminal" to almost all (98%) understanding "vomit." Only 35% of these patients understood the word "orally," 22% understood "nerve," and just 18% comprehended "malignant." Older patients tended to have fewer years of education and were less likely to recognize words or give an incorrect or vague answer.

Patients and providers may think they are communicating adequately with a shared basic understanding of common medical terms. However, patients' ubiquitous misunderstanding of medical terms leads to miscommunication. Examples from this study exemplify the worrisome extent of the misunderstanding. "Pulse" was commonly identified as a "bad hurt or sickness," "a nerve" as "the pressure of nerves," "temperature" as "too much fever," or "check for high blood pressure," as "blood rushing through the nerves," and the like (Samora et al., 1961). In focus groups conducted in a walk-in clinic of a public hospital, Mayeaux et al. (1996) found patients with low-literacy skills were likely to think "fat in the diet" meant anything fattening, including potatoes, rice, and bread, and most were not certain what "three times a day" meant.

Patients' misunderstanding of medical terms also interferes with the utility of patient education pamphlets. Gibbs et al. (1987) found that nearly half of the family practice patients interviewed defined the word "hypertension" as meaning nervous or easily upset. One in four thought "orally" meant "how often" one takes medicine and that "sodium" referred to multiple items in the diet.

A study of the most common adult medical problem, hypertension, clearly illustrates the problems inherent in using terms perceived by health care providers to be understood by all patients. Interviews with 75 low-income patients receiving treatment for hypertension at Louisiana State University

(LSU) Medical Center in New Orleans revealed disparate interpretations for the terms applied to this disease. Most (72%) conceptualized their disease as "pressure trouble" or "pressure." Sixty percent of these patients described their disease with the terms "high blood" or "high pretension." Physicians commonly used these colloquial phrases when communicating with their patients. However, careful interviewing revealed that many of these patients thought that "high blood" was a physical disease in which the blood was too hot, too rich, or too thick. They thought "high blood" was caused by heredity, poor diet, and heat—either one's temperature, the temperature outside, or a combination of these. They believed that the way to treat "high blood" was to abstain from pork, hot or spicy foods, and grease and by various folk remedies, such as drinking lemon juice, vinegar, and garlic water (Centers for Disease Control, 1990a, 1990b).

Patients believed "high pretension" or pressure trouble was a disease of the nerves caused by stress, worry, or an anxious personality. These patients believed that during times of emotional excitement, blood pressure would shoot up rapidly toward the head and then fall back slowly. They believed the way to treat "high pretension" was to rest and relax—to take it easy (Centers for Disease Control, 1990a, 1990b). A common and dangerous misconception of these patients was that they did not need to go to the doctor or take their prescribed medicines as long as they did what they believed was the right health behavior (e.g., taking home remedies or relaxing). Thus, patients who misunderstand their diagnosis and treatment plan may be poorly compliant with their medicines and their appointments. This case illustrates the disparity in physicians' and patients' health logic and health language.

The Medical Interview.   Patients with low literacy, limited health knowledge, and insecurity in using medical terminology have hidden barriers to being effectively interviewed by health care providers. Sixty percent to 80% of the diagnostic information that physicians get is from what patients are saying (i.e., the history; Hampton, Harrison, Mitchell, Prichard, & Seymour, 1975; Kassirer, 1983; Lazare, Putnam, & Lipkin, 1995; Sandler, 1980). Problematically, patients with low literacy may not realize what information doctors need to know or they may lack the health vocabulary to report their symptoms. Checking to ensure information gathered from the patient is accurate and ensuring the patient understands information provided by the physician is the most important interviewing skill a physician has; however, it is the least utilized (Cohen-Cole & Bird, 1991; Cox, Hopkinson, & Rutter, 1981).

Low literacy may also interfere with the validity of mental status tools frequently used to screen for cognitive impairment (Mayeaux et al., 1995). Because of its brevity and ease of use, the Mini-mental State Examination

(MMSE; Folstein, Folstein, & McHugh, 1975) is commonly used to screen and follow patients in nursing homes. Physicians who rely on the MMSE should be aware that patients may score in the demented range because they cannot read or count well enough to accurately complete some of the items on the test, such as writing a complete sentence, following instructions to close their eyes, or counting backwards from 100 by sevens.

Comprehension of Instructions and Compliance. Patients with low literacy and inadequate knowledge of health vocabulary and concepts obtain much less information from health care instructions (Doak, Doak, & Root, 1996). They may feel overwhelmed with information, yet they tend to ask fewer questions (Mayeaux et al., 1996). Moreover, providers may give too much detailed information or information that is not relevant or useful to them (Cacioppo & Petty, 1982; Doak, Doak, & Root, 1996; Mayeaux et al., 1996; Reid et al., 1995). These problems, which are often hidden, may lead to poor compliance. Patients with poor literacy skills may often take medications at the wrong dosage or frequency and are not always cognizant of important side-effects or the need for follow-up testing (Baker, Parker, Williams, Pitkin et al., 1996; Mayeaux et al., 1996). Even when patients are motivated, their inadequate literacy may still be a barrier to compliance.

A real clinical case illustrates the complications and morbidity resulting from a patient's inadequate literacy:

A 66-year-old patient with high blood pressure, angina, diabetes, and mild heart failure presented to a Medicine clinic for her routine appointment. She was taking four separate oral medicines as well as insulin. Her blood pressure and diabetes were poorly controlled, so her medications were adjusted, and she was scheduled to be seen the following week. At the second visit, her blood pressure and diabetes remained poorly controlled, and she had suffered two episodes of angina. Her medicines were again adjusted, and a fifth oral medicine was added. At the third clinic visit, her blood pressure and diabetes were still poorly controlled, and because of worsening angina and heart failure she required admission to the hospital. After initial emergent treatment, subsequent therapy with her prescribed outpatient medical regimen promptly caused hypoglycemia and hypotension with prolongation of the hospitalization. Careful review with the patient of her medication regimen revealed she could not read her prescription labels, the numbers on the insulin syringes, or any educational material given to her. She had no idea how to take any of her medicines! Usually she took far less than the prescribed amounts. Finally, she was provided appropriate one-on-one education that ensured her understanding of the medications and proper dosing. Her blood pressure and diabetes were well controlled at subsequent outpatient visits. (R. Jackson, personal communication, March 13, 1991)

This case illustrates that, in the treatment of chronic disease, a patient's literacy may be a fundamental yet hidden barrier to their compliance. A study in general medical clinics at public hospitals in Los Angeles and Atlanta supports the implications of this anecdote. Researchers evaluated 402 patients with hypertension and 114 with diabetes mellitus to determine the association of patients' literacy skills with knowledge about their conditions. Patients' functional health literacy strongly correlated with knowledge of their illness. For example, among patients with inadequate literacy and diabetes, only half knew the symptoms of hypoglycemia, compared to 94% of those with adequate literacy. Similarly, fewer low-literate patients with hypertension, compared to literate patients, knew that a blood pressure of 160/100 is high, or that blood pressure can be lowered with weight loss and exercise (Williams et al., 1998).

Another study of 483 patients with asthma yielded similar results; poor literacy skills correlated with less knowledge of asthma and improper metered-dose inhaler skills. When statistical adjustments were made for education and other sociodemographic covariables, literacy level was the strongest correlate of health knowledge and disease management skills (Williams et al., 1998).

Preventive Health. Inadequate literacy also serves as a barrier to preventive health measures. Public health messages, patient education materials, and provider recommendations concerning disease prevention and screening are usually not aimed at patients with limited literacy. To participate in health prevention behaviors and screening, patients need to have a basic understanding of these concepts. Davis, Arnold et al. (1996) found a common lack of accurate information about mammography among patients with limited literacy skills; 39% of women reading below a fourth-grade level did not know why women are given mammograms, compared with 12% of those reading at or above a 9th-grade level. Patients who had inadequate reading skills did not know that mammography was associated with cancer, looking for a lump, or an examination of the breast. Conversely, women with adequate literacy skills who read on at least a 9th-grade level appeared to be adequately informed about mammography.

Further, patients with poor literacy skills cannot adequately access the vast array of public health information available. They are outside the societal flow of information that brings people to health care. For example, they cannot read and understand messages about the value of screening mammography or flu shots commonly found in magazine articles, displayed on posters in supermarkets and clinics, or on billboards along highways. It is unlikely that television can fully counterbalance this lack of access (Miles & Davis, 1995).

Patient autonomy, the cornerstone of American medical ethics in the 1990s, requires patients to be knowledgeable in order to gain full advantage from the myriad of available treatments. Health care increasingly relies on patients to make their own decisions about the risk and benefits of procedures, disease screening, and treatment. As these issues become more complex and patients' responsibility expands for full participation in their health care, disparity grows between patients' abilities and needed health literacy skills.

Impact of Literacy on Written Health Communication

For patients with poor literacy skills, health care is becoming ever more complex with increasing reliance on written materials for patient communication. Many health maintenance organizations (HMOs) rely on newsletters to communicate with patients suffering from chronic diseases such as asthma or diabetes. Technologic advances in health care also require greater patient participation in and understanding of their treatment. For example, patients discharged from the hospital 25 years ago after a heart attack were only given words of support and counseling to "take it easy." Today, such patients are commonly prescribed four or more medications (e.g. aspirin, beta-blocker, cholesterol lowering agent, ACE inhibitor, other anti-hypertensives such as a diuretic, nitrates, or any combination of these) and counseled to adjust their diet and begin an exercise regimen.

However, numerous studies document that health materials such as patient education brochures are often written at levels exceeding patient reading skills (Cooley et al., 1995; Davis, Crouch, Wills, Miller, & Abdehou, 1990; Davis et al., 1994; Dollahite, Thompson, & McNew, 1996; Glazer, Kirk, & Bosler, 1996; Jackson et al., 1991; Jackson, Davis, Murphy, Bairnsfather, & George, 1994; Meade, Diekmann, & Thornhill, 1992; Petterson, Dornan, Albert, & Lee, 1994). Emergency department discharge instructions contain pertinent information on home health care; yet they are written on too high a level for a majority of American adults (Chacon, Kissoon, & Rich, 1994; Jolly et al., 1993; Powers, 1988). Contraception instructions are often not easy to read or user-friendly for target audiences (Ledbetter, Hall, Swanson, & Forrest, 1990; Swanson et al., 1990; Wells, Ruscavage, Parker, & McArthur, 1994).

Providers have an ethical as well as legal responsibility to ensure that individuals understand the procedures, options, risks and benefits, and other elements of informed consent for invasive procedures, research, or both (Department of Health and Human Services, 1991). However, numerous studies have found that consent documents are written at too high of a reading level for many patients to understand (Baker & Taub, 1983; Grossman, Piantadosi, & Covahey, 1994; Grundner, 1980; Hopper, TenHave, & Hartzel, 1995; LoVerde, Prochazka, & Byyny, 1989; Meade & Howser, 1992; Morrow, 1980; Rivera, Reed, & Menius, 1992). Williams et al. (1995) found that fewer than half of participants in public hospitals in Atlanta and Los Angeles could comprehend the standard consent document used for invasive procedures at the Atlanta hospital. Cassileth, Zupkis, Sutton-Smith, and March (1980) found that 60% of patients participating in a study conducted in Philadelphia understood the purpose and nature of medical procedures to which they had signed written consent just one day before and that only 40% of the participants reported they had read the form carefully. Cassileth et al. concluded that the difficulty of the material and its legalistic wording imposed barriers to the patients' comprehension of information intended to facilitate informed decisions. However, Davis, Holcombe et al. (1998) and Davis, Fredrickson et al. (1998) found that simplifying consent documents to a 7th-grade level, shortening them, and adding graphics made the forms more appealing and easier to read, but this did not improve comprehension significantly. Comprehension of the forms was virtually the same for each form (58% simplified form vs. 56% standard form).

Reading the consent document is only one element in an interactive, multifaceted informed consent process; however, we know surprisingly little about which type of messages, approaches, and patient education materials will enhance the comprehension of patients with inadequate literacy skills (Davis, Holcombe et al., 1998).

Identification of Patients with Low Literacy

Any attempt to overcome the barrier of patients' inadequate literacy first requires identifying those who need extra help. With this knowledge, health practitioners can adjust the delivery of verbal messages, written materials, and new technologies to aid the illness explanation process. Providers cannot assume they can recognize patients with poor literacy skills. People with limited literacy may not realize they have a problem (Kirsch et al., 1993) and often will attempt to hide it if they do (Davis, Long et al., 1993; Doak, Doak, & Root, 1996; Parikh, Parker, Nurss, Baker, & Williams, 1996). A remarkable two thirds of people in Level 1 on the NALS describe themselves as being able to read "well" or "very well" and more than 90% of those in Level 2 believe this (Kirsch et al., 1993). Parikh et al. (1996) found that low literacy was a tremendous source of shame. Among patients with low literacy, 67.2% had never told their spouse, 53.4% had never told their children, and 19% had never disclosed their difficulty to anyone. Lack of recognition of limited literacy skills or profound shame complicates the task of health care professionals who want to recognize and tailor health education messages to low-literate patients.

Assessment of patients' reading skills is helpful if health care providers want to effectively communicate with their patients (Davis, Long et al., 1993; Doak, Doak, & Root, 1996). Testing a sample of patients in a clinic or hospital system can guide health professionals in fine tuning communication skills and selecting and developing educational materials and clinical interventions (Davis, Michielutte, Askov, Williams, & Weiss, 1998; Weiss, Coyne, & Michielutte, 1998). Individual testing alerts providers that a particular patient may have problems with basic clinician–patient communication and need simple verbal and written instructions that focus on providing basic information (Doak, Doak, & Root, 1996).

The Rapid Estimate of Adult Literacy in Medicine (REALM; Davis, Crouch, & Long, 1993; Murphy, Davis, Jackson, Long, & Decker, 1993) and the Wide Range Achievement Test–Third Edition (WRAT-3; Jastak & Wilkinson, 1993) are the most commonly used reading assessments in medical settings. Both are quick and easy to administer and score. REALM was developed especially for use in health care settings. However, recognizing reading difficulties does not always require a test. An Internist in Atlanta asks patients to read the label on a pill bottle she keeps in her lab pocket (R. Parker, personal communication, May 1, 1996); other physicians ask patients to read instructions. Pediatric nurse practitioners in Milwaukee are alerted to the possibility of low literacy in mothers who fill out intake forms incorrectly, incompletely, or misspell or misuse common terms such as "step throat" (Davis, 1997). Public health nurses in Wichita, Kansas are suspicious when mothers return immunization risk forms with all the items checked (Davis, Cross, & Fredrickson, 1998). Clinicians have reported numerous strategies used by their patients to hide their poor reading ability, including use of statements such as, "I forgot my reading glasses," "I don't need to read this through now. I'll read it when I get home," or, "I'd like to discuss this with my family first. May I take the instructions home?" (Doak, Doak, & Root, 1996).

IMPROVING ILLNESS EXPLANATIONS TO PATIENTS WITH LIMITED LITERACY

Discovering that a substantial portion of a patient population has low-level reading skills may require evaluation and revision of the overall educational approach used in a clinic. Providers need to be aware that patients with inadequate literacy skills may be anxious and feel ashamed about being expected to read and fill out intake questionnaires, sign consent forms, or communicate with providers. Instituting a system in which someone routinely offers help in completing forms and relatives who are invited to participate in the medical interview or patient education sessions can circumvent this problem.

Standard patient educational materials, which are generally written at a high school or college level, will rarely be useful in heath care settings that serve families with low literacy skills. Simpler, easy-to-read materials, written in the everyday language of the target population are usually needed. A few studies have shown that such materials can improve knowledge (Dowe, Lawrence, Carlson, & Keyserling, 1997; Jolly et al., 1995; Overland, Hoskins, McGill, & Yue, 1993; Young, Hooker, & Freeberg, 1990). However, even the simplest material may not be understood by individuals who have very limited literacy (Davis, Fredrickson et al., 1998; Davis, Holcombe et al., 1998). Alternative approaches such as radio, television, videotapes, audiotapes, multimedia, lay health educators, or any combination of these may be effective (Davis, Berkel et al., 1998; Meade, McKinney, & Barnas, 1994; Said, Consoli, & Jean, 1994; Sweeney & Gulino, 1988). Providers need to work with patients to develop nontraditional approaches that are helpful for both parties (Davis, Berkel et al., 1998; Rudd & Comings, 1994). As new materials and approaches are introduced, they will need to be evaluated to determine if, in fact, they are more effective in providing patients with the needed information.

Improving Delivery of Verbal Messages to Explain Illness

Despite the lack of research identifying the best method of patient education for low-literate patients, health care providers can improve their communication skills with this population. A few simple things, such as slowing down, using simple language, and including a family member in the discussion clearly help (Baker, Parker, Williams, Pitkin et al., 1996; Mayeaux et al., 1996). Communication of essential messages can be enhanced if the provider will confirm the patient's or family member's understanding of essential points at every visit. Providers may also want to confirm that medical instruction makes sense to the patient.

Providers can schedule repeat patient visits so all the messages do not have to be given during the first visit (P. Lewis, personal communication, September 30, 1997). Short sessions with limited information are more effective for people with limited literacy and limited health knowledge (Doak, Doak, & Root, 1996), and relevant stories or pictures focusing on patient behavior may be more memorable than a mini lecture of instructions (Doak, Doak, & Meade, 1996).

It is often best for providers to demonstrate desired skills (e.g., using an asthma inhaler) rather than having patients read about the skills. Furthermore, clinicians should then have the patient demonstrate the skills to assure they have been adequately understood (Doak, Doak, & Root, 1996; Mayeaux et al., 1996; McMahon, Rimsza, & Bay, 1997; Plimpton & Root, 1994). This "show me" technique applies to many health care behaviors. For example, health care providers should not assume low-literate patients are able to read their instructions on medication bottles. Rather, they should ask the patient to "show me" how to take the medication. Health care providers may need to routinely ask patients to demonstrate their comprehension. Patients' lack of adequate knowledge will not be detected unless sought. Yet, physicians rarely, only 2% of the time in one study (Braddock, Fihn, Levinson, Jonsen, & Pearlman, 1997), assess patient understanding of their instructions.

Clinicians and health educators can inadvertently hinder communication by giving too much detailed information especially in areas that are not particularly useful to patients. Clinicians are often quick to reveal their knowledge by spewing out medical information to patients but rarely, if ever, ensure patient understanding. Patient educators also tend to want to give all the information up front. However, a person with a new diagnosis of diabetes, for example, does not need to know at the first visit about foot or eyesight complications; it is too overwhelming. However, diabetes nurse educators often hand out all of the brochures outlining everything (J. Keenan, personal communication, April 22, 1998).

Information overload can also be a problem with written materials. When 170 patients of a Sleep Disorder clinic were asked how brochures that they had been given could be improved, the patients indicated they wanted less information, fewer polysyllabic words, and that they needed medical terms defined (Chesson, Murphy, Arnold, & Davis, 1998). Cacioppo and Petty (1982) found that patients who were not professionals did not have as great a need for cognitive information as their physicians believed. Low-literacy patients often feel overwhelmed with a lot of information. With these high-risk patients, health care providers need to remember not only to use simpler words but also to slow down, check for understanding, and to give smaller bits of information.

Providers can encourage a dialogue with patients by sitting down, removing distractions, fully attending to them, and eliciting and listening to their concerns. Providers also need to consider the patients' explanation of their problem(s), their thinking and beliefs about causes and treatments, and so forth (Lazare, 1995; Lazare et al., 1995; Novack, 1995; Quill, 1995). Many barriers could be lowered with continuity of care and providers promoting an on-going dialogue that encourages patients to ask for clarification when confused or when medical advice does not seem logical, achievable, or worthwhile. However, asking patients if they understand the message is a poor question, as is "Do you have any questions?" Patients with low-literacy skills may not be able to frame questions rapidly or have the vocabulary to ask the necessary questions. Cultural directives may also prohibit some patients from questioning their physician. To check comprehension, providers need to ask patients to voice their understanding and concerns about the message or treatment plans. They might also ask patients what is important to them, what they think, what they are going to do, and how they would describe this to family members.

Patient and provider emotions also need to be considered when delivering messages about illness (Cohen-Cole, 1991; Kaplan, Greenfield, & Ware, 1989). Providers may be anxious about delivering such messages, and patients may be anxious about hearing them. In addition, patients with low literacy may be anxious about seeing a physician, in general, as well as being anxious about discussing their illness, so they may not hear essential health messages. Patients with low-literacy skills may experience the additional anxiety of not being able to read or write well enough to handle ordinary tasks expected of patients in a hospital or clinic. Providers can help decrease patient anxiety by sitting down, making eye contact, not rushing, using a calm reassuring tone of voice, and being mindful of giving nonverbal cues that send the powerful body message that the physician does care and is not distracted or rushed (Levinson, 1994; Mayeaux et al., 1996; Quill & Townsend, 1991). Asking patients if they would like a trusted family member or friend in the room may also help lower their anxiety and facilitate communication and patient education (Mayeaux et al., 1996).

Improving Written Materials to Explain Illness

With cost effectiveness as a value and goal, health care is increasingly a written culture. Persons at all literacy levels prefer to have a better understanding of simple, written materials compared to complex materials (Joint Commission on Accreditation of Health Care Organizations, 1996). For persons with limited reading skills, however, simplicity is particularly important (Davis, Bocchini et al., 1996; Doak, Doak, & Root, 1996; Ley, Jain, & Skilbeck, 1976; Meade, Byrd, & Lee, 1989). Individuals with limited reading skills take words literally rather than in context. They read slowly and either skip over or become confused by unfamiliar words. They tire quickly and often miss the context in which words are presented (Doak, Doak, & Meade, 1996; Doak, Doak, & Root, 1996).

Interviews with sleep disorder patients found that if questionnaires or patient education materials are mailed to patients with low literacy, they will not be read unless the patients have help. Many patients reported they would not ask for help. Further, in households with just marginal readers, patients could not be assured that the help they might receive was accurate (Chesson et al., 1998). Written material for such persons must be carefully constructed to assure its reading ease and comprehensibility. The 5th-grade readability level is an appropriate goal for most health care materials intended for the public, but clinicians should keep in mind that even this level will be too difficult for up to one fourth of the population (National Work Group on Literacy and Health, 1998). In addition, materials written on a

5th-grade level may still not be "user friendly" or "easy to read" (J. Keenan, personal communication, April 22, 1998).

Improving Nonwritten Materials to Explain Illness

Many individuals, even those who can read, frequently depend on nonwritten means of communication to obtain health-related information. Among persons who do not speak English, oral communication may be the primary method of obtaining health information (Baker, Parker, Williams, Coates, & Pitkin, 1996).

A variety of nonwritten health education materials are either available now or are currently being developed. Some are simple: picture books, slide and tape presentations, audiotapes, videotapes, models (National Work Group on Literacy and Health, 1998), and street plays (C. Kohler, personal communication, October 19, 1996). Others use highly sophisticated computer-based, multimedia technologies.

Some computer-based materials designed for adults with limited literacy assess the patients' answers and create a customized presentation for each viewer based on those responses. Interactive educational tools have been used to prepare patients' for surgical procedures (Adler, Seibring, Bhaskar, & Melamed, 1992), to communicate informed consent (Llewellyn-Thomas, Thiel, Sem, & Woermke, 1995), and to convey practical information about a variety of other health issues (Campbell et al., 1994; Kasper, Mulley, & Wennberg, 1992; Kumar, Bostow, Schapira, & Kritch, 1993; Randall, 1993). To our knowledge, nonwritten materials have not been widely studied.

Sensitivity to What Patients Need to Know

Reid et al. (1995) found that physicians and patients differed on what they felt was important to include in written illness explanations and treatment descriptions. Turner, Maher, Young, Vaughan-Hudson (1996) found that physicians did not identify outcomes that were the most important to cancer patients. For example, patients said acute side-effects were as important as long-term side-effects, and side-effects such as energy loss and change of appearance, not routinely emphasized by physicians, were more significant to them. Individual interviews with sleep-disorder patients revealed both high and low readers wanted patient education materials that briefly and simply explained treatments and side-effects (Chesson et al., 1998).

Focus groups of parents and physicians concerning immunization information revealed differences in perception of the importance of risk communication. Parents wanted to know why the immunizations were being given, the immunization schedule, common side-effects, and a little bit about rare, severe risks of immunization. Family physicians and pediatricians did not believe that most parents wanted to know about severe risk of vaccines that vaccine risks could be explained in a timely manner, or in a way that most parents could understand (Davis, Cross, & Fredrickson, 1998).

Focus groups of patients with a particular illness may help providers identify messages that are most useful (Davis, Berkel et al., 1998; Mayeaux et al., 1996). Focus groups of diabetic patients concerning oral medication instructions indicated many patients felt that doctors usually just said, "take this medicine" and gave very little helpful, patient-centered instructions with the prescription. The patients indicated they wanted to know the name of the medicine, using both the generic and trade name (doctors used the trade name and pharmacists asked if they wanted the generic). Patients also requested explicit and practical step-by-step information on how to take the medication from the patient's point of view (i.e. with food or not, what time, and how often). Patients requested information that was direct and to the point about common side-effects and the few rare side-effects for which they needed to see the physician (Davis, BeDell, & Rabbit, 1997).

Given the position of power held by health care providers over patients, providers should not expect most patients to expose their confusion with explanations, complain about wordy brochures, complicated intake forms, or reveal their own limited health knowledge (Doak, Doak, & Root, 1996; Kaplan et al., 1989). Novel approaches to patient communication and education may provide solutions to this conundrum. For instance, Davis, Berkel et al. (1998) evaluated written versus nonwritten health communication to patients providing insight into the various factors affecting patient understanding and compliance.

They evaluated the relative effectiveness of three approaches, varying from a personal recommendation to a low-literate brochure to a custom-made interactive small group program to increased mammography utilization by women in a public hospital. The custom-made program, developed and designed in partnership with target women and cofacilitated by a peer and cancer nurse, proved to be at least 30% more effective than the National Cancer Institute (NCI) brochure combined with a personal recommendation or recommendation alone. The use of a colorful, easy-to-read (5th-grade) NCI brochure in addition to a personal recommendation was no more effective than that of a recommendation alone. The results suggest that simply giving patients in public hospitals low-literate, culturally appropriate brochures will not be effective in improving mammography utilization. In fact, efforts spent creating and distributing written educational materials for low-literate audiences may do little more than foster a false sense of security among health care providers.

Davis, Berkel et al. (1998) found that the personal, woman-to-woman, warm and humorous video developed for use in small groups significantly influenced mammography utilization in the short term. This supports recent findings by Yancey, Tanjasiri, Klein, and Tunder (1995), who reported that culturally sensitive videos increased cervical cancer screening in public health centers. Such videos may influence health behavior through affective as well as cognitive channels. In Davis, Berkel et al.'s (1998) study, both the content and format of the video and the patient education program were designed and executed in collaboration with target women. This reinforces Rudd and Commings' (1994) finding that patient involvement in developing health education materials ensures that the content is relevant to the patients' situation and is presented from their viewpoint. Women in the Davis, Berkel et al. (1998) study focus groups helped write and acted in the video; in addition, a woman in one of the focus group was hired as the peer educator. Clearly, health care providers need more input from patients concerning what information they need, how they want to receive it, and from whom they want to receive it.

CONCLUSION

Clinicians, hospitals, and clinics must become more sensitive to the prevalence, significance, and management of low literacy. Low literacy is a pervasive problem in the United States and its impact on health care is just beginning to be realized. This chapter gives examples of the hidden impact of low literacy, limited health vocabulary, and misunderstanding of health concepts on provider–patient communication and patient education. Patients may not understand or may misunderstand common words or concepts such as "orally," "hypertension," "screening mammogram," "fat in the diet," or "take three times a day." Compliance may be jeopardized because patients are not certain how to dose or administer medication. Most written health care materials, such as patient-education brochures, clinic intake forms, emergency department discharge instructions, and standard consent documents are written above the reading level of over half of U.S. adults and are, therefore, not helpful to many patients.

This chapter provides strategies to identify patients with low literacy skills as well as how such knowledge might be used to improve the health care system and to refine health care messages and instructions. For example, clinics may need to evaluate and revise their overall approach to patients, including the appropriateness of their written materials and current patient education practices. More time with providers may be needed so messages can be confirmed and patients can demonstrate prescribed dosing, and the like. Family members may need to be invited to the clinic appointments, and more frequent visits may need to be scheduled so the clinician or the patient educator does not feel pressured to give too much information on the first or any other visit.

Differences in physician and patient conceptualization of illness and perception of instructions need to be considered. Physicians' health logic is based on factual information. Patients' health logical and decision making may be based on experience, stories, or hearsay. When physicians explain illness or give advice using only factual information, patients may not perceive the information as logical, relevant, or worthwhile or be able to infer needed behavioral information. Patients request simple, to-the-point instructions given from the patients' point-of-view that include explicit but brief information on how to take prescribed medication, common side-effects, risks, and what symptoms indicate the need to return for evaluation. Despite health care providers' beliefs, patients do not need to be told everything all at once. Providers are advised that patients with low literacy are likely to ask few, if any questions, and checking comprehension by asking, "Do you understand?" or "Do you have any questions?" is not useful for either the provider or the patient. To check for understanding, providers need to ask patients to voice what they are going to do and how they would describe their situation to family members.

Patients' shame and anxiety about limited reading, health vocabulary, and health knowledge limits their ability to communicate. Providers must be cognizant of these issues as they instruct patients. Finally, simpler materials, experimentation with nonwritten materials, and novel approaches to explaining illness need to be explored. Providers and clinics need to work with patients to gather their input to design materials and approaches that are relevant and useful for them. Optimizing patient–provider communication to provide high-quality health care through explaining illness can be accomplished only through collaborative efforts.

REFERENCES

Adler, D. N., Seibring, B. S., Bhaskar, D. M. D., & Melamed, B. G. (1992). Information seeking and interactive videodisc preparation for third molar extraction. *Journal of Maxillofacial Surgery, 50,* 27–31.

Baker, D., Parker, R. M., Williams, M., Coates, W., & Pitkin, K. (1996). Use and effectiveness of interpreters in an emergency department. *Journal of the American Medical Association, 275,* 783–788.

Baker, D. W., Parker, R. M., Williams, M. V., Pitkin, K., Parikh, N. S., Coates, W., & Imara, M. (1996). The health care experience of patients with low literacy. *Archives of Family Medicine, 5,* 329–334.

Baker, M. T., & Taub, H. A. (1983). Readability of informed consent forms for research in a Veterans Administration medical center. *Journal of the American Medical Association, 250,* 2646–2648.

Braddock, C. H., Fihn, S. D., Levinson, W., Jonsen, A. R., & Pearlman, R. A. (1997). How doctors and patients discuss routine clinical decisions: Informed decision making in the outpatient setting. *Journal of General Internal Medicine, 12,* 339–345.

Campbell, M. K., DeVellis, B. M., Strecher, V. J., Ammerman, A. S., DeVellis, R. F., & Sandler, R. S. (1994). Improving dietary behavior: The effectiveness of tailored messages in primary care settings. *American Journal of Public Health, 84,* 783–787.

Cacioppo, J. T., & Petty, R. E. (1982). The need for cognition. *Journal of Personality and Social Psychology, 42,* 116–131.

Cassileth, B. R., Zupkis, R. V., Sutton-Smith, K., & March, V. (1980). Informed consent—why are its goals imperfectly realized? *New England Journal of Medicine, 302,* 896–900.

Centers for Disease Control. (1990a). Health beliefs, compliance—hypertension. *Morbidity and Mortality Weekly Report, 39,* 701–704.

Centers for Disease Control. (1990b). Health beliefs, compliance—hypertension. *Journal of the American Medical Association, 264,* 2864.

Chacon, D., Kissoon, N., & Rich, S. (1994). Education attainment level of caregivers versus readability level of written instructions in a pediatric emergency department. *Pediatric Emergency Care, 10,* 144–149.

Chesson, A. L., Jr., Murphy, P. W., Arnold, C. L., & Davis, T. C. (1998). Presentation and reading level of sleep brochures: Are they appropriate for sleep disorder patients? *Sleep, 21,* 406–412.

Cohen-Cole, S. A. (1991). Why "three" functions? In S. A. Cohen-Cole (Ed.), *The medical interview: The three-function approach* (pp. 4–10). St. Louis, MO: Mosby.

Cohen-Cole, S. A., & Bird, J. (1991). Function 2: Building rapport and responding to patient's emotions (relationship skills). In S. A. Cohen-Cole (Ed.), *The medical interview: The three-function approach* (pp. 21–27). St. Louis, MO: Mosby.

Cooley, M. E., Moriarty, H., Berger, M. S., Selm-Orr, D., Coyle, B., & Short, T. (1995). Patient literacy and the readability of written cancer education materials. *Oncology Nurse Forum, 22,* 1345–1351.

Cox, A., Hopkinson, K., & Rutter, M. (1981). Psychiatric interviewing techniques: II. Naturalistic study: Eliciting factual information. *British Journal of Psychiatry, 138,* 283–291.

Davis, T. (1997, June). *Assessing parent literacy and tailoring your patient education.* In Focus '97 National Pediatric Conference. Workshop conducted at the National Pediatric Conference, Milwaukee, Wisconsin.

Davis, T. C., Arnold, C., Berkel, H., Nandy, I., Jackson, R. H., & Glass, J. (1996). Knowledge and attitude on screening mammography among low-literate, low-income women. *Cancer, 78,* 1912–1920.

Davis, T. C., Berkel, H. J., Arnold, C. L., Nandy, I., Jackson, R. H., & Murphy, P. W. (1998). Intervention study to increase mammography utilization in a public hospital. *Journal of General Internal Medicine, 13,* 230–233.

Davis, T., BeDell, S., & Rabbit, K. (1997). Focus group of medication handouts given by the physician. Unpublished raw data.

Davis, T. C., Bocchini, J. A., Jr., Fredrickson, D., Arnold, C., Mayeaux, E. J., Murphy, P. W., Jackson, R. H., Hanna, N., & Paterson, M. (1996). Parent comprehension of polio vaccine information pamphlets. *Pediatrics, 97,* 804–810.

Davis, T. C., Cross, J. T., & Fredrickson, D. D. (1998). Focus group of parents and providers concerning vaccine risk communication. Unpublished raw data.

Davis, T. C., Crouch, M., & Long, S. (1993). *Rapid estimate of adult literacy in medicine.* Shreveport: Louisiana State University Medical Center.

Davis, T. C., Crouch, M. A., Wills, G., Miller, S., & Abdehou, D. M. (1990). The gap between patient reading comprehension and the readability of patient education materials. *The Journal of Family Practice, 31,* 533–538.

Davis, T. C., Fredrickson, D. D., Arnold, C., Murphy, P. W., Herbst, M., & Bocchini, J. A. (1998). A polio immunization pamphlet with increased appeal and simplified language does not improve comprehension to an acceptable level. *Patient Education and Counseling, 33,* 25–37.

Davis, T. C., Holcombe, R. F., Berkel, H. J., Pramanik, S., & Divers, S. G. (1998). Informed consent for clinical trials: A comparative study of standard versus simplified forms. *Journal of the National Cancer Institute, 90,* 668–674.

Davis, T. C., Long, S. W., Jackson, R. H., Mayeaux, E. J., George, R. B., Murphy, P. W., & Crouch, M. A. (1993). Rapid Estimate of Adult Literacy in Medicine: A shortened screening instrument. *Family Medicine, 25,* 391–395.

Davis, T. C., Mayeaux, E. J., Fredrickson, D., Bocchini, J. A., Jr., Jackson, R. H., & Murphy, P. W. (1994). Reading ability of parents compared with reading level of pediatric patient education materials. *Pediatrics, 93,* 460–468.

Davis, T. C., Michielutte, R., Askov, E. N., Williams, M. V., & Weiss, B. D. (1998). Practical assessment of adult literacy in health care. *Health Education and Behavior, 25,* 613–624.

Department of Health and Human Services, 45 C.F.R. § 46.101–46.124 (1991).

Doak, C. C., Doak, L. G., Friedell, G. H., & Meade, C. D. (1998). Improving comprehension for cancer patients with low literacy skills: Strategies for clinicians. *CA - A Cancer Journal for Clinicians, 48,* 151–162.

Doak, C. C., Doak, L. G., & Root, J. H. (1996). *Teaching patients with low literacy skills* (2nd ed.). Philadelphia: Lippincott.

Doak, L. G., Doak, C. C., & Meade, C. D. (1996). Strategies to improve cancer education materials. *Oncology Nursing Forum, 23,* 1305–1312.

Dollahite, J., Thompson, C., & McNew, R. (1996). Readability of printed sources of diet and health information. *Patient Education and Counseling, 27,* 123–134.

Dowe, M. C., Lawrence, P. A., Carlson, J., & Keyserling, T. C. (1997). Patients' use of health-teaching materials at three readability levels. *Applied Nursing Research, 10,* 86–93.

Folstein, M. F., Folstein, S. E., & McHugh, P. R. (1975). Mini-mental state: A practical method for grading the cognitive state of patients for the clinician. *Journal of Psychiatric Research, 12,* 189–198.

Gibbs, R. D., Gibbs, P. H., & Henrich, J. (1987). Patient understanding of commonly used medial vocabulary. *The Journal of Family Practice, 25,* 176–178.

Glazer, H. R., Kirk, L. M., & Bosler, F. E. (1996). Patient education pamphlets about prevention, detection, and treatment of breast cancer for low literacy women. *Patient Education and Counseling, 27,* 185–189.

Grossman, S. A., Piantadosi, S., & Covahey, C. (1994). Are informed consent forms that describe clinical oncology research protocols readable by most patients and their families? *Journal of Clinical Oncology, 12,* 2211–2215.

Grundner, T. (1980). On the readability of surgical consent forms. *New England Journal of Medicine, 302,* 900–902.

Hampton, J. R., Harrison, M. J. G., Mitchell, J. R. A., Prichard, J. S., & Seymour, C. (1975). Relative contributions of history-taking, physical examination, and laboratory investigations to diagnosis and management of medical outpatients. *British Medical Journal,* 486–489.

Hopper, K. D., TenHave, T. R., & Hartzel, J. (1995). Informed consent forms for clinical and research imaging procedures: How much do patients understand? *American Journal of Roentgenology, 164,* 493–496.

Jackson, R. H., Davis, T. C., Bairnsfather, L. E., George, R. B., Crouch, M. A., & Gault, H. (1991). Patient reading ability: An overlooked problem in health care. *Southern Medical Journal, 84,* 1172–1175.

Jackson, R. H., Davis, T. C., Murphy, P., Bairnsfather, L. E., & George, R. B. (1994). Reading deficiencies in older patients. *The American Journal of the Medical Sciences, 308,* 79–82.

Jastak, S., & Wilkinson, G. S. (1993). *Wide range achievement test* (3rd ed.). Wilmington, VA: Jastak Associates.

Joint Commission on Accreditation of Health Care Organizations. (1996). Patient and family education. In: *Joint Commission on Accreditation of Health Care Organizations. Accreditation Manual for Hospitals.* Chicago: (pp. 211–224.)

Jolly, B. T., Scott, J. L., Feied, C. F., & Sanford, S. M. (1993). Functional illiteracy among emergency department patients: A preliminary study. *Annals of Emergency Medicine, 22,* 573–578.

Jolly, B., Scott, J., & Stanford, S. (1995). Simplification of emergency department discharge instructions improves patient comprehension. *Annals of Emergency Medicine, 26,* 443–446.

Kaplan, S. H., Greenfield, S., & Ware, J. E. (1989). Impact of the doctor–patient relationship on the outcome of chronic disease. In M. Stewart & D. Roter (Eds.), *Communicating with medical patients* (pp. 228–245). Thousand Oaks, CA: Sage.

Kasper, U. F., Mulley, A. G., & Wennberg, J. E. (1992). Developing shared decision-making program to improve the quality of health care. *QRB Quality Review Bulletin, 18,* 183–190.

Kassirer, J. P. (1983). Teaching clinical medicine by iterative hypothesis testing. *New England Journal of Medicine, 309,* 921–923.

Kirsch, I., Jungeblut, A., Jenkins, L., & Kolstad, A. (1993). *Adult literacy in America: A first look at the results of the national adult literacy survey.* Washington, DC: U.S. Department of Education.

Kitagawa, E., & Hauser, P. (1973). *Differential mortality in the United States: A study in socioeconomic epidemiology.* Cambridge, MA: Harvard University Press.

Kumar, N. B., Bostow, D. E., Schapira, D. V., & Kritch, K. M. (1993). Efficacy of interactive automated programmed instruction in nutrition education for cancer prevention. *Journal of Cancer Education, 8,* 203–211.

Lazare, A. (1995). The interview as a clinical negotiation. In M. Lipkin, Jr., S. M. Putnam, & A. Lazare (Eds.), *The medical interview: Clinical care, education and research* (pp. 50–62). New York: Springer-Verlag.

Lazare, A., Putnam, S. M., & Lipkin, M. J., Jr. (1995). Three functions of the medical interview. In M. Lipkin, Jr., S. M. Putnam, & A. Lazare (Eds.), *The medical interview: Clinical care, education, and research* (pp. 3–19). New York: Springer- Verlag.

Ledbetter, C., Hall, S., Swanson, J. M., & Forrest, K. (1990). Readability of commercial versus generic health instructions for condoms. *Health Care Women International, 11,* 295–304.

Levinson, W. (1994). Physician–patient communication: A key to malpractice prevention. *JAMA, 272,* 1619–1620.

Ley, P., Jain, V. K., & Skilbeck, C. E. (1976). A method for decreasing patients' medication errors. *Psychological Medicine, 6,* 599–601.

Llewellyn-Thomas, H. A., Thiel, E. C., Sem, F. W. C., & Woermke, D. E. H. (1995). Presenting clinical trial information: A comparison of methods. *Patient Education and Counseling, 25,* 97–107.

Logan, P. D., Schwab, R. A., Salomone, J. A., & Watson, W. A. (1996). Patient understanding of emergency discharge instructions. *Southern Medical Journal, 89,* 770–774.

LoVerde, M. E., Prochazka, A. V., & Byyny, R. L. (1989). Research consent forms: Continued unreadability and increasing length. *Journal of General Internal Medicine, 4,* 410–412.

Mayeaux, E. J., Davis, T. C., Jackson, R. H., Henry, D., Patton, P., Slay, L., & Sentell, T. (1995). Literacy and self-reported educational levels in relation to mini-mental status examination scores. *Family Medicine, 27,* 658–662.

Mayeaux, E. J., Murphy, P. W., Arnold, C., Davis, T. C., Jackson, R. H., & Sentell, T. (1996). Improving patient education for patients with low literacy skills. *American Family Physician, 53,* 205–211.

McMahon, S. R., Rimsza, M. E., & Bay, R. C. (1997). Parents can dose liquid medication accurately. *Pediatrics, 100,* 330–333.

Meade, C. D., Byrd, J. C., & Lee, M. (1989). Improving patient comprehension of literature on smoking. *American Journal of Public Health, 79,* 1411–1412.

Meade, C. D., Diekmann, J., & Thornhill, D. G. (1992). Readability of American Cancer Society patient education literature. *Oncology Nurse Forum, 19,* 51–55.

Meade, C. D., & Howser, D. M. (1992). Consent forms: How to determine and improve their readability. *Oncology Nurse Forum, 19,* 1523–1528.

Meade, C. D., McKinney, P., & Barnas, G. P. (1994). Educating patients with limited literacy skills: The effectiveness of printed and videotaped materials about colon cancer. *American Journal of Public Health, 84,* 119–120.

Miles, S., & Davis, T. (1995). Patients who can't read: Implications for the health care system. *JAMA, 274,* 1719–1720.

Morrow, G. R. (1980). How readable are subject consent forms? *Journal of the American Medical Association, 244,* 56–58.

Murphy, P. W., Davis, T. C., Jackson, R. H., Long, S. W., & Decker, B. C. (1993). Rapid estimate of adult literacy in medicine: Using a novel reading recognition test. *Journal of Reading, 37,* 124–130.

Novack, D. H. (1995). Therapeutic aspects of the clinical encounter. In M. Lipkin, Jr., S. M. Putnam, & A. Lazare (Eds.), *The medical interview: Clinical care, education and research* (pp. 32–49). New York: Springer-Verlag.

Overland, J. E., Hoskins, P. L., McGill, M. J., & Yue, D. K. (1993). Low literacy: A problem in diabetes education. *Diabetes Medicine, 10,* 847–850.

Parikh, N. S., Parker, R. M., Nurss, J. R., Baker, D. W., & Williams, M. V. (1996). Shame and health literacy: The unspoken connection. *Patient Education and Counseling, 27,* 33–39.

Parker, R. M., Baker, D. W., Williams, M. V., & Nurss, J. R. (1995). The test of functional health literacy in adults: A new instrument for measuring patients' literacy skills. *Journal of General Internal Medicine, 10,* 537–541.

Petterson, T., Dornan, T. L., Albert, T., & Lee, P. (1994). Are information leaflets given to elderly people with diabetes easy to read? *Diabetes Medicine, 11,* 111–113.

Plimpton, S., & Root, J. (1994). Materials and strategies that work in low literacy health communication. *Public Health Representative, 109,* 86–92.

Powers, R. D. (1988). Emergency department patient literacy and the readability of patient-directed materials. *Annals of Emergency Medicine, 17,* 124–126.

Quill, T. E. (1995). Barriers to effective communication. In M. Lipkin, Jr., S. M. Putnam, & A. Lazare (Eds.), *The medical interview: Clinical care, education and research* (pp. 110–121). New York: Springer-Verlag.

Quill, T. E., & Townsend, P. (1991). Bad news: Delivery, dialogue, and dilemmas. *Archives of Internal Medicine, 151,* 463–468.

Randall, T. (1993). Producers of videodisc programs strive to expand patients' role in medical decision-making process. *Journal of the American Medical Association, 270,* 160–162.

Reid, J. C., Klachko, D. M., Kardash, C. A., Robinson, R. D., Scholes, R., & Howard, D. (1995). Why people don't learn from diabetes literature: Influence of text and reader characteristics. *Patient Education and Counseling, 25,* 31–38.

Rivera, R., Reed, J. S., & Menius, D. (1992). Evaluating the readability of informed consent forms used in contraceptive clinical trials. *International Journal of Gynaecology and Obstetrics, 38,* 227–230.

Rudd, R. E., & Comings, J. P. (1994). Learner developed materials: An empowering product. *Health Education Quarterly, 21,* 313–327.

Said, M. B., Consoli, S., & Jean, J. (1994). A comparative study between a computer-aided education (ISIS) and habitual education techniques for hypertensive patients. *Journal of the American Medical Association,* (Suppl.), 10–14.

Samora, J., Saunders, L., & Larson, R. F. (1961). Medical vocabulary knowledge among hospital patients. *Journal of Health and Human Behavior,* 83–92.

Sandler, G. (1980). The importance of the history in the medical clinic and the cost of unnecessary tests. *American Heart Journal, 100,* 928–931.

Seligman, A. W., McGrath, N. E., & Pratt, L. (1957). Level of medical information among clinic patients. *Journal of Chronic Disease, 6,* 497–505.

Spandorfer, J. M., Karras, D. J., Hughes, L. A., & Caputo, C. (1995). Comprehension of discharge instructions by patients in an urban emergency department. *Annals of Emergency Medicine, 25,* 71–74.

Stamler, R., Hardy, R., & Payne, G. (1987). Educational level and five-year all-cause mortality in the hypertension detection and follow-up program. *Hypertension, 9,* 641–646.

Stedman, L. C., & Kaestle, C. F. (1991). Literacy and reading performance in the United States from 1880 to the present. In C. F. Kaestle, H. Damon-Moore, L. C. Stedman, K. Tinsley, & W. V. Trollinger, Jr. (Eds.), *Literacy in the United States* (pp. 75–128). New Haven, CT: Yale University Press.

Swanson, J. M., Forrest, K., Ledbetter, C., Hall, S., Holstine, E. J., & Shafer, M. R. (1990). Readability of commercial and generic contraceptive instructions. *Image Journal of Nursing School, 22,* 96–100.

Sweeney, M., & Gulino, C. (1988). Interactive video in health care: Blending patient care, computer technology, and research results. *Journal of Biocommunication, 15,* 6–11.

Turner, S., Maher, E. J., Young, T., Vaughan-Hudson, G. (1996). What are the information priorities for cancer patients involved in treatment decisions? An experienced surrogate study in Hodgkin's disease. *British Journal of Cancer, 73,* 222–227.

Weiss, B. D., & Coyne, C. A. (1997). Communicating with patients who cannot read. *New England Journal of Medicine, 337,* 272–273.

Weiss, B. D., Coyne, C., & Michielutte, R., (1998). Communicating with patients who have limited literacy skills: Concensus statement from the National Work Group on Literacy and Health. *The Journal of Family Practives, 46,* 168–176.

Weiss, B. D., Hart, G. H., & Pust, R. E. (1991). The relationship between literacy and health. *Journal of Health Care for the Poor and Underserved, 1,* 351–363.

Weiss, B. D., Reed, R. L., & Klingman, E. W. (1995). Literacy skills and communication methods of low-income older persons. *Patient Education and Counseling, 25,* 109–119.

Wells, J. A., Ruscavage, D., Parker, B., & McArthur, L. (1994). Literacy of women attending family planning clinics in Virginia and reading levels of brochures on HIV prevention. *Family Planning Perspectives, 26,* 113–115, 131.

Williams, D. M., Counselman, F. L., & Caggiano, C. D. (1996). Emergency department discharge instructions and patient literacy: A problem of disparity. *American Journal of Emergency Medicine, 14,* 19–22.

Williams, M. V., Baker, D. W., Honig, E. G., Lee, T. M., & Nowlan, A. (1998). Inadequate literacy is a barrier to asthma knowledge and self-care. *Chest, 114,* 1006–1015.

Williams, M. V., Baker, D. W., Parker, R. M., & Nurss, J. R. (1998). Relationship of functional health literacy to patients' knowledge of their chronic disease: A study of patients with hypertension and diabetes. *Archives of Internal Medicine, 158,* 166–172.

Williams, M. V., Parker, R. M, Baker, D. W., Parikh, N. S., Pitkin, K., Coates, W. C., & Nurss, J. R. (1995). Inadequate functional health literacy among patients at two public hospitals. *Journal of the American Medical Association, 274,* 1677–1682.

Young, D., Hooker, D., & Freeberg, F. (1990). Informed consent documents: Increasing comprehension by reducing reading level. *Institutional Review Board, 12,* 1–6.

Yancey, A., Tanjasiri, S., Klein, M., & Tunder, J. (1995). Increased cancer screening behavior in women of color by culturally sensitive video exposure. *Preventive Medicine, 24,* 142–148.

Explaining Illness:
An Examination of Message
Strategies and Gender

Anne S. Gabbard-Alley
School of Speech Communication
James Madison University

Until recently, researchers in health communication have assumed that the gender of the physician and of the patient had little, if any, impact on the communication interaction between the two parties. Although there is serious concern about sex differences in health care and health research, gender was one of the first variables discarded by researchers studying communication and its relation to health care (Gabbard-Alley, 1995). However, as women have become more involved in health care, both as patients and as health care providers, health communication researchers have begun to focus on the influence of patient and physician gender when people are communicating about illness. The impetus for these studies is most likely the increase in the number of women being trained as physicians. Over 42% of students now entering medical school programs are female, compared to 25% in 1980 and 9% in 1970 (American Medical Association; AMA; 1998). It is projected that by the year 2010, 33% of the physicians in the United States will be female compared to 19% in 1994 (AMA, 1998). Some researchers have been motivated by their concern about possible discrimination toward women in the health care arena. Whatever the motivation, the communication strategies used to communicate about illness have become an important issue for health professionals and communication scholars.

This chapter examines the different types of communication strategies used by male and female patients and physicians when communicating about illness. This includes (a) a review of the research findings about gender and the communication strategies used when communicating about illness, (b) suggestions for new epistemological approaches to the study of gender and communication about illness, and (c) identification of a model of illness communication that includes the variables that need to be considered when explaining illness.

GENDER, MORBIDITY AND MORTALITY

As a background for a review of health communication research on gender and how gender impacts health communication interactions, it is important to discuss the differences in health behaviors by females and males. The division of gender into female–male does not imply a feminine, masculine, or other role. It simply reflects the language used in the majority of studies conducted. The use of the term gender to imply male–female is not intended to deny the psycho-social dimensions of the masculine–feminine distinction.

Factors Contributing to Gender Differences

Historically, health statistics have shown significantly more reported female morbidity than male morbidity, with the mortality rate for men being consistently higher (McCracken, 1998). Recent statistics show an overall life expectancy for females of 80.2 years and for males, 73.5 years (McCracken, 1998). The gender differential in morbidity is more pronounced among less severely ill patients than among sicker patients (Safran, Rogers, Tarlov, McHorney, & Ware, 1997).

Sociobiological Differences. The prevailing theory among medical sociologists for explaining the higher reported female morbidity is the socialization hypothesis, which posits that sociological factors that tend to suppress or inhibit the sick role for males do not operate in a similar fashion for females (Hohmann, 1989; Marcus & Seeman, 1981). Marcus and Seeman (1981) suggested females may report more illness because adopting the sick role is more socially acceptable for them and therefore is a role easier for them to assume. The socialization hypothesis presumes sick-role behavior is more compatible with traditional female roles and, thus, women may feel less constrained than men in defining and reporting mild symptoms as illness.

Lewis and Lewis (1977) conducted a number of longitudinal studies on health-related beliefs and gender behaviors and found that children start learning gender-role health behaviors at an early age. For instance, they examined an elementary school where children ages 5 through 12 were allowed to visit the school nurse without permission from their teachers. Before this, when the children had to seek permission, boys and girls visited the nurse about an equal amount of times. After the children were allowed to visit the nurse without permission, it was found for each visit that a boy made to the nurse, girls made 1½ visits (Lewis & Lewis, 1977). This ratio of health care visits is similar to that of adults in the 35 to 54 age group (Roter & Hall, 1992). Lewis & Lewis (1977) also found that a variety of adult role models and the media teach women at an early age to seek care for medical complaints, whereas men are taught to disregard pain. Johnson and Meischke (1993) said "the public perceives the media to be the source of most of its health-related information" (p. 42). Weisman (1987) found women are more likely than men to report being influenced by health information in the media.

A second hypothesis for women reporting more illness than men is the fixed-role hypothesis that is based on the traditional role expectations of males and females. Specifically, as Grove and Hughes (1979) explained, "women, as compared to men, typically have more role obligations that require constant ongoing activities vis-a-vis their spouse, children, and others living in the home ... these obligations can interfere with self-care and have a negative effect on one's health" (p. 132). This is especially true today because most women hold a job outside the home while still being responsible for the many female jobs in the home such as child care, cleaning, and shopping.

Grove and Hughes suggested that filling the varied roles could lead to self-neglect or fatigue. This would, in turn, lower bodily resistance and account for more reported illnesses in women. Marcus and Seeman (1981) took this a step further by speculating that because a woman typically cares for ill family members, she risks increased exposure to various infections. Therefore, women may have higher morbidity rates because they are more likely to be exposed to communicable illnesses.

A third explanation for females reporting more illness is the physician-bias hypothesis that argues that societal biases, shared by physicians, lead to differential diagnosis and treatment of female patients. The specific societal biases on which this hypothesis is based are: (a) females are weaker and therefore more vulnerable to illness than males, and (b) society tends to devalue female role responsibilities. This hypothesis was strongly supported by research reported by Safran et al. (1997). They found all physicians were significantly more likely to prescribe restriction of activities, based on reported illness, for female patients than for male patients. Furthermore, they found the observed differences in activity restriction were not explained by differences in male and female patients' health or role responsibilities. In addition, they found that male physicians were four times more likely to prescribe activity restriction for female patients than for male patients. They speculated that "a devaluation of female role responsibilities might ... make physicians less concerned about advising temporary activity suspension" (p. 719). Also, based on their research findings, physicians with such attitudes were more likely to be male, older, and–or subspecialists rather than female, younger, and–or generalists.

Finally, a fourth hypothesis for females reporting more illness is the biomedical hypothesis based on the premise that sex-related differences in biophysiology result in females being more susceptible to illness. This hypothesis has been largely discarded in the past decade (Cioffi, 1991; Safran et al., 1997). Whereas the first three hypotheses discussed provide some explanation for women reporting more illness than men, it is probably a combination of the three that accounts for this phenomena.

Power Differences.   A second phenomena that may contribute to differences in this context is power. Specifically, power differences must be briefly discussed in terms of the role that power plays in the communication interaction between physicians and patients when communicating about illness. There are a number of researchers who have discussed the physician paternalism versus patient autonomy spectrum of power as it relates to medical decision making (Koch, Meyers, & Sandroni, 1992; Quill & Brody, 1996), but little is known about how power impacts on the interpersonal communication interaction during the medical visit.

Traditionally, *power* is the ability to control the agenda in a situation, including the control of discussion issues and decision making (Bachrach & Baratz, 1962). The power one person holds over another is usually determined by the dependence of one person on another. Because the patient is inherently dependent on the knowledge and ability of the physician, she or he holds the power in the relationship. Kalish (1975) noted that physician authority is derived from expert power. As simple a behavior as an internist unnecessarily wearing a white lab coat is a power behavior indicating to the patient that "I am the expert in this situation," and "I have the power to control this communication interaction." Doctors need to be aware that patients may choose to use, or not use, various communication strategies simply because of the power imbalance in the relationship. Beisecker and Beisecker (1990) noted that due to the status difference between patient and physician, most patients are unlikely to express verbally their desire for involvement in the communication interaction that occurs during a medical visit.

Although power is available to patients through noncompliant behavior strategies or lawsuits, this power does not impact on the immediate communication interaction when discussing illness.

COMMUNICATION PATTERNS
OF FEMALE AND MALE PATIENTS

Roter and Hall (1992), in a review of 61 published studies in health communication prior to 1987 divided the communication that takes place during the medical visit into the following categories. The first category, *information giving*, is where the patient presents symptoms, answers questions, and the like. They found information giving consumed 46.9% of the communication interaction by the patient. The second category, *question asking*, made up 7.0% of the patient communication interaction. *Social conversation* made up 13.4 % of the patient communication interaction. *Positive talk* (laughter, shows of approval, etc.) made up 18.7% of the patient communication interaction and 8.3% of the patient communication was negative talk (showing antagonism, disagreements).

Gabbard-Alley (1989) suggested that three major communication goals need to be accomplished in the patient–physician visit. First is the exchange of information. The patient needs to effectively communicate the nature of his or her illness to the physician. The physician needs to effectively communicate her or his understanding of the patient's illness, a diagnosis of the illness and suggestions for ways to solve the illness problem. The second goal is the exchange of relational or affective information when pertinent. This is accomplished by the physician using communication strategies that provide evidence of compassion, caring, and concern in order that the patient can feel she or he can safely discuss psychosocial issues with the physician. The third goal is negotiation between the patient and the physician toward a workable and mutually agreeable solution to the problem.

Disclosure and Inquiry in Health-Related Interactions

Documentation from communication investigations shows that females generally disclose more information about themselves than do males (Gabbard-Alley, 1995). This characteristic is also supported by gender findings in health communication. For example, Wallen, Waitzkin, and Stoeckle (1979) found that female patients asked more questions of the physician and talked more than male patients. This finding was supported by Waitzkin (1984, 1985), who found that women asked more questions and talked more than males in health-related interactions. It should be

noted that Beisecker and Beisecker (1990), in a study of patient information-seeking behaviors, did not find gender to be a significant variable.

One explanation for women asking more questions and talking more
than men in health related interactions is based on women being more
knowledgeable about health matters than men (Coope & Metcalfe, 1979;
Gabbard-Alley, 1995). A study of pharmacist–patient communication by
Schommer and Wiederholt (1997) found that males received more instructions about medications than females. They suggested pharmacists
may perceive that females are more familiar with medications due to the
frequency with which they use pharmacies. Wartman, Morlock, Malitz,
and Palm (1983) found that being female correlated significantly with understanding drug instructions. Buller and Buller (1987) suggested that female patients may be more knowledgeable about medical techniques and
treatments than male patients. If females have more knowledge about
health matters than males, this could give them the confidence to discuss
health concerns in more detail and to expect more information from
health professionals.

Another explanation for higher female communication rates in
health-related interactions is that physicians of both sexes tend to verbally interact more with females than with males, thereby encouraging
more communication from female patients (Gabbard-Alley, 1995). Sen
(1997) found that females were given more information than males and
they were more accurately informed about their treatment methods and
results than males. Waitzkin (1884, 1985) found women tended to receive
more explanations and more nondiscrepant responses from physicians
than did males. Hooper, Comstock, Goodwin, and Goodwin (1982) found
that in physician–patient interaction, ratings of physician information
giving were significantly higher with female patients than with male patients. Hall, Roter, and Katz (1988) conducted a meta-analysis of 41 studies published between 1967 and 1986 involving health care professionals
and patient–client communication interaction in which they found that
health providers gave more information to female than to male patients.
In a later study, Hall, Irish, Roter, Ehrlich, and Miller (1994a) found that
female and male physicians did not differ in the total amount of information given to patients, either medical or psychosocial. No study has shown
less information being given to adult female patients (Roter & Hall,
1992). However, in one pediatric study, Bernzweig, Takayama, Phibbs,
Lewis, and Pantell (1997) found that male physicians gave more information to boys and that female physicians gave more information to girls in
all categories of resolution of problems (i.e., "this is not a serious problem
and will probably clear up in a few days"; medication management, i.e.,
"take these pills 4 times a day"; and nonmedication management, i.e.,
"drink lots of fluids"). Their findings also revealed that male physicians

engaged in the least amount of conversation with girls in substantive medical communication.

Communication Partnership Patterns

When discussing illness, female patients use more partnership communication than male patients (Hall et al., 1994a). Partnership communication consists of statements that emphasize the "we" nature of the relationship between the communicating parties (e.g., "we need to do more about this problem"). The use of this communication strategy by females is probably due to the fact that women, in all their roles, tend to use more partnership communication as opposed to the power communication interactions preferred by many males. For example, Meeuwesen, Schaap, and van der Staak (1991) found that during the medical visit, male patients make more interpretations (judgments, labeling) than females.

Patients direct more partnership statements to female physicians than male physicians (Hall et al., 1994a). However, when the patient is male and the physician female, the patient makes the greatest number of partnership statements (Hall et al., 1994a). In addition, Hall et al. (1994b) found that patients liked positive, partnership communication strategies when there were male patient–male physician and female patient–female physician dyads. They suggested that:

> this may signify that when positive feelings are conveyed by the physician in a same-gender dyad, patients may interpret such cues unambiguously as showing warmth and regard, whereas in opposite-gender encounters such communication may be met with some tension because such cues also can convey flirtation or sexual interest. (p. 1223)

Evidence has been found to indicate that general medical providers feel more comfortable communicating about issues of feelings and emotions with female patients than with male patients (Mant, Broom, & Duncan-Jones, 1983; Verbrugge, 1984). Hohmann (1989) suggested this could be due to an "artifact of the greater expressiveness and responsiveness of women" (p. 479). Female patients appear to like the use of psychosocial communication with both female and male physicians, particularly if the communication consists of emotionally supportive statements (Hall et al., 1994b). The extra communication interaction with female patients may be spent in affective communication interaction rather than communication directed toward specific medical concerns.

Overall, female patients spend more time with physicians and communicate more than do male patients. Evidence suggests that the extra time is most likely spent in psychosocial communication interaction. Patients communicate more with female physicians than they do with male physicians (Roter, Kipkin, & Korsgaard, 1991), with the female patient–female physician having the most communication interaction (Hall, Roter, Milburn, & Daltroy, 1996). Specifically, patients engage in more positive talk and partnership building and ask more questions and give more information (both biomedical and psychosocial) with female physicians (Roter et al., 1991). Female patient–female physician pairings result in more statements of medical information from the patients.

COMMUNICATION PATTERNS OF FEMALE PHYSICIANS AND MALE PHYSICIANS

In their review of health communication studies prior to 1987, Roter and Hall (1992) found the communication interaction by physicians during the medical visit could be categorized by the following variables: information giving by the physician, which utilized 35.3% of the communication interaction time; information seeking, 22.6% of the communication time; social conversation, 6.0%; positive talk, 15%; negative talk, 1.3%; and partnership building, 10.6%. Partnership-building communication, which was not represented in the patient's communication interaction, is the physician's attempts to engage the patient in the communication interaction. These percentages vary according to whether the patient is male or female.

Length of Medical Consultation

The length of a medical visit is usually longer for female patients than for males (Hall et al., 1994a; Hooper, Comstock, Goodwin, & Goodwin, 1982; Meeuwesen, Schaap, & van der Staak, 1991), with the combination of female patient–female physician having longer visits (Britt, Miles, Meza, Sayer, & Angelis, 1996). Roter, Lipkin, and Korsgaard (1991), in a nationwide study of 11 primary-care sites, found that female physicians averaged 22.9 minutes per medical visit with their patients, compared to 20.3 minutes for male physicians. In a study of pediatric visits, Bernzweig et al. (1997) found that female physicians conducted visits 29%, or 8 minutes, longer than male physicians. Bertakis, Helms, Callahan, Azari, and Robbins (1995) found no significant differences in total length of visit between male and female physicians although the average female physician did spend 1.05 minutes more with patients. Despite females having more time with physicians, one investigation found that male and female physicians are more attentive to male patients (Meeuwesen et al., 1991).

Differences in Amount and Type of Interaction

Female physicians engage in significantly more communication during the medical visit than do male physicians (Roter et al., 1991). However, physicians and patients contribute equal amounts of verbal communication in female patient–female physician pairings (Hall et al., 1994a). When the dyad is composed of male physicians and male patients, the physician contributes more verbal communication (Hall et al., 1994a).

Meeuwesen et al. (1991) found female physicians gave more *edification* (statements of objective information) than male physicians, and more objective information was given to female patients than to male patients. This was supported by Roter et al.'s (1991) finding that female physicians communicate with more task-focused exchanges (e.g., question asking and information giving). Female physicians ask more questions with biomedical content (e.g., how often do you have these episodes?) than do male physicians (Hall et al., 1994a).

One continuing problem with effective interpersonal communication in medical visits has been the use of technical language, or jargon, by physicians. It has been found that female physicians use less technical language than male physicians (Gabbard-Alley, 1985). Evidence is inconclusive as to whether or not the communication strategies used by physicians for giving information is more technical with female patients or male patients. Waitzkin (1985) found that physicians matched their language-level responses to female patients' questions, thereby avoiding the implication that they were talking up or talking down to female patients. Some researchers have interpreted this finding as evidence that physicians do talk down to female patients. However, Hall et al. (1994a) found that physicians used more technical language with female than with male patients and less technical language was used in the female-physician–male-patient dyad than in any other combination. Roter and Hall (1992) speculated that the use of technical language by physicians could be a means of maintaining control over the encounter. This use of technical language reinforces the physician–patient power imbalance discussed earlier.

Male physicians use more interpretations and advisements in their communication than do female physicians (Meeuwesen et al., 1991). Interpretation and advisement communication strategies are used to attempt to control the behavior of the patient. Interpretation communication strategies occur when the physician makes judgments about the patient and consequently labels the behavior of the patient, for example, "You aren't dealing with this very well." Advisement communication strategies consist of advice, commands, and suggestions (e.g., "You must get more rest").

Female physicians give more time to discussing family information or social matters (Bertakis et al., 1995). Also, there is more communication about family information when the patient is female. Bertakis et al. (1995) noted that "female physicians displayed greater interest in learning more about the patient's family and social milieu" and suggested that "these differences in communication are not mere artifacts of differential patient populations: male and female physicians exhibit consistently different approaches to the practice of medicine" (p. 414). In addition, Meeuwesen et al. (1991) found that female physicians talked longer with psychosocial patients, compared to somatic patients, whereas male physicians did not. Generally, female physicians have more psychosocial content in their communication than do male physicians (Hall et al., 1994a; Roter et al., 1991).

In a study conducted in a pediatric context, Bernzweig et al. (1997) found there was 41% more social exchange communication when the physician was female. Because the patients were children, such communication consisted of statements like "what grade are you in now?"—statements unrelated to the patients' illness or statements intended to establish rapport. However, Hall et al. (1994a) did not find that female physicians engaged in more social communication than male physicians when the patients were adults.

Female physicians give more disclosures (revealing of thoughts, subjective information) than do male physicians (Meeuwesen et al., 1991) and make more use of partnership statement communication. Corollary to this, female physicians engaged in more positive communication than male physicians (Hall et al., 1994a; Roter et al., 1991) with the female patient–female physician combination having the highest number of positive communication instances (Hall et al., 1994a). In addition, physicians demonstrate more tension release (i.e., laughter) with female patients and are more likely to ask about female patients' opinions or feelings (Steward, 1983). Bernzweig et al. (1997) found that female physicians spend more time developing rapport with patients than do male physicians.

Hall et al. (1994a) found that female physicians use more facilitating responses such as back-channel responses, which includes the use of nods, "uh-huh," "yes," and "I see," than do male physicians. Furthermore, they found that these responses were used more with female patients by both male and female physicians, with the most back-channel responses occurring with female physician–female patient pairings.

Female physicians spend 36% more time discussing preventive services than male physicians (Bertakis et al., 1995). When the physician is female, regardless of the gender of the patient, Bernzweig et al. (1997) found there was 39% more communication about the history and nature of the illness.

Influence Strategies and Messages

One communication variable that has not been given much research attention is the type of influence strategy used by physicians. Some researchers have found the use of coercive influence strategies (scare tactics, scolding, threats, and rewards) leads to patients being more satisfied with communication interaction with their physician (Beck & Frankel, 1981; Schmidt, 1977). Other researchers have found that patients rate communication interaction higher when persuasive influence strategies are used by the physician (Gabbard-Alley, 1989; Leventhal, 1982). It is likely that persuasive-influence strategies work effectively for many types of patients in most contexts and coercive-influence strategies work effectively with other types of patients in other contexts. Gabbard-Alley (1985) found that male physicians are more likely to use coercive-influence strategies when discussing illness than are female physicians; Weeuwesen et al. (1991) noted that male physicians expressed more controlling behaviors than female physicians.

Overall, it is known that female physicians give their patients more time, engage in more communication with their patients, and spend more time communicating about psychosocial issues than male physicians. Female physicians also give more information to patients and use less jargon and more back-channel responses than male physicians. Female physicians are less likely to use coercive communication strategies. Beisecker, Murden, Moore, Graham, and Helmig (1966) found that female medical students and primary care physicians advocated greater patient input into medical decision making than male medical students and primary care physicians.

Male physicians give their patients less time, engage in less communication with their patients, and spend less time communicating about psychosocial issues than female physicians. Male physicians are more likely to use communication strategies that attempt to control the communication interaction between the physician and the patients and are more likely to use coercive communication strategies. Corollary with these findings, Gross (1992) found that male physicians reported many more interpersonal difficulties with their patients than did female physicians.

Interruptions

One of the communication strategies that people use to obtain a speaking turn is interruptions. Interruptions have traditionally been used by physicians to maintain control during verbal exchanges with patients. Beckman and Frankel (1984) found that during the patient's opening comments of the medical visit, only one patient was allowed to complete the original statement before being interrupted by the physician. West (1984) found that male physicians interrupted patients significantly more than did female physicians. However, Irish and Hall (1995) found that patients interrupted physicians more than physicians interrupted patients and found no significant differences in the number of interruptions by female or male patients. They also found that when there are interruptions, patients are more likely to interrupt with statements, whereas physicians interrupt with questions. They suggested that the interruptions by physicians with questions could be an attempt to seek additional information and the interruptions by patients could be an attempt to answer the questions and thus give additional information.

Researchers have found that male patients do not like interruptions from male physicians but female patients do not appear to mind interruptions from female physician (Hall et al., 1994b). West (1984) found that patients were more likely to interrupt female physicians than male physicians and suggested this could be evidence of disrespect toward female physicians. Irish and Hall (1995) found support for this conclusion. Hall et al. (1994b) suggested that in male–male dyads, "interruptions may take on overtones of conflict or dominance, with associated negative implications" (p. 1224). They further speculated that "interruptions between female dyads have a different connotation, one that indicates positive involvement and enthusiasm" (p. 1224).

NONVERBAL COMMUNICATION BEHAVIOR AND GENDER

Being aware of the nonverbal communication behaviors of a patient may be one of the best diagnostic tools of a physician. A physician who appears to be rushing through the medical visit may convey to the patient that she or he is not really interested in the patient. For instance, Schneider and Tucker (1992) found that "nonverbal approachability" was a significant variable in doctor–patient communication interaction. Hall et al. (1996) noted that physicians' use of negative voice tone, although coupled with emotional concern and positive verbal statements, led to physicians "inadvertently revealing ... their negative affective reactions" to sicker patients (p. 1214).

Research concerning nonverbal communication during a medical visit is limited due to the nature of the medical visit. Although researchers can record medical visits with the permission of the patient, the use of videotapes or direct observations poses problems of patient confidentiality. Most of the researchers interested in nonverbal communication in medical visits either use filtered audiotapes or videotapes that focus primarily on the physician so the patient's identity will not be compromised.

An investigation by Hall et al. (1994a) illustrated the difficulty of nonverbal research in the health context. Visits were videotaped but the camera was covered during any physical examination, with the audio track left running. Two of the nonverbal communication behaviors they observed were smiling and nodding. Smiling is a nonverbal behavior generally used to convey positive affect, whereas nodding is a nonverbal behavior generally used to encourage continuing communication or to indicate agreement. They found that female physicians smiled more when interacting with patients than did male physicians, and female physicians smiled more with male patients than with female patients. In addition, female physicians nodded more than male physicians and the greatest number of nods occurred in female physicians–female patient encounters. They were unable to analyze the same behaviors for patients due to research constraints.

Hall, Roter, and Katz (1988), in their meta-analysis of 41 studies involving health communication, found that more nonverbal attention was given to female patients than male patients by health care providers. Street and Wiemann (1987) and Cartwright (1967) found that female patients prefer health professionals who display nonverbal cues of attentiveness and responsiveness more than do male patients.

Voice Quality

Hall et al. (1994a) were able to obtain information about nonverbal communication by analyzing voice quality of the soundtracks of videotapes. Their subjects were 50 internists (25 women and 25 men) from a large group practice at a teaching hospital and 100 patients (50 women and 50 men). The patients were mostly White, with an average age of 62. It cannot be assumed that these findings would correlate with other age and race groupings.

Their findings included the following. Male patients' voice quality was more boring (uninvolved) than female patients' voice quality and the voice quality of patients in the female physician–male patient group was rated as the most uninvolved of other groupings. Male patients' voices displayed lower anxiety than did female patients' voices and same-sex physician–patient pairs had less anxiety expressed in their voices than opposite sex pairings. Female patients' voices were rated as more submissive than male patients, whereas same-sex physician–patient pairings were rated as more submissive than opposite-sex pairings. Voices of patients in the female physician–male patient group were more dominant than patients in other groups and the physician's voice in the female physician–male patient pairing was less friendly than in other groupings.

Hall et al. (1994a) found that male physicians' voice quality was rated as less interested than female physicians' voices although all physicians spoke to female patients with a less interested voice tone than to male patients. Male physicians' voice quality was rated as calmer than that of female physicians. Female patients were spoken to in a calmer manner than were male patients, and the female physician–male patient grouping was found to be have a much more anxious voice quality than other pairings.

One of the findings of this study of voice quality is that in the female physician–male patient combination, the patients' voices were more dominant and more uninvolved. This could suggest a negative reaction by the male patients to having a female physician, or it could reflect the stereotypical communication reaction of middle-age males to any female who is in a power position. It would be interesting to see if these findings remained the same if the male patient population were younger. Roter and Hall (1992) found that physicians (male and female) used voices that had a more bored, calmer, and more submissive tone when communicating with female patients. They suggested that physicians' less active and less dominant manner with females reflects a more low-key manner of interaction.

Eye Contact

Another component of nonverbal communication is the amount of, or lack of, eye contact between the communicating parties. In Western cultures, people are encouraged to engage in eye contact during communication encounters. Eye contact is usually taken to mean the speaker and listener are interested in the topic under discussion. Heath (1984) observed that patients often stopped talking until the physician looked at them, rather than continuing to talk while the physician wrote notes. Relatedly, Bensing, Kerssens, and van der Pasch (1995) found that medical visits lasted longer and the patient talked more when the physician had a high level of eye contact with the patient. In addition, they found that when the physician had a high level of eye contact with patients, the patients were more inclined to talk freely about their problems and they gave more information about psychosocial issues.

Bensing (1991) found that in physician–patient visits that were rated positively, the physician gave more nonverbal attention, specifically eye contact. In addition, physicians who encouraged the patient by semiverbal utterances like "hm-hm" and "ah" were rated higher. Physicians were also rated more positively when they used verbal empathy, which was demonstrated by the physician reflecting on the words of the patient or paraphrasing what the patient said.

Touch

Much research in nonverbal interaction and health communication has focused on touching behaviors between patients and health care providers. Street and Buller (1988) found that physicians used significantly less task touch with female patients than with male counterparts. They modified this result by noting much of the task touching with female patients was gynecological, obstetrical, and breast exams and therefore not available for the researchers' camera. They did not find significantly more task touching with females when cameras were allowed to run.

In general, researchers have agreed that touching is particularly important in communicating with elderly patients. Despite the conventional wisdom that suggests affective touching of the elderly does improve provider–patient interaction (McCorkle, 1974), contrary evidence exists when the subjects are divided by gender. In a study of affective touching and elderly patients in nursing homes, DeWever (1977) found that the gender of the participants was correlated with perceived discomfort if being effectively touched by nurses. Specifically, females perceived they would experience more discomfort from affective touching than males perceived they would experience. Further, females perceived they would experience more discomfort from affective touching by male nurses. Gender was not related to perceived discomfort from affective touching by female nurses. A nurse, male or female, putting an arm around the patient's shoulders was the touching behavior perceived as most uncomfortable. McCann and McKenna (1993) also found that expressive touching behaviors involving the leg, face, and around the shoulders were perceived as uncomfortable by all elderly patients. The only touching behavior perceived as comfortable by the patients was instrumental touching of the arm and shoulder by a female nurse.

In addition, the physician's overall perception of the patient's nonverbal characteristics may have an influence on the communication interaction. Hooper et al. (1982) found that physician interpersonal behaviors were rated highest when they were interacting with "well-groomed, elderly Anglo-American women" and were lowest with "disheveled, young Spanish-American males" (p. 636). Hall, Milburn, and Epstein (1993) found that "physicians sometimes behave more negatively toward minority, low-income and female patients than toward white, higher income and male patients, even within the same care settings" (p. 93).

Due to the difficulties of conducting nonverbal communication research during medical visits, more is known about the nonverbal behaviors of physicians than those of patients when discussing illness. Evidence concerning the nonverbal communication behavior of physicians is limited. Consequently, one might conclude that the nonverbal communication behaviors people exhibit in other contexts of their lives probably carries over into the medical visit. If this is true, then it would follow that females, both patients and physicians, would be more effective in the use and interpretation of nonverbal communication cues when communicating about illness because general communication research findings indicate that women are more effective users of nonverbal communication strategies.

CONCERNS WITH PRESENT RESEARCH

Evidence from the research reviewed indicates females, both physicians and patients, are more effective communicators when discussing illness than are male physicians and male patients. Because it is also known that effective communication skills are a major determinant of patient satisfaction (Murphy-Cullen & Larsen, 1984), it would follow that patients who have female physicians would be more satisfied with the medical visit. Throughout this chapter, it has been shown that use of more effective communication strategies have been found in female physician–female patient dyads. However, Hall et al. (1994a) found both female and male patients were less satisfied with the medical visit when the physician was female, specifically when the physician was a "youthful appearing" female. Because they did not know the actual age of the physicians, they made educated judgments as to the relative age of the physicians. They did know the average age of the patients in this study, which was 62. They speculated that patients "may have discredited or devalued the younger female physicians based on prejudice alone or older patients might not respect younger female physicians" (p. 1228). Although their speculation might account for part of the reason for this finding, there are also other confounding variables that need attention before any strong general conclusions can be drawn concerning how the gender of the patient or physician affects the communication interaction in the medical visit.

Context of the Visit

One variable that is included in all communication models, but is not given enough serious attention, is the context in which the medical communication encounter occurs. For example, researchers have found that the location of the health care service has a gender component. Anderson and Bartkus (1973) studied the extent to which students used outside care in lieu of university health services available through prepaid student fees. They found male students with health problems requiring medical attention would use the campus medical center, whereas female students tended to use outside medical services to a greater extent. In addition, Todd (1989) found that the communication interaction between women and physicians in a neighborhood clinic differed from that in a private clinic. In another study where the data was collected from visits to internal medicine physicians at a large teaching hospital, Hall et al. (1994b) found that male patients did not like affective (psychosocial) communication from male physicians, although they did like positive–partnership communication. In a second study using data collected from a variety of differing contexts, Hall et al. (1994b) found that communication about psychosocial topics was not disliked by male patients.

McMahan, Hoffman, and McGee (1994) made the relation between context and communication even more direct when they noted that:

> different units of a hospital ... require different communication styles and strategies ... the interpersonal interaction in an emergency room differs, in certain respects, from the interpersonal interaction required for the day-to-day interaction on the floor of an oncology unit. (p. 104)

It is necessary to be even more specific because another variable that confounds the research findings about gender and the communication between patients and physicians are the segments of the total visit in which specific communication strategies are used. Noted earlier in this chapter are the various differences in use of communication strategies during particular segments of the medical visit that were found by Meeuwesen et al. (1991). Roter et al. (1991) found that most of the gender differences in communication strategies came during the history-taking segment of the visit. Bertakis et al. (1995) found that male physicians gave significantly more of the visit time to history taking than did female physicians. Hall et al. (1994a) found that there were no gender differences in the friendliness of physicians' voices in the early part of a medical visit but later in the visit, male physicians used friendlier voices than did female physicians.

It is necessary for health communication researchers to be aware of the contextual variables each person brings to the communication encounter (Gabbard-Alley, 1995). All models of effective communication include the environment (context) of the communication encounter as an important component. However, the definition of context in these models is too narrow. The consideration of context must include the historical, social, and personal variables of all parties involved in the communication encounter (Gabbard-Alley, 1995). For example, one personal contextual variable that should be considered is the nature of the disease and its effect on the communication interaction, as was suggested by Davis (1981) in a study of males and females with osteoarthrosis where no significant differences in symptom reporting between males and females were found. Davis noted that reporting of symptoms may be dependent on the type of illness and the specific experiences associated with a particular illness rather than on the gender of the patient. Sen (1997), in a study of cancer patients, found that female patients tended to be given more information than male patients, as have most studies. Sen also speculated that female patients were more informed because their disease (e.g., breast and genitourinary cancers) results in a high percentage of body-altering surgery and is, by its very nature, more difficult to avoid recognizing. Because the patients cannot avoid knowing they have the cancer, they want (and get) more information about the disease. It is logical that other personal contextual variables should also be considered.

Gender Versus Female–Male

Another variable that confounds the findings I reviewed here was suggested by Annandale and Hunt (1990). They argued that "research on gender and health needs to give empirical recognition to the possibility that sex and gender are not necessarily coincidental" because many people do not adopt socially defined gender roles (p. 26). In their continuing longitudinal study, they used Bem's (1974) Sex-Role Inventory to correlate gender orientations with assessments of health status. Annandale and Hunt found that high-masculinity scores were associated with improved health for men and women and high femininity scores were associated with poorer health outcomes with men and women. This certainly goes against the conventional findings that "women = feminine" live longer and have fewer health problems than "men = masculine." Weyrauch, Boiko, and Alvin (1990) noted that "biological sex is a genetic trait, whereas sex role, a psychological construct, is a set of preferences, skills, personality attributes, self-concepts, and behaviors that is felt to be appropriate for a man or a woman" (p. 559).

One study that lends some credibility to this argument was conducted by Weyrauch et al. (1990). In a study of patient sex role and physician preference, they found that 100% of the women who were classified as having an androgynous sex role (using Bem's Sex Role Inventory), and who expressed a preference between male or female physicians, preferred a female physician. In a study that considered only biological sex, Fennema, Meyer, and Owen (1990) found 31% of men and 43% of women preferred physicians of their own sex. These percentages vary in other studies depending on the type of illness complaint, but they reflect the general trend for physician preference when one considers biological sex but not gender orientation.

In this review of gender, communication, and illness, I have found evidence suggesting that male physicians are less effective communicators than female physicians and that female patients are more effective communicators than male patients when discussing illness. But if the claim is accepted that the biological sex of a person is not equal to their gender orientation or sex role, then it is possible the findings discussed here have been confounded by not paying attention to the possible gender orientation of participants involved in these studies. For example, it has long been understood that the socialization process during medical school training has traditionally been masculine in nature. But Dickinson and Tournier (1993) found that despite all the occupational-role socialization that going through the physician education–socialization process involves, physicians tended to graduate from medical school with the same gender-role socialization that had taken place prior to entering medical school. They also found that female physicians had more effective communication with dying patients than did male physicians and speculated that feminine gender characteristics lend themselves to better communication with dying patients and their families than do masculine traits. It could be that if the physicians involved in communication studies were divided by gender orientation rather than by biological sex, communication strategies of physicians of both sexes would be found to correlate more with gender orientation. Annandale and Hunt (1990) thought that "some situations are felt to require a 'feminine' and some a 'masculine' response, and individuals who are able to adapt to such situational demands are seen as superior in social skills (and) better adapted to the social environment" (p. 26).

It must also be noted that the matter of being an effective communicator in particular contexts might not be a function of gender but is rather a function of being rhetorically sensitive (see House, Dallinger, & Kilgallen, 1998). In response to this caveat, some have argued that those who use a feminine communication style are more rhetorically sensitive. It is also possible that physicians and patients whose gender orientation, or sex role, is androgynous would be more effective communicators, or more rhetorically sensitive, because they would use both feminine and masculine communication strategies, depending on the context of the communication encounter.

TOWARD FUTURE INQUIRY

One way research studies in health communication could be improved would be to adopt a more interpretative or rules-based approach (Gabbard-Alley, 1995). Smith (1982) stated that "a rule is a means-end generalization, describing people's beliefs about what behaviors are required in certain contexts if they are to achieve desired objectives" (p. 62). Specifically, rules "define appropriate actions in specified social settings" (p. 62). Smith suggested that people are self-directed and goal-oriented agents who strive to maximize rewards and minimize punishments. In other words, people have particular goals that they wish to achieve and they take the appropriate actions that are called for in particular contexts to accomplish these goals. Such an approach would be less concerned with effects and more concerned with describing how female or male communicators go about achieving their goals during a medical visit. Instead of noting that women are more aggressive in communicating with physicians, this approach would be interested in questions such as "what types of communication strategies do females–males use when interacting with physicians in context A in order to accomplish their goals?" A patient who goes to a walk-in clinic in order to get a yearly flu shot will use different communication strategies than a patient who goes to an internist to discuss an upcoming surgical procedure because these patients have different goals to achieve. More specifically, the patient who spontaneously goes into a walk-in clinic to get a flu shot is probably most concerned with fast and efficient service. The effectiveness of the communication strategies involved is of minor importance. On the other hand, when discussing surgery with one's personal internist, a number of possible historical, social and personal variables must be considered (by both patient and physician) when choosing communication strategies. In addition, the physician in varied contexts will use differing communication strategies.

Based on the previous discussion, a model including the differing variables that appear to impact on physicians and patients communicating about illness would contain the following elements.

In this model, the communication interaction about illness by both the patient and the physician takes place in an environment that is grounded in both parties' perceptions of the observed rules for effective communication in this context. The observed rules for communicating about illness to which each participant would adhere would be based on their expectations

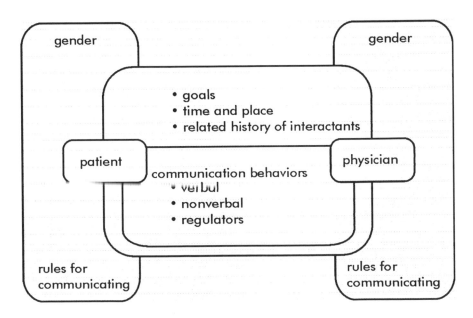

FIG. 6.1   Context of medical visit.

of the communication strategies they should use to obtain their respective goals, the time and place of the interaction and the related history of the interactants. Related histories would grow out of either personal prior experiences, observations of the experiences of others, or folklore experiences such as having observed a similar encounter on television or having read about a similar experience.

These rules may vary according to the gender orientation of the participants. For example, based on current research findings, those participants with feminine gender orientation would be more likely to think that a discussion of psychosocial issues connected with their illness would be a logical part of the communication interaction. Participants with masculine gender orientation probably would not be as likely to include a discussion of psychosocial issues. If the validity of an androgynous gender orientation is assumed, there is currently no research available to know what communication rules that participants with such orientation would observe when discussing illness.

This model can serve as a general indicator of the factors that need to be considered when illness communication between physicians and patients is studied. Although examined here are the findings of a number of studies on the impact of gender on the communication interaction that occurs when physicians and patients discuss illness, at this time, there is not a great deal of research information available. In addition, the research that has been conducted has concentrated on only a few of the many variables that impact communication interaction. It is very probable that future researchers will discover additional information that would impact on the validity of this model.

Because the discussion of illness is of a more serious nature than the discussion of many other topics, it is important that researchers continue to explore the manner in which gender impacts on illness discussions. It is also important for those persons who are physicians to be aware of the impact of gender on the communication interaction. Although it is not realistic to teach every patient that their gender has an impact on their discussion of illness, it is realistic to expect all physicians to become aware of how either their gender orientation or that of their patients will impact on communication interactions about illness. With this knowledge, physicians can adapt their communication strategies in a manner that will make explaining illness most effective for each patient.

REFERENCES

American Medical Association. (1998). [on-line]
Anderson, J. G., & Bartkus, D. E. (1973). Choice of medical care: A model of health and illness behavior. *Journal of Health and Social Behavior, 14,* 33–48.

168GABBARD-ALLEY

Annandale, E., & Hunt, K. (1990). Masculinity, feminity and sex: An exploration of their relative contribution to explaining gender differences in health. *Sociology of Health and Illness, 12*, 24–46.

Bachrach, P., & Baratz, M. (1962). Two faces of power. *American Political Science Review, 56*, 947–952.

Beck, K., & Frankel, A. (1981). A conceptualization of threat communication and protective health behavior. *Social Psychology Quarterly, 44*, 204–217.

Beckman, H., & Frankel, R. (1984). The effect of physician behavior on the collection of data. *Annuals of Internal Medicine, 101*, 692–703.

Beisecker, A. E., Murden, R. A., Moore, W. P., Graham, D., & Nelmig, L. (1966). Attitudes of medical students and primary care physicians regarding input of older and younger patients in medical decisions. *Medical Care, 34*, 126–137.

Beisecker, A. E., & Beisecker, T. D. (1990). Patient information-seeking behaviors when communicating with doctors. *Medical Care, 28*, 19–28.

Bem, S. (1974). The measurement of psychological androgyny. *Journal of Consulting and Clinical Psychology, 42*, 155–162.

Bensing, J. (1991). Doctor–patient communication and the quality of care. *Social Science and Medicine, 32*, 1301–1310.

Bensing, J. M., Kerssens, J. J., & van der Pasch, M. (1995). Patient-directed gaze as a tool for discovering and handling psychosocial problems in general practice. *Journal of Nonverbal Behavior, 19*, 223–242.

Bernzweig, J., Takayama, J. I., Phibbs, C., Lewis, C., & Pantell, R. H. (1997). Gender differences in physician–patient communication: Evidence from pediatric visits. *Archives of Pediatrics & Adolescent Medicine, 151*, 586–591.

Bertakis, K. D., Helms, L. J., Callahan, E. J., Azari, R., & Robbins, J. A. (1995). The influence of gender on physician practice style. *Medical Care, 4*, 407–416.

Britt, H. B. A., Miles, D., Meza, A., Sayer, G. P., & Angelis, M. (1996). The sex of the general practitioner: A comparison of characteristics, patients and medical conditions managed. *Medical Care, 34*, 403–415.

Buller, M. K., & Buller, D. B. (1987). Physicians' communication style and patient satisfaction. *Journal of Health and Social Behavior, 28*, 375–388.

Cartwright, A. (1967). *Patients and their doctors.* London: Routledge & Kegan Paul.

Cioffi, D. (1991). Beyond attentional strategies: Cognitive perceptual model of somatic interpretation. *Psychological Bulletin, 109*, 25–41.

Coope, J., & Metcalfe, D. (1979). How much do patients know? A MCQ paper for patients in the waiting room. *Journal of the Royal College of General Practice, 29*, 482–488.

Davis, M. A. (1981). Sex differences in reporting osteoarthritic symptoms: A sociomedical approach. *Journal of Health and Social Behavior, 22*, 298–310.

DeWever, M. (1977). Nursing home patients' perception of nurses affective touching. *The Journal of Psychology, 96*, 163–171.

Dickinson, G. E., & Tournier, R. E. (1993). A longitudinal study of sex differences in how physicians relate to dying patients. *Journal of the American Medical Women Association, 48*, 19–22.

Fennema, K., Meyer, D., & Owen, N. (1990). Sex of physician: Patients' preferences and stereotypes. *The Journal of Family Practice, 30*, 441–446.

Gabbard-Alley, A. S. (1985, November). *A study of the influence strategies of physicians.* Paper presented at the National Communication Association, Denver.

Gabbard-Alley, A. S. (1989, October). *Persuasive influence strategies versus coercive influence strategies in physician-patient communication: A test of Tedeschi's model.* Paper presented at the James Madison University Health Communication Institute, Harrisonburg, VA.

Gabbard-Alley, A. S. (1995). Health communication and gender: A review and critique. *Health Communication, 7*, 35–55.

Gross, E. B. (1992). Gender differences in physician stress. *Journal of the American Medical Women's Association, 47*, 107–112.

Grove, W., & Hughes, M. (1979). Possible causes of the apparent sex differences in physical health: An empirical investigation. *American Sociological Review, 44,* 126–146.

Hall, J. A., Irish, J. T., Roter, D. L., Ehrlich, C. M., & Miller, L. H. (1994a). Gender in medical encounters: An analysis of physician and patient communication in a primary care setting. *Health Psychology, 13,* 384–392.

Hall, J. A., Irish, J. T., Roter, D. L, Ehrlich, C. M., & Miller, L. H. (1994b). Satisfaction, gender, and communication in medical visits. *Medical Care, 32,* 1216–1231.

Hall, J. S., Milburn, M. A., & Epstein, A. M. (1993). A causal model of health status and satisfaction with medical care. *Medical Care, 31,* 84–94.

Hall, J. A., Roter, D. L., & Katz, N. R. (1988). Meta-analysis of correlates of provider behavior in medical encounters. *Medical Care, 26,* 657–675.

Hall, J. A., Roter, D. L., Milburn, M. A., & Daltroy, L. H. (1996). Patients' health as a predictor of physician and patient behavior in medical visits. *Medical Care, 34,* 1205–1218.

Heath, C. (1984). Participation in the medical consultation: The co-ordination of verbal and nonverbal behaviour between the doctor and patient. *Sociology of Health & Illness, 6,* 311–338.

Hohmann, A. A. (1989). Gender bias in psychotropic drug prescribing in primary care. *Medical Care, 27,* 478–490.

Hooper, E. M., Comstock, L. M., Goodwin, J. M., & Goodwin, J. S. (1982). Patient characteristics that influence physician behavior. *Medical Care, 20,* 630–638.

House, A., Dallinger, J. M., & Kilgallen, D. (1998). Androgyny and rhetorical sensitivity: The connection of gender and communicator style. *Communication Reports, 11,* 12–20.

Irish, J. T., & Hall, J. A. (1995). Interruptive patterns in medical visits: The effects of role, status, and gender. *Social Science and Medicine, 41,* 873–881.

Johnson, J. D., & Meischke, H. (1993). Cancer-related channel selection: An extension for a sample of women who have had a mammogram. *Women & Health, 20,* 31–44.

Kalisch, B. (1975). Of half gods and mortals: Aesculapian authority. *Nursing Outlook, 23,* 22–28.

Koch, K. A., Meyers, B. W., & Sandroni, S. (1992). Analysis of power in medical decision-making: An argument for physician autonomy. *Law, Medicine and Health Care, 20,* 320–326.

Lewis, C. E., & Lewis, M. A. (1977). The potential impact of sexual equality on health. *New England Journal of Medicine, 297,* 863–867.

Leventhal, H. (1982). Wrongheaded ideas about illness. *Psychology Today, 73,* 48–55.

Mant, A., Broom, D. H. J., & Duncan-Jones, P. (1983). The path to prescription: Sex differences in psychotropic drug prescribing for general practice patients. *Social Psychiatry, 19,* 185–192.

Marcus, A. C., & Seeman, T. T. (1981). Sex differences in reports of illness and disability: A preliminary test of the "fixed role obligations" hypothesis. *Journal of Health and Social Behavior, 22,* 174–182.

McCann, K., & McKenna, H. P. (1993). An examination of touch between nurses and elderly patients in a continuing care setting in Northern Ireland. *Journal of Advanced Nursing, 18,* 838–846.

McCorkle, R. (1974). Effects of touch on seriously ill patients. *Nursing Research, 23,* 125–131.

McCracken, S. (1998, September 29). Health news. *The Washington Post,* p. 37.

McMahan, E. M., Hoffman, K., & McGee, G. W. (1994). Nurse-physician relationships in clinical settings: A review and critique of the literature, 1966–1991. *Medical Care Review, 51,* 83–112.

Meeuwesen, L., Schaap, C., & van der Staak, C. (1991). Verbal analysis of doctor–patient communication. *Social Science and Medicine, 32,* 1143–1150.

Murphy-Cullen, C. L., & Larsen, L. C. (1984). Interaction between the socio-demographic variables of physicians and their patients: Its impact upon patient satisfaction. *Social Science and Medicine, 10,* 163–166.

Quill, T. E., & Brody, H. (1996). Physician recommendations and patient autonomy: Finding a balance between physician power and patient choice. *Annals of Internal Medicine, 125,* 763–768.

Roter, D., Kipkin, M., Jr., & Korsgaard, A. (1991). Sex differences in patients' and physicians' communication during primary care medical visits. *Medical Care, 11,* 1083–1093.

Roter, D. L., & Hall, J. A. (1992). *Doctors talking with patients/patients talking with doctors: Improving communication in medical visits.* Westport, CT: Auburn House.

Safran, D. G., Rogers, W. H., Tarlov, A. R., McHorney, C. A., & Ware, J. E. (1997). Gender differences in medical treatment: The case of physician-prescribed activity restrictions. *Social Science and Medicine, 45,* 711–722.

Schneider, D. E., & Tucker, R. K. (1992). Measuring communicative satisfaction in doctor–patient relations: The doctor–patient communication inventory. *Health Communication, 4,* 19–28.

Schommer, J. C., & Wiederholt, J. B. (1997). The association of prescription status, patient age, patient gender, and patient question asking behavior with the content of pharmacist–patient communication. *Pharmaceutical Research, 14,* 145–151.

Schmidt, D. D. (1977). Patient compliance: The effect of the doctor as a therapeutic agent. *Journal of Family Practice, 10,* 60–81.

Sen, M. (1997). Communication with cancer patients: The influence of age, gender, education, and health insurance status. *Annals of the New York Academy of Sciences, 809,* 514–524.

Smith, M. J. (1982). *Persuasion and human action: A review and critique of social influence theories.* Belmont, CA: Wadsworth.

Steward, M. (1983). Patient characteristics which are related to the doctor–patient interaction. *Family Practice, 1,* 30–36.

Street, R. L., & Buller, D. B. (1988). Patients' characteristics affecting physician–patient nonverbal communication. *Human Communication Research, 15,* 60–69.

Street, R. L., & Wiemann, J. M. (1987). Patient satisfaction with physicians' interpersonal involvement, expressiveness, and dominance. In M. L. McLaughlin (Ed.), *Communication yearbook, 10,* (pp. 591–612). Newbury Park, CA: Sage.

Todd, A. D. (1989). *Intimate adversaries: Cultural conflicts between doctors and women patients.* Philadelphia: University of Pennsylvania Press.

Verbrugge, L. M. (1984). How physicians treat mentally distressed men and women. *Social Science and Medicine, 18,* 1–9.

Waitzkin, H. (1984). Doctor–patient communication: Clinical implications of social scientific research. *Journal of the American Medical Association, 252,* 2441–2446.

Waitzkin, H. (1985). Information giving in medical care. *Journal of Health and Social Behavior, 26,* 81–101.

Wallen, J., Waitzkin, J. H., & Stoeckle, J. (1979). Physician stereotypes about female health and illness. *Women and Health, 4,* 1135–1145.

Wartman, S. A., Morlock, L. L., Malitz, F. E., & Palm, E. A. (1983). Patient understanding and satisfaction as predictors of compliance. *Medical Care, 21,* 886–891.

Weisman, C. S. (1987). Communication between women and their health care providers: Research findings and unanswered questions. *Public Health Reports* (Conference Proceedings Supplement), *1,* 147–151.

West, C. (1984). When the doctor is a "lady": Power, status and gender in physician–patient encounters. *Symbolic Interaction, 7,* 87–93.

Weyrauch, K., Boiko, P., & Alvin, B. (1990). Patient sex role and preference for a male or female physician. *The Journal of Family Practice, 30,* 559–562.

7

Explaining Illness to Older Adults: The Complexities of the Provider–Patient Interaction as We Age

Jon F. Nussbaum
Department of Communication
Pennsylvania State University

Loretta Pecchioni
Department of Speech Communication
Louisiana State University

Jo Anna Grant
Department of Communication
Arkansas State University

Annette Folwell
Department of Communication
Western Oregon University

The Oklahoma Geriatric Education Center located in the Oklahoma Center on Aging at the University of Oklahoma sponsors a Summer Geriatric Institute each year to provide an educational enhancement experience for health care providers who care for older adults. At one of the more well-attended sessions for the 1997 conference, a geriatrician began her talk with a story about one of her patients, who recently had undergone heart surgery. The geriatrician projected on a screen a plate full of food items the cardiologist had recommended for this patient to eat following surgery. The plate of food consisted of the most bland assortment of vegetables imaginable. This new diet represented a very common practice for patients recovering from heart surgery. The diet is meant to provide a healthy lifestyle to prevent further heart problems. This particular recovering patient was male, well over 70 years, who loved cake. The geriatrician next showed a slide depicting a wonderful tray of many slices of delicious cake. The geriatrician said that once or twice a week, she made sure her patient ate cake.

Although this story was meant to convey multiple messages, perhaps the most important message in the context of this chapter is that older patients may just not fit the typical mold of cookbook medicine and that health care providers may need to stop and rethink how health care is delivered and managed with individuals who are well into their sixth or seventh decade of life. The heart surgery was successful, but the patient need not enter into a routine to prevent heart disease for an additional 50 years.

It is clear that we are becoming an increasingly older society. In addition to our increased life span and the total number of individuals who are over the age of 65, persons aged 65 and older make greater use of the health care system than any other segment of the population (U.S. Senate Special Committee on Aging, 1991). This is in a context of a population of older adults who remain relatively healthy. However, when an older individual does visit the physician, that person is more likely to present chronic conditions complicated by comorbidities (Adelman, Greene, & Charon, 1991; Beisecker, 1996). The medical encounter becomes more of an illness-management process rather than a direct session of cure. This fact, combined with a lack of knowledge on the part of health care providers (especially physicians) of the aging process, can lead to a rather unproductive medical interaction. The difficulties associated with the health care provider–older patient interaction has spawned an impressive amount of scientific literature attempting to uncover the problems associated with the communication between formal caregivers and their older patients.

This chapter reviews the unique physical, cognitive, language, and interative–relationship characteristics of this particular medical interaction that must be considered when explaining illness to older adults. We frame our chapter within the Communication Predicament Of Aging Model, a perspective designed to help explain intergenerational communication.

COMMUNICATION PREDICAMENT OF AGING MODEL

Social gerontologists studying the interactive life of older adults noticed that, at times, communication problems seemed to occur during interactions between older adults and their younger interactive partners. These problems appeared to be most pronounced within medical encounters. In an attempt to explain and understand the process of problematic intergenerational communication, Ryan, Giles, Bartolucci, and Henwood (1986) created the Communication Predicament Of Aging Model. This model was first presented to explain how stereotypes might lead to problematic speech that may ultimately affect the health of older adults (Williams, Giles, Coupland, Dalby, & Manasse, 1990; Williams & Nussbaum, in press). According to this model, a younger individual, such as a health care provider, approaches the older individual to interact. The younger individual notices certain physical cues that trigger intergroup categorization and associated age stereotypes. These old-age stereotypes invoke certain types of speech behavior that may not serve the older individual or younger person well. In other words, the stereotypes associated with the age of the interactants have a profound effect on the communication within the interaction. This interaction pattern can lead to loss of self-esteem and control on the part of the older adult and at the same time reinforce negative stereotypic behavior on the part of younger interactants.

Hummert (1994) modified the original communication predicament model by proposing a Stereotype Activation Model that focuses more on the role of positive stereotypes. The exact stereotype that is activated is related to the perceivers' self-system, their age, frequency, and quality of contact with other older adults and the cognitive capacity of the other interactant. Like the original communication predicament model, Hummert's modification maintains that age-adapted speech will result as a function of stereotypes associated with the aging process.

The communication predicament that occurs when a younger individual interacts with an older adult is at the heart of what we are attempting to describe within this chapter. It is our contention that younger health care providers will experience this communication predicament when attempting to explain illness to their older patients. The process of recognizing old age cues, having stereotypic expectations, modifying speech behavior, and experiencing the consequences of this modified speech behavior must be understood and, in some instances, controlled if we are to competently explain illness to older adults. This process of communication entails several steps and permits us to separate the process into its communicative components. First, we review the physical manifestations of aging that signal to younger health care providers that they are about to enter an interaction with an older adult is reviewed. Next, the cognitive factors associated with communication and aging is reviewed. Third, the literature on language and aging, including how younger and older individuals modify their speech when entering an intergenerational interaction is reviewed. Then, the interactive–relationship findings that have emerged from studies to the dynamics of the physician–older patient relationship are discussed. Finally, the chapter is concluded with suggestions on how this literature should influence the design of effective illness explanations.

Physical Aging

When health care providers meet with older patients, they are bombarded with physical cues signifying that this patient is old. Clearly, graying hair, wrinkled skin, hair loss, slow movement, and numerous other external cues are linked to the aging process. The Baltimore Longitudinal Study on Aging, a project funded by the National Institute on Aging, has documented the physical, mental, and emotional effects of aging in healthy people (Shock et al., 1984; Sprott & Roth, 1992). Perhaps the most important findings from the study allow the separation of fact from myth. Persons do not manifest the markers of age at the same rate and chronological age is not the best predictor of who looks old. As we age, we do experience changes in our general appearance, dental condition, weight and metabolism, cardiovascular system, reaction time, the function of organs, strength, and changes in senses (Hayflick, 1994). However, these changes are less critical than biography in determining our current medical status (Stahl & Feller, 1990). In addition, the myth that old equals sick is a fallacy (Stahl & Feller, 1990). The National Health Interview Survey (1996) found that only 16.1% of community-dwelling individuals 65 and older reported serious limitations in instrumental activities of daily living (e.g., being able to do grocery shopping) or activities of daily living (e.g., eating or getting in and out of bed). Although a significant minority of the elderly (21.3%) have a chronic disability, the percentage of elderly in this category is declining (Duke University, 1997). Simply stated, older people are healthier, longer. In addition, the outward markers of aging, such as graying hair and wrinkles, often have no correlation to cognitive impairment or any type of slowed mental capacity. On the surface, none of the normal age-related physical changes people undergo for the great majority of their lives should interfere with competent interactions between a health care provider and an older adult. However, as the communication predicament model suggests, these markers of aging produce stereotypic expectations of what should transpire. These expectations have the potential to produce interactive problems.

The ability to communicate competently with another individual often assumes the ability of both interactants to hear. One physical change highly correlated with the aging process is presbycusis, age-related hearing loss. When compared with the entire population, older adults are more likely to have some degree of hearing impairment (Villaume, Brown, & Darling, 1994). Shewan (1990) reported that individuals aged 18 to 44 years have a 4.9% prevalence rate of hearing impairment, compared to a 38.1% rate for persons over the age of 75. Age-related hearing loss is typically greater for high-frequency than for low-frequency tones (Villaume et al., 1994). Diminished sensitivity for these higher-pitched sounds has significant implications for how older adults apprehend the content of speech by detecting, discriminating, and recognizing words, phrases, and sentences.

Simply stated, one's ability to hear is directly related to one's ability to successfully communicate. Beyond all other age-related physical changes, hearing loss directly affects the communicative encounter with older adults. Nussbaum, Thompson, and Robinson (1989) suggested that hearing loss may cause the older adult to have less confidence in his or her ability to communicate and may make it less likely that he or she will initiate communication or ask for clarification when the meaning is not clear. Hearing loss has also been associated with anxiety, depression, and social isolation (Darbyshire, 1984). At the same time, older adults do not simply accept hearing loss. Numerous adaptive strategies are available for the hearing impaired to cope with their hearing problems. In addition, not every older adult suffers from age-related hearing difficulties. Although presbycusis is common enough for us to be concerned about competent communication with an older adult, the younger health care provider must be competent enough within the communication encounter to adapt his or her strategy of communication to first discover if hearing is an issue and then to change behavior to deal with the hearing loss, if needed.

The Communication Predicament Of Aging Model states that the younger interactant must first recognize the behavioral cues of old age. We do physically change as we age. The one physical change that has a direct impact on our ability to communicate about illness is hearing loss. Beyond hearing loss, however, the physical changes of aging are only the first step in the communicative process of talking about illness. The second phase of the model centers on both the young adult and the older adult forming stereotypic expectations based on the physical cues. These stereotypic expectations involve the cognitive component of our communication experiences.

Cognition

The study of cognition within the process of communication and aging is quite extensive (Nussbaum, Hummert, Williams, & Harwood, 1996). Two major areas of cognitive study are of interest to this chapter on explaining illness to older adults. First, the actual cognitive abilities and cognitive decline with age have an impact on the communicative encounter. Much like the various physical changes we experience as we age may or may not directly affect our communicative abilities, the various age-related cognitive changes might impact the medical encounter. Second, the process of stereotyping during the interaction between a younger health care provider and an older adult can affect the communication within that encounter.

Three aspects of the cognitive system appear to exhibit age-related change and have an affect on language processing and production capabilities of older adults: Working memory, processing speed, and name retrieval. Research by Kemper and colleagues (Kemper, Kynette, Rash, O'Brien, & Sprott, 1989) has shown that working memory capacity and processing speed appear to affect the syntactic and discourse processing abilities of older adults. Age-related loss of syntactic complexity in both written and oral modalities was uncovered for individuals with advancing age. Kemper, Kynette, and Norman (1992) linked decline in working memory to significant declines in syntactic complexity for individuals in their late 70s and 80s. In addition, a decline in working memory has been linked to the processing of complex syntactic structures in conversation with others (Norman, Kemper, Kynette, Cheung, & Anagnopoulos, 1991). The results of this study showed that older participants had much poorer recall than young adults for the syntactically complex statements in a conversation.

As indicated previously, there is good evidence that working memory declines in older adults. However, the evidence is clear that semantic memory does not decline as we age (Salthouse, 1988). Therefore, older adults have no more problems finding words in their conversations than younger adults. However, older adults are plagued more than young adults by problems with retrieving proper names (Cohen, 1994). This problem has been associated with proper names having fewer and more arbitrary attribute links than do common nouns. The ability to retrieve a proper name from memory is not as easy as retrieving a common noun. Regardless, the inability to remember a name signals to the participants in a conversation that something may be terribly wrong with the cognitive abilities of the older adult regardless of whether cognitive impairment is an actual issue.

The decline in cognitive abilities associated with the production and processing of language needs to be placed in the context of competent communication. The important questions for those of us interested in the communication of illness with older adults is whether these cognitive declines have an impact on the general communicative competencies of older adults. Nussbaum et al. (1996) concluded that the cognitive impairments associated with the age-related changes discussed earlier do not reduce the communicative competence of older adults. Age differences in language performance, interestingly, sometimes favor older adults, who often have been found to produce more interesting and clearer narratives than younger adults. The problem with name retrieval on the part of some older adults, however, may interfere with perceptions of communicative competence. As an older individual struggles to retrieve the name of a friend or a town, this could cause a loss of self-esteem on the part of the older adult as well as serve to reinforce stereotypes associated with the aging process for the younger interactant.

The discussion thus far concerning cognitive changes and aging has concentrated on normal aging. Pathological changes in cognitive abilities, such as Alzheimer's dementia, are clearly connected to reduced communication competence. Kemper and Lyons (1994) provided a detailed discussion of the affects of Alzheimer's dementia on language and communication. It should be noted that the perception of Alzheimer's dementia as part of normal aging can produce negative stereotypes that once again place a barrier around competent communication between health care providers and their older patients. Of individuals 65 years and older, less than 9% suffer from senile dementia of the Alzheimer's type (Moody, 1994).

A second process of cognition that is of interest concerns whether attitudes, stereotypes, and communication-related beliefs influence perceptions of and communication with older people. There is evidence to suggest that age-related physical and cognitive decline in old age does not necessarily lead to communication difficulties for older adults. However, the Communication Predicament Of Aging Model proposes that communicative difficulty for older adults can be related to stereotypes associated with old age. Numerous literature reviews on attitudes toward, beliefs about, and stereotypes of older adults indicate that negative as well as positive evaluations do exist concerning the aging process (Nussbaum et al., 1996). Hummert, Garstka, Shaner, and Strahm (1994) categorized the negative stereotypes of older adults into the labels "severely impaired," "despondent," "shrew–curmudgeon," and "recluse." Positive labels include "golden ager," "perfect grandparent," and "John Wayne conservative." The results of numerous studies indicate that the stereotypes associated with older adults change depending on how much information an individual has about an older adult. Typically, the more positive an older adult is presented, the more positive a communication encounter with that older person is perceived. However, if the target older person is presented in a negative stereotypic way, subjects of all ages report the likelihood of communication problems. People are simply more positive about interacting with golden-agers and more negative about interacting with a curmudgeon.

Next, the process of communicating with an older adult concerns whether these negative and positive perceptions of older adults influence communication. The Communication Predicament Of Aging Model indicates that if a younger individual is presented with negative categorizations of an older adult, that younger individual should predict problems within a communication encounter for that older adult. Positive stereotypes of an older adult should lead to beliefs that the older adult is a competent communicator and would experience no age-related communication problems. Hummert and colleagues (Hummert & Shaner, 1994; Hummert, Shaner, Garstka, & Henry, in press) found that young people did, indeed, feel that negative targets required messages that were shorter, less complex, and more demeaning in tone than messages sent to positive targets. This evidence supports the prediction of the model that our stereotypes and attitudes toward older adults may influence our communicative behavior. The next section of this chapter examines the literature concentrating on how both younger individuals change their language when interacting with an older adult and how older individuals change their language when interacting with a younger person.

Language

When entering an interaction with an older adult, we first notice the physical cues that indicate that this individual is different than us—this person is old. These cues prompt us to consider stereotypic notions of old age that produce an initial projection of how the interaction with this older adult will proceed. At this point, it becomes important to understand whether the ensuing conversation between the two participants will be significantly affected by the age of the participants. Does the fact that a younger individual is interacting with an older individual change the talk? Communication Accommodation Theory allows for the exploration and prediction of the changes that occur to language within an intergenerational interaction (Nussbaum et al., 1996) Research concerning accommodation theory has focused on the natural pattern of converging toward a desirable conversational partner in such features as speech rate, volume, dialect, and formality (Giles & Coupland, 1991). When speech style is adapted in response to actual or perceived features of the other individual in an interaction, then accommodation has occurred (Harwood, Giles, & Ryan, 1995). Other forms of intergroup accommodation including divergence (moving away from the speech style of the other individual), overaccommodation (moving toward a stereotypic conception of the other person), underaccommodation (failing to be sensitive to the conversational needs of the other individual), and complementarity (divergence with positive intent) have been studied by Giles and his associates (Harwood et al., 1995). The most extensively investigated strategy of accommodation that has important implications for explaining illness to older adults is young-to-old overaccommodation.

Caporael (1981) noticed an extreme form of patronization to institutionalized older adults, irrespective of their functional ability, that was labeled "secondary baby talk." The much younger staff of nursing homes were found to drastically change their style of speaking to the older residents. The talk directed toward the older residents was very similar to talk directed to newborns. Caporael's work led to numerous studies both in nursing homes and in other contexts to identify the characteristics of this secondary baby talk or patronizing speech directed toward older adults. Patronizing speech is distinguished from normal adult speech by being slow, oversimplified, polite, and overly warm in combination with clarification strategies such as careful articulation and increased volume (Ryan et al., 1986). Researchers have now identified patronizing speech directed toward older adults in service settings as well as within the family (Kemper, 1994; Montepare, Steinberg, & Rosenberg, 1992). It has become clear that when younger adults talk to older adults, a patronizing speech style is likely to be utilized by the younger adults.

Grainger, Atkinson, and Coupland (1990) speculated that younger adults use a patronizing speech style with older adults in order to communicate nurturance and socioemotional support. However, in some cases, patronizing speech is also used as a strategy to communicate dominance and control over the older adult. Ryan and Cole (1990) investigated the appropriateness of patronizing speech from the perspective of the older adult. It appears as if older adults with certain life circumstances feel that patronizing speech may be acceptable. Older adults living in institutions were more tolerant and appreciative of some aspects of patronizing speech than were older adults living in the community. The dilemma faced by younger family members, friends, caregivers, and strangers when interacting with older adults is just how much to overaccommodate their speech style. At what point does patronizing speech become an irritant and work to disrupt competent communication?

A series of experimental studies have been published to determine how individuals respond to vignettes of patronizing speech in different contexts (for a detailed review of these studies see Nussbaum et al., 1996). The results appear quite clear that both older and younger adults feel that intergenerational communication is less satisfying when patronizing talk is present. In addition, when older adults were asked if they had ever been patronized by younger adults, they responded that they had and that it was extremely irritating. It is relevant to note that older adults rated residents of nursing homes as less competent, weaker, and less alert when patronizing speech was directed toward that older resident. This finding is of concern because patronizing speech can confirm stereotypes of weakness and lead to greater dependence on the part of the older adult.

The results from the series of investigations concerning younger-to-older overaccommodation indicate that patronizing talk is a common feature of intergenerational communication (Caporael, 1981; Kemper, 1994; Montepare et al., 1992; Ryan et al., 1986). This patronizing talk is not limited to nursing homes or older adults who are frail and ill. Patronizing talk occurs in most contexts and can be seen as a sign of respect and concern or as a sign of disrespect and an attempt to control the interaction. For health care providers who are attempting to explain illness to older patients, the ability to control an appropriate amount of patronizing speech will be an important feature of that interaction.

Because all interactions involve at least two participants, it is necessary to consider the talk of the older interactant within intergenerational communication. Thus far, we have reviewed literature that concentrated on the talk of the younger interactant directed toward the older adult. Even within a medical encounter where the health care provider may dominate the interaction, the older adult remains an active participant whose behavior will, to some extent, dictate the success of the communicative encounter. Research that has explored the interactive role of older adults within intergenerational discourse has identified old-to-young underaccommodation. An older individual who is not sensitive to a younger individual's viewpoint would be underaccommodating within the conversation.

Perhaps the most demonstrative study that has investigated old-to-young underaccommodation was an investigation of intergenerational discourse conducted in Wales by Coupland, Coupland, and Giles (1991). Younger women (30–40 years) were paired with older women (70–90 years) and told to get to know one another. The older women were members of adult day-care centers and the younger women were recruited through newspaper ads. The paired women were strangers and their conversations were videotaped. The most profound result from these taped conversations was the fact that the older women spent approximately one sixth of their time disclosing personally painful information. This phenomenon was termed painful self-disclosure (PSD). The older adults introduced the majority of the PSDs, although numerous PSDs were elicited by the younger person. Often, an initial PSD would lead to the chaining of other PSDs. In only one old–young dyad did the younger individual reciprocate with her own PSD. This interactive pattern of disclosing highly painful information, chaining this painful information to other painful information, and the lack of reciprocity of painful information all within an initial encounter is deemed to be highly unusual. During a follow-up study, young women listened to audiotaped extracts of PSD from the initial study. Most of the younger women reported that the older women who were disclosing painful information during this initial encounter were egocentric, focusing on their own problems, and were underattentive to the younger women and their conversational needs. In other words, the older women were underaccommodat ing within the conversation and this underaccommodation was evaluated as inappropriate.

The finding that older adults are underaccommodative in intergenerational communication has received support from Williams (1992). A large sample of undergraduate students were asked to describe and rate their satisfying and dissatisfying intergenerational interactions. One of the four factors found to differentiate satisfying from dissatisfying encounters was labeled "underaccommodative negativity." Two items that loaded high on this factor were "the older person talked excessively and exclusively about his/her own problems" and "I didn't know what to say in return to the older person's complaints." The undergraduate students who reported that age was a salient factor within their intergenerational communication also claimed to have endured more of this negative underaccommodation. In another study, Williams and Giles (1995) asked young adults to comment on dissatisfying conversations with older adults. The younger adults reported that the older adults would not listen to them, would interrupt, and would talk off-target.

Gold and colleagues (Gold, Andres, Arbuckle, & Schwartzman, 1988; Gold, Arbuckle, & Andres, 1994) investigated a phenomenon similar to that previously mentioned when an older adult produces an extreme amount of irrelevant speech in normal conversations. The authors stated that they were very impressed by the fact that they had never encountered children, and only infrequently observed younger adults, who performed such extremely verbose behavior. This abundance of talk with a lack of focus they labeled "off-target verbosity" (OTV). A conversation with an older adult who is OTV quickly turns into a monologue. This type of talk primarily consists of reminiscences about the speaker's past, presented in a disjointed manner. For speech to be categorized as OTV, it must be prolonged and lack coherence. It is simply not just too many words in a conversation, but the words must appear to be disjointed and irrelevant to the agreed-on topic of the conversation. The research by Gold and her colleagues does find a link between OTV and aging. Between 17% and 22% of older adults can be classified as extreme talkers. The stereotype of the older adult talking too much and on what appear to be random topics in a conversation actually does occur in a rather large minority of interactions with older adults. The implications for this socially irritating behavior have yet to be studied. However, it is not unreasonable to suggest that health care workers, or any individual for that matter, who must interact with an OTV person—and requires that person to provide important information in a timely manner—will likely have a difficult interaction. In addition, once a younger adult encounters an OTV older adult, the behavior exhibited by the older adult is likely to be remembered and generalized to future encounters with older adults.

Whether the younger interactant is patronizing the older adult within an interaction or the older adult is talking too much in a scattered monologue, intergenerational communication can be difficult at times. The literature is quite convincing that communication encounters between individuals of different generations is different from communication encounters of same-age peers. Because the great majority of provider–older patient encounters are intergenerational, the difficulties associated with overaccommodation and underaccommodation will be real and must be addressed if illness is to be explained in a competent manner. Beyond difficulties with language that can occur within the provider–older patient interaction, health communication researchers have investigated the uniqueness of the physician–older patient relationship. In the next section of this chapter, the results of numerous studies that have looked into the unique nature of the physician–older patient relationship will be reviewed.

Physician–Older Patient Relationship

Changes in the health care business have necessitated interaction between patients and numerous professionals beyond their physician. The purpose of managed care, for instance, is to maintain our health with fewer costly trips to the physician and shorter stays in the hospital. Thus, the way we do medical encounters is rapidly changing. However, to date, very little research has investigated the relationship between nurses, physician assistants, physical therapists, nutritionists, and numerous other medical professionals and older patients. Therefore, left are the rather impressive amount of empirical research that attempts to explain the unique attributes and outcomes of the physician–older patient relationship. Literature reviews do exist that discuss the major research programs investigating the physician–older patient relationship (Beisecker & Thompson, 1995; Haug & Ory, 1987). We simply wish to highlight several important conclusions and implications from that literature that have significant impact on how a health care provider explains illness to an older adult.

The first factor that appears to have impact on the physician–older patient relationship is the context of medical care (Greene, Adelman, Rizzo, & Friedmann,1994). Older individuals who visit a physician in a clinic, a hospital, or within a health maintenance organization will find physicians who are rushed and who must see a number of different patients of all ages in a required period of time. As we have mentioned before, older patients typically have more chronic diseases, have longer medical histories, may move slower, may be verbose, and are likely to be accompanied by a relative; thus, the visit may require more time than is allocated. In addition, the pressures of managed care may have an impact on how long the physician can interact with a patient, regardless of age. The rushed nature of the medical interaction or a perception that one is not being cared for because of time constraints will surely affect the communication between the physician and older adult. Factors such as the diagnosis, the reason for the visit, and whether the visit is an initial encounter or a repeat visit influences the nature of the interaction (Beisecker, 1996). Medical encounters also transpire in long-term care facilities or assisted living centers. Such interactions will be of a different nature than those taking place in a physician's office. Another context issue involves telemedicine. The technology that permits physicians and patients to interact over fiberoptic telephone lines is a priority in large, rural states. Research investigating the affect of telemedicine on the older patient–physician relationship has yet to be performed. Needless to say, the general context of the medical encounter may play a significant role in the process of explaining illness to an older patient.

One of the basic assumptions of this chapter is that the older patient–health care provider interaction is significantly different from interaction that transpires within a younger patient–health care provider encounter. Although we would argue that, in many ways, age is not a factor in such interactions, it should be clear that age-related physiological changes, cognitive changes, and life experiences of an older individual tend to complicate the physician–patient relationship. Ory, Abeles, and Lipman (1992) reported that the current cohort of older individuals have different attitudes toward health care than younger individuals. For instance, older women are more accepting of mammography, older people in general report higher frequencies of preventive health actions, are more compliant with treatment regimens, and are more responsive to health threats. In addition, there appear to be important communicative differences between older and younger patients within the medical encounter. Beisecker and Thompson (1995) concluded that younger patients ask questions of physicians more frequently, talk about their problems more, give information in more detail and are more assertive in their medical encounters. Beisecker and Beisecker (1990) reported that older patients do ask more questions in longer interactions with their physicians but these questions are asked during the later parts of the interaction.

Researchers have also investigated the importance of who raises medical issues the encounter (Adelman, Greene, Charon, & Friedmann, 1992). Results of coded interactions between physicians and their older patients revealed that physicians were more likely to raise medical topics, whereas patients were more likely to raise psychosocial topics and discussion of the physician–patient relationship. Of more importance, however, is the finding that physicians responded more positively and with more detail when they had initiated the topic. The authors reported that these results may signal a problem for older patients who wish to have their concerns addressed by the physician. If the older patient raised an issue, the physicians frequently did not respond with much information. Rost and Frankel (1993) found similar results with older diabetic patients whose personal medical concerns were not raised within the encounter. It is important to note that older patients who participated in a previsit interview asking the older patient about their problems raised more problems or issues in the medical encounter. Older patients appear to ask more questions and raise more relevant issues with their physicians if coached prior to the medical encounter.

An important relational issue in the medical encounter centers on medical decision making. Factors such as patient involvement and patient participation in decision making appear to differ for younger and older patients. Beisecker and Thompson (1995) cited substantial evidence that the current cohort of older adults does not want as much involvement in medical decision making as younger adults. Older patients want the physician to be in control and to make the medical decision. This finding is consistent with research conducted by Greene, Adelman, Charon, and Friedmann (1989), who reported that physicians are less likely to share medical decision making with their older patients. The complementary nature of this relationship is quite efficient. The older patient may not want to participate in the decision and the physician is more than willing to make each medical decision without the patient's participation. This lack of joint participation concerning the medical decisions is of special concern for older patients who have been shown to report less agreement with the physician than younger patients concerning the main goals and primary medical problems of the encounter (Greene et al., 1989).

An additional physician-centered issue that has an important impact on the physician–patient relationship is the presence of ageism in the medical encounter (Butler, 1975; Haug & Ory, 1987). Greene and Adelman (1996) reported that the majority of older adults receive their general medical care from internists and family practitioners, not from formally trained geriatricians. To illustrate this point, the University of Oklahoma College of Medicine has recently created only the third Department of Geriatric Medicine in the United States. The formal role of this department in the routine education of the medical students is still unclear. Yet, the university was persuaded that some more formal role of geriatric education was needed on the Health Science Center campus. Williams and Nussbaum (in press) went so far as to state that the health care industry—including medical schools, hospitals, and even insurance companies—are among the most ageist entities in our modern society. Ageist beliefs and attitudes within the medical profession (such as depression is a common occurrence as we age, that pain is a normal part of aging, or even that age is a disease) cannot help but complicate any medical interaction with an older adult. Medical students are not trained in the physical, psychological, or communicative correlates of the aging process. Although geriatricians are trained to attend to both the physical aspects of a disease and the psychosocial concerns of their patients, physicians not receiving such formal training in geriatrics may compromise quality of care for older adults because of a reliance on stereotypic notions of the aging process to diagnose illness and then to communicate that diagnosis to their older patients. Stahl and Feller (1990) reported that physicians may ignore disease-related symptoms, attributing them to old age and, therefore, pursue less aggressive treatments. Greene and Adelman (1996) made a sound case for the discussion of psychosocial factors in older patients' medical encounters so as to better inform the physician about the true nature and consequences of the aging process. These psychosocial factors, however, are not considered essential to the practice of medicine for any age group of patients by mainstream medicine. The discussion of the effect of psychosocial factors on the etiology, course, and outcomes of disease does not occur in most medical encounters. Without attention to the psychosocial domain of communication within older patient–physician encounters, Greene and Adelman (1996) felt that older patients' problems will remain unidentified and that the quality of their lives will be diminished.

The physician–older patient interaction is often researched and discussed as a dyadic encounter. However, it is not uncommon for an older adult to bring a companion with them into the medical encounter. This type of triadic medical interaction is much more common for older patients than for patients who are younger adults (Beisecker & Thompson, 1995). The presence of a companion, typically a spouse or an older adult child who is the family caregiver, is very likely to change the nature of the medical encounter. Beisecker (1989) determined that companions play several roles within a medical encounter. The watchdog role enables the companion to verify information for both patient and physician. The significant other role enables the companion to provide feedback regarding the appropriateness of various behaviors within the medical interaction to both patient and physician. Finally, the surrogate patient role is played by the companion when he or she answers questions directed toward the older patient. In addition, Beisecker (1989) reported that the companion frequently asks questions of the doctor on behalf of the patient. Companions initiate more comments to the doctor or respond to the doctor's questions even when those questions are not directed toward the companion. There appears to be some evidence that a companion brought to the medical encounter could take interactive time away from the patient. Coe (1987) also reported that the companion can be a very active participant in the medical encounter. Companions can elaborate on what the older patient is saying, explain to the older patient what the physician is saying, or negotiate with both the physician and older patient on appropriate strategies of health maintenance. The fact that a companion has accompanied the older patient to the medical encounter certainly has some positive consequences. The companion can help both the physician and older patient to conduct a more competent interaction. At the same time, however, a companion can become a rather awkward barrier to effective interaction. Regardless, physicians who see older patients must learn to interact with companions and in the best of circumstances turn the companion into a well-informed and motivated caregiver.

Researchers have also investigated numerous outcomes of the physician–older patient interaction. Beisecker (1996) summarized the research on the outcomes of the medical encounter for older patients by reporting that older patients are satisfied with the medical encounter. As a matter of fact, older patients often report higher levels of satisfaction with their medical care than younger patients. Factors that predict patient satisfaction include the physician's task-directed skills, the amount of information given to patients, the patients' perceptions that their needs were being met, emotional support and communication regarding psychosocial communication, perceptions of whether older patients are given an opportunity to ask questions regarding their own agenda, and the physician's ability to build a relational partnership with the older patient. Family caregivers do not report as much satisfaction with the physician as do older patients (Glasser, Rubin, & Dickover, 1989; Haley, Clair, & Saulsberry, 1992). Beisecker (1996) reported that caregiver dissatisfaction is related to the amount of information received, emotional support offered (to the caregiver and not the patient), and assistance in referrals to needed services. In addition, caregivers are more dissatisfied when they feel the doctor has asserted too much control during the medical encounter (Beisecker, 1996).

Additional outcome measures include patient recall and patient compliance to the treatment regimen. Roter and Hall (1989) found that as the amount of information the physician gives to the patient increases, the recall of information by the patient decreases. Physicians need to know when too much information becomes a burden and overloads the patient or that they need to provide information in written as well as oral form for later use by the patient. Beisecker (1996) reported that factors such as information giving, patient's volunteering of information, the type and amount of physician question asking, and patient response to those questions are related to patient compliance to treatment regimens. In addition, numerous physician characteristics such as job satisfaction, number of patients seen per week, and physician specialty are related to patient compliance. Perhaps most important for many older patients is the fact that a family caregiver will be working with the patient to follow the treatment regimen. Thus, compliance will be dependent on how well the caregiver understands and complies with the physician's recommendations.

Summary of Research

Proposed in this chapter is that the Communication Predicament Of Aging Model captures the complexity of the health care provider–older patient relationship and provides an excellent scheme for organizing the empirical literature directed toward explaining illness to older adults. The physical cues of aging—regardless of whether they are actual physical, psychological, or communicative behaviors or whether they are perceived to be real—will be recognized by the younger health care provider and will set into motion a communication process affected by numerous negative as well as positive stereotypes. The language utilized in the medical encounter will not only be caused by these stereotypes but will reflect these stereotypes and, at the same time, will define and shape the health care provider–older patient relationship. These language behaviors and the relationship in which the communication transpires will help to determine the outcomes of the medical encounter. The health care provider–older patient medical encounter deserves special attention from health communication scholars. This special attention is based on the empirical evidence cited previously and leads to the pragmatic suggestions for future research that can lead to more competent interaction within the medical encounter.

EXPLAINING ILLNESS TO OLDER ADULTS

We view the medical encounter as a dynamic communication process that demands attention to all participants in the interaction. Concentrating on the health care provider, the older patient or the caregiver–companion without accounting for what each member adds to the interaction fails to capture the richness of the medical encounter. It should be clear that explaining illness is not simply a matter of choosing one effective verbal strategy on the part of the physician. In addition, successful strategies to explain illness to older adults will require more than just a list of verbal commands. The communication process includes a very large cognitive component both before and after the actual exchange of messages. With these fundamental ideas in mind, the following key suggestions are offered on how the empirical literature can influence the design of effective illness explanations.

Knowledge of the Physical, Cognitive, and Social Correlates of the Aging Process

A series of surveys reveal that our individual knowledge of why we age and what the normal behaviors associated with aging really are remain a mystery to most individuals. It is the responsibility of all social scientists who study health-related behaviors, practitioners and health care providers who must care for older adults, and all aging individuals to familiarize themselves with the normal changes that occur during the aging process. These age-related changes will be physical, cognitive, and communicative. These changes will not occur at the exact same time in all people, and some of the changes will be more noticeable in some individuals.

The major point here is to educate ourselves to the aging process. Hayflick's (1994) *How and Why We Age* and Austad's (1997) *Why We Age* are recent books written by well- respected biomedical scientists who provide accurate information on how the body and mind change across the life span. These books would be quite useful for anyone interested in the fundamental facts of the aging process. However, social scientists who wish to study the older patient–health care provider encounter and health care providers who interact with older adults need to read well beyond the books just cited and educate themselves to the complexities and subtleties of growing older. As we mentioned previously, the great majority of health care workers, especially physicians, have no formal training in human development across the life span. Often, the only older adults these professions saw in their medical education were very frail, sick individuals. The normal and noticeable changes in aging may not be recognized or may signal great alarm in those who have only dealt with frail elderly people. Of more importance for this chapter are the normal age-related changes that directly affect our ability to communicate competently. Hearing loss, verbosity, language production, and name retrieval are a few factors mentioned in this chapter that do appear to be affected by normal aging. Older individuals as well as health care professionals need to recognize these changes, adapt their behavior to accommodate these changes, and not associate these changes with the onset of a devastating disease like Alzheimer's.

Awareness of Stereotypes of Aging

The myths of aging (e.g., pain is normal, Alzheimer's is inevitable for all of us, sexual activity will disappear, intelligence will decline; etc.) are excellent examples of stereotypes associated with old age. The communication predicament model places stereotypes of aging in a very important location within the communication process. These stereotypes, both negative and positive, will directly lead to problematic language in an encounter. It is important for scholars to continue their investigations into the exact nature of these stereotypes as well as the relationship between stereotypes and language.

Research to date has identified many negative stereotypes associated with aging within individuals of all ages. Williams and Nussbaum (in press) were emphatic in their appraisal of the health professions as one of the most ageist institutions in our society. Negative stereotypes of aging held by health care professionals could do great harm in the proper diagnosis and treatment of older adults. The same can be true for positive stereotypes of aging. In addition, it is important to understand the stereotypes of aging held by older adults. If an older adult feels that aging is a process of decline and physical discomfort, he or she may be unlikely to seek help or to explain his or her illness to the caretaker in an appropriate and competent manner.

Patronizing Speech

Communication scholars have described, investigated, and provided exemplars of patronizing speech that occur as a result of stereotypes within the medical encounter. It would not be an overstatement to suggest that patronizing speech will occur within an interaction between a younger health care provider and an older patient. In some of these interactions, patronizing speech will be tolerated and accepted (e.g., in nursing homes). In other interactions, the patronizing speech directed toward older adults will have unwanted consequences. Patronizing speech has also been found directed toward younger adults by older individuals. This, too, should be of concern for those interested in a competent, successful interaction.

The over- and underaccommodation of our communicative behavior that can result in patronizing speech needs to be further investigated. It is not unreasonable to speculate that health care workers using this speech style to older adults who are active and of general good health may severely infect the medical encounter. On the other hand, a limited amount of patronizing speech may signal respect and concern, thus helping the medical encounter. In all situations, health care providers and older adults need to be aware of their patronizing speech and attempt to utilize this particular speech style in the most appropriate manner.

Build a Communication Partnership

Explaining illness to an older adult will differ from explaining illness to a younger adult in several significant ways. As mentioned previously, there are physical, cognitive, and communicative changes as we age; negative and positive stereotypes about aging will affect language; the older adults will have more chronic problems and will have a long history of interacting with the health care industry; and the older adults may be less talkative and more respectful within the medical encounter or overly verbose and too self-disclosive. Both the health care provider and the older adult will need to adapt their communicative style and strategies to successfully cope with these factors. One way of adapting to this particular medical encounter is to frame the encounter as a partnership. The health care provider–older patient medical encounter may need more time. It is simply not a good strategy to assume that patients of all ages demand the same time from the provider. The provider may have to listen for longer periods, may have to answer more questions both about physical issues and psychosocial issues, and should be aware of information overload and not attempt to explain illness and treatment regimens without time set aside to make sure the older patient understands what was just presented and possibly provide written materials for later referral by the patient. The research evidence is quite clear that older adults will want to discuss psychosocial issues that are not typically discussed with younger patients. These psychosocial issues may have a direct impact on the causes and possible consequences of why the patient has visited the provider. Therefore, the provider may need to enter into interactions with older patients that may never transpire with younger patients and, thus, spend more time within each encounter.

Scholars researching medical encounters with older adults need to study the dynamics of building this time-consuming communicative partnership in this particular interaction. How much additional time will this medical encounter actually take? Will the medical management professions permit such a time-consuming and expensive encounter? Can older adults be educated to take a greater role in their part of the medical encounter? Research cited in this chapter provided evidence that older patients coached prior to their visit with the physician raised more topics of concern than those not coached. Can physicians be educated to understand the importance of active listening and answering questions in understandable ways? Finally, is it possible to change the dynamics and nature of the interaction from a physician in total control to one in which the older patient takes some control and responsibility for that control? Health communication researchers need to study whether a communicative partnership between the provider and older patient is both feasible and productive.

The Companion

Beyond all the age-related changes and the consequences of these changes, the one factor that sets apart the medical encounter for an older adult and a health care provider from other medical encounters is the probability that a companion will accompany the patient. The companion, who is often the informal caregiver, significantly alters the communication that transpires within this medical encounter. Research has shown that the companion can take up valuable time asking and answering questions. Although the companion may be providing protection for the older patient, the physician may not be comfortable addressing two people and answering direct questions from an active companion.

The companion, however, can be encouraged to join the communicative partnership discussed previously. The companion may be the health care provider's best chance to competently explain illness and assure compliance. The co-opting of the companion into this communication partnership is no easy task. Research needs to discover how best to utilize the companion as a lay interpreter of the medical information necessary for the older patient to understand his or her condition. The companion can also be utilized as a home health caregiver who is in the best position to maintain compliance and report back if problems continue. It may be that all patients, regardless of age, are best served when a companion accompanies them into a physician's office. We suggest that the health care provider view the companion as an opportunity to better communicate with and explain illness to the patient. Health care providers interacting with an older patient and a companion can turn what might be an awkward situation into a very competent interactive partnership assuring good quality medical care.

CONCLUSION

The Communication Predicament Of Aging Model suggests that a number of unique factors must be studied and understood for health communication scholars to competently explain illness to older adults. First, we must be aware of the age-related physical, cognitive, and language changes that occur throughout our life span. Second, these changes will be noticed in interaction and will lead to stereotypes concerning the aging process. These stereotypes, in turn, will influence over- and underaccommodation of speech behavior on the part of both older patients and the younger health care provider. These speech behaviors serve to define the older patient–health care provider relationship that eventually leads to successful diagnosis, explanation of illness, compliance with the treatment regimen, and overall quality of care.

The authors of this chapter believe that having an older individual as a patient of a younger health care provider significantly changes the interactive dynamics of the medical encounter. This intergenerational relationship and the communicative complexities associated with explaining illness in a competent manner to the older individual necessitates a much closer look at this interaction by communication scholars. This medical encounter is now situated in a changing medical–business environment that, on the surface, appears to work against the needs of older adults. Both the medical profession, which has long ignored the aging body and mind, and the older adults themselves must take on more interactive responsibilities to understand the nature of communication and how explaining illness plays a significant role in quality health care.

REFERENCES

Adelman, R. D., & Greene, M. G., & Charon, R. (1991). Issues in physician–elderly patient interaction. *Aging and Society, 2,* 127–148.
Adelman, R. D., Greene, M. G., Charon, R., & Friedmann, E. (1992). The content of physician and elderly patient interaction in the medical primary care encounter. *Communication Research, 19,* 370–380.
Austad, S. N. (1997). *Why we age: What science is discovering about the body's journey through life.* New York: Wiley.
Beisecker, A. E. (1989). The influence of a companion on the doctor–elderly patient interaction. *Health Communication, 1,* 55–70.
Beisecker, A. E. (1996). Older persons' medical encounters and their outcomes. *Research on Aging, 18,* 9–31.
Beisecker, A. E., & Beisecker, T. D. (1990). Patient information seeking behaviors when communicating with doctors. *Medical Care, 28,* 19–28.
Beisecker, A. E., & Thompson, T. L. (1995). The elderly patient–physician interaction. In J. F. Nussbaum & J. Coupland (Eds.), *Handbook of communication and aging research* (pp. 397–416). Mahwah, NJ: Lawrence Erlbaum Associates.
Butler, R. (1975). *Why survive? Being old in America.* New York: Harper and Row.
Caporael, L. R. (1981). The paralanguage of caregiving: Baby talk to the institutionalized aged. *Journal of Personality and Social Psychology, 40,* 876–884.
Coe, R. M. (1987). Communication and medical care outcomes: Analysis of conversations between doctors and elderly patients. In R. A. Ward & S. S. Tobin (Eds.), *Health in aging* (pp. 180–193). New York: Springer.
Cohen, G. (1994). Age related problems in the use of proper names in communication. In M. L. Hummert, J. M. Wiemann, & J. F. Nussbaum (Eds.), *Interpersonal communication in older adulthood: Interdisciplinary theory and research* (pp. 40–57). Thousand Oaks, CA: Sage.
Coupland, N., Coupland, J., & Giles, H. (1991). *Language, society, and the elderly.* Oxford, England: Blackwell.
Darbyshire, J. O. (1984). The hearing loss epidemic: A challenge to gerontology. *Research on Aging, 6,* 384–394.
Duke University. (1997). Chronic disability declines dramatically among U.S. elderly. *Population Today, 25,*(9), 3.
Giles, H., & Coupland, N. (1991). *Language: Contexts and consequences.* Pacific Grove, CA: Brooks/Cole.
Glasser, M., Rubin, S., & Dickover, M. (1989). Caregiver views of help from the physician. *The American Journal of Alzheimer's Care and Related Disorders, 4,* 11.
Gold, D. P., Andres, D., Arbuckle, T. Y., & Schwartzman, A. (1988). Measurement and correlates of verbosity in elderly people. *Journal of Gerontology: Psychological Sciences, 47,* P266–P272.
Gold, D. P., Arbuckle, T. Y., & Andres, D. (1994). Verbosity in older adults. In M. L. Hummert, J. M. Wiemann, & J. F. Nussbaum (Eds.), *Interpersonal communication in older adulthood: Interdisciplinary theory and research* (pp. 107–129). Thousand Oaks, CA: Sage.

Grainger, K., Atkinson, K., & Coupland, N. (1990). Responding to the elderly: Troubles talk in the caring context. In H. Giles, N. Coupland, & J. M. Wiemann (Eds.), *Communication, health and the elderly* (pp. 192–212). Manchester, UK: Manchester University Press.

Greene, M. G., & Adelman, R. D. (1996). Psychosocial factors in older patients' medical encounters. *Research on Aging, 18,* 84–102.

Greene, M. G., Adelman, R. D., Charon, R., & Friedmann, E. (1989). Concordance between physicians and their older and younger patients in the primary care medical encounter. *The Gerontologist, 29,* 808–813.

Greene, M. G., Adelman, R. D., Rizzo, C., & Friedmann, E. (1994). The patient's perception of self in an initial medical encounter. In M. L. Hummert, J. M. Wiemann, & J. F. Nussbaum (Eds.), *Interpersonal communication in older adulthood: Interdisciplinary theory and research* (pp. 226–250). Thousand Oaks, CA: Sage.

Haley, W. E., Clair, J. M., & Saulsberry, K. (1992). Family caregiver satisfaction with medical care of their demented relatives. *The Gerontologist, 32,* 219–226.

Harwood, J., Giles, H., & Ryan, E. B. (1995). Aging, communication, and intergroup theory: Social identity and intergenerational communication. In J. F. Nussbaum & J. Coupland (Eds.), *Handbook of communication and aging research* (pp. 133–160). Mahwah, NJ: Lawrence Erlbaum Associates.

Haug, M. R., & Ory, M. G. (1987). Issues in elderly patient–provider interactions. *Research on Aging, 9,* 3–44.

Hayflick, L. (1994). *How and why we age.* New York: Ballantine.

Hummert, M. L. (1994). Stereotypes of the elderly and patronizing speech. In M. L. Hummert, J. M. Wiemann, & J. F. Nussbaum (Eds.), *Interpersonal communication in older adulthood: Interdisciplinary theory and research* (pp. 162–184). Thousand Oaks, CA: Sage.

Hummert, M. L., Garstka, T. A., Shaner, J. L., & Strahm, S. (1994). Stereotypes of the elderly held by young, middle-aged, and elderly adults. *Journal of Gerontology: Psychological Sciences, 49,* 240–249.

Hummert, M. L., & Shaner, J. L. (1994). Patronizing speech to the elderly: Relationship to stereotyping. *Communication Studies, 45,* 145–158.

Hummert, M. L., Shaner, J. L., Garstka, T. A., & Henry, C. (in press). Communication with older adults: The influence of age stereotypes, context, and communicator age. *Human Communication Research.*

Kemper, S. (1994). "Elderspeak": Speech accommodation to older adults. *Aging and Cognition, 1,* 17–28.

Kemper, S., Kynette, D., & Norman, S. (1992). Age differences in spoken language. In R. West & J. Sinnot (Eds.), *Everyday memory and aging* (pp. 138–154). New York: Springer-Verlag.

Kemper, S., Kynette, D., Rash, S., O'Brien, K., & Sprott, R. (1989). Lifespan changes to adults' language: Effects of memory and genre. *Applied Psycholinguistics, 10,* 49–66.

Kemper, S., & Lyons, K. (1994). The effects of Alzheimer's dementia on language and communication. In M. L. Hummert, J. M. Wiemann, & J. F. Nussbaum (Eds.), *Interpersonal communication in older adulthood: Interdisciplinary theory and research* (pp. 58–82). Thousand Oaks, CA: Sage.

Montepare, J. M., Steinberg, J., & Rosenberg, B. (1992). Characteristics of vocal communication between young adults and their parents and grandparents. *Communication Research, 19,* 479–492.

Moody, H. R. (1994). *Aging: Concepts and controversies.* Thousand Oaks, CA: Pine Forge.

National Health Interview Survey. (1996). Atlanta: Center for Disease Control.

Norman, S., Kemper, S., Kynette, D., Cheung, H., & Anagnopoulos, C. (1991). Syntactic complexity and adults' running memory span. Journal of Gerontology: *Psychological Sciences, 46,* 346–351.

Nussbaum, J. F., Hummert, M. L., Williams, A., & Harwood, J. (1996). Communication and older adults. In B. Burleson (Ed.), *Communication yearbook 19* (pp. 1–48). Thousand Oaks, CA: Sage.

Nussbaum, J. F., Thompson, T., & Robinson, J. D. (1989). *Communication and aging.* New York: Harper and Row.

Ory, M. G., Abeles, R. P., & Lipman, P. D. (1992). *Aging, health and behavior.* Newbury Park, CA: Sage.

Rost, R., & Frankel, R. (1993). The introduction of older patients' problems in the medical visit. *Journal of Aging and Health, 5,* 387–401.

Roter, D. L., & Hall, J. A. (1989). Studies of physician–patient interaction. *Annual Review of Public Health, 10,* 163–180.

Ryan, E. B., & Cole, R. (1990). Evaluative perceptions of interpersonal communication with elders. In H. Giles, N. Coupland, & J. M. Wiemann (Eds.), *Communication, health and the elderly* (pp. 172–191). Manchester, UK: Manchester University Press.

Ryan, E., Giles, H., Bartolucci, G., & Henwood, K. (1986). Psycholinguistic and social psychological components of communication by and with the elderly. *Language and Communication, 6,* 1–24.

Salthouse, T. A. (1988). Effects of aging on verbal abilities: Examination of the psychometric literature. In L. L. Light & D. Burke (Eds.), *Language, memory, and aging* (pp. 17–35). New York: Cambridge University Press.

Shewan, C. M. (1990). The prevalence of hearing impairment. *ASHA, 32,* 62.

Shock, N., Greulich, R. C., Cosa, P. T., Jr., Andres, R., Lakatta, E. G., Arenberg, D., & Tobin, J. D. (1984). *Normal human aging: The Baltimore Longitudinal Study of Aging.* Washington, DC: Government Printing Office.

Sprott, R. L., & Roth, G. S. (1992). Biomarkers of aging: Can we predict individual life span? *Generations, 16*(4), 11–14.

Stahl, S. M., & Feller, J. R. (1990). Old equals sick: An ontogenetic fallacy. In S. M. Stahl (Ed.), *The legacy of longevity: Health and health care in later life* (pp. 21–34). Newbury Park, CA: Sage.

U.S. Senate Special Committee on Aging. (1991). Washington, DC: Government Printing Office.

Villaume, W. A., Brown, M. H., & Darling, R. (1994). Presbycusis, communication, and older adults. In M. L. Hummert, J. M. Wiemann, & J. F. Nussbaum (Eds.), *Interpersonal communication in older adulthood: Interdisciplinary theory and research* (pp. 83–106). Thousand Oaks, CA: Sage.

Williams, A. (1992). *Intergenerational communication satisfaction: An intergroup analysis.* Unpublished Master's Thesis. University of California, Santa Barbara.

Williams, A., & Giles, H. (1995). *Satisfying–dissatisfying intergenerational conversations: An intergroup perspective.* Unpublished manuscript.

Williams, A., Giles, H., Coupland, N., Dalby, M., & Manasse, H. (1990). The communicative contexts of elderly social support and health: A theoretical model. *Health Communication, 2,* 123–143.

Williams, A., & Nussbaum, J. F. (in press). *Intergenerational communication across the life span.* Mahwah, NJ: Lawrence Erlbaum Associates.

8

Explaining Illness to Children: Theory, Strategies, and Future Inquiry

Bryan B. Whaley
Department of Communication
University of San Francisco

"Adults often assume that if they tell a child something—explaining it calmly and rationally—the child will comprehend." —Steward & Regalbuto (1975, p. 146)

Explaining illness is a communicative demand of increasing necessity for health practitioners (Dorn, 1984; Francis, Korsch, & Morris, 1969; Korsch & Negrete, 1972; Ley, 1988). Research suggests that this seemingly simple communicative process is, indeed, formidable and complex. Contrary to the quote that opens the chapter, when the receivers of illness explanations are children, the task of explicating medically related information is rendered more difficult (Bibace & Walsh, 1980; Eiser, 1984; Eiser & Eiser, 1987).

The arduous nature of explaining illness to children makes the task of pursuing theory and effective strategies extremely challenging. Moreover, this venture is founded on the premise that children's comprehension of their illness is an integral aspect of their medical care experience and thought to aid in their reduction of stress, self-management, and compliance with medical advice and regimens (Burbach & Peterson, 1986; Eiser,

195

1985; Eiser & Eiser, 1987; Potter & Roberts, 1984). For instance, Dorn (1984) suggested:

> How effectively one communicates can affect children's reactions to procedures, compliance with therapy, and knowledge about health and illness. ... How one approaches the child, the techniques used, and the language employed determine the degree of success or failure in these interactions. (p. 325)

Understanding existing theory and research, ascertaining the strengths and weaknesses of this literature, and determining future directions are necessary to enhance our understanding of illness explanation to youngsters.

The aim of this chapter, therefore, is to review the published works concerning message factors for explaining illness to children. Specifically, the following details the existing theory, strategies, and messages that have been offered for engaging in the communicative task of explicating the nature of illness to youngsters. This discussion concludes with suggested avenues to enhance this literature.

EXPLAINING ILLNESS TO CHILDREN

As important as explaining illness to children is said to be, research about strategies for this specific communicative task is extremely sparse (for literature concerning other issues on children and illness, see Bibace & Walsh, 1981; Eiser, 1985; Eiser & Kopel, 1997). Moreover, existing research concerning children and illness explanation has been dominated by focusing on children's conceptualization of illness (Eiser, 1985; Eiser & Eiser, 1987; Eiser, Patterson, & Tripp, 1984; Goldman, Whitney-Saltiel, Granger, & Rodin, 1991) and adults' estimations of children's understanding of illness (Perrin & Perrin, 1983). This research is based on the premise that knowing how children process and understand illness (i.e., give their answers about what causes illness), adults can extrapolate this knowledge into credible strategies and effective messages for explaining illness to children.

The foundation for illness explanation strategies to children has been the cognitive developmental (stage) approach (Bibace & Walsh, 1979, 1980, 1981; see Eiser, 1985 for reviews of sociological approach contributions to children's concepts of illness). Bibace and Walsh (1979, 1980) suggested that children's conceptualization of illness corresponds to the cognitive-developmental maturation posited by Piaget (1930) and Werner (1948).

Cognitive-Developmental (Stage) Approach

The work of Bibace & Walsh (1979, 1980, 1981) has served as the foundation for research concerning strategies for explaining illness to children.

They suggested that children's conceptualization or explanation of illness falls into six categories, on a continuum, that differ developmentally and qualitatively. The source of these categories are the investigations conducted on children ages 4 to 14 (e.g., Bibace & Walsh, 1979).

Their data yielded three primary illness conceptualizations, which Bibace and Walsh (1981) suggested align with the three stages of cognitive development of Piaget—prelogical, concrete logical, and formal logical. Further, two subtypes of explanations constitute each of the major categories, rendering six types of explanations of illness. Bibace and Walsh (1981) employed children's responses to a cold for illustrative purposes and will be used here, as well.

Prelogical Explanations. Characteristic of children between the ages of 2 and 6, prelogical thought is typified by children's incapacity to separate themselves from their social and physical environment. As a result, children in the prelogical phase of cognition offer explanations for cause–effect relationships by way of the myriad of spatial and temporal perceptual experiences or cues that are ambient in their lives (Bibace & Walsh, 1981; Piaget, 1930).

Developmentally, the most puerile explanation of illness is *phenomenism*. Children functioning in this stage perceive illness as being caused by an external concrete phenomenon that may coincide with an illness but is inaccessible spatially or temporally. In this stage, children are incapable of explaining how a phenomenon caused an illness:

How do people get colds? "From the sun." How does the sun give you a cold? "It just does, that's all."

How do people get colds? "From trees." How do people get measles? "From God," How does God give people measles? "God does it in the sky." (Bibace & Walsh, 1981, p. 36)

Bibace and Walsh (1981) suggested that *contagion* is the most prevalent illness explanation offered by the more advanced children in the prelogical group. Here, the cause of illness is found in people or entities that are close to, but not in contact with, the agent. Simple adjacency to the cause of illness or magic is offered as the conduit between the cause and the illness:

How do people get colds? "From outside." How do they get them from outside? "They just do, that's all. They come when someone else gets near you." How? "I don't know—by magic I think." How do people get colds? "When someone else gets near them." (Bibace & Walsh, 1981, p. 36)

Concrete–logical Explanations. Approximately between the age of 7 and 10 years, children progress to reasoning at the concrete–logical level.

At this stage, it is thought that children begin to differentiate between self and other and distinctly demarcate internal and external to self phenomenon (Piaget, 1930).

The younger children in the concrete–logical stage have been typified as using *contamination* as their mode of reasoning. The child, in this stage, conceptualizes between the cause of the illness and the method of transmission. Sickness is perceived as an action, object, or person separate from the child that has aspects damaging for or injurious to the body. The method of contamination is physical contact (i.e., rubbing, touching) of the object or person or performing the harmful activity resulting in contamination:

> What is a cold? "It's like in the wintertime." How do people get them? "You're outside without a hat and you start sneezing. Your head would get cold, the cold would touch it, and then it would go all over your body." (Bibace & Walsh, 1980, p. 36)

As children progress within the concrete–logical stage, their explanations reflect *internalization*. The agent of illness, here, is external to children's bodies but the effects or illness reside internally. The harmful agent gained internal access by way of swallowing or inhaling. However, children's depiction of internal illness is nebulous. Bibach and Walsh suggested that this is evidence for an unclear understanding of how organs function.

> What is a cold? "You sneeze a lot, you talk funny, and your nose is clogged up." How do people get colds? "In winter, they breathe in too much air into their nose, and it blocks up the nose." How does this cause colds? "The bacteria gets in by breathing. Then the lungs get too soft [child exhales], and it goes to the nose." How does it get better? "Hot fresh air, it gets in the nose and pushes the cold air back." (Bibace & Walsh, 1981, p. 37)

Formal–Logical Explanations.   At this stage, children about 11 years and older demonstrate formal–logical thought, exhibiting the most disparity between self and other. However, Bibace and Walsh (1981) noted: "the organism is least likely to manifest the effects of stimulus-boundedness because of the compensatory character of operational or logical thinking" (p. 37). This stage renders two types of explanations for illness—physiological and psychophysiological—that Bibace and Walsh suggested children reflect the "greatest amount of differentiation between the external and internal world, so that the source of the illness is located within the body even though an external agent is often described as the ultimate cause" (1981, p. 37).

Physiological explanations, usually provided by the callow children in this stage, render illness in terms of internal body organs and functions manifested by external agents. The source of illness is frequently accounted for by a failure or malfunctioning of an internal physiological process or organ. Children's explanations are very detailed "as a step by step internal sequence or events culminating in that illness" (Bibace & Walsh, 1981, p. 37):

> What is a cold? "It's when you get all stuffed up inside, your sinuses get filled up with mucus. Sometimes your lungs do too, and you get a cough." How do people get colds? "They come from viruses, I guess. Other people have the virus, and it gets into your blood stream and it causes a cold." Have you ever been sick? "Yes." What was wrong? "My platelet count was down." What's that? "In the blood stream they are like white blood cells. They help kill germs." Why did you get sick? "There were more germs than platelets. They killed the platelets off." How did you get sick? "From germs outside. They killed off the platelets." (Bibace & Walsh, 1981, p. 37)

Psychophysiological explanations exemplify the most mature grasp of illness. The explanations still focus on internal processes but can now incorporate a perception of psychological agents of illness as well. At this stage, children discern that thoughts and feelings can impact the workings of the body:

> What is a heart attack? "It's when your heart stops working right. Sometimes it's pumping too slow or too fast." How do people get a heart attack? "It can come from being all nerve-racked. You worry too much. The tension can affect your heart." (Bibace & Walsh, 1981, p. 38)

The literature about explaining illness to children has relied heavily on Piagetian stage theory and Bibace and Walsh's (1979, 1980, 1981) application of this supposal to children's conceptualization of illness (see Burbach & Peterson, 1986; Eiser, 1989; Eiser & Eiser, 1987, for critiques of stage approach). Most of the advice offered and the empirical investigations conducted have been in an effort to create and categorize explanatory strategies for explaining illness to children at different cognitive levels. I now detail what the literature has provided, of which portions have been similarly explicated elsewhere (i.e., Whaley, 1999).

Message Strategies for Explaining Illness to Children

Given the noted importance of children understanding illness, the proposed need for explanation strategies, and the dominance of Bibace and Walsh's (1979, 1980, 1981) efforts, there are surprisingly few investigations concerning message strategies for explaining illness to children. The literature at hand, however, concerns general suggestions, attention to terms used, employing figurative language, and scripts to consider when creating messages to explain illness.

General Strategies for Explaining Illness to Children.   Broad
guidelines and considerations have been posited when constructing an illness explanation for children. Basal to the process, the explainer is encouraged to regard the cultural, religious, intellectual functioning, personality,
and experience of the child (Bannard, 1987; Beales, Holt, Keen, & Mellor,
1983; Elsberry & Sorensen, 1986). Dorn (1984) emphasized assessing
each child's degree of understanding prior to explaining or the carrying out
of medical procedures, and outlined explanatory strategies for each
Piagetian stage. Moreover, an assessment of children's knowledge of their
illness is critical before structuring an appropriate illness explanation becomes similarly critical. Dorn promoted asking children to describe what
they believe is making them sick and, based on their responses, health care
personnel can better construct an explanation. Bannard (1987) proposed
having children draw pictures of what they believe to be the nature of their
disease or illness (e.g., diabetes) as a method of gauging their level of understanding. Including the parents in this process of designing illness explanations is also suggested (Whitt, Dykstra, & Taylor, 1979).
    The general guidelines offered for explaining illness to children are con-
ventional notions reflecting the importance of understanding base audience
characteristics prior to message construction. More specific suggestions
regarding message features are essential to designing effective illness explanations—vocabulary, figurative language, and scripts.

Vocabulary.   The multifaceted nature of language and word meaning
can serve to nullify the best illness-explanation intentions. For instance,
based on Piagetian theory, advice has been offered suggesting that medical
personnel govern their word choice and give considerable forethought
when explaining illness either to or in the presence of children. Whitt et al.
(1979) said that attention to vocabulary choice is especially important for
children who have yet to reach the concrete operational stage. Children at
this juncture have difficulty realizing that words may have multiple meanings or that some words may sound alike but denote different referents (i.e.,
homonyms). "Being concrete," suggested Whitt et al. (1979), demands
evading health-related explanatory nomenclature that may have multiple
meanings or may cause problems with ambiguity. Specifically, Bannard
(1987) suggested avoiding terms such as "dye," "drawing" blood, and
"burning" sugar internally. Further, Beales, Holt, Keen, and Mellor (1983)
told of a 5-year-old girl who was told her knee was "inflamed" and considered her joint to be "in flames" under her skin surface; hence, she had been
fearful that, in time, her entire leg would burn.
    Clearly, young children may lack the linguistic development, exposure,
and health–life experience to be held accountable for the intricacies of

word usage in the clinical setting. Hence, the recommendation that tacitly scrutinizing word choice to be incorporated into an illness explanation is sensible. In sum, such cautionary use of medical terms and other potentially ambiguous language is a theoretical and pragmatic development offered by this literature.

Figurative Language.   Incorporating the use of analogies, metaphors, or similes into illness explanations prevails as the linguistic suggestions for explaining illness to children. Granted, explaining with figurative language has pragmatic appeal and is commonly practiced (Analogies Enhance Teaching Efforts, 1996; Bannard, 1987; Beales et al., 1983; Eiser, Eiser, & Hunt, 1986a, 1986b; Harmon & Hamby, 1989; Nichter & Nichter, 1986; Potter & Roberts, 1984; Whaley, 1994; Whitt et al. 1979). Specifically, Elsberry and Sorensen (1986) recommended figurative language use when explaining portions of physical examinations and physiological pro-cesses—the pupil of the eye described as a small window, the tympanic membrane likened to a illuminated ice rink; abdominal percussion is com-pared to tapping on a wall to locate the stud for picture hanging; movement of an earthworm for peristalsis; and the variation in a balloon likened to gas in the bowel are among the comparisons suggested for explanatory pur-poses. They noted that comparisons should be used that are commonly fa-miliar; for instance, "just as a slicker protects you from the rain, your skin protects your body from infections" (p. 1172). Beales et al. (1983) added to the comparisons by suggesting blood vessels as being likened to pipelines and nerves being regarded as electric wiring. Moreover, Whitt et al. (1979) promoted comparing the nature of the telephone to the processes of epi-lepsy, the internal combustion engine (automobile) and its use of gasoline (fuel) for diabetes, and a large city and the myriad types of people (cells) that constitute it or the comparison to "outlaw" cells to elucidate the nature of cancer. In addition, Whitt et al. suggested employing the aspects of a gar-den hose for explaining problems associated with hydrocephalus and using characteristics of balloons for aneurysms. Finally, Harmon and Hamby (1989) suggested explaining the essentials of diabetes as:

> In insulin-dependent diabetes mellitus (IDDM), the pancreas does not make in-sulin. Insulin is needed to carry glucose from the blood into the cells where it is used as energy. Since there is no insulin, the glucose stays in the blood and the cells begin to starve. One way to understand this is to think of the blood vessels as streets, the cells as houses, and the glucose as cars that travel on the street. Insulin acts as the driveways which allow the cars to leave the street and go into the ga-rages. In IDDM, the cars stay on the street because there are no driveways (or in-sulin) to carry the glucose into the cell. (p. 413)

Several scholars have empirically examined the effectiveness of using the anecdotal, yet intuitive, suggestions of employing figurative language when explaining illness to children. For instance, Potter and Roberts (1984) investigated the effects of type of disease (diabetes vs. epilepsy), participants' cognitive maturity (preoperational vs. concrete operational), and amount–type of information provided about an illness (description vs. explanation) on several dependent variables. The investigators expected variance in participants' comprehension of illness, perceptions of vulnerability to the disease, understanding of condition severity, and the social attractiveness of a peer depicted in a vignette.

Participants were public school children in the first, third, and fourth grades. Children were in one of four experimental conditions in a 2 (disease; epilepsy vs. diabetes) x 2 (information; description vs. explanation). Participants in the descriptive information condition were read a vignette that reviewed only observable behaviors and symptoms of diabetes or epilepsy. Participants in the explanation condition received the same descriptive information (respective of disease) succeeded by an explanation of the disease. The explanation segment of the vignette used metaphors (i.e., telephone for epilepsy; car–fuel for diabetes) to aid the explanation process.

Pertinent findings suggested that participants' responses to comprehension measures in the explanation (metaphor) condition were significantly more advanced than the responses of participants in the descriptive condition. Also, findings suggested a more detailed retention of illness information by participants in the explanation (metaphor) condition than their descriptive condition counterparts.

Eiser, Eiser, and Hunt (1986a), in an effort to attenuate the findings of Potter and Roberts' (1984) efforts, investigated children's comprehension of metaphoric explanations of illness. Participants, aged 7 to 8 years and 10 to 11 years, were read one of four descriptions of a child who they were told would join their class. The descriptions varied in relation to type of illness—cancer or diabetes, and explanation—strictly medical or metaphorically aided. Eiser et al. (1986a) expected children in the analogy-type explanation condition to have a greater understanding of the illness, more attributions of positive qualities of the sick child, and preparedness to be friends with the sick child in the scenario than their strictly medical explanation peers. Eiser et al. posited that their data provided some evidence that portions of the messages were better comprehended with the aid of metaphors. Moreover, their findings indicate a positive relationship between increased age and greater understanding and recall of information.

Further examining the role of figurative language as a strategy for explaining illness to children, Eiser, Eiser, and Hunt (1986b) investigated children's and adults' production of metaphors–comparisons for the heart, lungs, brain, body, germs, blood and stomach. Children responded to "My heart is like. ... " Eiser et al. found that children's metaphors for the seven structures fell on a continuum ranging from perceptual (e.g., comparisons based on shape, color, texture) to functional (e.g., brain–computer, body–machine) and affective (e. g., germs are bad) comparisons. Moreover, their findings indicated that younger children produced and preferred the more perceptual comparisons and older children and adults prefer the more functional-oriented metaphors.

Finally, Whaley (1994), in a review of using figurative language to explain illness to children, posited that many of the suggestions forwarded in the literature are problematic. Specifically, Whaley surveyed the literature on explaining illness to children and compared the suggestions regarding figurative language use and the literature on when and how children process figurative language forms. Based on the comparison of both literatures, he contended that many of the offered suggestions regarding analogies and metaphors to explain illness to children are too advanced for the psycholinguistic competencies of children and that extreme caution should be employed when using comparisons to explain illness to children (see Spiro, Feltovich, Coulson, & Anderson, 1989, for the complexities involved in using figurative language to explain illness–disease to medical students).

Schemata–Scripts. Understanding the scripts children have of medically related events could aid in the illness explanation process. Eiser, Eiser, and Lang (1989) investigated scripts in children's reports of medical events. Participants (twenty 5-year-olds, twenty 8-year-olds) were asked to describe what happens when (a) you go to the doctor? (b) to the dentist? (c) to the hospital? (d) you don't feel well? (e) you have an operation? Responses were examined to determine how closely children's scripts coincided with the conventional sequencing of occurrences. Eiser et al. found that, in general, participants' scripts adhered to the customary order of events, with younger children responding with more list-like responses and older children providing more detailed and complex descriptions of sequential events.

Eiser, Eiser, and Jones (1990) continued this line of investigation by specifically examining children's scene schemata and scripts of hospitals. In experiment one, the authors showed children (3–5 years) a picture of a hospital scene with medically related objects depicted for 10 seconds. Then, after turning over the picture, the investigators asked the children to identify hospital items that were just presented to them. Results suggested a high level of accuracy in participants' responses. In the second experiment, Eiser et al. showed participants (3–5, 6–8, 9–10 years) five photographs of a hospital and five pictures of a school and asked the participants to organize them to "tell a story." Findings suggest that children's knowledge of hospital-related knowledge is fundamentally scripted and accurate, permitting for plausible inferences in this setting. These findings may prove helpful in designing illness explanations.

Using Existing Theory and Research to Design Illness Explanations. As inviting as it is to pursue stage theory, anecdotal suggestions, and findings from existing empirical investigations to explain illness to children, pragmatic and ethical considerations prohibit such practice. Simply, the literature is limited by a lack of cohesive theory and scant research to even make the most conservative of claims regarding the credence of existing strategies for explaining illness to children. Whitt et al.'s (1979) observation appears to still hold:

> In spite of commonplace admonitions to "speak at the child's level" and "be accurate," the clinical literature provides few illustrative examples for parents, physicians and pediatric nurses who seek to ameliorate children's distorted perceptions of bodily disorders. This dearth of information is not entirely surprising. For all the literature on the clinical phenomenon, there is little theoretical structure to guide the task of providing explanations of illness which are both accurate and within the child's cognitive capacity for understanding. (p. 331, italics added)

The existing literature does, however, provide a surplus of sound questions that offer a heuristic foundation for systematic inquiry for addressing the concerns posited by Whitt et al. (1979).

FUTURE INQUIRY

Evident from the scant empirical investigations and literature dominated by one theory, there is a considerable amount of work to be accomplished. The limited amount of theorizing and research about explaining illness to children renders this area of investigation prime for a plethora of theory-driven, well-designed investigations. Key to beginning systematic research concerning explaining illness to children is culling the literature and utilizing the strengths and balking at the residual.

Whaley (1999) suggested that efforts to advance knowledge of the strategies and messages for explaining illness to children should be pursued by addressing two issues. Initially, researchers must determine what illness-related information children *want* to know. The ample majority of the theory and research to date about illness explanation has been confined to explaining disease (etiology–biology) to children. That is, theorizing and investigations have focused on strategies for explaining to kids the biological nature of a particular disease. Thus, explanations have been based fundamentally on health providers' depictions of what children need to know—*disease*—rather than receiver-adapted messages of what children want to know—*illness*. This practice was noted by Williams and Wood (1986) concerning adults, " ... whereas the doctor's objective is to explain the etiology of the disease, the patient may be more concerned to make sense of the disruption [illness] caused by the disease" (p. 1435). Children, like adults, appear more concerned with what their condition means to the everyday nature, normalcy, fear and uncertainty of their lives than the physiology of the disease (see chap. 2, this volume; Eiser, 1994; Eiser & Eiser, 1987; Eiser et al., 1989, 1990; Solomon, 1986; Whaley, 1999). It is clear that future research should consider children's experience with a disease–illness, rather than their cognitive developmental stage, as a precursor for designing illness explanation strategies (e.g., Eiser, Havermans, & Casas, 1993).

Once researchers have a firm grasp of the type of illness-related information children may want and need (determined by them), the pursuit of *how* (i.e., strategies–messages) children want illness explained to them can ensue. In conjunction with using appropriate variations of several of the strategies already examined, this is where Eiser and her colleagues' (e.g., Eiser et al., 1989, 1990) efforts about children's scripts have considerable potential as strategies for illness explanation. Specifically, if children are concerned with how illness disrupts their lives, the use of scripts can be employed to explain their condition as it pertains to everyday living and their routine and can be used to reduce unwanted ambiguity that coincides with illness episodes and can also detail how their illness can be understood and managed.

Theorizing and researching how to explain illness to children is an extremely formidable endeavor. It appears at this juncture that considering "explanation" as both *content* of an illness explication and as *process* would be beneficial in framing what investigators to date have provided this literature. Holding this view of explanation can guide researchers in contributing to our understanding of how to explain illness to the youngest of the illness population.

REFERENCES

Analogies enhance teaching efforts. (1996). *Patient Education Management, 3,* 143–144.

Bannard, J. R. (1987). Children's concepts of illness and bodily function: Implications for health service providers caring for children with diabetes. *Patient Education and Counseling, 9,* 275–281.

Beales, J. G., Holt, P. J., Keen, J. H., & Mellor, V. P. (1983). Children with juvenile chronic arthritis: Their beliefs about their illness and therapy. *Annals of the Rheumatic Diseases, 42,* 481–486.

Bibace, R., & Walsh, M. E. (1979). Developmental stages of children's conceptions of illness. In G. Stone, F. Cohen, & N. Adler (Eds.), *Health psychology: A handbook* (pp. 285–301). San Francisco: Jossey-Bass.

Bibace, R., & Walsh, M. E. (1980). Development of children's conceptions of illness. *Pediatrics, 66,* 912–917.

Bibace, R., & Walsh, M. E. (1981). Children's conceptions of illness. In R. Bibace & M. E. Walsh (Eds.), *Children's conceptions of health, illness, and bodily functions* (pp. 31–48). San Francisco: Jossey-Bass.

Burbach, D. J., & Peterson, L. (1986). Children's concepts of physical illness: A review and critique of the cognitive-developmental literature. *Health Psychology, 5,* 307–325.

Dorn, L. D. (1984). Children's concepts of illness: Clinical applications. *Pediatric Nursing, 10,* 325–327.

Eiser, C. (1984). Communicating with sick and hospitalized children. *Journal of Child Psychology and Psychiatry, 25,* 181–189.

Eiser, C. (1985). *The psychology of childhood illness.* New York: Springer-Verlag.

Eiser, C. (1989). Children's concepts of illness: Towards an alternative to the "stage" approach. *Psychology and Health, 3,* 93–101.

Eiser, C. (1994). Making sense of chronic disease. The eleventh Jack Tizard Memorial Lecture. *Journal of Child Psychology and Psychiatry, 35,* 1373–89.

Eiser, C., & Eiser, J. (1987). Explaining illness to children. *Communication and Cognition, 20,* 277–290.

Eiser, C., Eiser, J. & Hunt, J. (1986b). Developmental changes in analogies used to describe parts of the body: Implications for communicating with sick children. *Child: Care, Health and Development, 12,* 277–285.

Eiser, C., Eiser, J., & Hunt, J. (1986a). Comprehension of metaphorical explanations of illness. *Early Child Development and Care, 26,* 79–87.

Eiser, C., Eiser, J. R.., & Jones, B. A. (1990). Scene schemata and scripts in children's understanding of hospital. *Child: Care, Health, and Development, 16,* 303–317.

Eiser, C., Eiser, J. R., & Lang, J. (1989). Scripts in children's reports of medical events. *European Journal of Psychology of Education, 4,* 377–384.

Eiser, C., Havermans, T., & Casas, R. (1993). Healthy children's understanding of their blood: Implications for explaining leukemia to children. *British Journal of Educational Psychology, 63,* 528–537.

Eiser, C., & Kopel, S. J. (1997). Children's perceptions of health and illness. In K. J. Petrie & J. A. Weinman (Eds.), *Perceptions of health and illness: Current research and applications* (pp. 47–76). Newark, NJ: Harwood Academic Publishers.

Eiser, C., Patterson, D., & Tripp, J. H. (1984). Illness experience and children's concepts of health and illness. *Child: Care, Health and Development, 10,* 157–162.

Elsberry, N. L., & Sorensen, M. E. (1986). Using analogies in patient teaching. *American Journal of Nursing, 86,* 1171–1172.

Francis, V., Korsch, B. M., & Morris, M. J. (1969). Gaps in doctor–patient communication: Patients' response to medical advice. *New England Journal of Medicine, 280,* 535–540.

Goldman, S. L., Whitney-Saltiel, D., Granger, J., & Rodin, J. (1991). Children's representations of "everyday" aspects of health and illness. *Journal of Pediatric Psychology, 16,* 747–766.

Harmon, C. C., & Hamby, J. (1989). Utilizing analogies in diabetes education. *Diabetes Educator, 15,* 413.

Korsch, B. M., & Negrete, V. F. (1972). Doctor–patient communication. *Scientific American, 227,* 66–74.

Ley, P. (1988). *Communicating with patients: Improving communication, satisfaction and compliance.* London: Croom Helm.

Nichter, M., & Nichter, M. (1986). Health education by appropriate analogy: Using the familiar to explain the new. *Convergence, 19,* 63–71.

Perrin, E. C., & Perrin, J. M. (1983). Clinicians' assessments of children's understanding of illness. *American Journal of Diseases of Children, 137,* 874–878.

Piaget, J. (1930). *The child's conception of physical causality.* London: Kegan Paul International.

Potter, P. C., & Roberts, M. C. (1984). Children's perceptions of chronic illness: The roles of disease symptoms, cognitive development, and information. *Journal of Pediatric Psychology, 9,* 13–27.

Solomon, J. (1986). Children's explanations. *Oxford Review of Education, 12,* 41–51.

Spiro, R., Feltovich, P., Coulson, R., & Anderson, D. (1989). Multiple analogies for complex concepts: Antidotes for analogy-induced misconception in advanced knowledge acquisition. In S. Vosniadou & A. Ortony (Eds.), *Similarity and analogical reasoning* (pp. 498–531). New York: Cambridge University Press.

Steward, M. & Regallouto, G. (1975). Do doctors know what children know? *American Journal of Orthopsychiatry, 45,* 146–149.

Werner, H. (1948). *Comparative psychology of mental development.* New York: Science Editions.

Whaley, B. B. (1994). "Food is to me as gas is to cars??": Using figurative language to explain illness to children. *Health Communication, 6,* 193–204.

Whaley, B. B. (1999). Explaining illness to children: Advancing theory and research by determining message content. *Health Communication, 11,* 185–193.

Whitt, J. K., Dykstra, W., & Taylor, C. A. (1979). Children's conceptions of illness and cognitive development: Implications of pediatric practitioners. *Clinical Pediatrics, 18,* 327–339.

Williams, G., & Wood, P. H. (1986). Common-sense beliefs about illness: A mediating role for the doctor. *Lancet, 2,* 1435–1437.

Pharmacists' New Communicative Role: Explaining Illness and Medicine to Patients

Jon C. Schommer
College of Pharmacy
University of Minnesota

Over the last several decades, pharmacists have been trained in a more clinically oriented fashion. Researchers have established that communication between pharmacists and patients is important for improving appropriate medication use and achieving desired patient outcomes. Patient-centered care has been embraced as the mission of pharmacy and pharmacists have become required by law to talk with patients about medications. Recent estimates show, however, that approximately 60% of the patients who receive prescriptions in pharmacies do not talk with their pharmacist about health-related aspects of their medications.

The transition from dispenser of pharmaceutical products to dispenser of information has been slow and there is a need for strategies to improve communication between pharmacists and patients. The objectives of this chapter are to: (a) describe the pharmacist's emerging role and current status of explaining illness and medicine to patients, (b) review participant and environment effects on pharmacist–patient communication, and (c) propose strategies for improving our understanding of pharmacist–patient communication about illness and medicine.

PHARMACIST'S EMERGING ROLE IN EXPLAINING ILLNESS AND MEDICINE TO PATIENTS

Historical Background

Pharmacists' place in U.S. culture is strongly tied to the vision of the pharmacist as the proprietor of a drug store. The drugstore itself, a special combination of soda shop, prescription department, and general emporium is something of a cultural icon (Higby, 1996). In the early 1900s, the position of the pharmacist in the U.S. health care system was firmly established. Physicians had agreed to dispense medicines only rarely and pharmacists reciprocated by limiting their diagnosing and prescribing to cases of minor ills and emergencies.

During the post World War II era, new, effective drugs emerged (Higby, 1996). New antibiotics such as tetracycline (1950) and erythromycin (1952) joined the penicillins. Other new drugs of note included hydrocortisone (1952), warfarin (1954), dextromethorphan (1954), and hydrochlorothiazide (1959). Post-war pharmacists were dispensing tablets and capsules that actually cured diseases rather than just ameliorated symptoms.

During the 1950s, the number of prescriptions dispensed by pharmacists increased over 50%, transforming the prescription department into the economic engine of the drug store (Higby, 1996). Pharmacists gained respect from their connection with new, effective drugs coming on the market but were restricted to machine-like tasks in which they "counted and poured" these medications into bottles. The 1952 Durham-Humphrey amendment to the Food, Drug and Cosmetic Act removed much of the pharmacist's autonomy in practice and the American Pharmaceutical Association Code of Ethics made the pharmacist's limited role quite clear:

> The pharmacist does not discuss the therapeutic effects or composition of a prescription with a patient. When such questions are asked, he suggests that the qualified practitioner [that is, a physician or dentist] is the proper person with whom such matters should be discussed. (Elliott, 1950, p. 58)

The 1960s was a period of turmoil for U.S. society. The civil rights and anti-war movements shook the social order and new rules of thinking and behavior replaced the old. So it went for pharmacy as well (Higby, 1996).

The era of clinical pharmacy (1965 to 1990) emerged in which pharmacists asserted themselves as drug information experts. During this period of change, Brodie and Benson (1976) stated that:

> the ultimate goal of the services of pharmacy must be the safe use of drugs by the public. In this context, the mainstream function of pharmacy is clinical in nature, one that may be identified accurately as drug-use control. (p. 507)

Rooted in hospitals, clinical pharmacy came to encompass unit dose distribution systems, the use of pharmacy technicians, the establishment of drug information centers, and the development of patient drug profiles. As clinical pharmacy demonstrated its utility, the number of pharmacists in institutional practice more than doubled to about 40,000, or nearly one fourth of all practitioners, during the 1970s and 1980s (Pharmacy Manpower Project, 1993).

In the community pharmacy practice sector, the change to clinical pharmacy was more gradual, but the person who stood across the counter from the pharmacist was undergoing a transformation from "the customer" to "the patient." After 150 years of caring about the wants of customers, pharmacists were beginning to care about the needs of patients (Higby, 1996). Such a paradigm shift prompted a revision of the American Pharmaceutical Association Code of Ethics in 1969. The new code began, "A pharmacist should hold the health and safety of patients to be of first consideration; he should render to each patient the full measure of his ability as an essential health practitioner" (The Challenge of Ethics in Pharmacy Practice, 1985, p. 62).

The clinical pharmacy era is best characterized as a transitional period between the years of "count and pour" practice and the dawning era of "pharmaceutical care," which is considered the new period in pharmacy's history (Higby, 1996). The concept, which grew out of Brodie's drug-use control (Brodie, 1967), has developed into a generally accepted definition. Pharmaceutical care is "the responsible provision of drug therapy for the purpose of achieving definite outcomes that improve a patient's quality of life" (Hepler & Strand, 1990, p. 539).

The Emergence of Pharmaceutical Care

Justification for the provision of pharmaceutical care is targeted at correcting the problem of "drug misadventuring," which covers the broad array of phenomena associated with negative drug experiences (Manasse, 1989a, 1989b). Drug misadventuring is a hazard or incident: (a) which is an inherent risk when drug therapy is indicated, (b) which is created through either omission or commission by the administration of a drug or drugs during which a patient is harmed, (c) whose outcome may or may not be independent of the pre-existing disease process, (d) which may be attributable to error, immunological response, or idiosyncratic response, and (e) which is unexpected and thus unacceptable to patient and prescriber. According to Hepler and Strand (1990), drug misadventuring can result from: (a) inappropriate prescribing, (b) inappropriate delivery, (c) inappropriate behavior by the patient, (d) patient idiosyncrasy, and (e) inappropriate monitoring. Thus, drug misadventuring not only includes issues of harm (safety), but also issues of treatment failure (efficacy). For example, a patient who took tetracycline with an antacid, which inhibits the absorption of the drug, would have experienced a drug misadventure if the treated condition was not cured.

Reported research provides evidence of the seriousness of drug misadventuring. In a summary of reviewed literature, Schommer (1992) reported that noncompliance with drug regimens ranged between 4% and 77%, medication errors between 25% and 90%, and the incidence of adverse drug reactions between 2% and 51% of the subjects studied. These wide ranges may be due to differences in study methods but also to the variety of medications, disease types, and populations investigated. Other estimates suggest that over half of the 2 billion medications prescribed each year may be taken incorrectly and result in one sixth of all hospital admissions, over one fourth of nursing home admissions, almost 2.5 million serious medical emergencies per year, and about 28% of all malpractice suits (National Council on Patient Information and Education, 1990, 1991; Perrin, 1988). The abuse of prescription drugs results in more injuries and deaths to Americans than all illegal drugs combined (Perrin, 1988). Also, improper use may be related to over 50% of the failures of prescription medication therapy (American Pharmaceutical Association, 1990). Overall, the estimated cost of drug-related morbidity and mortality for the ambulatory setting in the United States is $76.6 billion per year (Johnson & Bootman, 1995).

Hepler and Strand (1990) suggested that "pharmaceutical care" can improve health care outcomes and decrease costs by preventing or detecting and resolving drug-related problems that can lead to drug misadventures, both by increasing the effectiveness of drug therapy and by avoiding adverse effects. They outlined three major functions of pharmaceutical care. identifying potential and actual drug-related problems, resolving actual drug-related problems, and preventing potential drug-related problems.

There is evidence to justify pharmacy's claim of a mandate to help the patient obtain the best possible drug therapy and especially to protect the patient from harm (Brushwood, 1991; Hepler & Strand, 1990; Kessler, 1991). Literature reviews of the effects of pharmaceutical care based on over 400 studies showed that its provision to patients can increase appropriate use of medications, compliance, patient knowledge, understanding and recall of medication regimens, therapeutic outcomes (e.g., blood pressure control), patient satisfaction, patient acceptance of medical care, and quality of life (e.g., increased school attendance; Hatoum, Catizone, Hutchinson, & Purohit, 1986; Lipton, Burns, Soumerai, & Chrischilles, 1995; Schommer, 1992). Also, pharmaceutical care can decrease adverse drug reactions, number and cost of medications, emergency room visits, hospitalizations, length of stay in hospitals, and overall health care costs. Most of these studies were limited in scope, utilized different methods, and compared the provision of a component of pharmaceutical care with doing nothing at all. However, the results of these diverse studies do support the assumption that pharmaceutical care can improve outcomes and reduce costs of health care.

A key component of pharmaceutical care is communication between pharmacists and patients. For example, most prescription errors detected by pharmacists are discovered during verbal communication between the pharmacist and patient (Davis & Cohen, 1992). Communication between pharmacist and patient is an important precursor to patient understanding, acceptance, and appropriate use of medication and improved therapeutic outcomes (Hammarlund, Ostrom, & Kethley, 1985; McKenney, Brown, Necsary, & Reavis, 1978; Wiederholt & Schommer, 1991).

Researchers reported that compliance with a drug regimen primarily is determined by the nature and quality of practitioner–patient communication (Svarstad, 1986). Ley (1988) reported that improved communication between a practitioner and his or her patient increased: (a) patient knowledge and recall, (b) patient satisfaction, (c) genuinely informed consent, (d) patient compliance, and (e) the speed of recovery from illness. Based on these findings, pharmacist–patient verbal communication is a central component of effective pharmaceutical care.

Current Status of Pharmacist–Patient Communication

Health professionals endorse communication between practitioners and patients (Kimberlin, 1989) and recent federal and state regulations now mandate that pharmacist–patient communication services be offered to all patients who purchase prescriptions in community pharmacies (Kusserow, 1990; Omnibus Budget Reconciliation Act, 1990). Despite the mandate for communication between pharmacists and their patients, researchers report that the prevalence of pharmacist–patient communication often is low. Wiederholt, Clarridge, and Svarstad (1992) reviewed relevant literature and reported that the proportion of patients who received no verbal consultation for original prescriptions ranged between 17% and 30% for physicians and between 30% and 87% for pharmacists in the studies they reviewed.

In results from a 12-year longitudinal study (data collected in 1982, 1984, 1992, and 1994) of verbal counseling about prescribed medication, Morris, Tabak, and Gondek (1997) showed that counseling by physicians remained fairly stable with a range from 66% of patients who reported receiving counseling in 1984 to 70% in 1994. Respondents to their survey reported a slight reduction in having a pharmacist transfer their completed prescription to them (50%, 47%, 43%, and 44% over the four surveys), and the proportion of patients counseled by pharmacists remained fairly stable over the 12-year period (37%, 31%, 37%, and 42% over the four surveys).

It is clear that educating patients about prescription medications is an important, but not yet achieved, public health goal. Despite the pharmaceutical care movement and regulations stemming from the Omnibus Budget Reconciliation Act of 1990 that placed pharmacists in a new communicative role, progress to date on pharmacist–patient communication has been moderate. The next section of this chapter provides a brief outline of the limited theory underlying the pharmacist's role in health communication and then reviews reported research about participant and environment effects on the occurrence of such communication.

PARTICIPANT AND ENVIRONMENT EFFECTS ON THE OCCURRENCE OF COMMUNICATION

Theoretical Frameworks

Numerous theoretical frameworks have been proposed and used in the study of physician–patient communication. Some of these include: Health Communication Model (Svarstad, 1986), Social Learning Theory (Bandura, 1986), Interaction and Role Theory (Mathews, 1983), Communications Theory (Wasserman & Inui, 1983), Biomedical Model (Engel, 1977), Rational Decision Making Theory (Bandura, 1977), Health Belief Model (Strecher, Champion, & Rosenstock, 1997), Theory of Reasoned Action (Maddux & DuCharme, 1997), and Self Regulative Systems (Leventhal & Cameron, 1987), which have been useful for investigating how practitioner–patient communication can affect subsequent patient behaviors. However, these frameworks may be of limited utility when applied to understanding the pharmacist–patient encounter.

For instance, Morris, Grossman, Barkdoll, and Gordon (1987) cautioned that pharmacist–patient communication and physician–patient communication are different with respect to practitioner roles and the environment in which communication takes place (e.g., private physician office versus retail pharmacy setting). Therefore, pharmacy-specific frameworks are needed to help understand and explain pharmacist–patient communication. The development of pharmacist–patient communication in pharmacy practice is still in its infancy. Therefore, the most useful theoretical frameworks are those that propose factors that can affect the occurrence of pharmacist–patient communication.

Six models related to the occurrence of pharmacist–patient communication were identified by the author. For example, Dickson and Rodowskas (1975) used a modified work-sampling technique to collect data on pharmacist–patient communication in chain pharmacies. These data were used to test a model of pharmacist–patient communication. This was accomplished by developing a causal model that related six independent variables to the percentage of time that pharmacists engaged in patient communication per hour. The six independent variables were: (a) date of pharmacist's graduation, (b) day of the week, (c) time of day, (d) pharmacist's job title, (e) average hourly prescription volume, and (f) prescription department staffing.

The largest direct effect on pharmacist–patient communication was prescription department staffing. As the number of staff increased (professional and nonprofessional) in the prescription department, the amount of time pharmacists devoted to patient communication decreased. The direct effect of the other variables on communication was low. Other significant path relationships were between prescription volume and prescription department staffing, day of the week and prescription volume, and time of day and prescription volume. Dickson and Rodowskas' model provided a general view of pharmacist–patient communication that used the pharmacy practice setting as the unit of analysis.

Svarstad, Mason, and Shuna (1979) observed six pharmacists and four clerks dispense 1,637 prescriptions to 588 outpatients at a Veterans Administration Hospital. They reported that pharmacists' communication behavior was affected by patients' and pharmacists' backgrounds; the setting in which their interaction took place; physicians', co-workers', and patients' expectations and behavior; and other situational pressures such as prescription volume. These researchers used each pharmacist–patient interaction as the unit of analysis and identified how participants and the pharmacy environment can affect communication.

Russell, Wilcox, and Hicks (1982) proposed an interactionist approach for the study of pharmacist–patient communication. They defined communication as "a complex process that includes formulating thoughts into stimuli, transmitting the stimuli, and responding to the stimuli of the other person" (p. 11). They proposed that each communication dyad is unique. Therefore, if the pharmacist remains the same person but the patient is different in each dyadic communication, each communication episode should be considered unique. Also, they used the term "communication climate" to describe what affects the process and–or outcome of communication dyads. Based on their arguments, the investigation of pharmacist–patient communication should consider: (a) each unique dyadic encounter as the unit of analysis, (b) both pharmacist and patient roles in communication, and (c) the climate in which the communication occurs.

Another model of pharmacist–patient communication was tested by Morris et al. (1987) using data from a national telephone survey of 974 adult subjects. Using path analysis to test the model, they reported that age has both direct path and indirect path relationships to pharmacist–patient communication (counseling). Older subjects were less likely to be counseled by their pharmacist. However, two indirect paths led to increased counseling. First, the elderly were likely to patronize independent pharmacies rather than chain pharmacies, which was related to improved counseling rates. Second, the elderly were less likely to perceive the pharmacy counter as a barrier, which was related to higher counseling rates. Although the direct path relationship showed lower counseling rates with increased age, choice of an independent pharmacy and having a more positive attitude about overcoming the pharmacy counter barrier led to greater counseling by the pharmacist. Morris et al. also tested a model of doctor–patient communication and reported that the model was very different from that of pharmacist–patient communication.

Wiederholt et al. (1992) utilized data from a statewide survey and developed a model to predict occurrence of pharmacist–patient communication in community pharmacies. Predictive variables for the model were patient age and prescription type (new or refill). They reported that pharmacy personnel were 50% more likely to communicate with patients about medications for new prescriptions than for refill prescriptions. Moreover, pharmacy personnel were less likely to communicate with older patients. Patients aged 55 to 75 and 75 or older were less likely (50% and 42%, respectively) to communicate with pharmacy personnel when compared to the youngest age group (18–29 years).

Schommer and Wiederholt (1995) developed a predictive model for pharmacist–patient communication based on participant and pharmacy environment variables. They reported that Prescription Transfer by the Pharmacist (i.e., the pharmacist, rather than clerk, transferred the completed prescription to the patient) had the strongest direct effect on occurrence of pharmacist–patient communication. Another variable that affected occurrence of communication was Importance of Information (a 3-item measure comprised of the new or refill status of the prescriptions purchased, the patient's perceived importance of communication with a pharmacist at that pharmacy visit, and the pharmacist's perceived importance of communicating with the patient on that pharmacy visit).

No other variable they studied exerted a direct effect on occurrence of communication. However, three variables did directly influence the likelihood of prescription transfer by the pharmacist: (a) importance of information (already discussed as having a direct effect on communication), (b) the pharmacist's role orientation toward counseling patients, and (c) time barriers to communicating with patients. Pharmacists with more favorable attitudes about their role as medication counselor were more likely to transfer prescriptions directly to patients. Also, pharmacists who encountered time barriers in their practice were less likely to transfer prescriptions to patients themselves and relied on clerks or technicians to serve that function.

These pharmacy-specific models have only been developed to the point that they are descriptive in nature. No model was identified that could be considered a theoretical framework. In order to understand the effects that variables can have on the pharmacist–patient communication process, some general categories have been outlined and studied within the specific domain of pharmacist–patient communication—participant (pharmacist and patient) and environment variables. These are reviewed next.

Overview of Pharmacists' and Patients' Roles in Pharmacist–Patient Communication

Because patients initiate about 40% of pharmacist-patient communications (American Pharmaceutical Association, 1990), both the pharmacist and patient are important participants who can affect the occurrence of communication. Solomon, Surprenant, Czepiel, and Gutzman (1985) applied role theory to dyadic interactions in service encounters and argued that communication between a service provider and a customer is interactive (reciprocal) and that the socially defined structure of service encounters renders provider–customer interchanges especially amenable to role-theoretical analysis.

For both provider and customer, the enactment of the service scenario involves the mastery of a wide range of behaviors. On the provider side, the learning process often is explicit in the form of a training program or apprenticeship. However, the customer's burden typically is implicit. In the case of a customer's encounter with a novel situation, an idealized script may have been internalized through vicarious socialization or other past experiences.

Problems arise when there is an inconsistency with role expectations (Schommer, 1994; Sleath, 1996; Solomon et al., 1985). These can be exhibited in one of two ways: the provider's perception of job duties differs from the customer's expectations of those duties or the customer's conception of the customer role differs from the provider's notion of that role. For example, a patient may resent an overly familiar manner in a doctor, and a doctor in turn may bristle at the patient who performs self-diagnosis. In these examples, the role players are not reading from the same script.

Solomon et al. (1985) proposed that most expectations of roles are for ranges of behavior rather than for specific microbehaviors. Expectations may change over time as a script becomes redefined, although acceptance of a new service script probably is facilitated by integration with the old one. People familiar with situations often interact by rote with little conscious attention at the time. As long as the structure of a transaction is familiar, acting by rote appears to be the norm. Communication between a pharmacist and patient can be viewed as a service encounter. In such an encounter, perceived roles of the pharmacist and patient can be important determinants for the occurrence of communication.

Pharmacists' Roles in Pharmacist–Patient Communication. There have been a number of studies conducted in which the pharmacist's role in communication has been investigated. The last two decades of reported research is reviewed chronologically to highlight the development of research in this area. Mason (1979, 1983) developed and tested a 20-item Counselor Role Orientation (CRO) scale to measure community pharmacists' perceived role (an attitude) toward patient medication counseling. Pharmacists' CROs were related positively and significantly to the incidence of verbal instruction, interaction time, and pharmacist approachability.

Using the same data, Mason and Svarstad (1984) reported a link between pharmacists' attitudes toward medication counseling and measures of pharmacist–patient communication. These attitudes may be perceived by patients through how approachable the pharmacist seems. Also, Kirking (1984) reported that pharmacists' attitude toward counseling was the major explanatory variable of pharmacist–patient communication. Carroll and Gagnon (1984) concluded that provision of patient-oriented services by a pharmacist is affected as much by pharmacists' perceptions of consumer demand for them as by actual consumer demand.

Zelnio, Nelson, and Beno (1984) reported a significant relation between pharmacists' willingness and ability to provide services and the extent to which they provided services. Pharmacists providing services not only were more willing and able to do so but worked longer hours, tended to work in apothecary or independent pharmacies, held advanced degrees, and were more involved in continuing education.

Fink, Draugalis, and McGhan (1989) reported that a sample of 244 pharmacists ranked "counseling patients" as the most important of 16 pharmacy practice activities. Beardsley (1989) suggested that there are personal pharmacist barriers and patient barriers to the communication process. These include fears and anxieties about communication on both the pharmacist's and patient's part.

Anderson-Harper, Berger, and Noel (1992) surveyed a national sample of 771 pharmacists. Pharmacists reported spending about 20% of their time on patient education and counseling but desired to spend about 33% of their time on it. Pharmacists who were the most satisfied and most willing to communicate were owners and manager–directors. These groups also reported they had the most influence over their jobs. Respondents who did not desire to counsel were more satisfied than those who did desire to counsel. The staff pharmacist group reported a greater desire to counsel, less influence over their jobs, and lower job satisfaction than owners and manager–directors. It appears that pharmacists desire communication with their patients but practice constraints may contribute to role conflict for pharmacists.

Schommer and Wiederholt (1994b) reported that pharmacists reject the view that their role as counselor is one in which they merely provide factual, objective, drug-oriented information that is uniform for every patient. Rather, they view their role as providing subjective, patient-oriented advice that is the pharmacist's reasoned opinion. Pharmacists tailor their communication to meet the needs of their patients.

A predictive model of pharmacist–patient communication was tested in 12 community pharmacies (Schommer & Wiederholt, 1995). The results showed that a pharmacist's attitude toward counseling patients influences the likelihood of that pharmacist personally transferring completed prescriptions to patients and, in turn, communicating with them.

In summary, pharmacists have reported that they have a favorable orientation toward communicating with patients about medications and health and would like to spend more time in this professional activity. Pharmacists apparently see value in their role as providing subjective, patient-oriented advice that is based on the pharmacist's reasoned opinion.

Patients' Roles in Pharmacist–Patient Communication. A stream of research also has been reported for the patient's role in pharmacist–patient communication. For example, Spencer (1974) reported low-patient expectations of pharmacist consultation services may be a reason for the lack of communication between pharmacists and patients. Yellin and Norwood (1974) reported that respondents who replied that their pharmacist offered health information without being asked had a significantly higher mean attitude score about the pharmacy than those who answered they had to ask for information or did not seek information at their pharmacy. Other variables that yielded higher attitude scores were increased age and lower education level. The type of pharmacy patronized was not related significantly to a respondent's attitude toward pharmacy.

Gagnon (1978) reported that consumers rated the importance of most professional services given by a pharmacist as less important, on average, than pharmacists did. He suggested that consumers may have been uninformed about the value of professional services given by a pharmacist.

Schondelmeyer and Trinca (1983) reported that some patients did not want more information about their medications and others were not willing to pay for such information. However, more than one third of a certain category of patients (those purchasing new antibiotic prescriptions) paid an amount for a counseling service that was sufficient to cover the direct costs of providing the service.

Mackowiak and Manasse (1984) reported that patrons of an office practice pharmacy expressed significantly higher expectation scores for pharmaceutical services than patrons of a traditional pharmacy. Patrons of the office-practice pharmacy also reported more frequent counseling by a pharmacist than patrons of the traditional pharmacy. Wiederholt and Rosowski's (1996) findings also supported the notion that that type of pharmacy practice site can influence patients' expectations for counseling.

Carroll (1985) reviewed the literature on consumer demand for patient-oriented services in community pharmacies. He commented that these studies should be interpreted with caution because they are based on the assumption that consumers are familiar with pharmacy services. It may be that consumers have not had a chance to evaluate, try, or even become aware of pharmacy services because pharmacists have not provided them.

Results of a study conducted by Hibbard and Weeks (1987) showed that a minority of respondents engaged in information seeking about their health care but more than half were categorized as knowledgeable about the health care system. The elderly, who are the greatest users of health care per capita, were substantially less likely to seek information about their health. Culbertson, Arthur, Rhodes, and Rhodes (1988) reported a majority of patients (62%) preferred both written and verbal information from their pharmacist. Patients preferring verbal communication with their pharmacist more likely patronized an HMO pharmacy, were high-school educated, or had prescriptions for a new medication. Patients preferring written information more likely patronized a community pharmacy, were postgraduate educated, or had prescriptions for a renewal medication.

Mackowiak and Manasse (1988) reported a significant difference in expectations for pharmaceutical services based on age. Respondents categorized as "less than age 35" and those categorized "age 35 to 49" both reported significantly higher expectations than those categorized as "greater than age 65" for some services.

According to Schering Laboratories (1992), only 27% of the patients surveyed reported that they thought a pharmacist should talk to them personally about their prescription every time a prescription is filled. Thirty-six percent reported that the pharmacist should talk with them only if they ask and 32% reported that the pharmacist should talk with them only if the pharmacist thinks it is necessary. In the same study, 64% reported that nothing should be added to the cost of a prescription as a pharmacist's consultation fee if a law required all pharmacists to consult with their patients every time they filled a prescription. Twenty-three percent answered "don't know" to the question. Of the remaining 13% who did report a dollar amount, the average was only $2.17.

Chewning and Schommer (1996) collected data from pharmacy patrons about why people might not ask their pharmacist questions. The most common responses were patient fear–intimidation, patients' lack of awareness about pharmacists' expertise, lack of pharmacist accessibility (barriers), and patients trust their physicians to tell them what they need to know. Some respondents said they would feel disloyal to their doctor if they asked questions to a pharmacist.

Schommer (1996) investigated the pharmacist's role in health care as viewed by pharmacists and patients. Three aspects of the pharmacist's communicative role were studied: (a) the pharmacist's responsibility for providing risk management and risk assessment counseling to patients, (b) the pharmacist's role as counselor about medications, and (c) the pharmacist as a source for answering patients' questions. For that study, risk management counseling was defined as providing information about appropriate use of medications once the prescribing decision is made (i.e., how to correctly use medications). Risk assessment counseling was defined as providing information related to the appropriate choice of medications (i.e., the most appropriate medication to prescribe).

Data were collected via mailed survey from randomly selected samples of 600 pharmacists and 600 adults from the same geographic region. The results showed that pharmacists view themselves as primarily being responsible for providing risk management counseling but sharing the responsibility with physicians for providing risk assessment counseling. Patients' views differed from pharmacists, however. Patients more likely viewed the physician as the individual who should be responsible for providing both types of counseling, with pharmacists only sharing the responsibility for risk management counseling with physicians.

Regarding the pharmacist's role as a counselor about medications, pharmacists' and patients' viewpoints differed as well. Patients reported a greater agreement than did pharmacists with items that reflected greater reliance on the physician for information about medications. Finally, pharmacists and patients did not agree on the reasons why patients do not ask their pharmacist questions. Pharmacists most frequently listed pharmacy environment barriers (40% of responses), patient barriers (22% of responses), and fear–intimidation on the patients' part (17% of responses). Patients, on the other hand, most frequently listed lack of awareness by patients (31%), pharmacy environment barriers (26%), and trust in and loyalty to their physician (20%). Although patients did report pharmacy barriers as problematic, they most frequently cited a lack of awareness on their part about the availability of the pharmacist as counselor as the reason for why patients do not ask pharmacists any questions.

Schommer and Wiederholt (1997) reinforced the importance of patients in the communication process. They reported that patient question asking served as an important cue to pharmacists to provide information about administrative elements (e.g., generic availability), continuity of therapy, contraindications, purpose of medication, side-effects, interactions, and monitoring. However, only 26.8% of the 358 individuals in the study asked their pharmacist a question about medications or health during their pharmacy visit.

The important role that patients appear to play in the legitimization of pharmacists' communication services led to the investigation of how patients' expectations for these services are formed. A study was conducted to determine if experientially based factors or individual traits exert a strong influence on patients' expectations for counseling from pharmacists (Schommer, Sullivan, & Haugtvedt, 1995). The results showed that an individual trait—need for cognition (the tendency to engage in and enjoy thinking)—exerted the strongest effect on patients' expectations. Individuals who had a low need for cognition exhibited low expectations for counseling from a pharmacist. These individuals may not have an intrinsic need to know about how their medications work and may not wish to put much thought into their medication taking. Thus, they may perceive no need to exert any effort in talking with their pharmacist to get more information about their medications. Older individuals were more likely to comprise the low need for cognition group.

The next most significant predictor for patients' expectations was previous experience with counseling. Therefore, pharmacists may have some influence over patient's expectations for communication services by providing these services at a level that will be appreciated by their patients. The result showed that both individual traits and experiential variables can affect patients' expectations for communicating with their pharmacist.

In summary, the results of these studies suggest that patients have low expectations and knowledge of communication services offered by pharmacists. The pattern of responses shows that pharmacists and patients do not share common expectations about pharmacists' roles in health care. Also, it appears that whereas pharmacists view their role as one that adds value to a patient's health care above and beyond a level that can be provided by a physician alone, patients view the pharmacist's role as one that fits into their overall health care plan and is controlled by their physician. Subsequently, patient question-asking behaviors appear to be limited in community pharmacies.

It has been shown that pharmacists and patients serve important roles in the communication process between them. The next section of this chapter provides a review of reported research related to the effects of the pharmacy environment on pharmacist–patient communication.

Effects of Pharmacy Environment on Communication. Kotler (1973–1974) suggested that environments can be designed to produce specific emotional effects in the consumer that enhance desired behaviors. Several examples he gave in which this has been successful included shoe retailing, furniture retailing, bargain basement retailing, antique retailing, new homes, restaurants, airports and airplanes, psychiatric offices, and advertising agency offices.

Most modern pharmacies do not look or smell like the drug store of old. With prescription compounding almost nonexistent in today's community pharmacy, the olfactory distinctiveness of the pharmacy has disappeared, replaced by the commercial environment of front-end merchandise and its related olfactory characteristics (Pathak, 1979). Researchers have investigated how cues in a pharmacy environment can affect pharmacist–patient communication behaviors. These environmental cues can be categorized as physical environmental cues (e.g., presence or absence of a consultation area, stationary fixtures between the pharmacist and patient, distance between pharmacist and patient, lighting, height of prescription area counter, height of prescription area platform, physical appearance of the pharmacy practice setting, proportion of pharmacy devoted to the prescription department) or process environmental cues (e.g., privacy, new or refill prescription status, type of prescription, time, number of interchanges–transfers of the prescription that are not between the pharmacist and patient, transfer of prescription to patient by a pharmacist, noise). A chronological review of research that reported associations between components of the pharmacy environment and pharmacist–patient communication is presented next.

Spencer (1974) reported that patients' attitudes toward pharmacy were not formed in isolation but tended to be interrelated with facets of their pharmacy experience. Spencer found little evidence to support much of a relationship between patients and pharmacy staff members. Physical constraints, high volume demands on the staff's time, and an assembly line process that depersonalized the service were given as possible reasons for the lack of communication between pharmacists and patients.

Watkins and Norwood (1977) reported that pharmacists practicing in service, traditional, and discount pharmacy environments displayed no significant differences in knowledge or attitude but did differ significantly in regard to consulting behavior (discount lowest, service highest). This effect was independent of the age of the pharmacist. However, it was unclear whether the pharmacists' behavior in service pharmacies was the result of the pharmacist her- or himself or due to the effect of the environment.

Ludy, Gagnon, and Caida (1977) reported significantly more pharmacist–patient communication in satellite pharmacy settings with a private consultation room than in centralized traditional pharmacies with an open-window setting. Patients were significantly more satisfied with the satellite pharmacy and seemed to favor the private setting over the open window. Beardsley, Anderson, Johnson, and Wise (1977) also reported that higher privacy pharmacy environments increase the amount of pharmacist–patient communication. Ranelli (1979) reported that patients have a significantly more positive attitude toward the pharmacist when he or she was closer, at eye level, and without an obstacle between the pharmacist and patient.

Kirking (1980) found that environmental factors such as work load and type of drug dispensed may serve as cues and affect the amount of pharmacist–patient communication. Polanski and Polanski (1982) reported that patients perceive their surroundings and react favorably or unfavorably as a result of the environment. They suggested that pharmacy environments should ensure contextual cues such as privacy; a comfortable waiting area; soft, soothing colors; soft light; and soft music to facilitate communication.

Mason (1982) reported three factors that explained about 30% of the variance in the provision of patient-oriented dispensing services. They were independent pharmacy practice (vs. chain), conducive work environment, and time available. Windle, Hadsall, and Grouley (1982) reported that patients who patronized a clinic pharmacy reportedly were more likely to ask their pharmacist questions about their medication than those who patronized a community pharmacy. Nelson, Beno, and Davis (1983) reported that pharmacists in family medicine environments spent almost twice the amount of time in clinical activities as had been shown for pharmacists in chain store environments.

Carroll and Gagnon (1983) found that pharmacists were available to answer patients' drug-related questions, that pharmacists usually did not provide counseling to patients voluntarily, and that pharmacists were more likely to counsel patients who had lower educational attainment and higher drug expenditures. Cosler (1984) discovered that for certain drug categories of lower perceived importance by patients, there was no difference between the percentages of patients preferring the advice of a physician or a pharmacist. Overall, the pattern of preferences for the pharmacist as a source of drug information more closely resembled the pattern of a friend, neighbor, or relative but was dissimilar to the pattern for a physician.

Kirking (1984) reported that pharmacists' attitude toward counseling was the major explanatory variable of pharmacist–patient communication but environmental variables were important predictors as well (practice setting, prescriptions per hour, and neighborhood pharmacy location). Framm (1984) reported that use of a consultation room improved pharmacist–patient communication. Shepherd and Crawford (1987) reported patrons of independent pharmacy-practice environments had higher expectations of pharmacist counseling than patrons of chain store or grocery–drug practice settings.

Beardsley (1989) suggested a number of environmental barriers to pharmacist–patient communication. One of the most obvious barriers is the level of the prescription counter separating the patient from the pharmacist. Although an elevated counter may be necessary for security reasons, this barrier may give patients the message that the pharmacist does not want to be bothered by them. Another related physical barrier is the height of the pharmacist's platform. This may convey the perception of authority or superiority to patients that can intimidate some patients and inhibit communication. Also, he proposed that administrative and time barriers can lead to communication failure.

Hammel (1989) asked pharmacists what barriers hinder providing oral consultation to patients in their practice setting. The greatest reported barrier was inadequate time. Pharmacists practicing in high-volume pharmacies (100 or more prescriptions per day) reported this most often. Excessive work loads, inadequate staffing, interruptions, lack of reimbursement, and paper work are common reasons reported for the lack of time made available for communication with patients. Other barriers reported were: nondispensing duties, do not see patient, patient disinterest or impatience, physical layout of the prescription area, third party pick-ups or delivery, prescriptions given to patients by clerk, and not knowing the patient's medical or personal history.

Crowded, noisy prescription areas can inhibit pharmacist–patient communication. Fifty-nine percent of the respondents of one study reported there is not enough privacy in their pharmacy to speak with their pharmacist confidentially (Starr, 1990). Bergin (1990) found that the presence of pharmacy employees or other customers reportedly stops three out of 10 patients from seeking advice about their prescriptions. Smith (1990) reported factors important to patients when seeking the advice of their pharmacist were convenience of the service, approachability, interest, and concern of the pharmacist.

Kitching and Jones (1990) emphasized the importance of a proper climate (environment) for communication. A pharmacy environment with noise, poor lighting, uncomfortable seats, a telephone conversation going on in the background, and a tired looking pharmacist present some contextual cues that inhibit pharmacist–patient communication.

A draft report of the Office of the Inspector General (Kusserow, 1990) proposed that a number of barriers exist that limit the range of clinical services provided by pharmacists. These barriers were economic (product-based reimbursement and underutilization of supportive personnel), interprofessional (environmental, hesitancy to communicate, and struggles for power and autonomy), informational, training, and uneven patient demand (lack of patients' knowledge about pharmacists' expertise, lack of pharmacist availability, situational impediments, and patient lack of communication skills).

Kawahara (1991) proposed a number of barriers to effective counseling. They were structural design of the pharmacy, division of labor, patient population cultural background, information gap, pharmacist's perception of patient needs, and pharmacists' communication skills. Gardner, Boyce, and Herrier (1991) also identified barriers to communication. They identified environmental barriers (lack of privacy, phones, clerks, other customers, interruptions, counter, glass partition, displays, and distance from patient area), pharmacist barriers (being too close or too far from patient, inappropriate body movements, and inappropriate vocal characteristics), and patient barriers (emotional displays and impaired comprehension). Cardinale (1991) proposed that some barriers to pharmacist–patient communication include lack of time, invasive music, lack of privacy, counseling distance, interruptions, and distractions.

Sitkin and Sutcliffe (1991) studied the impact of professional, organizational, and legal factors on two pharmacist behaviors: information giving and advice giving. Data were collected from 94 community pharmacists practicing in Texas. Results showed that both professional and organizational factors influence a pharmacist's tendency to provide patients with information. A pharmacist's sense of professional responsibility and the pharmacist's assessment that a patient's individual case was sufficiently problematic affected advice-giving behavior. Legal controls aimed at the organization did not significantly influence pharmacist behavior.

Raisch (1993) studied relationships between pharmacist–patient communication (counseling), prescription payment methods, and practice settings for community pharmacy. Data were collected for 3,766 counseling events at 26 independent and 47 chain pharmacies in New Mexico. Self-pay and Medicaid patients more frequently were counseled than capitation patients. Chain pharmacists performed higher rates of counseling than independents, but more prescriptions were dispensed by independent pharmacists than chain pharmacists in this sample.

Schommer and Wiederholt (1994a) reported that the most frequently cited barriers that make it more difficult for pharmacists to provide consultation to patients were not enough time, no private consultation area, patients who do not want consultation, patients not available, and lack of technical support. On the other hand, the most frequently reported factors that make it easier to provide consultation to patients were pharmacist professionalism, patient demand and receptivity, privacy, enough time available, and the importance of the information.

Schommer and Wiederholt (1995) identified pharmacy environment variables that affected the occurrence of communication in community pharmacies. They were: time available for communication, the dispensing situation (e.g., new versus refill prescription), and having a dispensing process in which the pharmacist personally transferred the completed prescription to the patient.

A field experiment was conducted by Schommer (1995), in which two pharmacies were matched by pharmacy type, geographic location, patient mix, and daily prescription volume. An electronic message display was installed in one pharmacy and the other pharmacy served as a control. The display showed messages such as "our pharmacist is your best information source about medications" and was programmed to repeat the series of messages every 8 minutes. After a period of 6 months, patients in the experimental pharmacy displayed more aggressive information seeking from their pharmacist compared to the control group, in that they were more likely to initiate communication with their pharmacist.

In summary, physical and process cues in the pharmacy environment can affect the occurrence of pharmacist–patient communication. The most common cues reported in the literature related to the time available for communication, the dispensing situation (e.g., new versus refill prescription), and having a dispensing process in which the pharmacist personally transferred completed prescriptions to patients. It appears that some environmental barriers, such as physical layout of the pharmacy, can be overcome if prescription dispensing processes are designed in ways that favor opportunities for communication between patients and pharmacists.

STRATEGIES FOR IMPROVING OUR UNDERSTANDING OF PHARMACIST–PATIENT COMMUNICATION

Based on the literature reviewed in this chapter, a useful model for describing the occurrence of pharmacist–patient communication would reflect pharmacists' and patients' attitudes towards pharmacist–patient communication. Also, the model should reflect the role the pharmacy environment may have on the occurrence of communication.

There is a need for more research to develop standardized measures and explanatory models for pharmacist–patient communication in pharmacy practice settings. For example, fruitful areas for research could include investigating the mediating or moderating effect that the pharmacy environment might have in the communication process between pharmacist and patient dyads. Research to date suggests that prescription-dispensing processes that influence whether it is a pharmacist or a clerk who personally transfers the completed prescription to the patient play a significant role in pharmacist–patient communication. In the future, automation might develop to the point where pharmacists are removed from the preparation of prescriptions altogether. Such developments have important ramifications for face-to-face, pharmacist–patient communication. In addition, distance technology such as teleconferencing might become the norm for pharmacist–patient interaction. Thus the effects of technology on the occurrence and quality of pharmacist–patient communication are worthy of research. Along with these changes, the financing of health care continues to evolve. Larger, integrated corporations are becoming both the providers and payers of health care in the U.S. health system. Cost savings and better patient outcomes that pharmaceutical care can provide could be realized within an integrated health system entity. Such an evolution might help solve the problem of individual pharmacy reimbursement for communication services because pharmacies and related services could become parts of an integrated health system.

Research related to the participants in the communication process is needed as well. Pharmacists are highly trained medication experts. Colleges of pharmacy that wish to be nationally accredited are now mandated to phase out their 5-year bachelor of science pharmacy degrees and offer only the Doctor of Pharmacy degree, which is a 6- to 8-year professional degree. Such highly trained experts presumably will have the skills to provide pharmaceutical care and communicate effectively with patients. However, research is needed to determine if pharmacists' professional knowledge can be translated into usable, valued advice for patients (Sleath, 1996).

It appears that pharmacists are poised to engage in their new communicative role. However, patients do not seem to be aware of these communication services or do not wish to have a pharmacist interfere with the relationship with their physician. A great deal of work is needed to learn if patients view pharmacists as a legitimate source of drug information (Chewning & Schommer, 1996) and how the relationships between pharmacists and patients can be strengthened to foster communication about medications and health (Worley, 1996). Only when a patient is informed about the services pharmacists are able to provide and about the fact that these services are not being provided by others will he or she come to have a view of pharmacists that is congruent with how pharmacists are viewing themselves. It might only be then that pharmaceutical care will become a reality and pharmacists will achieve their new communicative role.

A recent advance for developing models specific to the unique nature of pharmacist–patient communication has been set forth by Chewning and Sleath (Chewning, 1997; Chewning & Sleath, 1996), in which they introduced a more participatory model of medication management called the Client-Centered Model. In their published work, Chewning and Sleath examined the potential therapeutic alliance between client (patient) and pharmacist and proposed that a client perspective should be taken. In the Client-Centered Model, clients collaborate with the pharmacist to: (a) identify treatment goals, (b) choose from regimen options, (c) monitor symptoms and evaluate regimens, and (d) revise regimens if problems occur (Chewning & Sleath, 1996). The pharmacist serves as a consulting partner in the decision process influenced by the client's desires and abilities, generating options based on these desires as well as the pharmacist's expertise.

It is yet to be seen if Chewning and Sleath's Client-Centered Model will replace the Medical Model (in which the pharmacist, rather than the patient, would be the dominant decision maker and the focus is on the patient's clinical status rather than overall well-being) as the conceptual framework for pharmacy practice and pharmaceutical care services. Regulations that govern pharmacy practice, pharmacists, and pharmacy environments have evolved so that pharmaceutical care and associated pharmacist–patient communication could become the new standard of pharmacy practice. The results of research reviewed in this chapter point to the importance of patients' response to the new roles of pharmacists as the factor that might make the pharmaceutical care era complete. A client-centered approach is an important next step for pharmacy in the future.

REFERENCES

American Pharmaceutical Association (1990, October 1). When adults take medicine: Improper use a national health problem. *Pharmacy Update*, 5–6.

Anderson-Harper, H. M., Berger, B. A., & Noel, R. (1992). Pharmacists' predisposition to communicate, desire to counsel and job satisfaction. *American Journal of Pharmaceutical Education, 56*, 252–258.

Bandura, A. (1977). Self-efficacy: Toward a unifying theory of behavioral change. *Psychological Review, 84*, 191–215.

Bandura, A. (1986). *Social foundations of thought & action: A social cognitive theory.* Englewood Cliffs, NJ: Prentice Hall.

Beardsley, R. S. (1989). Barriers in communication. In W. N. Tindall, R. S. Beardsly, & C. L. Kimberlin (Eds.). *Communication skills in pharmacy practice* (pp. 32–40). Philadelphia: Leas & Febiger.

Beardsley, R. S., Anderson Johnson, C., & Wise, G. (1977). Privacy as a factor in patient counseling. *Journal of the American Pharmaceutical Association, NS17*, 366–368.

Bergin, D. M. (1990). The high price of medication errors. *Drug Topics, 134*(20), 54–60.

Brodie, D. C. (1967). Drug use control: Keystone to pharmaceutical service. *Drug Intelligence and Clinical Pharmacy, 1*, 63–65.

Brodie, D. C., & Benson, R.A. (1976). The evolution of the clinical pharmacy concept. *Drug Intelligence and Clinical Pharmacy, 10*, 507.

Brushwood, D. B. (1991). The pharmacist's duty to warn: Toward a knowledge-based model of professional responsibility. *Drake Law Review, 40,* 1–60.

Cardinale, V. (1991). Patient counseling: Overcoming the barriers. *Drug Topics, 135*(23), 12–13.

Carroll, N. V. (1985). Consumer demand for patient oriented services in community pharmacies—A review and comment. *Journal of Social and Administrative Pharmacy, 3*(2), 64–69.

Carroll, N. V., & Gagnon, J. P. (1984). Pharmacists' perceptions of consumer demand for patient-oriented pharmacy services. *Drug Intelligence and Clinical Pharmacy, 18,* 640–644.

Carroll, N. V., & Gagnon, J. P. (1983). The relationship between patient variables and frequency of pharmacist counseling. *Drug Intelligence and Clinical Pharmacy, 17,* 648–652.

Chewning, B. (1997). Patient involvement in pharmaceutical care: A conceptual framework. *American Journal of Pharmaceutical Education, 61,* 394–401.

Chewning, B., & Schommer, J. C. (1996). Increasing clients' knowledge of community pharmacists' roles. *Pharmaceutical Research, 13,* 1299–1304.

Chewning, B., & Sleath, B. (1996). Medication decision—making and management: A client-centered model. *Social Science and Medicine, 42,* 389–398.

Cosler, L. E. (1984). *Consumer preferences for drug information.* Unpublished masters thesis, West Virginia University, Morgantown.

Culbertson, V. L., Arthur, T. G., Rhodes, P. J., & Rhodes, R. S. (1988). Consumer preferences for verbal and written medication information. *Drug Intelligence and Clinical Pharmacy, 22,* 390–396.

Davis, N. M., & Cohen, M. R. (1992).Counseling reduces dispensing accidents. *American Pharmacy, NS32*(10), 22.

Dickson, W. M., & Rodowskas, C. A. (1975). Verbal communications of community pharmacists. *Medical Care, 13,* 486–498.

Elliott, E.C. (1950). *The General Report of the Pharmaceutical Survey: 1946–1949.* Washington, DC: American Pharmaceutical Association.

Engel, G. L. (1977). The need for a new medical model: A challenge for biomedicine. *Science, 196,* 129–136.

Fink, R. J., Draugalis, J., & McGhan, W. F. (1989). Commitment to the profession of pharmacy: Are there sex differences? *American Pharmacy, NS29,* 28–34.

Framm, J. (1984). About a consultation room in a traditional pharmacy. *Journal of Social and Administrative Pharmacy, 2,* 34–36.

Gagnon, J. P. (1978). Store-distributed surveys as a source of consumer feedback on pharmacy services. *The Journal of Consumer Affairs, 12,* 333–342.

Gardner, M., Boyce, R. W., & Herrier, R. N. (1991). Setting the stage for optimal communication. In M. Gardner, R. W. Boyce, & R. N. Herrier (Eds.). *Pharmacist—patient consultation program* (pp. 2–8). Washington, DC: U.S. Public Health Service.

Hammarlund, E. R., Ostrom, J. R., & Kethley, A. J. (1985). The effects of drug counseling and other educational strategies on drug utilization of the elderly. *Medical Care, 23,* 165–170.

Hammel, R. W. (1989). Barriers to appropriate consultation. *Wisconsin Pharmacist, 58,* 14–15.

Hatoum, H. T., Catizone, C,, Hutchinson, R. A., & Purohit, A. (1986). An eleven-year review of the pharmacy literature: Documentation of the value and acceptance of clinical pharmacy. *Drug Intelligence and Clinical Pharmacy, 20,* 33–48.

Hepler, C. D., & Strand, L. M. (1990). Opportunities and responsibilities in pharmaceutical care. *American Journal of Hospital Pharmacy, 47,* 533–549.

Higby, G. J. (1996). From compounding to caring: An abridged history of American pharmacy. In C. H. Knowlton & R. P. Penna (Eds.), *Pharmaceutical care* (pp. 18–45). New York: Chapman & Hall.

Hibbard, J. H., & Weeks,. E. C. (1987). Consumerism in health care, prevalence and predictors. *Medical Care, 25,* 1019–1032.

Johnson, J. A., & Bootman, L. (1995). Drug-related morbidity and mortality: A cost-of-illness model. *Archives of Internal Medicine, 155,* 1949–1956.

Kawahara, N. (1991). Creating the environment for patient counseling. *Drug Topics, 135*(15), 77–83.

Kessler, D. A. (1991). Communicating with patients about their medications. *New England Journal of Medicine, 325,* 1650–1652.

Kimberlin, C. L. (1989). Communications. In A. I. Wertheimer, & M. C. Smith (Eds.). *Pharmacy practice: Social and behavioral aspects* (pp. 159–196). Baltimore: Williams & Wilkins.

Kirking, D. M. (1984). Evaluation of an explanatory model of pharmacists' patient counseling activities. *Journal of Social and Administrative Pharmacy, 2,* 50–56.

Kirking, D. M. (1980). *Pharmacists' perceptions of their role in outpatient drug therapy counseling.* Unpublished doctoral dissertation, The Ohio State University, Columbus.

Kitching, J. B., & Jones, I. F. (1990, January 20). Communicating with patients. *The Pharmaceutical Journal,* 82.

Kotler, P. (1973–1974). Atmospherics as a marketing tool. *Journal of Retailing, 49,* 48–64.

Kusserow, R. P. (1990, November). *The clinical role of the community pharmacist.* Washington, DC: U.S. Government Printing Office.

Leventhal, H., & Cameron, L. (1987). Behavioral theories and the problem of compliance. *Patient Education and Counseling, 10,* 117–138.

Ley, P. (1988). The benefits of improved communication. In P. Ley (Ed.). *Communicating with patients* (pp. 157–171). London: Croom Helm.

Lipton, H. L., Burns, P. J., Soumerai, S. B., & Chrischilles, E. A. (1995). Pharmacists as agents of change for rational drug therapy. *International Journal of Technology Assessment in Health Care, 11,* 485–508.

Ludy, J. A., Gagnon, J. P., & Caiola, S. M. (1977). The patient-pharmacist interaction in two ambulatory settings. *Drug Intelligence and Clinical Pharmacy, 11,* 81–89.

Mackowiak, J. I., & Manasse, H. R. (1988). Expectation vs. demand for pharmacy service. *Journal of Pharmaceutical Marketing & Management, 2,* 57–72.

Mackowiak, J. I., & Manasse, H. R. (1984). Expectations for ambulatory services in traditional and office-practice pharmacies. *American Journal of Hospital Pharmacy, 41,* 1140–1146.

Maddux, J. E., & DuCharme, K. A. (1997). Behavioral intentions in theories of health behavior. In D. S. Gochman (Ed.), *Handbook of health behavior research* (pp. 133–151). New York: Plenum.

Manasse, H. R. (1989a). Medication use in an imperfect world: Drug misadventuring as an issue of public policy, Part 1. *American Journal of Hospital Pharmacy, 46,* 929–944.

Manasse, H. R. (1989b). Medication use in an imperfect world: Drug misadventuring as an issue of public policy, Part 2. *American Journal of Hospital Pharmacy, 46,* 1141–1152.

Mason, H. L. (1983). Using attitudes and subjective norms to predict pharmacist counseling behaviors. *Patient Counseling and Health Education, 4,* 190–196.

Mason, H. L. (1982, June). *Factors affecting patient-oriented services provided by community pharmacists.* Paper presented to the Section of Teachers of Pharmacy Administration, American Association of Colleges of Pharmacy Annual Meeting, Kansas City, MO.

Mason, H. L. (1979). *The pharmacist's medication counseling role: Attitudes and behavior of community practitioners.* Unpublished doctoral dissertation, University of Wisconsin, Madison.

Mason, H. L., & Svarstad, B. L. (1984). Medication counseling behaviors and attitudes of rural community pharmacists. *Drug Intelligence and Clinical Pharmacy, 18,* 409–414.

Mathews, J. J. (1983). The communication process in clinical settings. *Social Science and Medicine, 17,* 1371–1378.

McKenney, J. M., Brown, E. D., Necsary, R., & Reavis, H. L. (1978). Effect of pharmacist drug monitoring and patient education on hypertensive patients. *Contemporary Pharmacy Practice, 1,* 50–56.

Morris, L. A., Grossman, R., Barkdoll, G., & Gordon, E. (1987). Information search activities among elderly prescription drug users. *Journal of Health Care Marketing, 7*(4), 5–15.

Morris, L. A., Tabak, E. R., & Gondek, K. (1997). Counseling patients about prescribed medication: 12-year trends. *Medical Care, 35,* 996–1007.

National Council on Patient Information and Education (1991, October 1). October is 'Talk About Prescriptions' month. *Talk About Prescriptions Month Newsletter,* insert.

National Council on Patient Information and Education (1990, October 1). Smart medicines need smart patients. *Talk About Prescriptions Month Newsletter, 1.*

Nelson, A. A., Beno, C. E., & Davis, R. E. (1983). Task and cost analysis of integrated clinical pharmacy services in private family practice centers. *The Journal of Family Practice, 16,* 111–116.

Omnibus Budget Reconciliation Act. (1990). Washington, DC: U.S. Government Printing Office, 152.

Pathak, D. S. (1979, January/February). Atmospherics: A valuable marketing tool. *The Journal of Postgraduate Pharmacy, 6–7,* 60.

Perrin, F. V. (1988). Improving communication with your patients. *Drug Topics, 132* (9), 48, 50, 52, 54, 56.

Pharmacy Manpower Project. (1993). Ann Arbor, MI: Vector Research.

Polanski, R. E., & Polanski, V. G. (1982, October). Environment for communication. *American Pharmacy, NS22,* 33–34.

Raisch, D. W. (1993). Patient counseling in community pharmacy and its relationship with prescription payment methods and practice settings. *Annals of Pharmacotherapy, 27,* 1173–1179.

Ranelli, P. L. (1979). The utility of nonverbal communication in the profession of pharmacy. *Social Science and Medicine, 13,* 733–736.

Russell, C., Wilcox, E. M., & Hicks, C. I. (1982). *Interpersonal communication in pharmacy: An interactionist approach* (pp. 11–41, 75–105). New York: Appleton-Century-Crofts.

Schering Laboratories (1992). Schering Report XIV. *Improving Patient Compliance: Is There a Pharmacist in the House?* Kenilworth, NJ: Author.

Schommer, J. C. (1996, March). *The pharmacist's role in health care as viewed by pharmacists and patients.* Paper presented to the 143rd Annual Meeting of the American Pharmaceutical Association, Nashville, TN.

Schommer, J. C. (1995). The use of contextual cues for improving pharmacist consultation services. *Journal of Ambulatory Care Marketing, 6,* 73–86.

Schommer, J. C. (1994). Effects of interrole congruence on pharmacist-patient communication. *Health Communication, 6,* 297–309.

Schommer, J. C. (1992). *The roles of pharmacists, patients, and contextual cues in pharmacist-patient communication.* Unpublished doctoral dissertation, University of Wisconsin, Madison.

Schommer, J. C., Sullivan, D. L., & Haugtvedt, C. L. (1995). Patients' role orientation for pharmacist consultation. *Journal of Social and Administrative Pharmacy, 12*(1) 33–42.

Schommer, J. C., & Wiederholt, J. B. (1997). The association of prescription status, patient age, patient gender, and patient question asking behavior with the content of pharmacist-patient communication. *Pharmaceutical Research, 14,* 145–151.

Schommer, J. C., & Wiederholt, J. B. (1995). A field investigation of participant and environment effects on pharmacist patient communication in community pharmacies. *Medical Care, 33,* 567–584.

Schommer, J. C., & Wiederholt, J. B. (1994b). Pharmacists' views of patient counseling. *American Pharmacy, NS34*(7), 46–53.

Schommer, J. C., & Wiederholt, J. B. (1994a). Pharmacists' perceptions of patients' needs for counseling. *American Journal of Hospital Pharmacy, 51,* 478–485.

Schondelmeyer, S. W., & Trinca, C. E. (1983). Consumer demand for a pharmacist conducted prescription counseling service. *American Pharmacy, NS23,* 321–324.

Shepherd, M. D., & Crawford, S. Y. (1987). An investigation of what factors are important to the elderly in selecting a pharmacy and purchasing drug products. *Journal of Pharmaceutical Marketing & Management, 2,* 63–82.

Sitkin, S. B., & Sutcliffe, K. M. (1991). Dispensing legitimacy: The influence of professional, organizational, and legal controls on pharmacist behavior. *Research in Sociology of Organizations, 8,* 269–295.

Sleath, B. (1996). Pharmacist-patient relationships: Authoritarian, participatory, or default? *Patient Education and Counseling, 28,* 253–263.

Smith, F. J. (1990, June 9). Factors important to clients when seeking the advice of a pharmacist. *The Pharmaceutical Journal,* 692–693.

Solomon, M. R., Surprenant, C., Czepiel, J. A., & Gutman, E. G. (1985). A role theory perspective on dyadic interactions: The service encounter. *Journal of Marketing, 49,* 99–111.

Spencer, E. (1974). The attitudes of ambulatory patients toward a hospital-based pharmacy service: The patient as consultant. *Drug Intelligence and Clinical Pharmacy, 8,* 710–716.

Starr, C. (1990). Patients may not want advice if they can't talk in private. *Drug Topics, 134*(13), 13–14.

Strecher, V. J., Champion, V. L., & Rosenstock, I. M. (1997). The health belief model and health behavior. In D. S. Gochman (Ed.), *Handbook of health behavior research* (pp. 71–91). New York: Plenum.

Svarstad, B. L. (1986). Patient–practitioner relationships and compliance with prescribed medical regimens. In L. H. Aiken & D. Mechanic (Eds.), *Applications of social science to clinical medicine and health policy* (pp. 438–459). New Brunswick, NJ: Rutgers University Press.

Svarstad, B. L., Mason, H. L., & Shuna, A. (1979, July). *Factors affecting the pharmacist's consultation behavior: An observational study.* Paper presented at the American Association of Colleges of Pharmacy Annual Meeting, Denver, CO.

The challenge of ethics in pharmacy practice. (1985). Madison, WI: American Institute of the History of Pharmacy.

Wasserman, R. C., & Inui, T. S. (1983). Systematic analysis of clinician-patient interactions: A critique of recent approaches with suggestions for future research. *Medical Care, 21,* 279–293.

Watkins, R. L., & Norwood, G. J. (1977). Impact of environment and age on quality of consultant behavior. *American Journal of Pharmaceutical Education, 41,* 19–22.

Wiederholt, J. B., Clarridge, B. R., & Svarstad, B. L. (1992). Verbal consultation regarding prescription drugs: Findings from a statewide study. *Medical Care, 30,* 159–173.

Wiederholt, J. B., & Rosowski, P. G. (1996). Antecedents of expectations for pharmacist information services measured in naturalistic settings. *Marketing Theory and Applications, 7,* 296.

Wiederholt, J. B., & Schommer, J. C. (1991). Improving pharmacist-patient verbal communication. Belmar Mall, NJ: H & R Communication.

Windle, M. J., Hadsall, R. S., & Grouley, D. R. (1982, December). *Attitudes of pharmacy patrons towards contemporary pharmacy services.* Paper presented at the American Society of Hospital Pharmacists Midyear Clinical Meeting, Los Angeles.

Worley, M. M. (1996). *Exogenous, endogenous, and outcome components of relationship quality between pharmacists and patients.* Unpublished masters thesis, The Ohio State University, Columbus.

Yellin, A. K., & Norwood, G. J. (1974, February). The public's attitude toward pharmacy. *Journal of the American Pharmaceutical Association, NS14,* 61–65.

Zelnio, R. N., Nelson, A. A., & Beno, C. E. (1984). Clinical pharmaceutical services in retail practice I. Pharmacists' willingness and abilities to provide services. *Drug Intelligence and Clinical Pharmacy, 18,* 917–922.

COCULTURAL ISSUES
AND EXPLAINING ILLNESS

10

Native Americans Explaining Illness: Storytelling as Illness Experience

Lillian Tom-Orme
Huntsman Cancer Institute
The University of Utah

Indigenous peoples of North America suffer from certain life-threatening diseases and illness more frequently than other ethnic or cultural group (Burhansstipanov & Tenny, 1995; Indian Health Service, 1996; Young, 1994). Complicating the healing process is Western culture's insistence that Native Americans be treated or remedied in Western facilities, with a lack of Western-trained Native American health care personnel or Western personnel aware of the nuances of illness patterns among Native Americans.

Health and illness are defined and explained differently by people throughout the world, often painted very colorfully in accordance with cultural norms and values. Native Americans, as with the other groups addressed in this book, view health and illness distinctly from other cocultures. For instance, in the Native American view, illness cannot be discussed separately from health. Problems of misunderstanding arise between Native peoples and untrained Western health personnel; Native

American outlooks and explanations of health and illness are unknown to the Western medical and health care providers.

A solution to the aforementioned situation is to improve understanding of cultural premises of health and illness shared by Native American populations. Although there is very limited research suggesting appropriate means of explaining illness to Native Americans, reviewing the research that is available will aid the facilitation of appropriate illness explanations to Native Americans and, hopefully, foster further inquiry.

The following, therefore, details the cultural premises and illness beliefs of Native Americans, discusses the primary means of understanding and explaining illness—storytelling—and offers recommendations to health care professionals to better understand and assist native people during their illness experiences who are seeking health care.

NATIVE AMERICANS

Frequently, the term *Native Americans* applies to American Indians, Alaska Natives, and Pacific Islanders. However, in this chapter, *Native Americans* will include only American Indians and Alaska Natives (AI–AN).

There are over 545 federally recognized tribes of American Indians and Alaska Natives, sometimes referred to as Native Americans, in the United States. It has been estimated that up to 10 million indigenous peoples speaking over 1,000 languages inhabited North America at the time of the first European contact in the 1400s (Indian Health Services, IHS, 1995a). Over 2,000 distinct languages may have existed 15,000 to 30,000 years previously in the "new world" (McNickle, 1971). Today, approximately 2 million indigenous people are found in every state, in cities and rural areas, and speaking over 200 different languages in addition to English. Less than one half of the native population continues to live on reservations or hold traditional values that tie them to their land. At least 60% have moved to towns and cities across the country; many have intermarried with other races and become acculturated, are members of tribes not formally recognized by the federal government, or may not live on federally designated reservations (Burhansstipanov & Tenney, 1995; Still & Hodgins, 1998). It is common knowledge that economics and federal Indian policies of forced relocation, education, and assimilation in the early 1900s are reasons for the large exodus from reservation lands. However, because of native ties to the land and the spiritual beliefs as caretakers of the land, many refer to their reservation as "home" and continue to return periodically.

There is great diversity among AI–AN populations. In addition to diversity in language, there are different cultural values, beliefs, and practices that define distinct tribes or regional groups. Simultaneously, however, there are similarities concerning these factors. For instance, the tribes in the Southwest use corn and its products for food and in ceremonial practices, whereas Plains tribes use tobacco and the tribes from the Sonora desert use more beans in their food ways. Historically, traditions of the Plains people included hunting to a larger extent than Southwestern pueblo tribes, who participated in village-based lifestyles. Although culture is not static but is ever-changing, certain cultural patterns are slower to change than others. Indigenous peoples adapted to the pressures of outside influence as well as altered their cultures to the environment and changing social, economic, political patterns over time. This change has also affected the health practices and status of Native Americans.

Contemporary Health Status

American Indian and Alaska Natives have mortality and morbidity figures that are disproportionately higher than many ethnic and cultural groups in the United States. The reasons for this are not easily explained but could be attributed to a combination of history, social, economic, cultural, and political factors.

The AI–AN population is relatively young. Of the nearly 2 million indigenous peoples, about one half are under 27 years of age as compared to 22.8% among Euro-Americans and almost 12% of AI–AN are under age 5, compared to 7.7 % for the U.S. All Races population (IHS, 1996; U.S. Bureau of the Census, 1990). The average life span has improved among IHS users. For instance, the difference in average life span between Navajo IHS users and the general U.S. population has decreased dramatically from a deficit of 27 years (Kane & Kane, 1972) to 2.5 years IHS, 1996). Since 1972 through 1974, infant mortality and maternal mortality have decreased 58% and 68%, respectively (IHS, 1996).

Another indicator of improved health status is the dramatic decrease in tuberculosis mortality from 57.9 per 100,000 population in 1955 to 2.2 per 100,000 population in 1992 (Indian Health Service, 1995b). Tremendous strides have been made in the health care and health status of native peoples, particularly in the past 50 years. However, morbidity and mortality from preventable chronic diseases and conditions have gradually increased over the same time period. Moreover, according to the U.S. Bureau of the Census (1990), Native Americans are poorer and less educated with a median household income of $19,897 as compared to U.S. All Races of $30,056 and 65.3% of those at least 25 years of age were high school graduates as compared to U.S. All Races of 75.2%.

American Indian and Alaska Native women have the lowest cancer survival rate as compared to other ethnic women in the country (Bacquet & Ringam, 1996; Bleed, Risser, Sperry, Hellhake, & Helgerson, 1992). Cancer rates in which Indian morbidity exceed U.S. rates include stomach, cervix, colon–rectum, liver, and gall bladder (Cobb & Paisano, 1997). Breast cancer is considered rare in AI–AN women; however, 1- and 5-year survival rates are extremely poor. Overall cancer rates in both males and females are lower among Native Americans, although regional variations depict a different picture of cancer morbidity and mortality (Cobb & Paisano, 1997). For instance, Alaska Natives are at significantly greater risk for cancers of the nasopharynx and colon–rectum and have experienced the most dramatic increase in lung cancer since the1970s (Lanier et al., 1996).

Type 2 diabetes among Native Americans has had increasingly devastating effects since about 1940, when it was first documented (West, 1974). The Pima Indians are considered to have the highest prevalence of diabetes in the world with one half of the adult population over age 35 suffering from diabetes and its complications. Overall, the incidence of type 2 diabetes ranges between 5% and 50% in native communities. According to the Indian Health Service (IHS, 1995b), age-adjusted diabetes morality among AI–AN is 2.5 times the U.S. All Races rate (30.0 vs. 11.8 per 100,000 population). Once known as adult-onset diabetes, type 2 diabetes is now observed with more frequency among native children (Dean, 1998; Joe, 1994). Complications from kidney failure, heart disease, and amputations are high among Native populations.

Morbidity and mortality from unintentional accidents remain higher than other population groups (IHS, 1996). Intentional accidents such as suicide and homicide among the younger age groups are higher, as well (IHS, 1996). The pendulum has dramatically swung from eating traditional foods high in fiber and nutrients to diets containing high fat, sugar, and total calories. Sedentary lifestyles have been adopted en masse, whereas moderate to strenuous physical activities once necessary for survival have been abandoned. Obesity has become widely accepted from childhood to adulthood and, as a contributing factor in the rising rates of cardiovascular disease and diabetes, has become a serious concern in the last half of the century due to dramatic changes in lifestyle patterns (Jackson, 1994). Obesity has also become widely accepted given the history of malnutrition, illness, and the difficulty in maintaining a stable food supply in early history to more contemporary practices of having an abundance of high-calorie foods (White et al., 1997; Wolfe, 1994). Recent population-based studies found that two thirds of Navajo women between 12 and 91 years, and 35 to 40% of Navajo adolescents (12–19 years old) were found to be overweight (Freedman, Serdula, Percy, Ballew, & White, 1997; White et al., 1997).

Health Care Systems Utilized by AI–AN Populations

Since 1954, Indian people residing on recognized reservations have received health care from the Indian Health Service, provisions made under P.L. 83–568 (IHS, 1995b). This is a federal responsibility, one of many promises made by the U.S. government in treaties signed with Indian tribes in exchange for lands taken. The existence of IHS program services has not always meant that services were accessible, acceptable, affordable, and available. Many tribes lived in isolated areas and could not reach health care facilities; this remains a challenge today in spite of modern transportation and telephones (Bell, 1994; Berry, 1997). The health care available has not always been understood due to cultural and language issues. These challenges remain today. Because Congress determines the IHS budget, funds allocated to local programs have not always met health care needs or rendered them comparable to the rest of the nation. Specialized care has not been available to Native Americans and, until recently, Indian people living in urban areas could not access Indian Health Services. Trained Indian health professionals remain few in number. This is an area of great need, as Indian people favor having their own kind explain their illness situation and to provide health care in ways that they prefer and understand. In the recent years, due to PL–638 Indian Self-Determination, tribes have finally begun to operate their own health care programs. As of October 1, 1995 the IHS reported tribes operating 11 hospitals, 129 health centers, 3 school health centers, 73 health stations, and 167 Alaska village clinics (IHS, 1996, p. 21).

World View

Spector (1991) viewed the concept of culture as "the sum of beliefs, practices, habits, likes, dislikes, norms, customs, rituals, and so forth that we have learned from our families during the years of socialization" (p. 50). These learned cultural nuances are passed on to our children either unaltered or modified by political, economic, and societal forces as we go through life. Culture influences how we view the world around us and how we define our health and illness experiences. Hultkrantz (1987) defined *worldview* as "a people's concept of existence and their view of the universe and its power" (p. 21).

Native people share a worldview of health and illness as occurring in a circular interaction of various cultural elements playing equally important parts in juxtaposition to each other, rather than in a linear continuum more characteristic to Western views (Bear Heart, 1996). Also, the native worldview is a larger, more expansive view or a holistic perspective, contrasting things or events such as death and life or male and female occurring as equal contributors to the pathways of life. For instance, a circular pattern of life is described such that life does not begin with birth and end with death, a linear perspective. In contrast, one might explain that death is a part of life; we all die, but a part of us is passed on to those who follow us; or that as we pass from physical living, through death we make a transition into another life. Similarly, male and female are physical and symbolic opposites but they make up a whole because one needs the other in life and cannot exist in isolation (Bear Heart, 1996; Bell, 1994; Kluckhohn & Leighton, 1962).

"There's a Reason for all Things"

Native people strongly believe that events do not occur out of happenstance. Whether planned or unplanned, "there's a reason for all things" to occur as they do is a prevalent view of native thought (Bear Heart, 1996; Spector, 1991). For instance, the Ojibwe people believe that health is promoted by "knowing oneself" and knowing his or her purpose in life (Turton, 1997). Searching out one's purpose in life reflects that "all things have a meaning," and this framework supports the harmony of the spiritual, psychological, physical, and emotional aspects of one's existence. Two stories illustrate this further.

In 1996, I met a young, energetic Indian man who described himself as living with the diagnosis of HIV. In his story, he told of how hard it was to deal with the diagnosis. The turning point for him to accepting his diagnosis as one major event in his pathway was when he visited and walked with a loving mother figure, an Indian medicine person. This woman took him out to nature, to the surrounding hillsides, and reintroduced him to the land and its bountiful supply of plants that had medicinal value. He was admonished for not looking around and seeing what nature had in store for health and healing. At the time I met this young man, he told how he did not take chemically derived drugs but had been taking the earth's natural healing products for 13 years and had not yet converted to AIDS. This vibrant person is now an advocate for culturally appropriate health education not only about HIV–AIDS but for native people to be personally more resourceful in their own health maintenance. He refers to his condition as a "gift" or "his purpose in life." Native people often take time to reflect on life's most difficult situations, particularly when they are afflicted with potentially life-threatening illnesses. Historically, native people went on a vision quest to seek answers to difficult questions or meanings of difficult life situations. Accordingly, this young man's interpretation of his illness was that this was a lesson to learn about the earth's natural medicines, which need to be valued by native people, and to be a spokesperson for prevention and safe lifestyle behaviors.

Mary learned her purpose in life through a different illness. Many native people and others have heard the story of Mary, a young woman who was diagnosed with leukemia in 1987 (Cobb & Lovato, 1995; M. P. Lovato, personal communication, January 8, 1998; Yuhas, 1998). Until her experience was made public, her local tribal village people were afraid of her and ostracized her for fear that they might catch the cancer. At that time, people did not talk about cancer openly for fear that they might "wish it upon themselves." Her family gave the much-needed support for a bone marrow transplant and she left the comfort of her sacred land and home to seek treatment in a large university medical center. She was unsure about her return. After experiencing an arduous period of treatment and blood transfusions, Mary recovered. At first, she could not understand the reason why she lived through this daunting experience when all odds were against her, except for the fact that her experience might have a lesson for others. She talked about a vision she had during her recovery period in which she was told of her role to work with her village and other Indian people. She contemplated this for some time and decided that she was saved because there was a need to educate her village members and other native people—that cancer needs to be better understood, that cancer does not have to kill, and openly talking about cancer will not bring demise to all. In a short time, Mary became a national spokesperson for people surviving and living with cancer. Her village council has since become a strong support system, is proud of its national recognition, and in time donated land to build a structure for Lovato's cancer support group work, for education, training sessions, and to improve the health of Indian people. Mary is short in stature but her words and her story are extremely powerful in captivating her audience in the need for cancer survivor support, education, and control. Where ever she speaks, she tells her story; a very poignant one. She integrates humor throughout her story as a very powerful element of her message.

Bear Heart (1996) advised, "Live hopefully. It does not matter what happens, what your circumstances are, you have something to connect with" (p. 139). He explained that we may get sick and almost die, but on recovering, one must say "thank you" because we realize that there is a lesson and one should be grateful for it.

Having the gift of humor and displaying your humorous side are ways that native people face many adversities in life. To Western cultures, poor people may be viewed with pity because they do not possess material things. However, materialism does not matter to traditional native people; what matters are health, spiritualism, humor, and kinship. One who has all these is considered wealthy and has a gift to share (Kluckhohn & Leighton, 1962).

Illness Beliefs and Nature

Briefly and simply, illness is generally defined as a disharmony in one's life, often caused by natural or unnatural means among Native Americans (Wing & Thompson, 1995). Natural causes may include violation of cultural taboo, failure to protect oneself from environmental or climatic changes, decreased immunity, animals, or other necessary change in the natural order of things. Unnatural causes of illness are inflicted through the work of sorcery, witchcraft, magic, and wizardry, which are used in envy or jealousy by others (Bear Heart, 1996; Wing & Thompson, 1995). When struck with a fatal illness or chronic debilitating condition, native people may initially experience the same sadness and frustration in attempts to sort through the meaning of these events.

Today, native people turn to traditional practices, the Native American Church, Christian churches, allopathic medicine, or a combination of any of these to seek relief from illness (Tom-Orme, 1988b). Traditional practices may involve elaborate ceremonies or seemingly simple acts of partaking of "sweats," sprinkling corn or tobacco, offering prayers to the Creator, use of sweet grass, or walking. Thus, to maintain a healthy balance, individuals can perform simple daily activities or may hold more elaborate rituals for more serious illness in which larger resources are needed. As in many traditional societies, a person and his or her family seek a shaman or curer to identify the source of ill health and perform ceremonies to correct the disharmony (Bear Heart, 1996; Spector, 1991).

Much of how native people describe their health and illness experiences are intertwined with their spiritual and religious views. Spirituality and–or religion have never been viewed as separate from other institutions; rather, they are actively integrated into all of life's powerful forces and activities. Thus, in explaining healthy states or illness situations, the role of spirituality and the power of a deity in either allowing for health or illness are considered. In explaining the reasons for the seemingly sudden appearance of some chronic health conditions, native people often explain that perhaps the deities are unhappy with us or that we are straying from what the Creator had provided us. In attempts to understand the increasing prevalence of diabetes and its complications, native people may ascribe its onset to eating too much White man's food and not enough traditional foods (Gittelsohn et al., 1996; Tom-Orme, 1988b). In most cultures, there are manifest and ideal cultural rules, written or oral, that are passed on to members of the cultural group. When these rules are not followed and disharmony results, people seek explanations to restore order to their lives.

Wing and Thompson (1995) found that Muscogee people attribute the causes of alcoholism to personal disharmony, lack of immunity, poor diet, and evil influences. Personal disharmony had to do with social pressure and psychological state of the person and his or her significant others. It was also related to intolerance and lack of immunity to alcoholic contents. Evil influence, considered an unnatural cause of alcoholism, is inflicted on a victim to cause disharmony in that person's life. Therapy for this type of illness is to neutralize the effect by removing the cause, taking medicine, and eating a specific diet.

In my research among the Navajo, people often described their understanding of the origin of diabetes illness in terms of taboos they might have violated (Tom-Orme, 1988a, 1988b). They told stories about their lives, how they initially began to feel ill, and how they came to experience more serious consequences of what health care professionals call diabetes complications. Health care providers describe diabetes in terms of pathophysiological events in the pancreas and the buildup of glucose or sugar in the bloodstream. These complications were viewed differently and given different meaning by health professionals and by the patient population. Navajo people did not attempt to describe diabetes as a disease but, rather, as an illness.

To the Navajo, diabetes is an illness rather than a disease. They explain their experience with diabetes in ways that seem to make sense to them so that they could map their existence vis a vis this dreadful illness. For example, Mrs. Nakaidinae attributed a diagnosis of Bell's Palsy to "sugar" and that the symptoms of drooping eyelids and facial paralysis she experienced must somehow be related. The most important and personal explanation to her was that she violated a cultural taboo by using firewood that had previously been struck by lightening. In addition, being a rug weaver, she had designed the eye of a Yei (powerful spiritual deity) figure in a manner that might have upset the spiritual figures. She talked about her numerous attempts to correct the weave in the eyes, but she was never satisfied with the outcome. She eventually left the Yei eyes as is, although she still felt uneasy throughout the weaving of the rug. Then one day, she experienced weakness on one side of her face; she immediately thought of her struggle to design to her satisfaction the eyes of the Yei, as well as the wood she used to cook a meal. Her first choice of health care was a private physician because, initially, she sought a simple answer. Her eyes watered profusely, one side of her face was distorted, and she lost feeling on that side of her face. It was the same side as the Yei face with which she had trouble weaving. The Western-trained health care providers' explanations were not heeded but, instead, she had a curing ceremony performed to correct her transgression. She will never understand the providers' explanation, but she had her own traditional cultural explanation for her misery. Once healing took place, she continued her life's journey as a weaver. The belief in reciprocity between humankind and the spirit world is extremely strong among traditional Navajo as well as other Indian people.

In the case of Mr. Begashi who also had diabetes, his explanation for retinopathy was attributed to placing a Yei mask on "the wrong way" and the spirits were angered by this violation of a very sacred rite (Tom-Orme, 1988b). Yeis are mighty spiritual deities personified in Yei bi Chei dances by select individuals. Mr. Begashi had been a dancer for many years and felt it his duty to participate in this annual healing ritual performed for the ill that also bestows good health inwardly. Because the Yei dance is a sacred ceremony, it is very important that all parts of the protocol are followed carefully, including the attire worn, the dance, and singing. Mr. Begashi admonished himself, saying that he should have known better; after all, he had been a dancer for some time. At the time of the interview, Mr. Begashi had not undergone a cleansing ritual to appease the spirits and to return to harmony, all in attempts to restore his failing vision. To restore balance in his life would require financial and emotional commitment by his extended family and for the whole community to participate in the cleansing ritual. He thought this would be a major undertaking and was daunted by the enormity of the entire celebration. Again, to him, the pathophysiologic explanation for how retinopathy develops from uncontrolled diabetes has no benefit; emphasis must be placed on the cultural explanation of how illness occurred in response to a taboo violation. Until this transgression, which is thought to have brought on the illness, is corrected, a Navajo person will continue to experience disharmony and the health professional's explanation will remain unheeded.

In these two examples, the worldview of the need to restore harmony or health is a goal and illness or disharmony is considered to be a part of one's life experience. However, to some extent illness is expected in the sense that it is a part of life events. When it does occur, all concerned seek explanations and perform rituals to restore harmony.

Again, among indigenous people, health is described in terms of balance in all aspects of life. Thus, health is defined in relation to how one feels mentally, socially, physically, and spiritually. So when persons are told they have diabetes or cancer, the effects are experienced in many ways. As such, one might describe the emotional or mental turmoil encountered by the extended family. Then, one might become involved in spiritual activities to search for the meaning of a devastating illness. Moreover, one might solicit the assistance of kin to endure the physical effects of pain or other symptoms. Based on observations and stories of other acquaintances, newly diagnosed people with diabetes know what it is like to have diabetes, cancer, or other chronic health problems. They tell about feeling sad, having sleep disturbances, being depressed, and an array of emotions that might not easily be explained to a harried and time-pressured health professional taking a medical history. The goal of attaining an acceptable level of health is to restore balance among these parameters. Therefore, it behooves the Western-trained health professional to learn cultural patterns, to understand them, and to participate actively in restoring health or balance. In the Westernized system of treatment, providers would prescribe treatment for the symptoms reported and for the elevated blood glucose. However, in the Navajo way of dealing with illness, the cause would be sought and all significant family or clan members involved in the therapy.

EXPLAINING ILLNESS TO NATIVE AMERICANS

Illness is a personal experience that needs to be explained when a person seeks health care from a provider. In a Westernized health care setting, providers rely on the ill person to offer a brief history and concise description of signs and symptoms so that an appropriate assessment could be made and proper treatment prescribed. When people from diverse cultures enter a Westernized health care setting, communication about illness and health care needs may be a challenging experience for both parties. Illness may be explained differently, in discordance with Western expectations or training of the health care provider. Moreover, the way illness is explained may depend on a person's childhood experience, personal physical or emotional experience, experience with certain health care systems or providers, traditional or acculturated adherence, or factors such as tribal affiliation or geographic patterns. For Native Americans, storytelling is the primary method of illness explanation. When health care providers state, "tell me about your illness," they will not receive an immediate description of physical complaints. If the provider shows compassion and the patience to listen to one's illness explanation, the Native person will always start with a story related to an event in the past. In addition, traditional rituals seek not only the physical causes but spiritual bases of an illness (Spector, 1991). Thus, Western medical and health practitioners may have to encourage or refer native clients for appropriate complementary services so that holistic care is provided. This may require referral to an herbalist, to a medicine person who might prescribe a vision quest or a sweat, a grief counselor, or any number of traditional practitioners.

Thus, a health care provider may not always need to explain illness to a native person but instead allow the person to unfold his or her views of illness through storytelling. How they view illness influences their responses to the intervention, treatment, and prevention of health problems (Gittelsohn et al., 1996).

Role of Culture in Illness Explanation

Paul (1955) depicted the culture concept as strongly influencing how people experience and perceive various life events, including health and illness. Often, health care providers do not understand a lay person's perception of health or an illness, particularly when the provider feels strongly that a condition needs immediate attention. Further, Paul stated that culture is learned inductively and unconsciously. Thus, individuals perceive a certain order or predictability based on this learned aspect of culture. When two people of different cultural backgrounds meet, they bring to this encounter certain orientations, experience, or behavior that are not only different but are potentially wrought with misinterpretation or discontinuity. For instance, American Indians and First Nations people of Canada did not traditionally consider pregnancy an unhealthy or illness condition requiring frequent clinic visits (Sokoloski, 1995; Still & Hodgins, 1998). Navajo people associate pregnancy with their traditional creation story, therefore viewing it as a time to keep all activity very sacred and natural. There are many rules to follow for physical activity, diet, thoughts, and rituals (Still & Hodgins, 1998). Before nurse midwives were introduced to provide maternal health care to pregnant Navajo women, all patients used the same outpatient clinic area that was physically attached to the hospital. Among the Navajo, the hospital is seen as a place where sick people go to die. Because pregnancy is a healthy state and all actions and thoughts of the pregnant women are directed to avoiding taboos or inappropriate thoughts, Navajo women avoided the clinic and hospital altogether.

Although illness is a universal phenomena, how one interprets or communicates the meaning or experiences of illness differs. In pregnancy, there is greater emphasis on health rather than illness. Among the Navajo, women are taught to avoid anything related to illness or death; therefore, a provider must be careful to explain healthy activities in positive ways. One must always beware that explanations are not perceived as "wishing" negative thoughts on the client. Also, both health and illness need to be discussed together as the worldview of native people stresses the role of opposites in daily life activities.

Storytelling to Convey Messages

Among American Indians–Alaska Natives, storytelling is a valued and basic vehicle for communication and for transmitting cultural information from one generation to the next. Most Indian languages are oral rather than written; thus, it is important to listen carefully to a story to ensure that important messages are heard and understood. The use of storytelling in Indian cultures is a very important method to convey ideas in their proper context. Often, messages conveyed in a story are not always obvious, requiring the receiver to be an active listener, a contemplative thinker, and interested participant in the interaction (Gilliland, 1995). Reitz (1986) stated that stories project one kind of truth and reality by mapping knowledge in memory.

Atkinson (1998) posited that storytelling is a fundamental form of communication, pervasive in daily events. Storytelling is not unique to native people; however, we tend to use storytelling more frequently and consistently as a method of communication than Western cultures. Andre (1997) stated, "stories are one of the joys of life. In some sense, stories are life, for through them we make sense out of what happens" (p. 346). Thus, we think and speak in story form and bring meaning to our lives through stories.

One important caution to a Western health care provider is to allow for periods of silence throughout the story. Silence is often very uncomfortable to many European cultures. To native populations, however, silence is the norm and highly respected. Bell (1994) explained that "long periods of silence are used to formulate thoughts so that the spoken word will have significance. Speech is not simply communication but power and wisdom" (pp. 234–235). In fact, hurried speech, direct eye contact, and pointing are considered rude and aggressive behaviors among the Navajo.

Explaining Illness as Story

Using storytelling to recreate illness experience is a method used commonly between patient and medicine person in traditional American Indian practice, although not a common occurrence in Western health care settings. Atkinson (1998) suggested storytelling as an important method to understand another person's position or description of her personal experience or his relation to others. It allows the person's voice to be heard and encourages her to speak for and about herself first.

Bell (1994) described how Anglo physicians are often impatient with Navajo patients who gather their extended family members for consultation rather than agreeing to have a quick conversation. What she calls long histories (stories) are preferred by traditional Navajo who would start with "events of the remote past and work up to current events" (p. 235). By constructing these stories, a circular view of the world is reconstructed whereby an illness today is connected with events of the past and all actions are seen as important parts of the larger world. Similarly, Sioux people perceive the world as a circle within which they practice and hold in deep regard the five great values: generosity and sharing, respect for elders, interdependence with nature, individual freedom, and courage (Sanchez, Plawecki, & Plawecki, 1996). Therefore, a health care professional needs to consider Native American cultural values and the role of storytelling in describing one's illness or state of health.

To illustrate the pervasiveness of storytelling to explain illness among native people, I would like to share a recent encounter. I had an interesting experience at a major Indian gathering where I spent much of my time at a education booth for the American Diabetes Association (ADA). Being a native person myself, I was very excited and curious to interact with conference attendees and to share my enthusiasm for a program that was promoting tribal community participation across the country. Understandably, many people avoided stopping at the booth when they read the ADA banner because of the tenacious and vicious nature of diabetes that wreaks havoc among our people. But I motioned for them to come by and talk. Those who stopped became immediately engaged in conversation; they told me stories about their own or a family member's experience with diabetes; they described their desire to overcome the deadly disease; they poignantly revealed their personal struggle, and they suggested ways to improve on the educational material I had at the booth. Unfortunately, I could not be as helpful as I would have liked, as the physical environment was not conducive to listening to the stories they wanted to share. I was exhausted after 2 days because it seemed that I became physically and emotionally involved in the work of meeting and listening to people's stories. Also, because of my passion to improve diabetes awareness and education, I exerted an enormous amount of energy in contemplating the messages behind the words and the feelings and emotions about living daily with diabetes.

Several factors contributed to this to make it a positive experience for those who shared their stories rather than making it an experience that might have ended in avoidance of anything related to diabetes, the enemy. First of all, I am an Indian person, a Navajo, and a health professional who has worked in diabetes for some time; therefore, credibility was immediately established. I also have relatives with diabetes who suffer similarly and hope for relief from the dreadful disease. Next, although the circumstances wrought by an exhibit hall gives an aura of sensory overload, my approach was still genuine interest in the person and what she or he had to share. Finally, I listened actively and became involved in the story that was unveiled. Active listening takes time, energy, and a subjective tour of the person's circular world.

Indigenous Language and Metaphors

To indigenous peoples of this country, life is viewed as a journey shared with others of their own kind. In fact, in native languages, the words used for "life" are often interpreted as a walk or pathway. Furthermore, the entire universe is always in motion and references are made to movement in speech patterns. One might talk about illness occurring in different segments of the journey, or a past experience in the journey might be described as "walking out of" or "shedding the cover of" illnesses. In the Navajo language, we talk about "walking into clothes" when referring to getting dressed, "walking to visit" when in actuality driving a car, "walking out of a cold" when overcoming a cold. In English, references are made to "walking the walk," or "choosing the right path," or "life's journey," but often we use these terms only metaphorically or to add color to speech, whereas indigenous people's speech is laden with words and terms that place figurative English references in an entirely different context.

An example from my diabetes research may help here (Tom-Orme, 1988a, 1988b, 1994). In interviewing older Navajo people with diabetes, references were made about "sugar is killing me." Navajo people described illness or disease as almost having a life force of its own and to which they felt helpless. One reason for this was that diabetes is not understood well in spite of its insistent presence among native peoples (Hickey & Carter, 1994). Many Navajo, as well as other Indian people, ponder the problem of diabetes when a person's health does not improve even while taking oral or injectable medications to treat diabetes. At the time of my study, one goal of diabetes counseling was for patients to admit that they have diabetes and "they can control their diabetes." In the language of the Navajo, this was not possible. So, to our way of thinking about this illness, we could never overcome the effects of diabetes as has been described by Westernized health professionals because our perceptions and communication patterns do not make this possible (Tom-Orme, 1988a, 1988b, 1994).

Frank (1995) argued that people are compelled to tell their stories in order to construct new maps and new perceptions of their relationship to the world. Thus, in his book, *At the Will of the Body: Reflections on Illness,* he told his story of living with cancer, constructing a map and perceptions of his relationship with cancer and the world around him. Similarly, Cousins (1979) told his story by reconstructing for himself and the reader the events leading up to his sudden hospitalization and the grave diagnosis of a disease. From narratives of personal experiences and life with certain conditions, we can better understand the balance between opposing forces, the power, and the meaning of the whole experience (Atkinson, 1998). Having this knowledge as health care practitioners, we can become more adept at feeling what the other person lives with, what needs exist, and how we can help. However, contemporary health care providers are taught to remain objective, unbiased, and to not become personally involved.

Problems Using Translators

Many American Indian tribal groups continue to use their native language exclusively while among their own kind. Communicating in their familiar language conveys exactly how they feel or what they experience through the use of stories. Elder people are endowed with a lifetime of experience and therefore are considered wisdom keepers and storytellers (Sanchez, Plawecki, & Plawecki, 1996). Storytelling is their natural method of communication. Unfortunately, too often in health care settings, untrained translators are used to convey messages between the ill native person and the nonnative health professional. Much of the meaning and feelings are lost in the translation. Quite frequently, certain words or terms used to describe body parts or illness cannot be translated, and vice versa from English to native language. One amusing example told by many Navajo people is about a young Navajo translator who told an elder to step on the scales "to be hung." This translator had used the literal term rather than the more appropriate one, which is a request to step on the scales "to see how heavy you are." The "hanging" term had come from an older method of weighing animals.

Problematically, in Westernized health care settings, young, untrained native people are requested to serve as translators for their elders who are non-English speakers. When young children are asked to translate for parents or grandparents, they become privy to certain personal information about adults who wish to maintain a level of confidentiality about their health status. Thus, health professionals may unknowingly contribute not only to a communication problem of receiving distorted information but also violating a special relationship where age and gender are respected through communication modes. Furthermore, the value of storytelling is minimized or altogether lost in this triad hit-or-miss approach.

Illness Explanation Recommendations for Health Care Professionals

In order to improve communication with clients or patients about health and illness states, health care professionals need to be mindful of cultural groups and their unique backgrounds. In this chapter, I examined the ways that Native American people structure their worldview about health and illness states, their explanations for why illness occurs, their views of health, and their preferred methods of communication. To improve communication when working with Native Americans, the following recommendations are made. However, each health care provider needs to avoid stereotyping by accommodating to the needs and orientation of each client or family encountered in the health care process.

Initially, the health care professional needs to be aware that his or her client will probably not share the same world view about health and illness. The professional will tend to value health highly and therefore advocate a rather immediate visit to an allopathic provider when illness happens. On the other hand, to the Native-American client, illness may be viewed not as an immediate concern but is one of many needs in the larger scheme of daily living. If the illness persists, self-care herbal therapy or traditional medicine, what Westerners call alternative therapy, may be attempted or family members may be consulted first. Or, Western therapy may be used first followed by traditional approaches. The professional needs to realize that native people desire health, that illness is a disharmony, but the perception of illness is distinct and may be acted on differently.

Second, the health professional needs to be open to whatever the client brings to the encounter. Having an open mind about the client's views, experiences, his or her attempted self-treatment, or a traditional therapy consultation helps to establish an acceptance for openness and respect. This is a beginning of a trust relationship, a goal for which one ought to strive to avoid a rather immediate closure to further communication.

Next, the health professional needs time to create the proper environment to receive stories related about illness. Storytelling does not take place in a prescribed amount of time and, moreover, understanding the story certainly cannot take place in a hurried environment. Granted, this approach is very different from what the health professional might have been taught through his or her professional training program; however, this approach fails to be conducive to the current managed-care climate in which time is of the essence.

Fourth, there are implications for communicating health information to native people. Health educators need to be mindful of appropriate learning styles, acceptable environments for communication, subtle body language used, and different modes and pace of communication that reflect Native American practice. Health education messages conveyed through stories, demonstrations, and colorful illustrations may be more appropriate than exclusive use of lectures and written material. Traditional native people avoid sustained direct eye contact, as it is considered rude and aggressive. Bicultural native people may be more accepting of direct eye contact. Often, native people are expected and thought always to portray a stoic demeanor (Hickey & Carter, 1994), but once respect has been gained and relationships are established, a very different character and background will be revealed. True, oral communication is often soft and fluid; often with a splash of humor, the relationship will blossom over time into a colorful and lively one. The therapeutic or accepting relationship may not develop immediately; therefore, patience is a virtue in this instance.

Another recommendation is the use of open-ended questions, rather than direct, probing ones or using a standard form. For instance, the statement, "Tell me how you feel today" rather than "What brings you in today?" sets a tone that you are prepared to listen to the client's personal experience. One patient's response to the latter question was "I don't know; you have been sending me postcards asking me to come to the clinic." Obviously, the person had missed a previous clinic appointment and several reminder postcards were sent. Adherence to a standard interview form may convey the subtle message of formality or even disinterest in the person. Nurses, increasingly more than other health professionals, include qualitative interview or study methods in their education (Tom-Orme, 1988a, 1988b, 1993, 1994). This practice will prove helpful in serving Native Americans.

Sixth, the use of talking circles is an acceptable communication style among native peoples. Often, in health research where one wishes to learn more about health and illness perceptions or to evaluate a project, the talking circle is used. In this setting, participants gathered in a circle take turns to speak to send a message. The message is usually delivered in a story format. Each knows this is a safe environment in which to share personal stories and feelings and there is no time limit for each person. The circle may be repeated several times, and the circle is opened with reverence to the Creator and closed likewise. Circles and stories are considered sacred and are treated accordingly. Talking circles for health education sessions can be a very effective and entertaining format to achieve a very important task. A talking circle for family could be called to make decisions about surgical procedures, to terminate life support, or to improve family support and communication. There are many opportunities in health care among native populations where the talking circle format could be utilized (Tom-Orme, 1993, 1995).

Finally, active listening cannot be stressed enough when interviewing people about their illness. Active and deep listening goes beyond hearing every word said; rather, it involves immersion into the story being told or the experience being recreated. Listening well bridges a trusting and accepting linkage between the listener and the storyteller. It is nonjudgmental communication that conveys caring, respect, and honor of the other person's life and story. Listening is an art to be learned and a gift to be given (Atkinson, 1998).

FUTURE DIRECTIONS

There is great need for continued research on the most effective methods to communicate between health care providers and Native-American clients or patients. Most Native Americans maintain some aspects of traditional health practices and explanations of illness, no matter their education or acculturation, as in the case of this author. However, others such as long-term urbanized, elder Native Americans may perceive and manage their health differently, incorporating aspects from other cultures and the predominant health care system (Hatton, 1994). Thus far, there has been limited research among a variety of Native Americans but there is a growing body of literature about the Navajo. However, there is a dearth of literature written by Navajo health professionals about Navajo people. Nursing has led the health care professions in attempting to understand cultural patterns of health communication; other professions need to follow this area. Research pertinent to culturally competent communication and health care, particularly explaining illness, is needed.

REFERENCES

Andre, J. (1997). Swapping stories: A matter of ethics. In D. E. Henderson, N. M. P. King, R. P. Strauss, S. E. Estroff, & L. R. Churchill (Eds.), *The social medicine reader,* (pp. 346–349). Durham, NC: Duke University Press.

Atkinson, R. (1998). *The life story interview.* Thousand Oaks, CA: Sage.

Bacquet, C., & Ringam, K. (1996). *Cancer among Blacks and other minorities: Surveillance, epidemiology and end results (SEER) report, Statistical profile* (NIH Pub. No. 86, 2785). Bethesda, MD: National Cancer Institute.

Bear Heart. (1996). *The wind is my mother: The life and teachings of a Native American shaman.* New York: Berkley.

Bell, R. (1994). Prominence of women in Navajo healing beliefs and values. *Nursing & Health Care, 15,* 232–240.

Berry, R. A. (1997). A nurse practitioner-managed after-hours clinic for a Native American reservation. *Journal of the American Academy of Nurse Practitioners, 9,* 165–170.

Bleed, D. M., Risser, D. R., Sperry, S., Hellhake, D., & Helgerson, S. D. (1992). Cancer incidence and survival among American Indians registered for Indian Health Service care in Montana, 1982–1987. *Journal of the National Cancer Institute, 84,* 1500–1505.

Burhansstipanov, L., & Tenney, M. (1995). Native American health issues. *Current Issues in Public Health, 1,* 35–41.

Cobb, N., & Lovato, M. P. (1995). A Pueblo cancer support group and education program. *The Indian Health Service Primary Care Provider, 20,* 21–24.

Cobb, N., & Paisano, R.E. (1997). Cancer mortality among American Indians and Alaska Natives in the Untied States: Regional differences within the Indian Health Service, 1989–1993 (Indian Health Service Pub. No. 97-615-23) Rockville, MD: Indian Health Service.

Cousins, N. (1979). *Anatomy of an illness as perceived by the patient: Reflections on healing and regeneration.* New York: Bantam.

Dean, H. (1998). NIDDM–Y in First Nation children in Canada. *Clinical Pediatrics 37,* 89–96.

Frank, A. W. (1995). *The wounded storyteller: Body, illness, and ethics.* Chicago: University of Chicago Press.

Freedman, D. S., Serdula, M. K., Percy, C. A., Ballew, C., & White, L. (1997). Obesity, levels of lipids and glucose, and smoking among Navajo adolescents. *The Journal of Nutrition, 127,* 2120S–2127S.

Gilliland, H. (1995). *Teaching the Native American* (3rd ed.). Dubuque, IA: Kendall/Hunt.

Gittelsohn, J., Harris, S. B., Burris, K. L., Kakegamic, L., Landman, L.T., Sharman, A., Wolever, T. M., Logan, A., Barnie, A., & Zinman, B. (1996). Use of ethnographic methods for applied research on diabetes among the Ojibway-Cree in northern Ontario. *Health Education Quarterly, 23,* 365–382.

Hatton, D. C. (1994). Health perceptions among older American Indians. *Western Journal of Nursing Research, 16,* 392–403.

Hickey, M. E., & Carter, J. S. (1994). Cultural barriers to delivering health care: The non-Indian provider perspective. In. J. R. Joe & R. S. Young (Eds.), *Diabetes as a disease of civilization: The impact of cultural change on indigenous peoples* (pp. 453–470). New York: de Gruyter.

Hultkranz, A. (1987). *Native religions of North America: The power of visions and fertility.* San Francisco: Harper.

Indian Health Service (1995a). *Comprehensive health care program for American Indian and Alaska Natives.* Washington, DC: U.S. Department of Health and Human Services.

Indian Health Service (1995b). *Trends in Indian Health—1995.* Washington, DC: U.S. Department of Health and Human Services.

Indian Health Service (1996). *Trends in Indian Health—1996.* Washington, DC: U.S. Department of Health and Human Services.

Jackson, M. Y. (1994). Diet, culture, and diabetes. In J. R. Joe & R. S. Young (Eds.), *Diabetes as a disease of civilization: The impact of cultural change on indigenous peoples* (pp. 381–406). New York: de Gruyter.

Joe, J. R. (1994). Perceptions of diabetes by Indian adolescents. In J. R. Joe & R. S. Young (Eds.), *Diabetes as a disease of civilization: The impact of cultural change on indigenous peoples* (pp. 329–356). New York: de Gruyter.

Kane, R. L. & Kane, R. A. (1972). *Federal Indian care (with reservations!).* New York: Springer.

Kluckhohn, C., & Leighton, D. (1962). *The Navajo.* Garden City, NY: Doubleday.

Lanier, A. P., Kelly, J., Smith, B., Amadon, C., Harpster, A., Peters, H., & Tanttila, H. (1996). *Cancer in Alaska Natives: A twenty-five year report: 1969–1993, Incidence and mortality.* Anchorage: Alaska Native Health Service, Indian Health Service.

McNickle, D. (1971). Americans called Indians. In E. B. Leacock & N. O. Lurie (Eds.), *North American Indians in historical perspective* (pp. 29–63). Prospect Heights, IL: Waveland Press.

Paul, B. D. (1955). *Health, culture and community: Case studies of public reactions to health programs.* New York: Russell Sage Foundation.

Reitz, S. A. (1986). Preserving Indian culture through oral literature. In J. Reyher (Ed.), *Teaching the Indian child: A bilingual/multicultural approach* (pp. 255–280). Billings: Eastern Montana College.

Sanchez, T. R., Plawecki, J. A., & Plawecki, H. M. (1996). The delivery of culturally sensitive health care to Native Americans. *Journal of Holistic Nursing, 14,* 295–307.

Sokoloski, E. H. (1995). Canadian First Nations women's beliefs about pregnancy and prenatal care. *Canadian Journal of Nursing Research, 27,* 89–100.

Spector, R. E. (1991). *Cultural diversity in health and illness.* San Mateo, CA: Appleton & Lange.

Still, O., & Hodgins, D. (1998). Navajo Indians. In L. D. Purnell & B. J. Paulanka (Eds), *Transcultural health care: A culturally competent approach* (pp. 423–447). Philadelphia: Davis.

Tom-Orme, L. (1988a). Chronic disease and the social matrix: A Native American diabetes intervention. *Recent Advances in Nursing, 22,* 89–109.

Tom-Orme, L. (1988b). *Diabetes in a Navajo community: A qualitative study of health/illness beliefs and practices.* Unpublished doctoral dissertation, University of Utah, Salt Lake City.

Tom-Orme, L. (1993, September). *Breast and cervical cancer knowledge, attitudes, and beliefs of Native American women: Findings from focus group interviews.* Paper presented at the annual meeting of the Transcultural Nursing Society, Flagstaff, AZ.

Tom-Orme, L. (1994). Traditional beliefs and attitudes among Navajos and Utes. In J. R. Joe & R. S.Young (Eds.), *Diabetes as a disease of civilization: The impact of culture change on indigenous peoples* (pp. 271–191). New York: de Gruyter.

Tom-Orme. L. (1995). Native American women's health concerns: Toward restoration of harmony. In D. Adams (Ed.), *Health issues for women of color: A cultural diversity perspective* (pp. 27–41). Thousand Oaks, CA: Sage.

Turton, C. L .R. (1997). Ways of knowing about health: An aboriginal perspective. *Advances in Nursing Science, 19,* 28–36.

U.S. Bureau of the Census (1990). *1990 census of population: General population characteristics, United States.* Washington, DC: U.S. Government Printing Office.

West, K. (1974). Diabetes in American Indians and other native populations of the New World. *Diabetes, 23,* 841–855.

White, L. L., Ballew, C., Gilbert, T. J., Mendlein, J. M., Mokdad, A. H., & Strauss, K. F. (1997). Weight, body image, and weight control practices of Navajo Indians: Findings from the Navajo Health and Nutrition survey. *The Journal of Nutrition, 127,* 2094S-2098S.

Wing, D. M., & Thompson, T. (1995). Causes of alcoholism: A qualitative study of traditional Muscogee (Creek) Indians. *Public Health Nursing, 12,* 417–423.

Wolfe, W. S. (1994). Dietary change among the Navajo: Implications for diabetes. In J. R. Joe & R. S. Young (Eds.), *Diabetes as a disease of civilization: The impact of culture changes on indigenous peoples* (pp. 436–449). New York: de Gruyter.

Young, T. K.(1994). *The health of Native Americans: Toward a biocultural epidemiology.* New York: Oxford University Press.

Yuhas, S.(1998). Mary Petroline Lovato—Courage and compassion conquer cancer. *Winds of Change, 13,* 60–62.

11

Explaining Illness to Latinos: Cultural Foundations and Messages

Denice Cora-Bramble
George Washington University Medical Center

LaShaun Williams
California School of Professional Psychology

Over the past several decades, the United States has undergone profound demographic changes, evidenced by the dramatic increase of ethnic and racial minority populations at rates exceeding those of nonminorites. Moreover, the trend toward greater racial and ethnic diversity is expected to continue (U.S. Bureau of the Census, 1997). Specifically, almost 1 in 11 (8.8%) Americans are foreign born and in 1995 almost half (46.7%) of these foreign-born Americans were of "Hispanic" origin (U.S. Bureau of the Census, 1997). Projections demonstrate that the Hispanic or Latino segment of the citizenry will be a substantial factor in the population growth into next millennium.

As the Latino population expands, health professionals will be increasingly engaged in cross-cultural delivery of health care services. Latinos bring diverse, yet distinct, traditions, religions, customs, and beliefs to the health care setting. In order for clinicians to optimize their role in the realm

259

of evaluation, diagnosis, and treatment, they must be able to communicate within frameworks viewed as culturally acceptable by patients.

In an attempt to facilitate this process, it is necessary to provide a foundation for accommodating Latinos in their health care endeavors. This chapter first delineates the demographic, cultural, and health status information of Latinos. Next, specific folk illnesses and traditional health practices are defined. Finally, verbal and nonverbal cross-cultural communication factors concerning explaining illness to Latinos is detailed.

THE PATIENTS

Hispanic–Latino

The terms *Hispanic* and *Latino* are often used interchangeably. A brief historical note, however, is necessary to understand the difference. *Latino(a)* is usually used to identify those individuals with ethnic origins from Spanish-speaking countries in Latin America as well as in the Caribbean. The word *Hispanic*, on the other hand, was created by the U.S. government in the 1970s in an attempt to provide a common denominator to a large but disparate population (Rodriguez, 1995). The U.S. Bureau of Census adopted the term to describe and categorize as Hispanic "a person of Mexican, Puerto Rican, Cuban, Central or South American or other Spanish culture or origin (such as Spain), regardless of race" (Rodriguez, 1995). The assumption behind the designation was that the only link between the diverse populations was a connection with Spanish language or culture (Rodriguez, 1995). Latino, however, emphasizes the origins and histories of those who are indigenous to Latin America rather than Spain (Aguirre-Molina & Molina, 1994). Albert (1996) suggested, "Some Latinos reject the term Hispanic, seeing it as a designator imposed on term from the outside, one that incorrectly denotes, Spanish rather than Latin American, origins" (p. 328). Although the term "Latino" is not without its problems, it offers the unique strength of being both racially and linguistically neutral (Aguirre-Molina & Molina, 1994). Most Latinos prefer to be identified by their country or origin, such as Puerto Rican, Salvadoran, or Peruvian, which identifies individuals from Puerto Rico, El Salvador, and Peru, respectively (Albert, 1996; Rodriguez, 1995). The multiplicity of identifiers used alludes to the incredible diversity of the Latino population. Whereas some people still refer to Latinos as "Spanish" (e.g., "Are you Spanish?"), the term should be reserved to describe the language spoken rather than the heritage.

Demographics

There are approximately 23 million Latinos in the United States, which comprises more than 9% of the total population. Between 1980 and 1990, the Latino population increased by 53% as compared to a 4.4% increase of Euro-Americans, 13.2% of African Americans, and 107.8% of Asian–Pacific Islanders. These data reflect only the Latino population that participated in the census. The actual total population includes a significant number of undocumented Latino immigrants who were not counted. Whereas the total number of undocumented Latino immigrants is unknown, the current estimates could easily add an additional 4 million to the census figure.

Currently, Latinos live in every state in the United States. However, approximately 90% have chosen to live in 10 states. In the west and southwest, the majority reside in California and Texas, respectively. On the east coast, the Latino population is concentrated in New York and New Jersey, whereas in the southern states, Florida has the highest concentration. Certain generalizations can also be made related to the choice of states in which many Latino subgroups have decided to reside. The majority of Latinos in California are of Mexican heritage; in New York and New Jersey, of Puerto Rican heritage; and in Florida, of Cuban heritage. Although these are broad generalizations, they represent the current geographic trends.

Latinos are an extremely heterogeneous group even though a common language and cultural and historical backgrounds are shared. Any thoughtful attempt to describe Latinos as a single community will contain the designators that can be used to describe it as a collection of multiple communities. For example, although Spanish is a common language in Latin American countries, there are a variety of dialects and colloquialisms present within and between each country. With the recognition of similar aspects of Latino cultural heritage, there must also come the recognition of where these aspects begin to diverge. Balancing these divergent concepts of Latino commonality and diversity is an often challenging but necessary tension to maintain in any discussion of cultural identity.

Because of these factors, any generalized statements made about Latinos as a group will be of limited value. The characterizations presented, however, will serve as a useful guide, being more likely to be applicable to Latinos than not. Barker (1992) reminded us of the limitations of labels, "individual members of any social group differ from each other, and often socioeconomic and educational differences can outweigh ethnic or cultural ones" (p. 249). This statement is true for Latinos in the United States. For example, Cuban Americans have the highest educational and income levels, followed in order by Latin-American immigrants, Mexicans, and Puerto Ricans (Rodriguez, 1995). These differences in social or legal status may restrict any commonality of experience.

In addition to intragroup variability, there is the element of cultural dynamism to be considered. Cultures are influenced by many factors, including the changing needs of the people. As the social environment changes, cultures evolve and adapt. Populations such as Latinos in America exist within a larger society that primarily controls the means of production and communication and that dictates and imposes social norms (Molina, Zambrana, & Aguirre-Molina, 1994). With such pressures on a community, it can be expected that some of the values and practices of the dominant society will be integrated (Heggenhougen & Shore, 1986; Molina et al., 1994). This pressure may also serve to reaffirm traditional Latino values. For example, the pressures of living in a society that marginalizes Latinos and Latino culture may make the custom of sustaining a cohesive extended family network a necessary strategy for survival.

LATINO HEALTH ISSUES

Health status measures of mortality and morbidity differentiate Latino populations from other groups and provide useful information for health care providers serving Latinos. The National Council of La Raza (1998) noted that Hispanics suffer a greater incidence of highly preventable diseases, such as AIDS–HIV infection, tuberculosis, diabetes, cardiovascular disease, and breast and cervical cancer, than other U.S. populations. This section discusses just a few of the health issues Latinos face, including disproportionate incidence of certain organ-specific cancers, excess mortality due to diabetes, AIDS–HIV infection, and lack of access to consistent preventive health care.

Mortality

The national data collection system as it relates to mortality rates has hindered efforts to accurately assess death rates among Latinos. Until 1988, the national model death certificate did not contain Latino identifiers. This has continued to be the case as recently as 1995 (Anderson, Kochanek, & Murphy, 1997). At the state level, there were attempts by some to incorporate Hispanic origin in their death certificates, but the attempt was not uniform and lacked precision (Council on Scientific Affairs, 1991). For example, funeral directors completing death certificates may indicate ethnic origin by observation rather than by inquiry with the family (Trevino, 1982).

Studies suggest that in spite of the economic, language, and cultural barriers to accessing the health care system, Latinos in the United States appear to have lower mortality rates than non-Hispanic whites (Anderson et al., 1997; Rosenwaike, 1987; Sorlie, Backlund, Johnson, & Rogot, 1993). This apparent paradox has been conjectured to be a result of social and cultural factors that promote health (Markides & Coreil, 1986).

The major causes of death are similar for Latinos and non-Latinos: namely, heart disease and cancer (Anderson et al., 1997). However, the incidence of certain organ-specific cancer, such as of the stomach and cervix, is higher among Latinos compared with other groups (American Cancer Society, 1997). The leading cancer sites for Latinos is the same as for Whites: prostate, lung, breast, colon, and rectum. In addition, cancers of the bladder and stomach are commonly diagnosed in Latino men as well as cancers of the uterine cervix and corpus in Latina women (American Cancer Society, 1997). Hispanic women have been reported to have the highest rate of cervical cancer of any group other than Vietnamese women (American Cancer Society, 1997).

Diabetes and cirrhosis of the liver have had a great impact on Latino populations. Although cause-specific mortality rates for many diseases are higher for non-Hispanics, this pattern does not hold for diabetes and cirrhosis (Centers for Disease Control and Prevention, 1992). In addition, public health programs are encouraged to utilize strategies to reduce alcohol consumption because of the strong association between heavy consumption and cirrhosis (Centers for Disease Control and Prevention, 1992). Substance abuse in the form of narcotic addiction has also translated into a disproportionate number of deaths among Hispanics (The National Coalition of Hispanic Health and Human Services Organizations, 1990, COSSMHO).

Deaths due to violence and HIV–AIDS infection are also of particular concern. Homicide and HIV infection have been consistently ranked higher for Hispanics than for non-Hispanic Whites for each age group reported between 1 and 4 years and 45 and 64 years (Anderson et al., 1997).

Morbidity

Diseases such as diabetes, tuberculosis, hypertension, and AIDS–HIV infection affect the Latino population in disproportionate numbers (National Council of La Raza, 1998; Public Health Service, 1987). Self-reported hypertension is the most prevalent chronic condition suffered by both Hispanic men and women (Centers for Disease Control and Prevention, 1992). Latinos are at increased risk for a greater frequency and severity from infectious diseases such as tuberculosis because a significant proportion of the population lives under suboptimal conditions and travel to and–or immigration from countries where the diseases are found in endemic proportions. Studies indicate that there has been an increased representation of Latinos in outbreaks of immunization-preventable diseases that has been directly related to the lower immunization rates in children as well as adults (Centers for Disease Control, 1989; Sumaya, 1991). Latinos, as well as other racial minorities, are overrepresented in cases of AIDS–HIV infection and syphilis, with its associated vertical transmission results of increased cases of pediatric AIDS–HIV infection and congenital syphilis.

Latinos have been identified as being at high risk for the development of mental health problems such as depression, anxiety, and substance abuse. Anxiety and depression may be the result of migration and subsequent culture shock (COSSMHO, 1990).

Access to Health Care Services

Latinos face a wide array of financial and nonfinancial barriers to accessing the health care system. The U.S. Bureau of the Census (1995) indicated, "Among race and ethnic groups, persons of Hispanic origin had the highest proportion of non-coverage in 1993 (31.6 percent). In comparison, 20.5 percent of African Americans and 14.2 percent of European Americans were without health insurance coverage" (p. 37). Although Latino males have the highest labor force participation in the United States, they are usually employed in low-wage occupations that typically do not provide health insurance coverage. Furthermore, many are not eligible for Medicaid or other entitlement programs because of their immigration status. Poverty and the lack of health insurance are the primary barriers to health care among Latinos.

In addition to financial obstacles to accessing the health care system, Latinos face other challenges. These barriers may be cultural or linguistic in nature and may include the lack of translation or interpretation services; health facilities that are geographically out of reach; complex, monolingual health forms; and fear of deportation.

Cultural Themes in Latino Health

Helman (1994) defined culture as:

> A set of guidelines (both explicit and implicit) which individuals inherit as members of a particular society, and which tells them how to view the world, how to experience it emotionally, and how to behave in it in relation to other people, to supernatural forces, and to the natural environment. (p. 3)

He stated that culture can be seen as "an inherited 'lens,' through which the individuals perceive and understand the world that they inhabit, and learn how to live within it" (p. 3).

Culture and health are intertwined. One cannot hope to fully understand various conceptions of health and illness without an understanding of the culture that informs it. Cultural beliefs, attitudes, and practices will be reflected in a common health culture (Aguirre-Molina & Molina, 1994; Hochbaum, 1970). However, providers often lack knowledge of diverse health cultures, beliefs, and practices. Mullavey-O'Byrne (1994) asserted that the lack of knowledge among health care professionals and the intercultural communication difficulties that often result are major issues in health care provision.

In order to communicate effectively about health and illness, one must understand something about how it is conceptualized and understand aspects of the paradigm in which explanations of health and illness are embedded. Failure to recognize and understand the divergent definitions of illness and conceptions of health will create distance between the health provider and the patient. As the cultural distance increases, so does the likelihood of communication difficulties (Pachter, 1994).

Explanatory models for health and illness can be thought of as a microcosm of the larger cultural paradigm. Like the larger cultural framework, explanatory models provide a mechanism for making sense of the world and dictating actions for operating within that world. Barker (1992) explained that not only do these models provide an explanation for and assign a rational basis to otherwise unpredictable and abnormal events with potentially serious consequences, they also they dictate a response.

Kleinman, Eisenberg, and Good (1978) asserted the centrality of explanatory models in cross-cultural discussions of illness. Specifically, they defined the encounter between patient and doctor as a transaction between the explanatory models of each. The models of illness, despite their differences, are concerned with the same issues: (a) what caused it (etiology); (b) what the symptoms are and when and how they commenced (timing and mode of onset of symptoms); (c) what changes have occurred in the body since the onset (pathophysiology); (d) what type of illness it is and its course (natural history and severity); and (e) how it should be treated (appropriate treatment).

Learning the patient's model can provide insight into beliefs about illness, the personal and social meaning of the illness, expectations about what will happen as a result of illness, how a healer is expected to intervene, and what therapeutic goals are held (Kleinman et al., 1978). Although there are some common themes in conceptions of health and illness among Latinos, there are many differences in the way that specific illnesses are perceived. This discussion presents elements that are likely to be encountered, but one can expect significant variability in real-life scenarios.

Balance.   Balance and harmony are common themes in Latino culture, generally, and are reflected in conceptions of health and illness. A personal sense of "bienestar" (well-being) is thought to depend on balance in emotional, physical, and social contexts (COSSMHO, 1990). Failure to maintain a proper balance may produce diseases. Latinos may try to prevent diseases by avoiding strong emotions such as anger or rage and sadness.

The role of balance is exemplified in Humoral or Hot–Cold Theories of health and illness, which is common among some Latinos (COSSMHO,

1990; Harwood, 1971; Logan, 1977; Spector, 1996; Westberg, 1989). According to this humoral theory, health is achieved by balancing four body fluids or humors, which vary in temperature and moistness: blood, hot and wet; phlegm, cold and wet; yellow bile, hot and dry; and black bile, cold and dry. An individual is in health when the four humors are in proper balance, which is reflected by a warm, slightly wet body. Illness results from an excess or deficiency in the humors, which is reflected in a body that was overly dry, cold, hot, or wet. Foods, herbs, and other medications can be used to restore the natural balance. What is considered a "hot" illness is therapeutically balanced with "cold" medications and food. This cultural-theoretic framework is important to understand when medications are prescribed (COSSMHO, 1990; Logan, 1977; Spector, 1996). Latinos who believe that the common cold is caused by a cold draft are unlikely to follow medical advice to drink cold fluids. An appropriate substitution would be to recommend hot herbal teas and broths instead of cold fluids, such as fruit juices.

Folk Illness. Rubel (1977) defined *folk illness* as "syndromes from which members of a particular group claim to suffer and for which their culture provides an etiology, a diagnosis, preventive measures and regimens of healing" (p. 120). Health care providers serving Latinos should be aware of the folk illnesses recognized within the culture. Knowledge of these folk illnesses can be utilized not only to establish rapport with patients and facilitate communication but also to enhance patient care (Harwood, 1971; Pachter, 1994; Trotter, 1987).

Conversely, provider prejudice regarding the validity of folk illness can impede proper care. Trotter (1987) illustrated the importance of respecting a patient's label of the folk illness "caída de mollera." Despite the general recognition of Latina mothers that caída de mollera is potentially fatal, the physicians interviewed by Trotter felt the condition was not to be taken seriously. However, once these same physicians were presented with the cluster of symptoms associated with caída de mollera, they recognized it as potentially life threatening with an identifiable medical diagnosis. Trotter noted, "A consequence [of this prejudice] is that people who use modern health care facilities for other illnesses are staying away from appropriate medical care because of their perception that their beliefs in caída de mollera will be ridiculed" (p. 2). He suggested, "the use of the term should be encouraged so that health professionals do not lose a good screening device for problems in seriously at risk infants" (p. 2).

Although folk illnesses may be considered outside the realm of biomedicine, patients often consult multiple sources of care for any one episode of illness (COSSMHO, 1990; Pachter, 1994; Westberg, 1989). Pachter (1994) noted, "Patients sometimes go to biomedical practitioners for relief of symptoms while simultaneously using a folk therapist to eliminate the cause of the illness" (p. 691). The most commonly known folk illnesses and most of the characteristics of the conditions experienced by a diverse Latino population are offered in Table 11.1. (Andrews & Boyle, 1995; COSSMHO, 1990; Spector, 1996; Trotter, 1987). Although the names of the illnesses may be shared among different groups of Latinos, the experience of such illnesses vary. The way in which Mexican Americans conceptualize and experience "empacho" may differ from how Puerto Ricans perceive the condition.

Traditional and Folk Healers

As previously mentioned, patients may consult multiple sources of health care. Patients may choose to utilize a traditional healer only, biomedical or mainstream health care only, or a combination of both. Likewise, they may access the traditional healer before, during, or after seeking care from a mainstream health care practitioner. The patient's relationship with the traditional healer is of a very personal nature and is enhanced by the ability to relate linguistically as well as culturally (Scott, 1974).

There is some controversy related to the extent of utilization of traditional healers by Latinos, but most studies point to a utilization rate of less than 10% of the Latino population studied (COSSMHO, 1990; Westberg, 1989). Molina et al. (1994) explained that folk practitioners have an approach to healing that is holistic and utilizes a variety of techniques. They stated, "Because they take a holistic approach to the process of healing, Latino folk practitioners use a variety of methods, including "sobos" (massages), "yerbas" (herbs), and spiritual practices, such as "limpias," "barridas," "baño" (cleansing), magical rituals and prayer" (p. 33). These folk practitioners respond to the social and emotional needs of their patients, operating beyond the scope of mainstream medical professionals. Pachter (1994) noted, "A phrase commonly heard when talking to folk healers is 'doctors are good at treating their types of illnesses, we are good at treating other types'" (p. 694).

It should be noted that some of the folk medicine may be harmless or may improve the symptoms but others have been associated with causing detrimental effects (Pachter, 1994). A complete clinical history must include questions about traditional treatments and healers, as well as about shared medication and alteration of dosages prescribed.

THEMES IN CROSS-CULTURAL COMMUNICATION WITH LATINOS

Latino culture is permeated by distinct themes that are transferable to the health care environment, such as "respeto" (enhanced respect),

TABLE 11.1

Common Folk Illnesses

Perceived Etiology	Symptoms	Traditional Treatment.
Mal de Ojo (Evil Eye)		
• results from excessive admiration or envy on the part of another (e.g., when a child is admired by a jealous adult) • prevention; babies wear charm	• sleeplessness, fatigue, severe headache, high fever, and excessive crying in the case of a child	• prayer; ritual cleansing, barrida (Puerto Rican) or limpia (Mexican
Empacho		
• caused by ball of raw or undigested food clinging to the wall of the stomach or intestine	• stomach pains and cramps, lack of appetite, diarrhea, vomiting • possibly resulting from psychological stress that occurred while eating	• massage, medicines, gently pinching and rubbing the spine
Ataque de Nervios		
• expression of strong emotion in response to stressful life events (i.e., funeral, accident, violence)	• characterized by shouting, swearing, striking out at others	• none, temporary affliction • immediate support in the form of prayer over the person or application of alcohol rub over the face
Susto (Fright Sickness)		
• prolonged chronic condition resulting from exposure to traumatic experience or fright, such as a death or witnessing violence	• lack of interest in living, disruption of eating and hygienic habits, restlessness in sleep, loss of strength	• prayers, body massage, relaxation

(continued on next page)

Pasmo

• caused by an upset in hot–cold balance; typically exposure to cold air when body is overheated	• paralysis-like symptoms of the face or limbs spasm of voluntary muscle, chronic cough or stomach pain, arrest of child growth and development	• prevention • massage

Caída de Mollera (Sunken Fontanelle)

• fontanelle dislodged from top of head due to trauma or rough handling	• sunken fontanelle, sunken eyes, crying, failure to suckle, vomiting restlessness, diarrhea	• hold child upside down over a pan of water • apply a poultice to depressed area of the head • insert finger in child's mouth and push up against palate

"personalismo" (warm nature of interpersonal relationships), "machismo," and "familia." Understanding these themes facilitates the illness explanation process.

Respeto

"Respeto" (respect) and "dignidad" (worthiness, dignity) are important values in Latino culture (Albert, 1996; Molina et al., 1994). For Latinos, respeto prescribes the appropriate deferential behavior toward others on the basis of age, sex, class, and position of authority. For instance, elders insist on respect from those who are younger, adults demand respect from children, and men anticipate respect from women. Although many value and seek the respect of others, the expression and symbols of respect vary across cultures (Molina et al., 1994). For example, mainstream Americans may appreciate a professional who dresses casually in order to appear more accessible, whereas Latinos may view it as a sign that this person does not take the profession or the clients seriously. What mainstream Americans may appreciate as a provider's recognition of the equality of the client may be interpreted by Latinos as "una falta de respeto" or lack of respect (Roll, Millen, & Martinez, 1980). Respeto may be better demonstrated from a Latino perspective by a provider who cares enough about the occupation and the client to dress in the expected, traditional, or customary attire of the profession (Molina et al., 1994). Health professionals, by virtue of their healing functions, education, and training, are seen as authority figures and, as such, are awarded respect. Younger providers, however, are still expected to show respect to elder Latinos, being especially formal in their interactions. This formality, however, should not be mistaken for distance. Latinos tend to emphasize "personalismo" (personal), rather that impersonal relationships.

Personalismo

"Personalismo" refers to the trust and rapport that is established with others by developing warm, friendly, and personal relationships. As a group, Latinos prefer to relate in a congenial personal manner as opposed to an impersonal, business-like mode. Although health care providers are respected and often admired, the optimal relationship and style of communication is viewed as warm, open, and sincere. The verbal and nonverbal language utilized in the professional setting embodies this concept of personalismo. Greetings are often accompanied by a hug or a handshake and the introductory remarks are likely to go beyond purely clinical issues to include inquiries about the family's well-being. It is not unusual for patients to express their gratitude by bringing handmade presents or food to a health care provider. A personal characteristic that is viewed as favorable in all settings is "simpático." Although there is no direct translation into English,

> A person is seen as "simpático/a" to the extent that he or she is perceived to be open, warm, interested in others, exhibits positive behaviors toward others, is in tune with the wishes and feelings of others, and is enthusiastic. (Albert, 1996, p. 333)

Machismo

In the United States, the term "machismo" often may conjure up images of aggressive males showing off, competing with each other, or dominating women (Hutchinson & Paznanski, 1987). A more accurate and useful interpretation would recognize the Latino cultural context, within which machismo represents a masculine ideal of strength, dignity, respectability, honor, and capacity for protecting and providing for women and family (Hutchinson & Paznanski, 1987; Lisansky, 1981). It is a collection of values, ideals, and behaviors that are appropriate for the realization of manhood (Lisansky, 1981). This cultural thread can become particularly relevant in various clinical situations. For example, the cultural value of machismo may motivate Latino men to demonstrate their virility through high-risk health behaviors such as sexual intercourse with prostitutes (Carrier, 1985; Marin, 1989). Machismo-influenced role assignments may also impact health care decision making for family members, for which Latino men perceive themselves ultimately responsible (Meleis, Douglas, Eribes,

Shih, & Messias, 1996). Out of respect for these role assignments, a female patient may be reluctant to make decisions about her health care or the care of her child without first consulting her husband.

La Familia

In Latino culture, the family or "la familia," is the primary social institution, and interdependence among its members tends to be highly valued (Marín, 1989; Molína et al., 1994; Randall-David, 1989; Westberg, 1989). La familia includes not only the nuclear family but also grandparents, aunts, uncles, cousins (often second- and third- degree), close friends (often considered honorary uncles or aunts), and "padrinos" (godparents).

La familia has a significant role in health decision making and the entire family may take responsibility for the healing process (Marín, 1989; Molina et al., 1994; Randall-David, 1989; Westberg, 1989). It is not uncommon for many family members to visit hospitalized patients, which, if not anticipated, can be problematic if hospitals limit the number of visitors. In a culturally sensitive health care system, the hospital could accommodate as many family members as space allows, with the understanding that the patient will ultimately benefit. Further, providers can acknowledge the role of la familia by directing illness explanations to them in addition to the individual patient.

The Latino familial network of support may be stressed with migration and geographic mobility. Recent immigrants are at particular risk, given that they often face the simultaneous stressors of adapting to a majority culture and the loss of familial and community support. Health care providers should, in a sensitive manner, inquire about the presence of family support. Care should be taken to avoid poignant questions about immigration as it relates to legal status.

Health professionals who hold a biomedical view of clinical reality are part of a unique cultural system (Engel, 1977; Helman, 1994; Kleinman et at., 1978). Helman (1994) asserted:

> Those who practice modern scientific medicine form a group apart, with their own values, theories of disease, rules of behavior and organization into a hierarchy of specialized roles. The medical profession can be seen as a healing "sub-culture," with its own particular world view. In the process of medical education, the students undergo a form of "enculturation" whereby they gradually acquire a perspective on ill-health that will last throughout their professional life. (p. 101)

As a group, health care professionals are informed by a belief system that can be described as both culture-specific and value-laden: It is based on particular Western explanatory models and value orientations that provide a very special paradigm for how patients are regarded and treated. This also translates into the type of illness explanation strategies and messages employed.

Messages Factors and Illness Explanation

Typical aspects of the health professionals' communication style may create cultural conflicts. Some characteristics that could potentially create difficulties include establishing an impartial professional role, using direct questioning to elicit information, conferring with colleagues in forming a diagnosis, and utilizing complex linguistic structures during interactions with clients.

Professional Role.   While it may seem appropriate to establish a distant, professional role with the client, this may be perceived as cold and aloof and conflict with values of personalismo. As mentioned earlier in the discussion of respecto, the appropriate formality expected of health care professionals should not be confused with interpersonal distance. Verbally establishing a warm, friendly environment should not be sacrificed in the name of professionalism. For instance, a culturally sensitive approach to establishing rapport may be to take a moment to inquire about the patient's family.

In the face of time constraints, mainstream U.S. physicians search for ways to minimize the demands on their time. In response to this pressure, physicians may focus on getting to the point and avoiding long conversation. Schreiber and Homaiak (1981) noted that such efforts may be perceived as rude or counterproductive. For instance, failure to acknowledge the family's role in decision making could ultimately result in noncompliance. This problem could be averted by an inquiry as to whether the patient needs time to discuss treatment options with the family before making a final decision.

Consultation.   Direct questioning as a time-saving technique could be particularly problematic. In addition to being perceived by Latinos as unfriendly and abrasive, it may be taken as a sign of ignorance (Fishman, Bobo, Kosub, & Womeodu, 1993; Ruiz & Ruiz, 1983; Trotter, 1987). Consultation with another provider may have the same effect (Fishman et al., 1993, Ruiz & Ruiz, 1983). It cannot, therefore, be assumed that the referral of a client to a specialist will be perceived as a sign of responsible and conscientious care.

Language Choice.   Mullavey-O'Byrne (1994) identified a common communication habit of English-speaking health professionals that may create misunderstandings with persons of other cultures. She noted that when providers seek information from their clients, they often use negative and double negative questions, such as "You don't want to be dependent on your family, do you?" Such linguistic constructions may be especially difficult to understand for those for whom English is a second language. This could create a situation in which the provider misinterprets the client struggle to respond to the question as a sign of limited English proficiency, and perhaps perpetuate stereotypes regarding the English language ability of Latinos.

Nonverbal Expression and Illness Explanation

Nonverbal communication is an extremely complex and powerful aspect of interaction and can be difficult to understand. Singelis (1994) suggested:

> Unlike verbal communication, which has relatively clear, agreed-upon meaning (and is verifiable), nonverbal communication usually can be interpreted in different ways. Even under the best circumstances, nonverbal communication can be difficult to interpret. Added to this inherent ambiguity are variations in individuals, contexts, and cultures. (p. 277)

Just as languages assign different meanings to words, cultures assign different meanings to nonverbal behaviors. Culture-specific uses and interpretations of nonverbal communication can lead to misunderstandings during cross-cultural interactions (Singelis, 1994). In addition to the different meanings of nonverbal behaviors, differences in the importance of such messages must be considered in cross-cultural encounters. For example, Latino cultures, like other collectivist cultures emphasizing harmony and relationship, tend to make nonverbal channels of communication a more important source of information (Albert, 1996; Hecht, Anderson, & Ribeau, 1989; Singelis, 1994).

The meanings of the messages sent and received by Latinos, as with other cultures, are often conveyed by gestures and other nonverbal signals. In general, Latinos are much more expressive in their nonverbal communication displays than mainstream Americans. The mainstream American baseline of what is appropriate in nonverbal communicative behavior cannot be used as a standard for judgment of those from other cultural backgrounds. Failure to understand this has, at times, led non-Latinos to misperceive the seemingly animated behavior of Latinos as a sign of being out of control (COSSMHO, 1990).

Nonverbal communication may take on added significance in cross-cultural interactions, particularly when language barriers exist. Singelis (1994) noted:

> The fact that at least one communicator is working in a second language means the verbal content may not be as clear as it would be in an intercultural interac-

tion. Consequently, the reliance on nonverbal communication may be even greater than normal. (p. 275)

Gesture. The use of gestures can be important in clarifying and enriching verbal communication. Generally, Latinos utilize gesture more frequently that mainstream Americans. Albert (1996) explained, "Gestures are used to express feelings, to answer questions, to call people or send them away, to greet them, and so on" (p. 343).

Proximity. Proximity is the distance that participants maintain between themselves during social interactions (Williams, 1997) or the amount of space we need around ourselves to feel comfortable (Yoder, Wallace, & Hugenberg, 1996). Latinos typically prefer being closer to others during interactions (Albert, 1996; COSSMHO, 1990; Randall-David, 1989). They may sit and stand much closer than is comfortable for mainstream Americans. Those who place themselves at a greater distance may be perceived as distant and detached (COSSMHO, 1990).

Touch. Often, physical touch indicates the kind of relationship and level of involvement of the participants in the relationship (Yoder et al., 1996). Touch can be used as a way of fostering an interpersonal connection with another or as a way of establishing rapport. The kinds of touch that are appropriate can be extremely complex and dependent on many factors, such as the relationship of the persons interacting and the specific context of the encounter. Latinos tend to physically touch people more frequently than mainstream Americans. Handshakes, introductory embraces, kisses on the cheek, and backslapping are common expressions of warmth and affection (Albert, 1996; COSSMHO, 1990; Randall-David, 1989).

Eye Contact. Gaze has many functions in communicative exchanges. It can open a channel for communication by cuing turn taking, it can be used to show attention or reflect concern. Traditionally, some Latinos have been socialized to avoid direct eye contact with authority figures as a sign of respeto (Albert, 1996, COSSMHO, 1990). Prolonged eye contact may be interpreted as disrespectful (Randall-David, 1989).

Expression of Pain. Expressions of pain may be conveyed much more openly than expected by those from different cultural groups. Latinos may express their pain by moaning loudly. Murillo-Rohde (1979) suggested that providers consider the meaning of such behavior within the specific culture. In this context, moaning may be a way of asking others to share their pain, or it may be a technique, like Lamaze breathing, used to reduce pain (COSSMHO, 1990). The expression of pain is of paramount importance in the health care environment because analgesics, or painkillers, may be prescribed based on the subjective expression of pain.

Explaining Illness Using Interpreters

Language differences may be the most immediate barrier to overcome in a cross-cultural encounter. To address this issue, interpreters may be relied on. It is the interpreter's responsibility to make possible communication that is mutually satisfying and successful for the parties involved. This task becomes more difficult in health care situations where participants are from different backgrounds, with different perceptions of reality and different goals, and in unequal relationships of power (Travillian-Vonesh, 1991). Despite the great need for quality interpretation services and the complexity of the task, this is not consistently available. It is not uncommon for the "[r]esponsibility for interpretation ... to fall on the shoulder of anyone who is bilingual and convenient to the scene" (Putsch, 1985, p. 3345). This could be a bilingual staff member, a friend, or family member brought by the monolingual client. Ideally, a qualified interpreter will be available who understands the cultural context of all participants involved in the encounter.

It is the interpreter's task not just to translate word for word what is said but to bridge cultural gaps. Interpretation is a complex process, requiring a great deal of ability and skill (Putsch, 1985)—a wide range of vocabulary, understanding of linguistic characteristics, and the ability to switch from the technical to the colloquial when necessary (Freimanis, 1994). Interpreters must often describe and explain terms, ideas, and processes that lie outside of the linguistic and cultural systems of clients and providers (Jackson-Caroll, Graham, & Jackson, 1995; Putsch, 1985).

Bilingual employees are frequently called on to serve as interpreter. Most are not formally trained or paid for their interpretation services. In such cases, the dual work roles that include interpretation can lead to job conflicts and confusion for the client. Employees who interpret may become uncomfortably suspended between doing their real work, for which they feel they were hired, and pressures to respond to the needs of monolingual clients (Putsch, 1985). If providing interpretation is viewed as an unwelcome, unpaid burden, relying on staff and untrained volunteers will be problematic. Bilingual health workers may also create confusion for the client by adapting the dual roles of interpreter and provider. This is especially relevant in situations where the bilingual provider is already involved in the care of the patient (Williams, 1997).

At times, patients will bring their own interpreter in the form of a friend or family member. This situation is also problematic. If patients bring their child or a friend to help communicate, they may feel embarrassed to talk about personal or intimate matters or fear that the information will not be kept confidential (Freimanis, 1994; Woloshin, Bickell, Schwartz, Gany, & Welch, 1995). Moreover, a family member or friend may be ill-prepared to deal with the complexity of interpreting (Putsch, 1985). Children should not be used as interpreters for the reasons mentioned and also because using children potentially exposes them to sensitive information and inverts family dynamics (Woloshin et al., 1995). For these reasons, a professionally trained interpreter should be provided whenever possible.

Although in many ways it is appropriate to think of the professional interpreter as a tool for improving communication, it should also be kept in mind that the inclusion of an additional person in the communication process will alter the dynamics. Health care professionals as well as interpreters bring a collection of personal issues that may impact the communication process. Even when an interpreter of the same ethnicity of the client can be found, it cannot be assumed that they will share the same life experiences. The same diversity of assumptions, dialect, lifestyle, and economic status will also prevail between interpreter and client (COSSMHO, 1990). Sometimes the implications of this are quite serious. For example, an interpreter may speak Spanish but disdain Latinos or a particular groups of Latinos. Such attitudes will undoubtedly hinder effective illness explanation (COSSMHO, 1990; Kline, Acosta, Austin, & Johnson, 1980). However, researchers have provided suggestions for alleviating many of the aforementioned concerns regarding the use of interpreters to explain illness and medically oriented information (Freimanis, 1994; Graham, 1995; Putsch, 1985; Randall-David, 1989; Westberg, 1989; Williams, 1997; see Appendix A, this chap.).

CONCLUSION

The area of cross-cultural communication with Latinos as well as with other cultural groups requires time, interest, flexibility, and a true commitment to provide culturally competent health care. We would like to stress that to effectively explain illness to Latinos, one must engage in extensive exploration of the larger Latino cultural context. Randall-David (1989) noted, "To isolate one component or subsystem is to ignore the cultural complexity of the group" (p. 3). She suggested that for effective cross cultural communication regarding health and illness, "it is necessary to learn about the broader socioeconomic, political, religious, and cultural context in which health is embedded" (p. 3).

Cross-cultural communication with Latinos should optimally encompass the cultural threads of respeto and personalismo. Clinicians should not only merely tolerate, but also understand and support, the cultural differences in communication style among Latinos, evidenced, for example, by increased proximity and physical touch. The language barrier that may be present between monolingual patients and their providers can be effectively addressed through a translator, by expressing phrases with clarity, maintaining eye contact with the patient, and carefully observing nonverbal cues.

Applying effective cross-cultural communication skills and techniques frequently adds time demands in a health care environment that increasingly focuses on productivity. Time spent understanding important cross-cultural dynamics or appropriately utilizing the services of a translator leads to the delivery of enhanced quality of health care services. However, many clinicians straddle the cultural needs of the individual patient and the pressure to accommodate more patients in their daily schedule. As cost containment becomes the overriding priority in our health care system, more attention must be focused in measuring the quality and cultural relevance of the care delivered. A fertile area for future research includes assessing the impact of time constraints in managed care as it relates to explaining illness in cross-cultural health care settings.

REFERENCES

Aguirre-Molina, M., & Molina, C. (1994). Latino populations: Who are they? In C. Molina & M. Aguirre-Molina (Eds.), *Latino health in the US: A growing challenge* (pp. 3–22). Washington, DC: American Public Health Association.

Albert, R. D. (1996). A framework and model for understanding Latin American and Latino/Hispanic cultural patterns. In D. Landis & R. S. Bhagat (Eds.), *Handbook of intercultural training* (2nd Ed; pp. 327–348). Thousand Oaks, CA: Sage.

American Cancer Society (1997). *Cancer facts and figures: 1997.* Atlanta: American Cancer Society.

Anderson, R. N., Kochanek, K. D., & Murphy, S. L. (1997). Report of final mortality statistics, 1995. *Monthly Vital Statistics Report, 45*(11) suppl. 2.

Andrews, M. M., & Boyle, J. S. (1995). *Transcultural concepts in nursing care* (2nd ed.). Philadelphia: Lippincott.

Barker, J. C. (1992). Cultural diversity—Changing the context of medical practice. *Western Journal of Medicine, 157,* 248–254.

Carrier, J. M. (1985). Mexican male bisexuality. In F. Klein & T. J. Wolf (Eds.) *Bisexualities: Theory and research* (pp. 75–85). New York: Harworth Press.

"COSSMHO." (1990) See The National Coalition of Hispanic Health and Human Services Organizations.

Centers for Disease Control (1989). Measles—Los Angeles, California, 1988. *Morbidity and Mortality Monthly Report, 38,* 49–57.

Centers for Disease Control and Prevention (1992). *Chronic disease in minority populations.* Atlanta: Author.

Council on Scientific Affairs. (1991). Hispanic health in the United States. *Journal of the American Medical Association, 265,* 248–252.

Engel, G. L. (1977). The need for a new medical model: A challenge for biomedicine. *Science, 196,* 129–136.

Fishman, B., Bobo, L., Kosub, K., & Womeodu, R. (1993). Cultural issues in serving minority populations: Emphasis on Mexican Americans and African Americans. *American Journal of the Medical Sciences, 306*(3), 160–166.

Freimanis, C. (1994). Training bilinguals to interpret in the community. In R. Brislin & T. Yoshida (Eds.), *Improving intercultural interactions: Modules for cross-cultural training programs* (pp. 313–341). Thousand Oaks, CA: Sage.

Graham, E. (1995). *Guidelines for interpreted visits.* EthnoMed, Ethnic Medicine Guide, Seattle, WA: University of Washington.

Harwood, A. (1971). The hot–cold theory of disease: Implications for treatment of Puerto Rican patients. *Journal of the American Medical Association, 216,* 1153–1157.

Hecht, M. L., Anderson, P. A., & Ribeau, S. A. (1989). The cultural dimensions of nonverbal communication. In M. K. Asante & W. B. Gudykunst (Eds.), *Handbook of international and intercultural communication* (pp. 163–185). Newbury Park, CA: Sage.

Heggenhougen, H. K., & Shore, L. (1986). Cultural components of behavioral epidemiology: Implications for primary health care. *Social Science Medicine, 22,* 1235–1245.

Helman, C. (1994). *Culture, health and illness* (3rd ed.). Boston, MA: Butterworth and Heinemann Ltd.

Hochbaum, G. (1970). *Health behavior.* Belmont, CA: Wadsworth.

Hutchinson, W. R., & Poznanski, C. A. (1987). *Living in Colombia.* Yarmouth, ME: Intercultural Press.

Jackson-Carroll, L. M., Graham E., & Jackson, J. C. (1995). *Beyond medical interpretation: The role of interpreter cultural mediators (ICMs) in building bridges between ethnic communities and health institutions.* Seattle, WA: University of Washington.

Kleinman, A., Eisenberg, L., & Good, B. (1978). Culture, illness and care: Clinical lessons form anthropologic and cross-cultural research. *Annals of Internal Medicine, 88,* 251–258.

Kline, F., Acosta, F. X., Austin, W., & Johnson, R. G. (1980). The misunderstood Spanish-speaking patient. *American Journal of Psychiatry, 137,* 1530–1537.

Lisansky, J. (1981). *Interpersonal relations among Hispanics in the United States: A content analysis of the social science literature.* (Tech. Rep. No. 3). Urbana: University of Illinois.

Logan, M. H. (1977). Humoral medicine in Guatemala and peasant acceptance of modern medicine. In D. Landy (Ed.), *Culture, disease and healing: Studies in medical anthropology* (pp. 119–128). New York: Macmillan.

Markides, K., & Coreil, J. (1986). The health of Hispanics in the southwestern United States: An epidemiologican paradox. *Public Health Report, 101,* 253–265.

Marín, G. (1989). AIDS prevention among Hispanics: Needs, risk behaviors and cultural values. *Public Health Reports, 104,*(5), 411–415.

Meleis, A. I., Douglas, M. K., Eribes, C., Shih, F., & Messias, D. K. (1996). Employed Mexican women as mothers and partners: Valued, empowered and overloaded. *Journal of Advanced Nursing, 23,* 82–90.

Molina, C., Zambrana, R. E., & Aguirre-Molina, M. (1994). The influence of culture, class, and environment on health care. In C. Molina & M. Aguirre-Molina (Eds.), *Latino health in the US: A growing challenge* (pp. 3–22). Washington, DC: American Public Health Association.

Mullavey-O'Byrne, C. (1994). Intercultural communication for health care professional. In R. Brislin & T Yoshida (Eds.), *Improving intercultural interactions: Modules for cross-cultural training programs* (pp. 171 196) Thousand Oaks, CA: Sage Publications.

Murill-Rohde, I. (1979). Cultural sensitivity in the care of the Hispanic patient. *Washington State Journal of Nursing, 51,* 25–32.

The National Coalition of Hispanic Health and Human Services Organizations. (1990). *Delivering preventive health care to Hispanics—A manual for providers.* Washington, DC: Author.

The National Council of La Raza. (1998). *Health.* Washington, DC.

Pachter, L. M. (1994). Culture and clinical care: Folk illness beliefs and behaviors and their implications for health care delivery. *Journal of the American Medical Association, 271,*(9), 690–694.

Public Heath Service (1987). *Diabetes and minorities: Closing the gap.* Washington, DC: U.S. Department of Health and Human Services.

Putsch, R. W., III. (1985). Cross-cultural communication: The special case for interpreters in health care. *Journal of the American Medical Association, 254*, 3344–3348.

Randall-David, E. (1989). *Strategies for working with culturally diverse communities and clients.* Bethesda, MD: Association of the Care of Children's Health.

Rodriguez, S. (1995). *Hispanics in the United States: An insight into group characteristics.* Department of Health and Human Services. Washington, DC.

Roll, S., Millen, L., & Martinez, R. (1980). Common errors in psychotherapy with Chicanos: Extrapolations from research and clinical experience. *Psychotherapy Theory, Research and Practice, 17*(2), 158–168.

Rosenwaike, I. (1987). Mortality differentials among persons born in Cuba, Mexico and Puerto Rico residing in the United States, 1979–81. *American Journal of Public Health, 77*, 603–606.

Rubel, A. J. (1977). The epidemiology of a folk illness: Susto in Hispanic America. In D. Landy (Ed.), *Culture, disease and healing: Studies in medical anthropology* (pp. 119–128). New York: Macmillan.

Ruiz, P., & Ruiz, P. P. (1983). Treatment compliance among Hispanics. *Journal of Operational Psychiatry, 14*, 112–114.

Scott, C. S. (1974). Health and healing practices among five ethnic groups in Miami, Florida. *Public Health Reports, 89*,(6), 524–532.

Schreiber, J. M., & Homiak, J. P. (1981). Mexican Americans. In A. Harwood (Ed.), *Ethnicity and medical care* (pp. 264–336). Cambridge, MA: Harvard University Press.

Singelis, T. (1994). Nonverbal communication in intercultural interactions. In R. Brislin & T. Yoshida (Eds.), *Improving intercultural interactions: Modules for cross-cultural training programs* (pp. 268–294). Thousand Oaks, CA: Sage.

Sorlie, P., Backlund, E., Johnson, N., & Rogot, E. (1993). Mortality by Hispanic status in the United States. *Journal of the American Medical Association, 270*, 2464–2468.

Spector, R. (1996). *Cultural diversity in health and illness* (4th ed.). Stamford, CT: Appleton & Lange.

Sumaya, C. V. (1991). Major infectious diseases causing excess morbidity in the Hispanic population. *Archives of Internal Medicine, 151*, 1513–1520.

Travillian-Vonesh, A. (1991, February). Recruiting community interpreters from an unexpected source. *The ATA Chronicle, 20*,(2), 22.

Trevino, F. M. (1982). Vital and health statistics for the U.S. Hispanic population. *American Journal of Public Health, 72*, 979–981.

Trotter, R. T. (1987). Caida de mollera: A newborn and early infancy risk. *Migrant Health Newsline 4*,(5) 2.

U.S. Bureau of the Census (1997). How we are changing: Demographic state of the nation: 1997. *Current Population Reports* (Series P23–193). Washington, DC: U.S. Government Printing Office.

U.S. Bureau of the Census (1995). Population profile of the United States: 1995. *Current Population Reports* (Series P23–189). Washington, DC: U.S. Government Printing Office.

Westberg, J. (1989). Patient education for Hispanic Americans. *Patient Education and Counseling, 13*, 143–160.

Williams, D. (1997). *Communication skills in practice: A practical guide for health professionals.* Pennsylvania, PA: Jessica Kingsley Publishers.

Woloshin, S., Bickell, N., Schwarts, L., Garry, F., & Welch, G. (1995). Language barriers in medicine in the United States. *Journal of the American Medical Association, 273*, 724–728.

Yoder, D. D., Wallace, S. P., & Hugenberg, L. W. (1996). *Creating competent communication.* Dubuque, IA: Kendall/Hunt.

APPENDIX A
USING INTERPRETERS TO EXPLAIN ILLNESS

1. Get to know your interpreters through regular meetings to facilitate understanding and open communication. Getting to know the strengths and weaknesses of the interpreters available may allow you to match the interpreter to the situation. Regular meetings may also provide an opportunity to learn from interpreters about the target population. The interpreter may be able to provide insight into local beliefs and customs as well as relevant community issues.

2. If you are not able to meet regularly with interpreters, a previsit conference is recommended. Before the interpreted visit, it is important to establish the purpose of the visit, learn about the interpreter's style, determine if there are any time constraints on the interpreter, and learn if he or she has any concerns that need to be addressed before the visit.

3. Whenever possible, provide an opportunity for the interpreter to meet with the client prior to the interview. This will allow interpreters to establish a rapport with the client and explain general interpretation practices.

4. Learn the interpreter's approach, whether he or she interprets short phrases at a time, translates simultaneously, or summarizes long statements of the patient and the provider.

5. If the encounter includes more than three persons (e.g., family members and–or other health professionals are present), it will be necessary to establish ground rules for turn taking because all messages must go through the interpreter(s).

6. Look at the patient and direct all statements and questions to him or her unless what you say is actually meant for the interpreter. In such cases, the patient should be told that you intend to ask the interpreter a question.

7. Be deliberate in your speech, keeping in mind the goal of clarity. Comments and questions should be short and simple. Avoid complex sentences, technical terminology, acronyms, colloquialisms, abstractions, and idiomatic expressions. This will help make the information manageable for the interpreter and the client.

8. Emphasize important information by repeating it more than once.

9. Check for understanding and interpretation accuracy by asking the client to repeat back explanations and instructions in his or her own words.

10. Carefully observe the client, listening for tone of voice and inflection and watching for nonverbal expressions. Although the professional interpreter will attempt to express all nuances, it is important to watch for nonverbal cues.

11. Obtain feedback from the interpreter. Encourage the interpreter to alert you when he or she suspects that there has been a misunderstanding. Address any concerns about the interpreted visit to the interpreter as soon as possible .

Becoming More Involved in Interpreted Visits:

1. Learn appropriate forms of address in the client's language. A warm, "Buenas Dias, Señora" (Good Morning, Mrs. _____) can go a long way in establishing rapport.

2. Become familiar with characteristics of the language. It is particularly useful to become aware of special terminology used by clients, and which English terms do not exist or have different connotations in the target language.

3. Learn basic words and sentences in the target language. This knowledge can be used for the benefit of you and the interpreter: Recognizing words and phrases during the interpreted visit helps you to maintain your concentration and asking questions about words and phrases that were not translated prompts the translator's attention to detail.

12

Explaining Illness to Asian and Pacific Islander Americans: Culture, Communication, and Boundary Regulation

Gust A. Yep, Ph.D.
Department of Speech and Communication Studies
San Francisco State University

Tome Tanaka, a Japanese man in his sixties, was a patient in the rehabilitation unit. A stroke had left him with significant weakness on his left side. Self-care was an important part of his therapy. He had to relearn to feed himself, dress, shave, use the bathroom, and do other daily activities. Kathy, his nurse, spent a great deal of time carefully explaining to Mr. Tanaka how the staff would work with him on these tasks. The patient and his wife listened passively. … Several hours later … Kathy came into the room and discovered Mrs. Tanaka waiting on her husband as though he were an invalid.   —Galanti (1991, p. 57)

[Vietnamese] words that translate "feeling hot" don't mean "fever." What they mean is "I don't feel well" and generalized malaise. And if you should ask your Vietnamese patients, "Have you ever had hepatitis?" the translator [may] translate that into "liver disease," and liver disease in Vietnam means itching.   —Fitzgerald (1988, p. 67)

283

"Asian and Pacific Islander Americans"[1] are the fastest growing ethnic group in the United States (Mineta, 1994; Takeuchi & Young, 1994; Yep, 1993; Yu & Liu, 1992). As a result of this growth, the health care system is providing services to an increasing number of Asian and Pacific Islander Americans with a variety of illnesses—cancer, hepatitis, HIV/AIDS, tuberculosis, and health-related conditions like obesity, diabetes, and substance use and abuse. However, Asian and Pacific Islander Americans do not constitute a homogeneous ethnic category; there are many different ethnic groups within this cultural classification, including Chinese, Filipino, Japanese, Korean, Laotian, Native Hawaiian, Samoan, Thai, Tongan, and Vietnamese, among many others (Takeuchi & Young, 1994; Yu & Liu, 1992).

Unfortunately, health promotion, disease prevention, and health service delivery tend to be Eurocentric (Airhihenbuwa, 1995; Choi, Yep, & Kumekawa, 1998), culturally insensitive (Geist, 1997; Kreps & Kunimoto, 1994; Mayeno & Hirota, 1994), and linguistically inappropriate (Geist, 1997; Mayeno & Hirota, 1994; Rumbaut, Chavez, Moser, Pickwell, & Wishnik, 1988; Yep, 1997) for cocultural communities including Asian and Pacific Islander Americans. Mayeno and Hirota (1994) noted that in addition to structural problems in the health care system:

> [there] is a lack of culturally appropriate practices at the provider level. There is a lack of bicultural and culturally competent staff to provide appropriate care. This is perpetuated by an educational system for preparing health professionals in which cultural awareness is almost entirely absent. (p. 355)

The purpose of this chapter is to examine cultural factors influencing the process of communication associated with explanation of illness to Asian and Pacific Islander Americans. To accomplish this, the chapter is divided into five sections. First, a description of some common Asian and Pacific Islander American cultural attributes is offered. Next, common cultural beliefs associated with health and illness in these groups are examined. Third, how communication boundary regulation, as postulated by the theory of communication management of privacy (CMP), appears to be a relevant theoretical framework for communicating about illness in this context is detailed. Then, application of such a model to the process of explanation of

---

[1]The term "Asian and Pacific Islander American" is a label of convenience used by the Asian and Pacific Islander American Health Forum, a national advocacy organization dedicated to promoting policy, program, and research for improving health status of Asians and Pacific Islanders in this country. I problematize it by using quotation marks around the label, initially, to remind the reader that this is not a singular and homogeneous ethnic category. According to the U.S. Census Bureau, there are over 40 Asian and Pacific Islander groups from over 40 countries and territories, who speak more than 100 different languages. Asian and Pacific Islander Americans are characterized by tremendous linguistic, historical, geographical, and cultural diversity; therefore, Asian and Pacific Islander Americans may be more appropriately viewed as a conglomeration of communities with a set of distinctive as well as common fundamental features.

illness to Asian and Pacific Islander Americans by focusing on some of their common cultural characteristics and health beliefs is performed. Finally, discussed is the future directions for theory development, research, and health care delivery to Asian and Pacific Islander Americans.

CULTURAL ATTRIBUTES

Although Asian and Pacific Islander Americans represent a diverse group of individuals, some cultural commonalities have been identified (Chung, 1992; Yep, 1997, 1998, in press-b). Some of these cultural patterns include: (a) collectivistic orientation, (b) indirect mode of communication, (c) shame orientation, and (d) face maintenance. To illustrate these cultural attributes, I use the following case study reported by Galanti (1991):

> A middle-aged Chinese patient named Patrick Chung refused pain medication following cataract surgery. When asked, he replied that his discomfort was bearable and he could survive without any medication. Later, however, the nurse found him restless and uncomfortable. Again, she offered pain medication. Again he refused, explaining that her responsibilities at the hospital were far more important than his immediate comfort and he did not want to impose on her. Only after she firmly insisted that a patient's comfort was one of her most important responsibilities did Mr. Chung finally agree to take his medication. (p. 26)

Collectivistic Orientation

Asian cultures are generally collectivistic—cultures that emphasize the goals, needs, and perceptions of the group rather than the individual, therefore focusing on the "we" identity (i.e., the family and the larger group; Hofstede, 1984; Yep, 1997). In collectivistic cultures, the self is situationally and relationally defined; that is, the presentation of oneself is contingent on the nature of the context, situation, and the relationship with the interactant. Tu (1985) discussed this notion of self in relationship to Confucian philosophy, "a distinctive feature of Confucian ritualization is an ever-deepening and broadening awareness of the *presence of the other* [italics added] in one's self-cultivation" (p. 232). In most collectivistic cultures, the self is defined and maintained through a complex and dynamic interaction of social and personal relationships; the self is never free (Chung, 1992). This is in direct contrast with individualistic societies (e.g., Western cultures) in which the self is a perfectly free entity—autonomous and free to go after its own personal and unique wishes, needs, and desires. In the previous case study, it is clear that Mr. Chung saw his needs (physical discomfort) as secondary to those of the group (the nurse's responsibilities at the hospital).

Indirect Communication

Asian cultures generally use more indirect modes of communication (Chung, 1992; Yep, 1997, 1998) than Western cocultures. Hall (1976) maintained that cultures may be differentiated on the basis of their modes of communication by introducing the low–high context continuum. A low-context communication message is one in which most of the information is directly and explicitly stated in the verbalized message (e.g., a direct request for an explanation about medication side-effects). On the other hand, a high-context communication message is one in which most of the information is either implied in the social and physical context or internalized in the person, leaving little information in the verbalized message. Communicatively, Asian cultures generally fall on the high-context end of the continuum (Hall, 1976; Yep, 1998). Context affects all aspects of communication within a culture including language (both written and spoken), patterns of social organization, and conflict resolution. More specifically, Hall (1976) stated:

> High-context cultures make greater distinctions between insiders and outsiders than low-context cultures do. People raised in high-context systems expect more of others than do participants in low-context systems. When talking about something that they have on their minds, a high-context individual will expect his [or her] interlocutor to know what's bothering him [or her], so that he [or she] doesn't have to be specific. The result is that he [or she] will talk around and around the point, in effect putting all the pieces in place except the crucial one. Placing it properly—this keystone—is the role of his [or her] interlocutor. To do this for him [or her] is an insult. (p. 98)

To put it more simply, Western cultures tend to value direct interactional styles, whereas Eastern cultures value more indirect forms of communication. In the previously mentioned case study, it appears that Mr. Chung expected the nurse to "read between the lines" when he told her that "his discomfort was bearable and he could survive without any medication."

Shame Orientation

Shame is a powerful influence among Asian cultures (Benedict, 1946/1989; Yep, 1997). Abramson (1986) suggested that "shame is a life long burden" (p. 4), and many Asian and Pacific Islander Americans are concerned about behaviors that might bring embarrassment and loss of honor to themselves and their families. As Chung (1992) noted, "Asians have a lot to lose if they fail because their identities are rooted in their families and groups. Thus the whole family or organization feels disgraced collectively when one of its members does something shameful" (p. 32). Mr.

Chung's behavior, in the previous case study, could have been driven by shame: It might be embarrassing for an adult male to ask for pain medication when his age and gender role might indicate that pain and discomfort should be endured.

Face Maintenance

The concept of face is present in all cultures (Brown & Levinson, 1978; Ting-Toomey, 1988; Yep, 1998). Facework, or the behaviors that people engage in to make their actions consistent with their face, however, varies across cultures. In Asian cultures, communication practices tend to focus on supporting another person's face, at the same time not bringing shame to one's own self-face. In Western cultures, communication behaviors tend to focus on the preservation of one's individuality, autonomy, and space while respecting the other's need for autonomy and territory. Imposition on others can be viewed as a face-threat (Ting-Toomey, 1988). In the previous case study, Mr. Chung stated that "he did not want to impose on [his nurse]" and in doing so, he was preserving his own self-face and the nurse's face.

BELIEFS ASSOCIATED WITH HEALTH AND ILLNESS

Like other cocultural groups, Asian and Pacific Islander Americans hold a number of cultural beliefs related to health and illness (e.g., Kleinman, 1988; Ying, 1990). Although these beliefs appear to be different from one Asian group to another (e.g., Chinese and Samoan) and from one generation to the next (e.g., Issei, Nisei, Sansei, and Yonsei—first, second, third, and fourth generation Japanese American, respectively), some merit discussion as they are relevant to the process of explaining illness. In particular, four cultural beliefs associated with health and illness have been identified in this context: (a) discussion of illness, death, and dying, (b) discussion of taboo health topics, (c) perception of lucky and unlucky numbers, and (d) cultural beliefs of hot and cold.

Illness, Death and Dying

In Asian cultures, discussion of illness, death, and dying is considered bad luck, particularly when the disease is serious or terminal (Aoki, Ngin, Mo, & Ja, 1989; Yep, 1997, in press-b). In addition, it is believed that too much discussion about a serious health condition can become a self-fulfilling prophecy; that is, one can bring on the occurrence of the illness (Yep, 1997). Clearly, this belief can create cultural misunderstandings between non-Asian health care providers and Asian and Pacific Islander American patients. For example, a Western health care provider might interpret the

Asian patient's reluctance to discuss his or her condition as unhealthy denial, whereas the Asian patient might view the health care practitioner's discussion as bad luck.

Taboo Health Topics

As in all cultures, certain health topics appear to carry tremendous social and cultural stigma. The degree of stigma associated with certain illnesses can also change over time; for example, the stigma attached to people with cancer has diminished in some ways over the last several decades. However, there are some taboo health topics that persist among Asian and Pacific Islander Americans including sexually transmitted diseases and drug abuse (Aoki et al., 1989; Yep, 1997; Zane & Kim, 1994). Discussion of these topics with anyone, including health care providers, might be perceived as inappropriate, as they can bring shame and loss of face to the Asian patient and his or her family system (Aoki et al., 1989; Yep, 1997). One way to overcome this potential problem is to use figurative or indirect language (Yep, in press-b).

Lucky and Unlucky Numbers

Many Euro-Americans are superstitious about the number 13. For example, most, if not all, hospitals—or any building for that matter—do not have a thirteenth floor or room number 13. Galanti (1991) reported on the significance of numbers in Japanese culture:

> A young Japanese woman named Kieko Ozawa was being wheeled into operating room 4 when she noticed the number over the door. She began to cry softly. The nurse became concerned and asked what was wrong. Kieko was embarrassed but explained that the Japanese character for the number 4 was almost identical to that for the word "death." Already concerned about her health, Kieko was disturbed to be wheeled into a room labeled "death." (p. 48)

Through this same lens, Galanti (1991) noted that the Chinese believe that numbers 8 and 9 are lucky because they symbolize health and longevity, respectively.

Beliefs of Hot and Cold

In a number of Asian cultures, foods are believed to be either hot or cold (Galanti, 1991). These are not temperatures but rather qualities associated with specific types of food. For example, hot foods include beef, pork, and potatoes, whereas cold foods include chicken, fish, and fruit. If a person has a "cold condition" (e.g., lung cancer), it is believed that this person should receive "hot foods" to restore health balance (e.g., a diet full of beef, pork, and potatoes). Understanding this health belief can help the health care practitioner provide appropriate dietary suggestions for an Asian patient who might otherwise refuse to eat if he or she perceives them to be inconsistent to, or contradictory of, the "hot and cold" food–illness belief system.

In these previous two sections, some common Asian and Pacific Islander American cultural attributes and beliefs associated with health and illness have been examined. But how does culture affect the process of explaining illness? In the remaining sections of this chapter, I explore this question in detail. First, an examination of the notion of boundary regulation is offered, then how this notion can be used in the context of explaining illness to Asian and Pacific Islander Americans is explored.

BOUNDARY REGULATION

According to CMP, individuals regulate disclosure of private information in their relational systems (Petronio, 1991, in press; Petronio & Kovach, 1997; Petronio, Reeder, Hecht, & Mon't Ros-Mendoza, 1996). Disclosure regulation has been viewed as critical for satisfying relationships. For example, Petronio (1991) maintained that regulation of disclosure protects the individual in the relational system from personal vulnerabilities associated with risky information. During this course of regulation, individuals manage their communication boundaries: "Management is critical because it is the process through which the partners balance giving up autonomy by disclosing and increasing intimacy by sharing private information" (Petronio, 1991, p. 312). In short, communication boundary regulation is a strategic balance between self-revelation and self-restraint.

CMP is based on three fundamental assumptions (Petronio, 1991). First, partners in a relational system (like a doctor–patient dyad) erect boundaries to maintain a balance between autonomy and vulnerability when disclosing and receiving private information from the other. Next, individuals in a relational system strategically regulate their communication boundaries to minimize risks and potential vulnerability. Third, partners coordinate the intersection of their own individual boundaries by following specific relational rules that determine the sending and receiving of disclosure information, like explanation of illness, in terms of timing, amount, and context to establish an equilibrium between personal autonomy and relational knowledge.

CMP appears to be particularly relevant to explaining illness to Asian and Pacific Islander Americans for several reasons. First, Asian cultures, as stated in the previous section, tend to be more collectivistic in their cultural orientation. A corollary of this cultural attribute is the sharp distinction between in-group (e.g., one's extended family) and out-group (e.g., the community at large). Kim (1994) elaborated:

In collectivistic societies, one of the most important differentiations made about individuals is whether a person is part of an in-group or an out-group. Collectivistic cultures emphasize a *we* versus *they* distinction [italics in the original]. The emphasis on collective welfare, harmony, and duties typically applies only to the in-group and usually does not extend to out-groups. (pp. 32–33)

It is apparent that privacy and boundary regulation—in the context of explaining illness—are particularly salient to Asian and Pacific Islander cultural constituents who are characterized by clear in-group–out-group distinctions and tighter communication boundaries between in-group and out-group.

Second, CMP focuses on disclosure of private information potentially involving high levels of risk. In the case of explanation of illness and health conditions, the potential risks of disclosure are great—ranging from sadness, embarrassment, and discomfort to complete hopelessness like telling a patient that he or she has a terminal condition. This notion of privacy and boundary regulation appears to be especially relevant for explaining illnesses that are perceived as distressing, shameful, or stigmatizing in the patient's cultural context. For example, Takahashi (1990) noted that Japanese physicians often do not disclose a patient's terminal condition or explain the diagnosis to avoid patient distress, maintain their interdependent doctor–patient relationship, and to conceal their own fears and anxieties associated with death and dying.

Third, CMP introduces the notion of communication boundaries as a protective mechanism for both discloser and disclosee. In other words, this approach emphasizes the transactional nature of disclosive communication, like a health care practitioner disclosing diagnostic test results to his or her patient, in which both interactants actively exchange, negotiate, manage, and process information. More simply stated, Petronio's (1991, 1996, 1997, in press) model directs attention to both partners—as opposed to only one member of the dyad—in a disclosure situation. For example, Alex, a health care provider, might be apprehensive to disclose and explain to Kayo, a Japanese patient, that she has a sexually transmitted disease because he is uncomfortable discussing sexuality with the opposite sex. Kayo might experience loss of face and shame as a result of a stigmatizing health condition.

Finally, CMP is a new theoretical framework with considerable promise. It has been applied in the interpersonal (Petronio, 1991, in press), social (Petronio, in press; Petronio & Magni, 1996), and health contexts (Greene & Serovich, 1996; Petronio & Kovach, 1997; Petronio et al., 1996; Yep, in press-a). The current application of CMP in the intercultural health communication context appears to be another extension of its theoretical and practical potential.

BOUNDARY REGULATION
AND EXPLANATION OF ILLNESS

According to Petronio (1991, in press), disclosive messages—like telling a patient his/her medical diagnosis and explaining the implications of the condition—inherently contain a demand or expectation for appropriate response. Petronio (1991) outlined a number of factors that must be taken into consideration before disclosure takes place. In the context of explaining illness to Asian and Pacific Islander American patients, the health care provider (the discloser) needs to take into account three potential issues: (a) expectations communicated through the disclosive message regarding desired receiver's response, (b) selection and production of appropriate message strategy to disclose, and (c) content of the message in terms of both breadth and depth. Similarly, the patient (receiving partner) needs to consider several factors before responding to the disclosure and explanation of his or her illness including: (a) evaluation of expectations associated with the response, (b) search for attributions and motives behind the disclosure, and (c) determination of message response strategy. Boundary coordination is the extent to which health care provider and patient match between demands expressed in the disclosive message and meeting of those demands in the response message.

To illustrate boundary regulation and explanation of illness, I borrow another case study from Galanti (1991), who collected a number of anecdotes from American hospitals. This case involves a Japanese businessman:

Hiroshi Tomita ... was admitted to the hospital with a 102-degree fever of unknown origin ... his nurse, Jean, removed the blankets from the bed, leaving only a sheet to cover him. She explained that it was to keep his temperature from going up. She gave him a glass of cold apple juice, but he only took two sips ... when his temperature rose to 103 degrees ... Jean ordered a cooling blanket.... At this point, Mr. Tomita asked for his blankets, but Jean refused, once more explaining why. She put the ice blanket under him and left the room. In a few minutes, Mr. Tomita complained that the ice blanket was too cold and asked for his regular blankets. For the third time, Jean patiently explained the treatment. He did not say anything; he simply curled up under his sheet. When Jean returned ... he was sitting up in the chair with all the blankets wrapped around him, covered with goose bumps and shivering ... [and] his temperature was up to 105 degrees. Mr. Tomita continued to ask for his blankets and to get out of bed. Jean was at the point of putting restraints on him to keep him in bed. (pp. 97–98)

Health Care Provider's Expectations

When a health care provider explains a diagnosis or a health condition to a patient, it usually entails an implied expectation of a response from the patient. When Jean, in this example, explained to Mr. Tomita that she intended to keep his temperature from going up and gave him a glass of cold apple juice, the expectation was for him to drink the juice. Although Mr. Tomita seemingly understood the expectation, he took two sips from the glass, but he did not follow through completely (i.e., drinking the entire glass of juice). Through his actions, Mr. Tomita was saying "no" in an indirect, high-context way of communicating. Jean, on the other hand, presumably following a more direct and low-context style of communication, did not seem to assign as much importance to the nonverbal behaviors and the context of this communication situation and proceeded with her treatment plan.

Health Care Provider's Message Strategy Selection and Production

Once the health care provider has determined his or her expectation for communicating with the patient, he or she needs to select specific message strategies that will enhance the accomplishment of the expected goals. After consideration of the process of selecting a specific message strategy, the health care provider needs to encode his or her message. According to Petronio (1991), such message strategies can be either explicit or implicit.

Explicit message strategies are those communication tactics that contain high-certainty demand characteristics (Petronio, 1991). Such messages contain clear intentions, low ambiguity, obvious demands, and low uncertainty. In terms of communication boundaries, these messages give little autonomy to the recipient. In other words, less control is given to the receiver; therefore, the listener is placed in a more threatening position where protection from vulnerabilities is more difficult to attain. Because less autonomy is given to the recipient of the communication message, he or she has fewer options available as a response to the information delivered. In the most recent situation, when Jean was about to put restraints on Mr. Tomita to keep him in bed, he had few response options.

Implicit message strategies are those communication tactics that are characterized by low-certainty demand features (Petronio, 1991). These messages contain a high degree of ambiguity and uncertainty, allowing the listener more autonomy to respond to the implicit demand in the communication. Implicit message tactics protect the communication boundaries of both the sender and the recipient. The receiving partner has the freedom to probe for clarification, continue exploring the subject, or simply acknowledge the original message. If, in the previous example, Jean talked about different ways to reduce Mr. Tomita's fever, he could have asked questions, listened to her, or simply said nothing.

Message Content of Provider's Explanation

The health care provider, after assessing his or her expectations and message strategies, must make a decision about what to tell the patient. In other words, he or she needs to formulate the actual content of an explanation for the patient's illness or health condition. In the case study, Jean, the nurse, attempted to explain to Mr. Tomita why she was using an ice blanket to reduce his fever from 103 degrees. From her cultural perspective, her explanation seemed clear: A cooling blanket is used to cool her patient's body. Conversely, from Mr. Tomita's cultural perspective, Jean's explanation did not make any sense. In Japan, people with fevers require warm blankets and plenty of hot drinks to allow the body to "sweat it out." In this situation, the explanation of the medical intervention was fueled by a health belief that was in direct contradiction with the cultural belief of the client.

Patient's Evaluation of Expectations

Explanatory messages contain specific demands regarding appropriate responses to them. To assess the expectations for responding to the health care provider's explanation, the receiver must consider his or her sense of obligation to act and the extent to which he or she has autonomy in responding (Petronio, 1991). Further, this sense of responsibility to act is inversely related to perceived autonomy. More specifically, the greater the receiving partner experiences a sense of responsibility to act on the basis of the explanation, the lesser the perceived autonomy or choice; conversely, the lesser the sense of obligation, the greater the freedom the patient has for deciding on available options to respond. In the earlier example, Mr. Tomita was given little autonomy to act, as he was expected to sleep on top of an ice blanket and a single sheet over him. He attempted to object to the instructions using high-context communication methods and when they failed, he stopped listening to the nurse's instructions.

Patient's Attributional Searches

For the patient to respond appropriately, he or she must assess the motivation behind the health care provider's communication of medical information. To evaluate the reasons for the explanation, the receiver needs to consider relational memory or related past experiences with the health care provider, the message content or the information conveyed, the situation or context in which the explanation was given, the physical and psychological context, and the nonverbal behavior accompanying the verbal explanation (Petronio, 1991). In the previous case study, the patient appeared to be confused—there was no relational memory with a health care provider who was providing information inconsistent with his own cultural health beliefs in a medical emergency situation.

Patient's Determination of Message Response

Once the receiver of the medical explanation has examined the expectations of the message, he or she must decide on how to appropriately respond. According to Petronio (1991), there are two possible types of response strategies. The first, direct message response, is characterized by high certainty, directness, and clarity in the fulfillment of the obligations implied in the original message (e.g., a patient telling the health care provider that he or she will do certain things after listening to the explanation of the health condition). The second, indirect message response features high degrees of ambiguity and uncertainty in relationship to the demand associated with the original message (e.g., a patient telling the health care provider that he or she was feeling good about the explanation). Mr. Tomita, in the earlier case, attempted to first communicate indirectly by not drinking the cold apple juice that the nurse provided.

Health Care Provider–Patient Communication Boundary Coordination To the extent to which the response matches the demand of the explanatory message, there is boundary coordination or "satisfactory fit" in the communication episode, in particular, and the relationship in general (Petronio, 1991). Because of cultural differences, medical explanations might be met with cultural misunderstandings (Geist, 1997; Kreps & Kunimoto, 1994). When boundary coordination is attained, the communication is satisfying. Galanti (1991) described the conclusion of the previous case study:

> Reflecting on [Mr. Tomita's situation], Jean asked herself what she did when suffering from a temperature and chills. She realized that she did exactly what her patient wanted—she piled lots of blankets on herself, turned up the electric blanket … and drank hot liquids! [After Jean changed her intervention] Mr. Tomita was extremely happy and grateful. … His temperature came down after about three hours and eventually he removed the blankets on his own. (pp. 98–99)

CONCLUSION AND FUTURE DIRECTIONS

As the population of Asian and Pacific Islander Americans continues to grow in this country, more and more health care providers are expected to interact with Asian and Pacific Islander American patients, which naturally includes explaining a variety of illnesses and health-related conditions. In this chapter, outlined are several common cultural attributes that characterize members of Asian cultures including collectivistic or group orientation, indirect mode of communication, shame orientation, and face-maintenance concerns. Several cultural beliefs associated with health and illness are also identified: discussion of illness, death, and dying; taboo health topics; lucky and unlucky numbers; and the "hot and cold" system. I then proposed that communication boundary regulation, as postulated by CMP, might be a relevant theoretical framework to examine and understand the process of explaining illness to Asian and Pacific Islander Americans. Finally, how health care providers and patients might interact in the process of disclosing medical results and explaining the diagnosed condition by focusing on both interactants in a health communication episode are explained.

Although the notion of boundary coordination appears to be theoretically and pragmatically promising for understanding explanation of illness in intercultural health communication settings, Petronio's CMP needs to be tested in this context. Future research needs to examine how culturally different health care provider–patient dyads negotiate and regulate their boundaries according to their degree of intra–interculturalness (Sarbaugh, 1988), cultural expectations of health care provider and patient roles, type of illness and health condition (acute vs. chronic), and degree of cultural stigma associated with the condition, among others. In terms of health service delivery, the notion of boundary regulation can provide health care practitioners with some guidelines to understand the complexity of provider–patient interactions and to increase their intercultural sensitivity with patients who are culturally different from themselves when explaining illness.

REFERENCES

Abramson, P. R. (1986). The cultural context of Japanese sexuality: An American perspective. *Psychologia, 29,* 1–9.

Airhihenbuwa, C. O. (1995). *Health and culture: Beyond the western paradigm.* Thousand Oaks, CA: Sage.

Aoki, B., Ngin, C. P., Mo, B., & Ja, D. Y. (1989). AIDS prevention models in Asian-American communities. In V. M. Mays, G. W. Albee, & S. F. Schneider (Eds.), *Primary prevention of AIDS: Psychological approaches* (pp. 290–308). Newbury Park, CA: Sage.

Benedict, R. (1989). *The chrysanthemum and the sword: Patterns of Japanese culture.* Boston: Houghton Mifflin (original work published 1946).

Brown, P., & Levinson, S. (1978). Universals in language usage: Politeness phenomenon. In E. Goody (Ed.), *Questions and politeness: Strategies in social interaction* (pp. 56–289). Cambridge, England: Cambridge University Press.

Choi, K., Yep, G. A., & Kumekawa, E. (1998). HIV prevention among Asian and Pacific Islander American men who have sex with men: A critical review of theoretical models and directions for future research. *AIDS Education and Prevention, 10,* 19–30.

Chung, D. K. (1992). Asian cultural commonalities: A comparison with mainstream American culture. In S. M. Furuto, R. Biswas, D. K. Chung, K. Murase, & F. Ross-Sheriff (Eds.), *Social work practice with Asian Americans* (pp. 27–44). Newbury Park, CA: Sage.

Fitzgerald, F. T. (1988). How they view you, themselves, and disease. *Consultant, 28,* 65–77.

Galanti, G. (1991). *Caring for patients from different cultures: Case studies from American hospitals.* Philadelphia: University of Pennsylvania Press.

Geist, P. (1997). Negotiating cultural understanding in health care communication. In L. A. Samovar & R. E. Porter (Eds.), *Intercultural communication: A reader* (pp. 340–348). Belmont, CA: Wadsworth.

Greene, K., & Serovich, J. M. (1996). Appropriateness of disclosure of HIV testing information: The perspective of PLWAs. *Journal of Applied Communication Research, 24,* 50–65.

Hall, E. T. (1976). *Beyond culture.* New York: Doubleday.

Hofstede, G. (1984). *Culture's consequences: International differences in work-related values.* Newbury Park, CA: Sage.

Kim, U. (1994). Individualism and collectivism: Conceptual clarification and elaboration. In U. Kim, H. C. Triandis, C. Kagitcibasi, S. Choi, & G. Yoon (Eds.), *Individualism and collectivism: Theory, method, and applications* (pp. 19–40). Thousand Oaks, CA: Sage.

Kleinman, A. (1988). *Rethinking psychiatry: From cultural category to personal experience.* New York: The Free Press.

Kreps, G. L., & Kunimoto, E. N. (1994). *Effective communication in multicultural health care settings.* Thousand Oaks, CA: Sage.

Mayeno, L., & Hirota, S. M. (1994). Access to health care. In N. W. S. Zane, D. T. Takeuchi, & K. N. J. Young (Eds.), *Confronting critical health issues of Asian and Pacific Islander Americans* (pp. 347–375). Thousand Oaks, CA: Sage.

Mineta, N. (1994). Preface: Beyond "Black, white, and other." In N. W. S. Zane, D. T. Takeuchi, & K. N. J. Young (Eds.), *Confronting critical health issues of Asian and Pacific Islander Americans* (pp. vii–viii). Thousand Oaks, CA: Sage.

Petronio, S. (1991). Communication boundary management: A theoretical model of managing disclosure of private information between marital couples. *Communication Theory, 1,* 311–335.

Petronio, S. (in press). *The boundaries of private disclosures.* New York: State University of New York Press.

Petronio, S., & Kovach, S. (1997). Managing boundaries: Health providers' perceptions of resident care in Scottish nursing homes. *Journal of Applied Communication Research, 25,* 115–131.

Petronio, S., & Magni, J. (1996, November). *Being gay and HIV positive: Boundary regulation of disclosure discourse.* Paper presented to the Annual Meeting of the Speech Communication Association, San Diego, CA.

Petronio, S., Reeder, H. M., Hecht, M., & Mon't Ros-Mendoza, T. (1996). Disclosure of sexual abuse by children and adolescents. *Journal of Applied Communication Research, 24,* 181–199.

Rumbaut, R. G., Chavez, L. R., Moser, R. J., Pickwell, S. M., & Wishnik, S. M. (1988). The politics of migrant health care: A comparative study of Mexican immigrants and Indochinese refugees. *Research in the Sociology of Health Care, 7,* 143–202.

Sarbaugh, L. E. (1988). A taxonomic approach to intercultural communication. In Y. Y. Kim & W. B. Gudykunst (Eds.), *Theories in intercultural communication* (pp. 22–38). Newbury Park, CA: Sage.

Takahashi, Y. (1990). Informing a patient of malignant illness: Commentary from a cross-cultural viewpoint. *Death Studies, 14,* 83–91.

Takeuchi, D. T., & Young, K. N. J. (1994). Overview of Asian and Pacific Islander Americans. In N. W. S. Zane, D. T. Takeuchi, & K. N. J. Young (Eds.), *Confronting critical health issues of Asian and Pacific Islander Americans* (pp. 3–21). Thousand Oaks, CA: Sage.

Ting-Toomey, S. (1988). Intercultural conflict styles: A face-negotiation theory. In Y. Y. Kim & W. D. Gudykunst (Eds.), *Theories in intercultural communication* (pp. 213–235). Newbury Park, CA: Sage.

Tu, W. M. (1985). Selfhood and otherness in Confucian thought. In A. Marsella, G. DeVos, & F. Hsu (Eds.), *Culture and self: Asian and western perspectives* (pp. 231–251). New York: Tavistock.

Yep, G. A. (1993). HIV/AIDS in Asian and Pacific Islander communities in the United States: A review, analysis, and integration. *International Quarterly of Community Health Education, 13*(4), 293–315.

Yep, G. A. (1997). Overcoming barriers in HIV/AIDS education for Asian Americans: Toward more effective cultural communication. In D. C. Umeh (Ed.), *Confronting the AIDS epidemic: Cross-cultural perspectives on HIV/AIDS education* (pp. 219–230). Trenton, NJ: Africa World Press.

Yep, G. A. (1998). Safer sex negotiation in cross-cultural romantic dyads: An extension of Ting-Toomey's face negotiation theory. In N. Roth and L. K. Fuller (Eds.), *Women and AIDS: Negotiating safer practices, care, and representation* (pp. 81–100). Binghamton, NY: Haworth.

Yep, G. A. (in press-a). Disclosure of HIV infection in interpersonal relationships: A communication management of privacy approach. In S. Petronio (Ed.), *Balancing disclosure, privacy, and secrecy*. Mahwah, NJ: Lawrence Erlbaum Associates.

Yep, G. A. (in press-b). "See no evil, hear no evil, speak no evil": Educating Asian Americans about HIV/AIDS through culture-specific health communication campaigns. In L. K. Fuller (Ed.), *Media-Mediated AIDS*. Cresskill, NJ: Hampton Press.

Ying, Y. (1990). Explanatory models of major depression and implications for help-seeking among immigrant Chinese-American women. *Culture, Medicine, and Psychiatry, 14,* 393–408.

Yu, E. S. H., & Liu, W. T. (1992). US national health data on Asian Americans and Pacific Islanders: A research agenda for the 1990s. *American Journal of Public Health, 82,* 1645–1652.

Zane, N., & Kim, J. H. (1994). Substance use and abuse. In N. W. S. Zane, D. T. Takeuchi, & K. N. J. Young (Eds.), *Confronting critical health issues of Asian and Pacific Islander Americans* (pp. 316–343). Thousand Oaks, CA: Sage.

13

Explaining Illness to African Americans: Employing Cultural Concerns with Strategies

Carolyn A. Stroman
Department of Human Communication Studies
Howard University

Prayer and repentance, not penicillin, cure sin. —Snow (1978, p. 73)

This quotation cogently illustrates the central theme of this chapter; indeed, of this book: Culture is a key variable in the health care arena and specifically in the explanation and understanding of illness. As used here, *culture* refers to the world views, values, beliefs, attitudes, and behaviors that one acquires as a member of a given social group (Brown, 1963; Harwood, 1981). Culture has also been defined expansively to include "a broad range of social factors that lead people to think and act in very unique ways" (Kreps & Kunimoto, 1994, p. 2).

Cultural differences abound in the health care system; such variance manifests in the medical encounter on various levels. Differences in world views exist between health care practitioners who hold notions character-ized and expressed by medical terminology and patients who enter the situation with world views distinguished and expressed by their colloquial communication. In particular, patients and health care providers interpret the etiology of illness differently (Helman, 1994; Kreps & Kunimoto, 1994). As a result, differences in explaining illness and perspectives in assessing the most efficacious treatment exist (Helman, 1994; Kreps & Kunimoto, 1994).

Obviously, these differences may emerge as barriers to effective patient–health care provider communication. As was noted by Brown, Ballard, and Gregg (1994), the interactions that take place in the medical encounter may be viewed as "cross-cultural communication, with each participant struggling to understand the worldview of the other" (p. 98). Indeed, the ability of health care providers to understand the patient's point of view and to effectively communicate with patients from different cultural backgrounds has been characterized as a major challenge to the practice of medicine (Brown et al., 1994). This challenge would thwart illness explanations with the health care provider, who might be potentially unable to respond appropriately to the personal needs of patients for information, reassurance, and effective treatment (Harwood, 1981). As Haug (1996) suggested, age, sex, class, ethnic, or religious differences are potentially injurious to the patient–health care practitioner relationship. Kreps and Kunimoto (1994) spoke to the seriousness of ineffective intercultural communication in the health context by noting that such communication can and often does result in unnecessary pain, suffering, and even death.

When race and ethnicity are factors in the patient–health care practitioner equation, cultural differences take on a different intensity. As evidence of this, a great deal of research points to the existence of sociocultural and socioeconomic differences in behavior and reactions to illness, both among and within racial and ethnic groups. Furthermore, racial and social class biases have been found in the diagnosis and treatment of illness (Blendon, Aiken, Freeman, & Corey, 1989).

These findings have implications for physical health, illness, and illness explanation among racial and ethnic minorities, particularly in view of the increasing diversity of the nation (i.e., the notion that minority racial and ethnic groups will soon comprise the nation's numerical majority). These considerations suggest that the field of health communication should be focusing attention on ethnic minorities; in addition, they offer a compelling rationale for examining illness explanations in the major racial and ethnic groups and, in this instance, among African Americans.

This chapter provides a framework for highlighting the pivotal role of culture in the explanation and understanding of illness by focusing on African Americans. Specifically, the chapter: (a) describes several features of African-American culture that have particular relevance for communicating about illness, with special attention focused on the role of religion, spirituality, and social support; (b) examines extant research on explaining illness to African Americans; and (c) offers communication strategies for explaining illness and improving health outcomes. The chapter concludes with suggestions for future research pertaining to illness explanation among African Americans.

AFRICAN-AMERICAN CULTURE AND ILLNESS

What is it about being African American that calls for different paradigms and models of illness and illness explanation? Clearly, the unique racial, cultural, and ethnic characteristics of African Americans, like other cultural groups, serve such a rationale. These characteristics also contribute to the uniqueness of illness and illness explanations in this population.

This portion of the chapter elucidates some of these distinctive aspects of African-American culture that are key to generating explanations of illness. Specifically, the role of religion and spirituality in the illness experience, folk and popular traditions of health care, and the role of the family, friends, and clergy in compliance with treatment, health care-seeking behavior, and sources of illness explanation will be detailed.

At the outset, the heterogeneity of African Americans' health beliefs, behaviors, communication patterns, and lifestyles should be acknowledged. Because of the African world view, African Americans share some common cultural beliefs about how to diagnose, treat, and prevent illness (Akbar, 1985; Bailey, 1987; Jackson, 1981). Because of gender, class, age, religious, and other differences, they also have vastly different ways of seeking optimal health and preventing illness (Haug, 1996; Jackson, 1981; Potts, 1994; Sylvester, 1998). Therefore, it is important in any examination of African Americans (or other ethnic group) to acknowledge the wide variance in culture.

In recent years, scholars have identified a number of protective factors that help foster resiliency for individuals in responding to risk in African-American life and culture (Hill, 1972; Taylor, Jackson, & Chatters, 1997). Two protective factors—strong religious orientation and strong kinship ties—hold particular significance for illness and illness explanation.

Religion

African-Americans' religiosity has been well researched and documented extensively in the literature (Levin, Taylor, & Chatters, 1994; Taylor & Chatters, 1991). Religion and church assume major places in the lives of African Americans; religious beliefs are at the core of African-American life (Gary, Beatty, & Price, 1983; Taylor & Chatters, 1991). A deep-seated, unshakeable health belief among some African Americans is that God is the best physician and He can heal any illness. Especially popular among elderly African Americans is the saying that "God is a doctor who has never lost a patient."

Religious paraphernalia permeates some African-American homes. Snow (1993) detailed the items she observed: religious pictures, the Bible and other holy books, and prayer cloths. She also noted that "prayer and the reading of Scripture and the recitation of biblical verses is just as important—perhaps more important—a part of health behavior as eating right or taking the doctor's medicine" (p. 91–92).

Spirituality, a related concept, is also a mainstay of African-American life (Landrine & Klonoff, 1996). Deeply ingrained in African-Americans' conceptualization of healing and recovery from illness, spirituality as a coping mechanism against illness has been noted (Taylor & Chatters, 1991). For example, in Potts' (1994) examination of the role of spirituality in the cancer experiences of African Americans, two themes emerged: a belief in God as the source of healing, and prayer as instrumental in coping with cancer. He noted:

> Healing in African American communities is more than the science of selecting a specific medicine to effect a specific disease entity within an isolated human organism. It is an art, experienced as a spiritual-social process that includes the work of medicines, usually those prescribed by physicians, healers, and practices within a community of faith, with God being the ultimate source of healing. (p. 18)

African Americans' spiritual beliefs have led them to seek physicians who are more likely to practice holistic medicine and to endorse spiritual healing, the laying on of hands, and self-healing (Potts, 1994; Snow, 1978). Long before the recent spate of articles in the popular press recognizing the potential role of spirituality and prayer in the illness experience (Kita, 1998; Rubin, 1998; Trafford, 1997), African Americans were convinced of the power of prayer. In fact, among some African-American subcultures, beliefs about the healing power of prayer far outweighs any pronouncements from doctors and other health care professionals (Potts, 1994; Snow, 1993).

Kinship and Social Support

Strong kinship ties are another key feature of African-American life that has particular significance for illness and illness explanations. Because of its centrality, the family plays an important role in promoting health outcomes for the ill person. In particular, African Americans' social construction of illness is heavily influenced by advice from family members and friends. Also, treatment is frequently prescribed by friends and relatives.

Seemingly aware of research indicating that the quantity and quality of social ties are among the most powerful determinants of health (House &

Kahn, 1985), African Americans rely heavily on family and friends for help and support during illness. In fact, research suggests that social support increases patient compliance. Indeed, social support influences the decision to visit a health care provider as well as choices about treatment options (Thomas, 1981; Zola, 1972).

Strong kinship ties may help to explain the confidence that many African Americans have in old home remedies. Such remedies, passed down from generation to generation, are thought to possess more medicinal power than over-the-counter or prescription medicine. As noted by Jackson (1981), "home remedies are administered on the basis of diagnoses made either by the person who is ill or by others he consults, and on the basis of beliefs about the efficacy of these remedies" (p. 88).

As one of the most distinct health features of African-American life, home remedies continue to be used extensively to treat illness, particularly among many elderly African Americans or as adjuncts to medical care (Jackson, 1981). Many African Americans take home remedies simultaneously with prescription medicines.[1] Home remedies are generally taken before the patient has seen a health care provider (Harwood, 1981).

As indicated, African Americans use both biomedical and alternative sources of health care. Research suggests that in addition to mainstream providers, some African Americans use nontraditional sources such as root doctors, truthsayers, faith healers, and God (Chatters, 1991; Ossege, 1993; Watson, 1984). Interestingly, folk healers often encourage patients to use both mainstream and alternative sources of treatment (Jackson, 1981).

Sources of Understanding Illness

African Americans utilize a range of sources for advice and illness explanation. Bailey (1987) found the following pattern of health care seeking among a sample of African Americans residing in the Detroit metropolitan area—after an illness occurred, the respondents initially waited for a certain period of time for the body to heal itself. If healing did not occur, they sought advice from a family member, friend, or even church leaders and–or a traditional healer. Finally, they would seek help from a physician.

Research suggests that there are intragroup differences in the extent to which African Americans rely on modern health practitioners to understand and treat illness (Jackson, 1981; Sylvester, 1998; Thomas, 1981). For example, elderly and rural African Americans are more likely to utilize folk or alternative medical practitioners as sources of understanding. Younger African Americans and those with higher education and higher socioeco-

---

[1]Watson (1984) provided useful information on how to avoid potentially dangerous interactions between prescribed medications and folk remedies.

nomic status rely more heavily on modern medical practitioners, although many of them have been exposed to alternative sources of health care.[2] Lay advisors are generally used heavily by all groups (Table 1).

The framework provided structures an understanding of the sociocultural context of health and illness among African Americans.[3] Admittedly, this framework centers on health-enhancing resources in African-American life and culture, including the culturally distinctive healing traditions, the deep belief in the power of prayer and faith, and the reliance on home remedies.

TABLE 13.1
Sources of Illness Explanation Among African Americans

Source	Examples	Components of Illness Explanation
Modern Medical Practitioners	Physicians Nurse Practitioners Physician Ass't Technicians	Technical terminology Disease-oriented Emphasis on treatment (e.g., drugs, surgery, radiation, Biomedical models)
Alternative Medical Practitioners	Herbalists Faith Healers Folk Healers Naturopaths Acupuncturist Root Doctor Spiritualists	Alternative treatments (e.g., meditation, acupuncture) Psychological models Herbs
Nonmedical Professionals	Clergy Social Workers	Culturally relevant terminology, including faith, hope, prayer, God, spirit
Lay Advisors, including Self	Family Friends Co-workers Neighbors Self-help Group Members	Psychosocial intervention Self-medication Home Remedies Nonprescription medicine Health Foods Self-care

Note. Source: Revised and adapted from Cockerham (1995, p. 114) and Pescosolido (1992, p. 1113).

[2]See Fontenot (1994), Snow (1993), Terrell (1990), and Watson (1984) for anthropological accounts of African-American folk beliefs and use of folk medicine. Also, see Landrine and Klonoff's (1996) African American Acculturation scale for a subscale that measures traditional health beliefs and contains such points as "Illness can be classified as natural types and unnatural types"; and "If doctors can't cure you-you should go to a root doctor or to your minister" (p. 73).

[3]See Secundy (1991) for a translucent discussion of the experience of illness as it is shaped by African-American culture.

However, one factor has a profound impact on health practitioners using this knowledge to explain illness to African Americans—the dissatisfaction that many African Americans feel with the qualitative ways the physicians treat them when they are ill. Some African Americans have a deep distrust for the health care system (Blendon et al., 1989; Green, Maisiank, Wang, Britt, & Ebeling, 1997). For instance, Potts (1994) found distrust in the health care system, expressed through a refusal of African Americans to take prescribed medicines or a fear or distrust of physicians. One patient expressed fear and distrust in this manner:

> I'm afraid of doctors. And that was the only fear about this whole thing, cancer ... I'm just scared of them ... A person with a white coat on, I'm scared. And do you know the medicine he gave me to take, you know where it's at? Sitting on the counter where I brought it in. I haven't taken it. Because I feel I've taken too many pills. And they've done me more damage than I was already having. (Potts, 1994, p. 75).

The features of African-American culture that have implications for illness explanation can be summarized succinctly: When explaining illness to African Americans, health care providers should take into consideration the culturally distinctive role of religion, spirituality, and kinship ties in African-American culture; to the extent possible, they should be guided by these precepts in the medical encounter.

RESEARCH ON ILLNESS EXPLANATION
AND AFRICAN AMERICANS

Every day in various health care settings (e.g., a hospital, clinic, or doctor's office), a health care provider explains a given illness to a patient. This patient–provider interaction, which typically involves a doctor but increasingly involves a nurse practitioner, physician assistant, or other such practitioner, varies from situation to situation. Generally, however, within this interaction, one of the following aspects of illness is explained: (a) the etiology or cause of the illness; (b) the timing and mode of onset of symptoms associated with the illness; (c) the severity of the illness; and (d) the appropriate treatments for the illness (Harwood, 1981; Helman, 1994).

Explaining illness is a complex, multifaceted activity. In this cross-cultural exchange, patients are expected to convey their symptoms in a manner understandable to the health care provider and in return, health care providers must provide clear, nontechnical information about the illness. Patients' concerns about aspects of the illness may serve to complicate the illness explanation process and prevent them from participating in the medical encounter.

Clearly, patient characteristics have a profound effect on medical interactions and illness explanations. Research in this area has revealed, for example, that women receive different treatment from physicians than do men (see chap. 6, this volume). Physicians' interpersonal involvement is greater for women who receive more time and more explanations from physicians than do men. Women patients also ask more questions and talk more than do male patients (Street & Wiemann, 1987).

The literature on health care provider–patient communication, especially doctor–patient, is voluminous. However, little of this research is theory-driven and the available literature has failed to provide a body of knowledge regarding illness explanation. As Cegala, McGee, and McNeilis (1996) noted, "relatively little is actually known about the dynamics of how doctors and patients seek and provide information during the medical interview" (p. 4). Thus, it is clear why the information on illness explanation to African Americans is scant.

The available research, however, suggests that health care providers do an inadequate job of explaining illness to African Americans (Blendon et al., 1989; Dutton, 1978, 1986; Green et al., 1997). For instance, Blendon et al. (1989) specifically asked respondents about these aspects of illness explanation: whether the physician asked about pain, explained the seriousness of the illness, explained how long it would take for the prescribed medicine to work, or discussed test or examination findings. African Americans were more likely than Whites to report that on their last visit to a physician, the physician did not do any of these things. This supports research suggesting that physicians are less supportive with African-American and Hispanic patients and give less information to African-American patients than Euro-American patients (Brown et al., 1994; Dutton, 1978).

Even when health care providers disseminate health information specifically targeted toward African Americans, illness is explained ineffectively. Guidry, Fagan, and Walker (1998) evaluated the Cancer Prevention Material and African Americans Project and found that in addition to being culturally insensitive, much of the information was written at inappropriate reading levels (see chap. 5, this volume).

Moreover, several researchers have reported differences in the treatment of low income patients as compared with middle and upper-income patients, especially the amount of time spent providing information. For example, Waitzkin (1984) noted that poorly educated and lower class patients were provided fewer explanations than were the more educated and those with higher incomes. Noting that patients with a high school education or less often talk less and ask fewer questions, Street and Wieman (1987) reported that they also receive less information and time from doctors than do more educated patients. Similarly, Pendleton and Bochner (1980) found that upper-class patients, both male and female, were given more explanations and information about their health problems than their lower strata counterparts.

The failure of health care providers to adequately explain illness to African Americans has resulted in a number of negative health outcomes, particularly patient distrust and patient dissatisfaction with relational aspects of health care delivery. This is evidenced in reports of some African Americans being highly suspicious of biomedical explanations of illness and feeling unfairly treated because of their ethnicity while seeking help for a health problem (Blendon et al., 1989; Green et al., 1997).

Some of African Americans' dissatisfaction may be related to the setting in which they receive some illness explanations. African Americans are more likely than Whites to receive care in an emergency room or outpatient department (Cockerham, 1995). The implications of receiving care in such settings is apparent in Helman's (1994) assertion that the setting helps to determine "what is said in the consultation, how it is said, and how it is heard and interpreted" (p. 142).

One of the goals of effective communication between patient and health care provider is to increase the likelihood of patients understanding the illness and their compliance with recommended treatments. Although the research literature regarding explaining illness to African Americans is very limited and fragmented among a number of disciplines, this review of literature indicates that the communication between African Americans and health care providers is not likely to have positive health outcomes.

African Americans frequently do not receive appropriate, adequate explanations of their illness (i.e., correct diagnoses, explanations of the progression of one's illness, potential future symptoms, and side-effects of prescribed drugs; Helman, 1994; Ley, 1982). Neither do they receive explanations that reflect cultural sensitivity or cultural competence (i.e., the ability to acknowledge and accept cultural differences) on the part of health care professionals. There are, however, suggestions for improving health care provider–patient communication about illness.

RECOMMENDATIONS FOR IMPROVING ILLNESS EXPLANATIONS

Improved communication between patients and health care providers (e.g., illness explanations) increases the likelihood of a number of positive outcomes, including patient compliance with medical advice and prescribed regimens. This section provides general and specific recommendations for improving illness explanations. In addition, the final portion of this section provides a number of suggestions for future research on illness explanations and African Americans.

Strategies

There are many strategies that can be employed to improve illness explanations to African Americans. Although some are specific to explaining illness to African Americans, some are appropriate and would be appreciated by people of any ethnicity.

General Strategies.   One of the most important things that health care providers can do to improve illness explanations is to acknowledge and respect patients' experience and interpretation of their illness. One highly useful tool for gaining access to a patient's interpretation of illness involves eliciting the patient's explanatory model of illness (Kleinman, Eisenberg, & Good, 1978). Included among the questions that will elicit a patient's explanatory model of illness are the following: (a) What are the chief problems your illness has caused you? (b) What do you fear most about your sickness? (c) What kind of treatment would you like to have? (Kleinman et al., 1978).

A sample conversation that could conceivably be used to elicit the patient's model of illness and improve illness explanation is provided:

> I know that patients and doctors sometimes have different ideas about diseases and what causes them. So it's often important in treating a disease to get clear on how both the doctor and the patient think about it. That's why I'd like to know more about your ideas on (whatever disease or symptom is relevant to the situation). That way I can know what your concerns are, and we can work together in treating your sickness. (Harwood, 1981, p. 486)

Such communication shows that, in addition to focusing on the biomedical aspects of a given illness, the health care provider is willing to take the time to become familiar with both the patient's interpretation of the illness and the patient's own methods of dealing with the illness, both mentally and physically.

Another method of improving the quality of illness explanations by health care practitioners is to allow the patient to participate in the decision-making process; this is easily accomplished by giving the patient an opportunity to ask questions and to express concern about a diagnosis or prescribed regimen. By allowing the patient to participate in the decision-making process, the health professional increases the likelihood that the health care provider and the patient will arrive at a treatment regimen that is acceptable to the patient and one with which the patient will comply.

Clearly, the patient-centered model of illness explanation is the most effective (Kreps, 1988; Thompson, 1994). Therefore, patients should be encouraged to ask questions, express concern, and share opinions about the diagnosis and treatment of an illness. Likewise, health care providers should express concern and interest in the patients. In doing so, health care providers display both empathy and respect for patients when explaining illness.

In summary, patients desire the following features in the medical encounter when an illness is explained. Providing such features will greatly improve illness explanation to African Americans: (a) a sensitive and caring health care provider who is mindful of the emotional components of serious illness and can discern the distress of his or her patients; (b) an egalitarian medical encounter in which the health care provider does not dominate the content and the direction of the encounter; (c) recognition of the patient as a person to be treated with the utmost respect; and (d) a health care professional who inspires trust (Kreps, 1988; Pendleton, 1983). In short, in the medical encounter, the patient-centered model of illness is employed.

Culturally Specific Strategies.   There are suggestions for improving illness explanations to African Americans and making interpersonal communication more effective in interactions between health care providers and African-American patients. One of the most important things that health care providers should do when explaining illness to African-American patients is to keep in mind the importance of religion and spirituality in African-American communities. To the extent possible, health professionals should embrace religious and–or spiritual concepts in treatment. In addition to obtaining information on religious beliefs of patients, health care providers should also talk about spiritual issues with their patients. Faith, prayer, and healing should all be a part of medical interactions involving African-American patients. For example, health professionals might ask patients if faith has been important in their experience with illness (Potts, 1994). Health care practitioners would do well to consider giving the following advice to their African-American patients: "As a medical doctor, I'm interested in the medical effects of prayer: physical, mental, spiritual.... To the extent it affects your physical health, I'm going to encourage you to pray, to worship, to read scripture for their medical benefits" (Rubin 1998, p. 26).

In essence, when explaining illness to African Americans, health care providers should practice the philosophy of holistic health and treat the whole person: body, mind, and spirit. The biomedical and the spiritual dimensions of illness must be reconciled in illness explanations and health care providers must be willing to "address, understand and affirm that which the patient finds essential in healing, and that which is sacred in the patient's life" (Potts, 1994, p. 107).

In addition to their religious beliefs, it is necessary for health care providers to have an understanding of African Americans' existing beliefs about a given illness. Research demonstrates that patients make sense of their illness in terms of their existing beliefs and, after consulting with a physician, they revert back to what they initially felt was their illness or problem (Helman, 1994; Hunt, Jordan, & Irwin, 1989). Furthermore, research indicates that patients are more accepting of illness explanations that do not conflict with existing cultural beliefs (Helman, 1994; Hunt et al., 1989). Therefore, health care providers should acknowledge cultural beliefs. For example, Jackson (1981) highlighted a possible interaction that recognizes an African-American cultural belief, "If a patient believes firmly that a given condition is caused by a hex, the understanding physician might work within that framework, asking, for example, 'Is someone working roots on you?'" (p. 80).

In explaining illness to African Americans, health care providers should look for ways of combining folk models with biomedical models of illness (Brown et al., 1994). Being aware of culturally preferred modes of treatment (e.g., home remedies) and including such preferences in prescribed regimens, health care providers may increase patients' understanding of prescribed regimens and promote compliance (Harwood, 1981). To the extent possible, health care providers should incorporate therapies that promote self-healing (see Myers', 1993, belief system analysis).

Other strategies involve acknowledging the mistrust that many African Americans feel with the health care system. Often, this mistrust may be diminished by bringing the patients' minister, family, and friends into the medical encounter when illness is being explained. Respect is also an antidote for African Americans' mistrust of health care providers. It is vitally important that health care practitioners try to temper the elderly African American's mistrust by being supportive and respectful. For example, one unambiguous and universally accepted way to show respect to elderly African Americans is to refer to them as Mr. or Ms. or Mrs.

Another recommendation pertaining to elderly African Americans is for the health care provider to understand the language patients may use in their explanations of illness (Helman, 1994; chap. 1, this volume). For example, the technical term for a common disease among African Americans is diabetes mellitus; among many African Americans; however, it is commonly referred to as to "sugar diabetes" or "sugar."

Likewise, it may be helpful to reinforce what was said orally with written instructions in the language spoken among African Americans. A good example of the use of culturally specific language appears in the American Diabetes Association's flyer publicizing its African American Program. In explaining the program, it was noted that "There is no such thing as 'a touch of sugar.' If you have sugar, you have diabetes" (American Diabetes Association, n.d.).

Moreover, it is recommended that whether health care professionals explain illness orally, in writing, or both, they should be certain that they: (a) simplify instructions, (b) use nontechnical language, and (c) provide explicit directions and consistent advice (Harwood, 1981; Svarstad, 1986; Sylvester, 1998). As Jackson (1981) observed: "physicians who provide adequate explanations of their diagnoses will find that many of their urban black patients understand them and have some awareness of the restrictions or consequences that may be involved" (p. 100; an adequate explanation would, for example, detail the etiology, severity, and possible progression of an illness in nontechnical terminology).

Of course, health care providers are not expected to be cognizant of everything about every ethnic group. Therefore, a final recommendation would be to have an African American as part of the health care team when explaining illness to African Americans; this reduces the likelihood that nonverbal behaviors such as body language and paralanguage will be misinterpreted and a medical encounter being thwarted by cultural insensitivity.

To conclude, repeated is Kreps and Kunimoto's (1994) admonition that health care providers must be willing to endure the discomfort of unfamiliarity and the uncertainty of illness views that are different from their own. Developing sensitivity to cultural factors is no easy task; furthermore, it is a continuous, ongoing process. However, this task can be made less difficult if health care providers, especially doctors, remain ever vigilant of: (a) how their own cultural backgrounds, including attitudes, prejudices, and perceptions, influence the medical interaction and their illness explanations, and (b) how a seemingly innocuous comment may demonstrate cultural insensitivity and ultimately end up harming the patient. By being open-minded and receptive, health care practitioners may improve their explanations of illness to African Americans.

FUTURE RESEARCH AND THEORY

In the area of health communication, research questions pertaining to race and ethnicity have been rarely addressed in the literature. Consequently, explaining illness to African Americans (and other ethnic minorities) is a fertile area for research.

Future research on illness explanation to African Americans should focus on the strengths and health-enhancing resources within African Americans that serve as protective factors against illness. For example, many African-American patients are convinced that religious beliefs influence health and illness. Future research should investigate how best to integrate faith, prayer, and spirituality into illness explanations and the impact that this integration has on health outcomes.

Closely related to this is the variable of social support. How does participation in social support networks influence the illness experience and practitioners' illness explanation to African Americans? As noted previously, the illness explanation process involves more than the health care provider and the patient; family, friends, and nonmedical professionals including the clergy and social workers are frequently involved. Therefore, their roles in the explanation of illness need to be further explored.

Young and Klingle (1996) noted that research has ignored the potential impact of patients' cultural background on their ability to effectively participate in the medical encounter. Research is needed also on how best to elicit the African-American patient's explanatory model of illness. There is scant research addressing the question of whether the ethnicity of the health care provider has a significant impact on the illness explanation process. Investigations should examine how the ethnicity of the health care practitioner influences the quality of communication between patients and providers. Is the illness explanation more effective and the medical encounter more productive when both the patient and the health care provider are African American?

The diversity within African-American populations and how this diversity is related to illness should receive empirical attention. For example, whereas some research has focused on urban–rural differences, additional research is needed on inner city–suburban differences as well as on how the setting of the explanation (e.g., emergency room) influences the illness explanation process.

A number of theoretical perspectives have been shown to have important implications for health message design. Few of these, however, have been tested using African-American populations. Future research should examine the applicability of these theories to African-American life and culture. Two models that readily come to mind are Witte's (1995) persuasive health message framework, which may be useful for constructing health messages that elicit positive behavioral responses in ethnic minorities, and Svarstad's (1986) health communication model. Both of these models should be explored more in relation to African Americans. For example, researchers might consider testing this hypothesis, which has its origins in the health communication model: Dissatisfaction with the health care professional–patient relationship is a key explanatory variable of noncompliance among African Americans.

A significant void in the literature is research focusing on what patients and health care providers say during the medical encounter (Cegala, McGee, & McNeilis, 1996). Future research should examine the communication between the patient and various sources of illness explanation, including lay advisors as well as modern medical practitioners. When doing so, the complex interrelationships that exist between sociocultural factors and illness explanations can only be addressed through multidisciplinary research with rigorous methodology and data analysis procedures. Furthermore, the conduct of research that is culturally relevant is quite complex and various quantitative and qualitative techniques would be useful in this endeavor. For example, a complete understanding of the role of social support in the illness-explanation process would ideally involve collecting ethnographic as well as survey data.

Finally, research that will advance our knowledge of how best to explain illness to African Americans must be broadened to include a focus on identifying how racial discrimination and other cultural forces promote illness among African Americans. Of particular concern are those illnesses that African Americans, in comparison to Euro-Americans, have higher incidence and prevalence for, including diabetes, hypertension, and prostate cancer—illnesses for which they are most likely to need explanations (Livingston, 1994). Resolving these questions will require continued research to increase the base of scientific knowledge and to elucidate factors that put African Americans at greater risk for illness and death. Dilworth-Anderson, Burton, & Johnson (1993) maintained that scholars must reframe existing theoretical perspectives and create new ways of thinking about ethnic minorities in order to advance understanding of cocultural families. Health communication scholars must do likewise if we wish to enhance culturally relevant conceptual frameworks on illness explanation and to explain the relationship between illness explanation and health outcomes, such as understanding and compliance among African Americans. Future research should advance toward these ends.

CONCLUSION

The major intent of this chapter has been to demonstrate how culturally induced attitudes and behaviors impact the communication between health care providers and patients in ways that enhance as well as negate health outcomes. A secondary intent has been to provide information that will help health care providers develop multicultural communication proficiency (i.e., skills in communicating with members of diverse cultural groups to achieve desired objectives; Kreps & Kunimoto, 1994). Such proficiency is a necessity for those working in the health care arena—an arena increasingly being called on to acknowledge and address issues related to race, ethnicity, and diversity.

A major premise of this chapter is that culturally induced health behaviors and beliefs must be recognized and addressed when illness is explained to African Americans. Therefore, this chapter has highlighted a number of factors thought to be of significance for explaining illness to African Americans; namely religion and spirituality, social support and strong kinship ties, health care seeking behaviors, and biomedical and folk sources of illness explanation.

This chapter has provided information and examples that should increase awareness among health care providers of the range of health beliefs and practices they may encounter in medical interactions with African Americans. Strategies that have taken into account both the patient and the health care provider's point of view have been presented.

Based on the information contained herein, it may be concluded that when explaining illness to African Americans, health care professionals must first identify the patient's explanatory models of illness and use this information to recommend culturally relevant health information and treatment. Also, health care professionals should keep in mind that because much of illness explanation among African Americans takes place in a social network, much of their explanations must be filtered through the prism of this network: religion and spirituality.

Effective illness explanation to African Americans begins with a clear understanding of the cultural influence of African Americans on health beliefs and practices. By adopting this major precept as well as the practical suggestions contained in this chapter, health care providers may ensure that the communication that takes place in the heath care setting is enhanced and the explaining of illness to African Americans, indeed, to all ethnic groups, is improved.

REFERENCES

Akbar, N. (1985). *The community of self.* Tallahassee, FL: Mind Productions and Associates.

American Diabetes Association (n.d.). Program for African Americans. Alexandria, VA: Author.

Bailey, E. J. (1987). Sociocultural factors and health-care seeking behavior among Black Americans. *Journal of the National Medical Association, 79,* 389–392.

Blendon, R. J., Aiken, L. H., Freeman, H. E., & Corey, C. R. (1989). Access to medical care for Black and White Americans: A matter of continuing concern. *Journal of the American Medical Association, 261,* 278–281.

Brown, I. C. (1963). *Understanding other cultures.* Englewood Cliffs, NJ: Prentice Hall.

Brown, P. J., Ballard, B., & Gregg, J. (1994). Culture, ethnicity, and the practice of medicine. In A. Stoudemire (Ed.), *Human behavior: An introduction for medical students* (2nd ed, pp. 84–104). Philadelphia: Lippincott.

Cegala, D. J., McGee, D. S., & McNeilis, K. S. (1996). Components of patients' and doctors' perceptions of communication competence during a primary care medical interview. *Health Communication, 8,* 1–27.

Chatters, L. M. (1991). Physical health. In J. S. Jackson (Ed.), *Life in Black America* (pp.199–220). Newbury Park, CA: Sage.

Cockerham, W. C. (1995). *Medical sociology* (6th ed.). Englewood Cliffs, NJ: Prentice Hall.

Dilworth-Anderson, P., Burton, L. M., & Johnson, L. B. (1993). Reframing theories for understanding race, ethnicity, and families. In P. G. Boss, W. J. Doherty, R. LaRossa, W. R. Schumm, & S. K. Steinmetz (Eds.), *Sourcebook of family theories and methods: A contextual approach* (pp. 627–643). New York: Plenum.

Dutton, D. B. (1978). Explaining the low use of health services by the poor: Costs, attitudes or delivery systems? *American Sociological Review, 43,* 348–368.

Dutton, D. (1986). Social class, health, and illness. In L. Aiken & D. Mechanic (Eds), *Applications of social science to clinical medicine and health policy* (pp. 31–62). New Brunswick, NJ: Rutgers University Press.

Fontenot, W. L. (1994). *Secret doctors: Ethnomedicine of African Americans.* Westport, CO: Bergin & Garvey.

Gary, L., Beatty, L., & Price, M. (1983). *Stable Black families. Final Report.* Washington, DC: Institute for Urban Affairs, Howard University.

Green, B. L., Maisiank, R., Wang, M. Q., Britt, M. F., & Ebeling, N. (1997). Participation in health education, health promotion, and health research by African Americans: Effects of the Tuskegee syphilis experiment. *Journal of Health Education, 28,* 196–200.

Guidry, J. J., Fagan, P., & Walker, V. (1998). Culture sensitivity and readability of breast and prostate printed cancer education materials targeting African Americans. *Journal of the National Medical Association, 90,* 165–169.

Harwood, A. (1981). Guidelines for culturally appropriate health care. In A. Harwood (Ed.), *Ethnicity and medical care* (pp. 482–504). Cambridge, MA: Harvard University Press.

Haug, M. R. (1996). The effects of physician/elder patient characteristics on health communication. *Health Communication, 8,* 249–262.

Helman, C.G. (1994). *Culture, health and illness: An introduction for health professionals* (3rd ed.). Oxford, England: Butterworth- Heineman Ltd.

Hill, R. B. (1972). *Strengths of Black families.* New York: Emerson-Hall.

House, J. S., & Kahn, R. L. (1985). Measures and concepts of social support. In S. Cohen & S. L. Syme (Eds.), *Social support and health* (pp. 83–108). Orlando, FL: Academic Press.

Hunt, L. M., Jordan, B., & Irwin, S. (1989). Views of what's wrong: Diagnosis and patients concepts of illness. *Social Science and Medicine, 28,* 945–956.

Jackson, J. J. (1981). Urban Black Americans. In A. Harwood, (Ed.), *Ethnicity and medical care* (pp.37–129). Cambridge, MA: Harvard University Press.

Kita, J. (1998, June). Soul training. *Men's Health, 12,* 96–98.

Kleinman, A., Eisenberg, L., & Good, B. (1978). Culture, illness and care: Clinical lessons from anthropologic and cross-cultural research. *Annals of Internal Medicine, 88,* 251–258.

Kreps, G. L. (1988). Relational communication in health care. *Southern Communication Journal, 53,* 344–359.

Kreps, G., & Kunimoto, E. N. (1994). *Effective communication in multicultural health care settings.* Thousand Oaks, CA: Sage.

Landrine, H., & Klonoff, E. A. (1996). *African American acculturation: Deconstructing race and reviving culture.* Thousand Oaks, CA: Sage.

Levin, J. S., Taylor, R. J., & Chatters, L. M. (1994). Race and gender differences in religiosity among older adults. *Journal of Gerontology: Social Sciences, 49*(3), S137–S145.

Ley, P. (1982). Giving information to patients. In J. R. Eiser (Ed.), *Social psychology and behavioral science* (pp. 339–373). New York: Wiley.

Livingston, I. L. (Ed.). (1994). *Handbook of Black American health.* Westport, CT: Greenwood.

Myers, L. J. (1993). *Understanding an Afrocentric world view: Introduction to an optimal psychology* (2nd ed.). Dubuque, IA: Kendall/Hunt.

Ossege, J. (1993). Health care seeking behavior in rural, southern, African-American adults. *Dissertation Abstracts International, 54*(7), 3553B.

Pendleton, D. (1983). Doctor–patient communication: A review. In D. Pendleton & J. Hasler (Eds.), *Doctor–patient communication* (pp. 5–53). London: Academic Press.

Pendleton, D. A., & Bochner, S. (1980). The communication of medical information in general practice consultations as a function of patient's social class. *Social Science & Medicine, 14A,* 669–673.

Pescosolido, B. A. (1992). Beyond rational choice: The social dynamics of how people seek help. *American Journal of Sociology, 97,* 1096–1138.

Potts, R. G. (1994). *Spirituality and the experience of cancer in an African American community: Implications for psychooncology.* Unpublished doctoral dissertation, Depaul University, Chicago.

Rubin, A. J. (1998, January 11). Pills & prayers. *The Washington Post Magazine, 26,* 12–16.

Secundy, M. G. (Ed.). (1991). *Trials, tribulation, and celebrations: African-American perspectives on health, illness, aging, and loss.* Yarmouth, ME: Intercultural Press.

Snow, L. F. (1978). Sorcerers, saints and charlatans: Black folk healers in urban America. *Culture, Medicine, and Psychiatry, 2,* 69–106.

Snow, L. F. (1993). *Walkin' over medicine.* Boulder, CO: Westview Press.

Street, R. L., Jr., & Wiemann, J. M. (1987). Patient satisfaction with physicians' interpersonal involvement, expressiveness, and dominance. In M. L. McLaughlin (Ed.), *Communication yearbook,* (pp. 591–612). Newbury Park, CA: Sage.

Svarstad, B. L. (1986). Patient–practitioner relationships and compliance with prescribed medical regimens. In L. Aiken & D. Mechanic (Eds). *Applications of social science to clinical medicine and health policy* (pp. 438–459). New Brunswick, NJ: Rutgers University Press.

Sylvester, J. L. (1998). *Directing health messages toward African-Americans: Attitudes toward health care and the mass media.* New York: Garland Press.

Taylor, R. J., & Chatters, L. M. (1991). Religious life. In J. S. Jackson (Ed.), *Life in Black America* (pp.105–123). Newbury Park, CA: Sage.

Taylor, R. J., Jackson, J. S., & Chatters, L. M. (Eds.). (1997). *Family life in Black America.* Thousand Oaks, CA: Sage.

Terrell, S. J. (1990). *This other kind of doctors: Traditional medical systems in Black neighborhoods in Austin, Texas.* New York: AMS Press, Inc.

Thomas, D. N. (1981). Black American patient care. In G. Henderson & M. Primeaux (Eds.), *Transcultural health care* (pp. 209–223). Menlo Park, CA: Addison-Wesley.

Thompson, T. L. (1994). Communication in health care. In M. L. Knapp & G. R. Miller (Eds.), *Handbook of interpersonal communication* (2nd ed., pp. 696–725). Beverly Hills, CA: Sage.

Trafford, A. (1997, December 23–30). Can the power of prayer be measured? *Health, 13,* 6.

Waitzkin, H. (1984). Doctor–patient communication: Clinical implications of social scientific research. *Journal of the American Medical Association, 252,* 2441–2446.

Watson, W. H. (Ed.). (1984). *Black folk medicine: The therapeutic significance of faith and trust.* New Brunswick, NJ: Transaction Books.

Witte, K. (1995). Fishing for success: Using the persuasive health message framework to generate effective campaign messages. In E. Maibach & R. L. Parrott (Eds.), *Designing health messages: Approaches from communication theory and practice* (pp. 145–164). Thousand Oaks, CA: Sage.

Young, M., & Klingle, R. S. (1996). Silent partners in medical care: A cross-cultural study of patient participation. *Health Communication, 8,* 29–53.

Zola, I. K. (1972). Studying the decision to see a doctor: Review, critique, correction. In Z. J. Lipowski (Ed.), *Psychological aspects of physical illness* (pp. 216–236). Basel, Switzerland: Karger.

14

Commentary
and Continued Concerns

Barbara Korsch
Children's Hospital, Los Angeles
University of Southern California School of Medicine

This collection of chapters includes contributions by some of the leading researchers in the field of communication about illness, consisting largely of communication specialists but also including a number of physicians, a psychologist, and a pharmacist. These carefully selected chapters represent the most comprehensive collection of information on this important subject that has yet been developed. Undoubtedly, discussing the foundational theoretical issues involved in explaining illness, while addressing the needs of specific, clearly defined subgroups in our society and presenting relevant anthropologic and cultural information about certain cocultural groups, their health beliefs, and communication needs, is an ambitious project. This volume outlines a number of theoretical models. More often, it deals with empirical studies of experiences with certain communication strategies in certain settings. Each chapter presents well-documented, general conclusions about communication issues and practical recommendations and also represents a different approach to communicating about illness.

The encyclopedic first chapter by Thompson includes a wealth of information concerning communication from physician to patient: the language used, the manner in which the information is given, the actual amount of content shared—be it cause, diagnosis, treatment, or prognosis—and the preparation for procedures. All of these are addressed and documented with a comprehensive series of research findings. The most consistent message, is that, in general, practitioners tend to give insufficient information to patients or, at least, less than the patients say they would like or need. Only a few of the studies cited specific outcomes related to increased information that is documented. However, a number of variables are not taken into account that might influence the amount and nature of information that improves the outcome for the patient and physician. Most of these variables are not in the cognitive area but have to do with the relationship between the practitioner and patient, the history of each, their personalities, and the context in which the information is given. In all aspects of education, be it physician–patient or teacher–student, most measurements traditionally deal with the amount of cognitive information that is transmitted and absorbed. At the same time, most workers in this field realize that the effect of the communication, the underlying relationship, the context, the illness, and many other variables are of great importance. Thompson acknowledges these but, still the practical take-home message deals primarily with the cognitive information that is transmitted. The reference section, which is the basis for this particular chapter, will be extremely helpful for any researcher in the field.

Chapter 2, the multi-authored effort dealing with managing uncertainty in illness explanation clearly demonstrates that complexity and uncertainty are significant challenges for practitioners of medicine. They make for endless fascination, continued interest and—if the practitioner is honest and insightful—a state of humility, curiosity, and often anxiety on the part of the practitioner as well as the patient. The focus on the problematic integration theory is a fascinating and thoughtful chapter that starts with several case illustrations and then proceeds with an analysis of the types of uncertainty that are, by necessity, part of medical communication. The authors take the original viewpoint of looking at the values patients place on uncertainty versus the undesirable side effects of the state. The authors also discuss the situations in which uncertainty is actually welcomed and those in which it is intolerable. Chapter 2 represents a very clear analysis of this aspect of medicine and communication that, although lacking any clear cut conclusions and operational guidelines, provides valuable insights for practitioners and researchers. Of utmost importance is the need for awareness of how this situation changes depending on the course of illness, the relationship with healthcare providers, and the patients' life experiences. This awareness should potentially make the practitioner better able to respond sensitively to the feels and needs of the patient.

One of the practical behavioral recommendations in chapter 2 is that care providers must teach their patients to understand that medicine is, in fact, principled gambling. The authors acknowledge that this approach may threaten patients who might then lose faith in medical certainty. This topic is a complex issue that cannot be resolved so easily. The authors advise that it can be dealt with by assuring the patient that there will be constant caring services from the health-care team. I am not certain that this would always be the case. As Katz (1984) claimed, and other authors agree, doctors are too often prone to deny uncertainty. On the other hand, patients with serious illnesses who are dependent on health care establishments cannot be held accountable for being fully aware of the uncertainties involved. There are many real-life situations, not only in medicine, when being aware of the uncertain would be counterproductive. When there is a necessary course of action to take and that is the best option to follow, the expert in this situation may not be able to share the full degree of uncertainty with many patients. Simple examples from everyday life, such as taking one's car to a mechanic and having an essential part replaced, which in the judgment of the mechanic will make the car safe to drive. To dwell on the fact that we do not actually know whether the car will break down at any moment may not be strategic. This is a somewhat patronizing, paternalistic attitude, but patients and others seeking expert advice do not necessarily have unrealistic expectations of learning the absolute truth but, at the same time, may not always be open to having the lack of certainty emphasized to them. Whether one absolutely agrees with the authors' recommendations, the speculations about this problem re most clarifying and should elicit more sensitive and appropriate responses from those practitioners who heed them. Chapter 2 is uniquely valuable because it offers a unified theory as a basis for an approach to the complex issues dealing with uncertainty for practitioners and patients. It does not provide easy solutions but is thought provoking and will stimulate further research leading to new insights in one of the most taxing problems in communication between physicians and patients.

In chapter 3, Rowan points out that the media are not simply a single device for communicating health information to the public. They have a number of roles that need to be clearly understood. The public, to whom mass media information is addressed, needs to be assessed, and their needs and levels of understanding must be taken in account, as done by individual physician–patient communicators, a challenge that is not easily met. The use of the mass media in transmitting every kind of information is here to stay, making chapter 3 valuable in helping us understand the complex issues involved. Unfortunately, there is no unifying theory or principle at the basis of the various recommendations that have been made. Using mass media advertising techniques for the sale of certain pharmaceutical products is potentially dangerous and problematic. In a country where almost all media are governed by private enterprises, ulterior motives, such as money and power, often prevail over health and safety. This view represents a large portion of mass media activity that tends to dominate one's impressions and experiences. Rowan stresses the importance of establishing trust on the part of the audience in the mass media message. This goal is obviously hampered by the realistic awareness that ulterior motives are behind these messages. Stressing the need for clear messages, taking in account the audience and being clear when conflicting influences are being presented, is certainly valid and admirable.

Chapter 4 contains a great deal of valuable information and sound, practical recommendations for explaining illness as bad news. The research on which some of the recommendations are based tends to consist exclusively of surveys of patients' responses to how this information was given. These studies deal with a variety of patients, settings, and kinds of bad news. There are no prospective studies in which a conscious effort was made to give this message in various ways as well as to keep some variables constant. It would be very difficult to find real-life situations in which this would be an ethical approach, but there may still be some possibilities for simulations and other kinds of modeling in which, in addition to the observed patient responses on the basis of opportunistic observations, there could be somewhat more systematic and sophisticated research. The most helpful section of chapter 4 is the discussion of person-centered orientation to communicative context. This discussion emphasizes the two-way nature of the communication, the importance of the interactional partner, and characteristics and autonomy of the particular listeners. This emphasis is especially valuable because, throughout the volume, the discussion focuses on the active part of giving bad news to a patient as it is implemented by the person who has the information to give (largely because of limited available information). The complex interactions and relationships are harder to include in the equation, but the authors' approach represents a worthwhile effort in this direction. A clear summary by the authors defines person- centered communication as: "person-centered communication reflects an ability to adapt effectively to another's individual perspective, grant autonomy to the other in the course of a reasoning process that focuses communication on a proactive effort to accomplish goals" (p. 113, this volume) It is also significant in discussing the results of constructivist research on person-centered communication in which the authors stress nonverbal as well as verbal behavior. Verbal communication has always been the easier aspect to study, document, measure, and teach. However, it is generally accepted that the nonverbal aspects are of tremendous importance and, in some situations, more so than the verbal. Chapter 4 is especially valuable because it provides a number of theoretical constructs and gives a good review of existing work in the area.

Part II of this volume is less theoretical and deals with what is known about specific population groups and the activity of explaining illness to them. It also deals with the emergence of a new communicator in doctor–patient communication: the pharmacist.

Chapter 5 represents a wealth of factual information on the prevalence and impact of literacy on health messages. Chapter 5, besides being extremely informative, should be brought to every practitioner's attention. Health-care providers need to assess the patient's willingness to listen, understand, and interpret and to understand that there are no techniques that are universally applicable. Clearly, written messages present a special challenge in this population, but even the verbal interaction is especially challenging with a patient with limited education, understanding, or illiteracy. Once again, so many of the conclusions and recommendations are relevant to all patient populations and not just to the illiterate. Informational overload, the complexity of messages, the lack of assessing patients' understanding, or getting feedback are ubiquitous, but they are certainly more dramatic in the population with limited literacy. This group of researchers has always contributed uniquely to our understanding of the importance of this problem and has once again added to our knowledge and insight.

Chapter 6 is extremely comprehensive in its inclusion of virtually all the relevant empirical studies on communication skills and methods used by women practitioners, including differences between them and the male practitioner, and differences between addressing female and male patients. As would be expected, the findings are not always consistent; there is a strong trend toward women practitioners utilizing more of the noninstrumental, relational receptive and effective communication skills. Such gender differences have, of course, been communicated in other interactions between men and women, although the power balance between the two communicators adds a unique feature.

In chapter 6, attention is given not only to gender-specific communication skills and their relative desirability and effectiveness but also to more generic communication issues. So, once again, there is a review of power imbalance, disclosure, and partnership building—all of which are germane to all communication—but, in some cases, these empirical studies focus on the differences rather than the universal findings. One might speculate that gender differences, in particular, would not be stable in the face of changing context and changing role assignments to women in general. It has been noted that the first women who chose to study medicine tended to have certain attributes that were not stereotypically considered feminine. As women have become socialized into the profession, this has not necessarily stayed consistent. The data in chapter 6 are interesting and, to the extent that they show differences, depict the female practitioner as a more effective communicator. I am not sure how helpful these findings will be from a practical point of view because the evidence does not suggest that, in order to achieve good outcomes from patients, female practitioners need to use specifically different strategies. However, using a sample in which some of the other personal variables are controlled as a female versus a male practitioner, the population does give strength to some of observations on effective communication.

In chapter 6, the discussion of nonverbal communication is of special interest as well. This has always been an aspect of health communication that has not been as well-documented, studied, measured, and programmed because it is much more difficult from a methodological point of view. On the other hand, there is suggestive evidence that nonverbal communication, although less researchable and less teachable, has a significant role in the patient–practitioner relationship and that a better understanding of these is highly desirable. It is interesting to speculate which aspects of nonverbal behavior can actually be taught or whether attitudinal changes are necessary before nonverbal behavior changes.

The discussion of older adults in chapter 7 is extremely comprehensive, practical, and raises a number of concerns that need to be addressed as our population gets older and as we have more medical modalities to offer the older patient. The discussion focuses on the communication predicament observed when younger individuals interact with older adults. The authors consider realistic difficulties in communication, such as hearing difficulties in the elderly as well as working memory, processing, speed, and name retrieval. There is emphasis on the important fact that, although some of the communication difficulties inherent in the aging process contribute to the communication predicament in working with older patients, more importantly, there are many stereotypes about older patients that get in the way of the most effective and satisfying communication with them in the context of illness. All too frequently, it is not observations or careful listening to the older patient but stereotypes that have guided the type of communication elected by the professional. The most distressing example of this is the act of "talking down" to older patients. In an attempt to be kind but not looking for much responsiveness from older patients, nurses and doctors use a type of "baby talk" or talking with a relative about the patient, which indicates that the patient is not being taken seriously. There is important evidence on the kind of patronizing speech that health-care providers use. In chapter 7, as well as in most of the others, there is extensive and helpful documentation of the points made on the basis of existing research or expert opinion.

Chapter 8, like most of this volume, is a well-documented, comprehensive review of what has been learned about explaining illness to children and emphasizes where further research is indicated. The examples of children's quotes on illness are not only entertaining but also very revealing of the manner in which children process information in light of their developmental stage. The section on some of the desiderata for explaining illness to children is rich and comprehensive and is especially valuable because it challenges some of the commonly held usages and platitudes. It is interesting that in the recommendations made by the author, for instance, he points out that health professionals tend to focus on explaining the disease, etiology, and biology to children, whereas children would like to understand about illness and their experiences. This is not different from one of the prevalent misunderstandings between physicians and their adult patients who often feel that their illness experience is bypassed in the communication over disease-specific information. It is obviously even more germane to communicating with children.

Chapter 9 is more interesting from the point of view of the changing role of individual health care providers than as a contribution to the basic knowledge of communication. The specific applications deal more with the content of pharmacist–patient communication than being helpful in elucidating the communication process as such. Clearly, there is a special challenge in terms of role expectation in that the pharmacist's role is changing and the patients are not necessarily aware of their pharmacist's potential in this respect. More than likely, there are also significant problems in interprofessional education as the pharmacist's role becomes more extensive. This is the time when it is recognized that all health professionals have an essential role to play, and it is admirable to see this particular aspect of health care communication emphasized.

Part III of this volume, addressing co-cultural issues in explaining illness, is clearly more anthropologic and descriptive than theoretical. The chapters in this section do not address new issues in communication as such. Importantly, however, they do elucidate specific problems in communication based on population groups' health beliefs, modes of communication that are comfortable and acceptable to them, and their relationship to the health professional and to medicine in general. Some of the quotes and specific data about health beliefs are intrinsically fascinating and should be studied and recognized by practitioners when they have an opportunity to care for individuals belonging to these ethnic groups and subcultures or are otherwise engaged in health education to these populations. Again, one striking finding is that many of the recommendations for communicating with some of the people have a great deal in common with general principles of communication, such as the need for assessing the particular patient's or population's health beliefs, readiness to learn language in which they can communicate, and the like. Obviously, it is more dramatic when you come to a unique population group, such as the Native Americans but, in fact, if we use the same open-minded attitude in communicating with many other individuals and groups, we would undoubtedly learn to be more effective in a responsive way rather than in a didactic predetermined approach to communication. This circumstance makes a strong recommendation, for instance, to communicate in a desirable environment and for the use of open-ended questions rather than direct probing questions or using standard forms, which are very familiar to those who have been interested in the general field of communication.

It is essential to remember that, in each group, there are many individuals who object to the generalizations made about the group as a whole because the subcultures are as different as the different countries in Europe. Although they have the common-language origin, individual differences are powerful. So, here again, although it is fascinating and important to learn content about health beliefs and cultural norms in a population such as the Latinos, this does not take the place of assessing the individual patient. I remember an encounter with a Japanese mother who was receiving a complex prescription for how to take care of her child's skin rash was told by the practitioner, "I know this is a complex regimen but I feel sure that you will be able to handle it." The mother retorted to the practitioner, "So you think I am compliant just because I am Japanese? Well I don't want you to think that all the Japanese are compliant." I have had the same kind of responses from African-American patients who are almost more fearful of being stereotyped than of not being understood. In spite of all this, there is interesting information in each of these chapters. The discussion of the use of interpreters is most useful by highlighting such issues as the important concepts of the family, authority, and machismo.

Chapter 12 is most welcome at a time when many of us are caring for increasing patient populations of this background. The descriptive information about the value system, the manner of thinking, and communicating about health among this cocultural group is essential for anyone who is hoping to afford optimal care to members of this population. The concept of privacy, the differences in freedom to discuss issues of death and dying, and the importance of family participation are just a few of examples of descriptions of a population that seem essential for anyone who wishes to practice medicine in a sensitive and effective way. The examples used in the chapter on the Asian and Pacific Islander Americans are very revealing.

One question raised by the series of chapters on culturally diverse groups of patients is how to address the pros and cons of having a native of the respective group participate in the health care process or actually be the provider. Aside from the practical difficulties of having a provider in each group that a particular health care service needs to deal with, there are issues that have emanated more from the patients' group than from the providers. For instance, in a clinic situation, assigning patients to a physician who is of the same ethnic background as the patients has an element of stereotyping and an element, in some cases, of patronization. I have encountered a number of patients, as well as physicians, who object when a patient assignment is governed by the respective backgrounds of patient and physician. This tendency has practical benefit when a language barrier can be removed by having a Spanish speaking physician take care of a family with limited English. Whether or not this person would have to be of Latino origin in order to achieve maximum effectiveness or whether a practitioner of a different ethnicity spoke their language could be as effective is a moot question. In the case of African Americans, there have been many individuals who protested and stated that they do not necessarily want to be assigned or look for African-American physicians. They are more concerned about having the best medical care. The color of the practitioner's skin should not be decided for them, as they would like the choice of a practitioner that (albeit limited under managed care) is available to other patients. Accepting the recommendation to have practitioners like the patients for whom they care only emanates from practicality and from the preference of some individual patients; on many occasions there have also been anecdotal observations that health professionals—especially younger health professionals—have certain problems in dealing with patients more like themselves—as they would with their own family members. There may actually be a tendency toward overidentification (i.e., assuming the patient will share the practitioner's feelings and opinions rather than true empathy if the patient and physician are too similar in many respects). On one hand, the social distance will be reduced; on the other hand, the ease of communication may actually be reduced, especially when it comes to the discussion of sensitive subjects.

In summary, this monumental text on explaining illness between practitioners and patients constitutes a treasure trove when it comes to a relatively uncharted aspect of health care practices. Through what is known and accepted in the field of health, communication is stressed, and many original ideas and approaches are included. In thinking of appropriate readers for this text it appears that an individual health practitioner would not necessarily be motivated to study this entire volume, although communication theory and practice are not part of the knowledge base of most practitioners. As there is increased recognition that communication with patients is the essential medium in which health care takes place and that this subject is researchable and teachable as are other aspects of health care practice, the interest and sophistication of practitioners should increase. In the meantime, anyone who is teaching in the area of health communication, anyone with a special interest, or anyone who is developing a research project in related subjects should absolutely study this volume carefully and refer to it repeatedly. Future research will be enhanced by taking in account the intelligent speculations as well as the theories incorporated in this volume. Medical education needs to include many issues that are discussed so well in this book. More in-depth studies are warranted for any teachers of this subject as well as for any practitioners to deal with some of the special groups and issues identified in this volume.

What makes this volume difficult to read is that there is no unifying theory in the field of health communication as of yet, and that so many of the studies deal with small samples in a particular context so that the conclusions are not readily generalized, yet the authors felt obliged, and rightly so, to include a wide variety of studies in spite of their conflicting conclusions. I think the book raises as many questions as it gives answers. However, it presents significant progress in this important field, which is of such basic importance for health care in all contexts, by varied practitioners caring for diverse patient populations. It is not an easy read, but absolutely worth the effort.

REFERENCES

Katz, J. (1984). *The silent world of doctor and patient*. New York: Free Press.

Author Index

327

Subject Index

349